A Sense of Inequality

Transforming Capitalism

Series Editors:
Ian Bruff, University of Manchester; Julie Cupples, University of Edinburgh; Gemma Edwards, University of Manchester; Laura Horn, University of Roskilde; Simon Springer, University of Victoria; Jacqui True, Monash University

This book series provides an open platform for the publication of path-breaking and interdisciplinary scholarship which seeks to understand and critique capitalism along four key lines: crisis, development, inequality, and resistance. At its core lies the assumption that the world is in various states of transformation, and that these transformations may build upon earlier paths of change and conflict while also potentially producing new forms of crisis, development, inequality, and resistance. Through this approach the series alerts us to how capitalism is always evolving and hints at how we could also transform capitalism itself through our own actions. It is rooted in the vibrant, broad and pluralistic debates spanning a range of approaches which are being practised in a number of fields and disciplines. As such, it will appeal to sociology, geography, cultural studies, international studies, development, social theory, politics, labour and welfare studies, economics, anthropology, law, and more.

Titles in the Series

The Radicalization of Pedagogy: Anarchism, Geography, and the Spirit of Revolt, Edited by Simon Springer, Marcelo de Souza and Richard J. White

Theories of Resistance: Anarchism, Geography, and the Spirit of Revolt, Edited by Marcelo Lopes de Souza, Richard J. White and Simon Springer

The Practice of Freedom: Anarchism, Geography, and the Spirit of Revolt, Edited by Richard J. White, Simon Springer and Marcelo Lopes de Souza

States of Discipline: Authoritarian Neoliberalism and the Contested Reproduction of Capitalist Order, Edited by Cemal Burak Tansel

The Limits to Capitalist Nature: Theorizing and Overcoming the Imperial Mode of Living, Ulrich Brand and Markus Wissen

Workers Movements and Strikes in the 21st Century, Edited by Jörg Nowak, Madhumita Dutta and Peter Birke

A Century of Housing Struggles: From the 1915 Rent Strikes to Contemporary Housing Activisms, Edited by Neil Gray

Renewing Destruction: Wind Energy Development, Conflict and Resistance in a Latin American Context, Alexander Dunlap

Towards a Political Economy of Degrowth, Edited by Ekaterina Chertkovskaya, Alexander Paulsson and Stefania Barca

Producing and Contesting Urban Marginality: Interdisciplinary and Comparative Dialogues, Edited by Julie Cupples and Tom Slater

A Sense of Inequality, Wendy Bottero

A Sense of Inequality

Wendy Bottero

**ROWMAN &
LITTLEFIELD**
───────INTERNATIONAL
London • New York

Published by Rowman & Littlefield International, Ltd.
6 Tinworth Street, London SE11 5AL
www.rowmaninternational.com

Rowman & Littlefield International, Ltd. is an affiliate of
Rowman & Littlefield
4501 Forbes Boulevard, Suite 200, Lanham, Maryland 20706, USA
With additional offices in Boulder, New York, Toronto (Canada), and London (UK)
www.rowman.com

Copyright © 2020 by Wendy Bottero

All rights reserved. No part of this book may be reproduced in any form or by any electronic or mechanical means, including information storage and retrieval systems, without written permission from the publisher, except by a reviewer who may quote passages in a review.

British Library Cataloguing in Publication Information
A catalogue record for this book is available from the British Library

ISBN: HB 978-1-78348-786-8
ISBN: PB 978-1-78348-787-5

Library of Congress Cataloging-in-Publication Data
Names: Bottero, Wendy, 1965- author.
Title: A sense of inequality / Wendy Bottero.
Description: London ; New York : Rowman & Littlefield International, [2019] | Series: Transforming capitalism | Includes bibliographical references and index. | Summary: "This book considers what provokes everyday 'views' or framings of inequality"-- Provided by publisher.
Identifiers: LCCN 2019040032 (print) | LCCN 2019040033 (ebook) | ISBN 9781783487868 (cloth) | ISBN 9781783487875 (paperback) | ISBN 9781783487882 (epub)
Subjects: LCSH: Equality.
Classification: LCC HM821 .B67 2019 (print) | LCC HM821 (ebook) | DDC 305--dc23
LC record available at https://lccn.loc.gov/2019040032
LC ebook record available at https://lccn.loc.gov/2019040033

This book is dedicated to my family, Kim, David, Ben and Grace, my very supportive friends Ang and Ian, and to all the staff at Wythenshawe Hospital and The Christie at Salford Royal. Defend the NHS!

Contents

Acknowledgements ix

1 Restricted Visions? 1
2 Attitudes to Inequality 25
3 Misrecognising Inequality 57
4 Affective Inequality 89
5 Protesting Inequality 119
6 Resisting Inequality 145
7 Making Sense of Inequality 175
8 Conclusion: Analysing Inequality 207

Bibliography 219
Index 243
About the Author 251

Acknowledgements

Any book is a work of many hands and multiple sources of inspiration—although I will be claiming the sole REF credit. Nonetheless, I must acknowledge the many colleagues and friends who have supported me, and not just through the process of writing the book.

I must first thank my editors, Ian Bruff and Gemma Edwards, and my publisher Rowman & Littlefield International, for their incredibly helpful and thoughtful advice and for their patience about this long-delayed book.

Many colleagues at Manchester offered advice and encouragement and allowed me to rehearse the book's arguments to them at what must have been very dull tea breaks, and for this I thank Andy Balmer, James Rhodes, Brian Heaphy, Nadim Mirshak, and Kevin Gillan. Bridget Byrne and Jackie O'Callaghan in particular were stalwarts and great friends. To those colleagues who read chapters in draft and offered detailed feedback, I am eternally grateful, so thank you, Sarah Irwin, Bridget Byrne, Owen Abbott, Charlotte Branchu, Laura Fenton and Kirsty Morrin. I am also deeply grateful for the help and support of Graeme Kirkpatrick and Alice Bloch. My good friend Claire Alexander was the source of many tea breaks, and while she undoubtedly lowered my productivity she did wonders for my spirits and morale.

My deepest debt of gratitude goes to the members of the University of Manchester pragmatism reading group: Owen, Charlotte, Laura and Kirsty. Our journey through pragmatist and pragmatist-adjacent authors was thought-provoking, enormous fun and made a major impact on the ideas in this book. Your collegiality and generosity in the exchange of ideas was so intellectually nourishing it reminded me of why I got into academia in the first place.

ONE
Restricted Visions?

We have a detailed picture of changing patterns of inequality and their impact on people's lives but a weaker sense of how people perceive, interpret and understand issues of inequality or of how such understandings are located in everyday concerns. At a time of stark inequality, it is important to understand what shapes everyday 'views' or framings of inequalities in terms of the practical and strategic significance that people place on inequality. In doing so, we also need to examine the everyday bases of protest, resistance and dissent. It is because the subjectivities of inequality matter for the practical tasks of tackling inequality that it is important to understand them better. But what do ordinary people think about inequality? Unfortunately, we have a relatively thin and disconnected understanding of this. Too often work on the subjectivities of inequality has been siloed into disconnected research traditions and is more often focused on why people *fail* to acknowledge or challenge inequality than in accounting for when and why they do. This book brings together a range of different literatures in order to better understand what provokes a sense of inequality. I examine a diverse set of empirical and theoretical work—on social attitudes and perceptions, symbolic legitimation and misrecognition, research on affect and struggles for recognition, social movements research, resistance studies and interactionist and pragmatist approaches to everyday sense-making—to consider how troubling social situations come to be regarded as inequalities and how inequalities come to be seen as susceptible to intervention and change.

What do I mean by a 'sense' of inequality? Different literatures adopt varying understandings of the subjectivities of inequality, so I adopt a deliberately expansive approach, exploring people's 'sense of inequality' through attitudes and perceptions, reflexive and self-conscious values and beliefs, expressions of injustice and indignity, struggles against inequality through organised protest, resistance and mundane noncompliance, but also through the more tacit, embodied and affective ways in which people 'know' and 'sense' the world. However, throughout this book I adopt the pragmatist stance that all knowledge, whether tacit or reflexive, takes a practical character which inevitably shapes and limits our sense of the world (Dewey, 1982 [1920]: 161).[1]

A key theme in work on subjective inequality is the question of how inequalities are rendered more or less visible, not least because analysts have long identified a 'problem' with the restricted visions of inequality that people often seem to have. People's subjective grasp of inequalities has been identified as problematic, restricted or distorted in a range of work, with an emphasis on the fragmentary, 'paradoxical' or contradictory nature of responses to inequalities. A recurrent argument in the work examined in this book is that people often do not react as expected and that 'the relationship between inequality and grievance only intermittently corresponds with . . . the extent and degree of actual inequality' (Runciman, 1966: 286). Perhaps the most troubling aspect is what appears to be widespread compliance, or 'acquiescence' in the face of stark inequality, with less dissent or conflict than analysts expect. Such 'acquiescence' is seen as a key factor explaining the persistence of inequality.

In many accounts, the problem of subjective inequality is explained by how the experience of inequality *itself* distorts everyday understandings and limits challenge or critique, as part of the symbolic legitimation of inequality. But are people's understandings really so restricted? Throughout this book I critically interrogate the claim that ordinary people's understandings of inequality are limited, paradoxical or mystified and consider whether the restricted visions found in ordinary people's sense of inequality are partly a reflection of the restricted vision of *analysts*. I argue that if we locate people's knowledge, beliefs and values about inequality within a more situated understanding of their practical engagements and concerns, then their sense of inequality seems less restricted and starts to make better sense.

However, I adopt a critical stance to those approaches to the subjectivities of inequality which analyse them in terms of the degree to which they operate as recognitions of underlying 'objective' structures of inequality—as identified by the analyst—and which partition people's sense of inequality into *either* recognition *or* misrecognition, tacit or reflexive modes, distorted or critical understandings. Accounts of people's sense of inequality as misrecognitions do focus attention on how inequality is often taken for granted, but throughout this book I argue that such accounts overstate the extent of tacit naturalisation and provide a much weaker account of critical capacity or of how challenges to social inequality and domination come about. Conventional approaches to the subjectivities of inequality often characterise 'recognition' as emerging from moments of 'crisis' or 'exception', and so they neglect the sheer extent of 'everyday' critique and 'ordinary' expressions of dissent, resulting in a restricted and selective account of the bases of social challenge and transformation.

One difficulty is that many analysts' real interest in subjective inequality rests in how people's understandings affect their consent or challenge to relations of inequality. This question is an important one, and it is a key focus of this book. But we must first analyse people's understandings of inequality *on their own terms*, locating them within their ordinary practical concerns and contexts of activity and emerging as part of their struggles to resolve their problems of experience. My central aim is not to explore how *well* people understand inequality but rather to examine how and why people's everyday sense of 'inequality' comes about. People's sense of inequality must be located within their daily negotiation of practical tasks in contexts of unequal relations. Viewpoints on inequality emerge within various kinds of practical engagements, and people's knowledge is formed to navigate given situations and shaped by their practical capacities for action.

As Chapters 2 and 3 examine, people are generally more aware of, and more concerned by, how unequal relations affect their own immediate situation and concerns. They are more alert to wider structural and economic processes than some analysis suggests but typically view these processes in terms of how they must be negotiated, seeing inequality as a 'given' feature of the environment to be managed in their daily lives. For some analysts this represents another form of symbolic legitimation, because such a taken-for-granted practical experience of inequality 'naturalises' it as inevitable or self-evident. But despite its situated and practical character, people's sense of inequality is 'good enough' for most people to want lower inequality, to fuel scepticism and dissent to legitimating ideologies and to generate significant levels of recalcitrance, resistance and protest. It is hard to sustain arguments of symbolic legitimation or naturalisation without substantial qualification because critique, dissent and struggle are so commonplace.

But if symbolic legitimation does not prevent discontent, suffering or dissent, why does inequality persist? The implication—a key argument of this book—is that the obdurate and persistent nature of unequal social relations has less to do with symbolic legitimation and people's restricted sense of inequality than many analysts have imagined. People are often sceptical of dominant values and beliefs, feel discontent and understand the constraints of their situation reasonably well, but they lack the capacity to change their situation. Compliance and acquiescence may be key factors in the persistence of inequality, but such conformity is often pragmatic. So the reproduction (and transformation) of unequal and unjust social relations is less a question of symbolic legitimation, or critical reflexivity, and more a question of the various kinds of practical constraint which bind people into social arrangements. Such constraint extends beyond coercion or symbolic legitimation. A sceptical response to this argument might be that people's sense of constraint and their feelings of powerlessness and resignation are *themselves* a feature of the symbolic legitimation of inequality. But people are not necessarily deluded if they feel a certain resignation about wider social relations being resistant to change, because collective challenge is both hard to achieve and risky, and particularly so for the poor and powerless. Yet people do manage to resist, protest and mobilise, even in the most authoritarian contexts, so we also need to think more broadly about the nature of constraint and see it not just as a question of power relations but also as a feature of practical action and of how collective practices are collectively sustained—and sometimes undermined.

WHY SHOULD PEOPLE CARE ABOUT INEQUALITY?

Inequality has remerged as a significant public concern. Since the 1970s there has been a dramatic and sustained increase in inequalities in income and wealth in many countries in the world. The scale of this inequality is truly remarkable—the wealthiest 1% in the world now owns more wealth than the remaining 99% of the world's population, while just eight men own the same amount of wealth as the poorest half of the globe, nearly 4 billion people (Oxfam, 2017). The drivers of rising economic inequality are complex, with some pointing to globalisation and technological change as the key factors, others seeing rising inequality as intrinsic to capitalist economies, while for others rent-seeking and the widespread adoption[2] of a range of neo-liberal policies[3] since the 1970s are more significant (Stiglitz, 2016; Piketty, 2013; Brankovic, 2016; Therborn, 2013). Inequality *within* many countries has risen, particularly in richer countries which previously saw declines in inequality from the 1930s to the 1970s (Duprat, 2018). However, *global inequality* has declined in recent decades as poorer countries have caught up with richer ones, though this has mainly been driven by the rapid economic growth of two very large countries, China and India (Brankovic, 2016).

   China's and India's 'impressive growth led to large-scale poverty reduction and major improvements in living standards in these two countries, which almost entirely explains the process of income convergence between developing and developed countries that has been under way in the last few decades' (Duprat, 2018: 5). But while these trends have started to reverse the stark global inequalities of the last 200 years, 'the gap between rich and poor people worldwide remains vast' as the convergence that has taken place 'still leaves the average citizen in developing countries, even in fast growing Asian countries, with less than one fourth of the average citizen's income in advanced countries' (Ibid.: 5–6). Global inequality remains high partly because the process of convergence has been largely limited to Asia, while elsewhere the income gap between 'centre' and 'periphery' economies 'has either increased or hardly changed over the past decades' (Ibid.: 6). But high global inequality also reflects the dramatic increases in inequality in richer countries, with stagnating incomes among lower- and middle-income groups and a surge in 'ultra-high-net-worth individuals' (Ibid.).

However, there is nothing inevitable about rising economic inequality. It cannot simply be the outcome of inexorable global economic forces or technological change, because rising inequality is not ubiquitous. Inequality has gone up in many countries but not at a uniform pace, while in some countries inequality has been stable or has even fallen (as in Russia, Mexico, Thailand, Algeria, Tunisia, the Philippines, Iran and most Latin American and Caribbean countries) (Hassell, 2018; Roser and Ortiz-Ospina, 2016; Salverda et al., 2014; Nolan et al., 2014). Such variation shows that national institutions, politics and policies (such as redistributive taxation, investment in public services, education and welfare, regulation of employment, a living wage and strong trade unions) can have a substantial impact on inequality. The problem of inequality 'is not so much a matter of technical economics. It's really a problem of practical politics' (Sitglitz, 2014: n.p.). However, practical challenges to economic inequality must—to be successful—draw on popular support and ordinary understandings of injustice, iniquity and grievance.

Many analysts assume ordinary people *should be* concerned about inequality and are troubled when they sometimes seem less concerned than expected. But is inequality something people should care about? Certainly some argue that if economic inequality spurs competition and economic growth which everyone benefits from then there is no problem. Others see poverty, rather than inequality, as the real problem and argue that if rising inequality produces growth which reduces poverty levels then inequality can actually be positive. This is the argument behind 'trickle down' economics, for example, but also the stance of some philosophical arguments that inequality can be justified if it improves the situation of the worst-off in society (Rawls, 1971). Others suggest that if people's rewards fairly reflect their hard work and productivity then again there is no problem, because equality of opportunity and procedural justice are more basic principles of fairness than equality of outcome (Nozick, 1974). However, the focus of recent debates has increasingly been on the negative consequences of rising inequality for *everyone* in a society, from top to bottom: negatively affecting our shared social lives through its disruptive impact on growth, social stability and cohesion, the environment and political accountability.

Far from stimulating growth, OECD research (2015: 26; 2019) indicates that high inequality has put a 'significant brake' on long-term economic growth in the Global North, because the incomes of the bottom 40% have remained stagnant, curbing opportunities for lower- and middle-lower-income groups. Even that bastion of neo-liberalism, the International Monetary Fund (2018), has warned that high inequality is *negatively* associated with macroeconomic stability and sustainable growth. Nor have there been fair shares or equal opportunities in the growth that has occurred, with little 'trickle down' of wealth and with rising inequality actually associated with reduced opportunities for social mobility. The World Inequality Report (Alvaredo et al., 2017) shows that from 1980 to 2016 the poorest 50% of humanity only captured 12 cents of every dollar of global income growth, while the top 1% captured 27 cents of every dollar. And rising income inequality 'can stifle upward social mobility', because countries with greater income inequality are also countries where a greater fraction of economic advantage (and disadvantage) is passed on from parents to children and where there is lower intergenerational earnings mobility (OECD, 2011: 40; Brunori, Ferreira and Peragine, 2013; Deaton, 2013; Corak, 2013; Andrews and Leigh, 2009).

Epidemiological research also suggests that all members of a society—not just the poor or the working class—are adversely affected by high inequality because of how it increases status anxiety and insecurity for everyone (Wilkinson and Pickett, 2009, 2018). As the gap between rich and poor increases, people are more likely to define themselves and others in terms of superiority and inferiority, success and failure, which reduces levels of social mixing and social mobility, generates higher levels of conflict, aggression and status anxiety and results in a stronger emphasis on conspicuous consumerism which degrades the environment (Ibid.). Certainly countries with higher levels of inequality have higher levels of crime, ill health, stress and mental illness, even when we control for GDP (Marmot, 2002; Dorling, 2017; Wilkinson and Pickett, 2009, 2018). The World Economic Forum (2019: 8–9) argues that the 'deep challenges' created by high inequality include 'poverty, environmental degradation, persistent unemployment, political instability, violence and conflict' and warns that people 'excluded from the mainstream end up feeling disenfranchised and become easy fodder of conflict'.

Analysts also warn that very high economic inequality is a danger to political equality, with the super-rich not only holding more political power but also using it to sway policy to advance their own interests, reducing political accountability and risking oligarchy (Domhoff, 2017; Oxfam, 2014). High inequality creates enormous power and influence for elites, and the impact of big money on the political system can be seen in the fact that both wealthy individuals and corporations have seen their tax bill slashed since the 1970s. In rich countries, the average top rate of personal income tax fell from 62% in 1970 to 38% in 2013; globally only four cents of every dollar of tax revenue comes from taxes on wealth; while in countries like Brazil and the UK, the poorest 10% are now paying a higher proportion of their incomes in tax than the richest 10% (Oxfam, 2019: 12). Cross-national research shows that the higher the income inequality in a country the more it affects not only the political power of elites but also the political engagement and civil liberties of the rest. An examination of access to political power[4] and respect for civil liberties[5] in 136 countries (1981–2011) shows that as income inequality increases, 'rich people command greater political power and enjoy stronger civil liberties than poor people', with these effects 'often strongest in high-income and democratic countries' (Cole, 2018: 377, 358). In high-inequality societies, 'governments represent the middle- and especially the high-income group best' (Rosset, Giger and Bernauer, 2013: 825), with political parties in highly unequal societies appearing to care less about the preferences of the poor and with governments also generally further away from the preferences of low-income groups.

Given this, it is perhaps unsurprising that increasing economic inequality also leads to lower levels of confidence in political elites and the democratic process. It is well known that in democracies poorer people are less likely to vote, but increasing inequality in a country sharpens this trend, increasing political disengagement by lowering 'political interest, the frequency of political discussion, and participation in elections among all but the most affluent citizens', with this negative effect especially strong for those on low incomes (Solt, 2008: 48–9; Nolan et al., 2014). Inequality raises political challenges 'because it breeds social resentment and generates political instability' when people 'feel that they are losing out while a small group of winners is getting richer and richer' (OECD, 2011: 40). In public debate, one often expressed concern is that rising inequality will not just result in political disengagement and disenfranchisement but also that the disenfranchised will be drawn into anti-establishment, extremist and destabilising 'populist' movements which reject 'politics as usual'.

Of course, from a left-wing perspective, if such movements represent a challenge to oligarchy and high inequality, this may be no bad thing, and some left-leaning movements have pursued anti-elite, anti-austerity and direct-democracy policies. However, analysts have also been concerned that rising inequality is producing the wrong kind of discontent, with a turn to right-wing populist movements which not only attack the rule of elites but also make appeals to the 'people' framed in exclusionary, homogeneous and frequently racist grounds (Müller, 2016). In Europe, for example, it has been argued that rising inequality may lead the disenfranchised to turn to emerging populist parties of the radical right, expressing narrow, racist and authoritarian views (Nolan et al., 2014) and pursuing protectionist and anti-immigration policies. But again, people's reactions to inequality do not follow expected patterns, as the people pursuing the wrong policies also seem to be the wrong people.

The widespread assumption that 'populism' is a working-class phenomenon that manifests itself in times of economic crises is deeply flawed. Mols and Jetten's (2017) analysis of long-term voter patterns (from the 1970s on) in Western European countries shows no correlation between economic conditions and populist anti-establishment voting, with populist parties often remarkably successful in times of economic growth and prosperity. Populist parties do attract support from working-class voters experiencing hardship, but they also attract significant support from middle-class voters with above average wealth and income (Ibid.). Mols and Jetten argue that support for populist parties among the better-off increases with their *status anxiety*, the more they feel a sense of entitlement and fear that they might lose their relative advantage over other groups.

For example, both Brexit and the US presidential election of Donald Trump have been characterised as a reaction against rising inequality in which those 'left behind' by globalisation, the 'economic have-nots' of deindustrialisation, have turned to support populist parties as part of a working-class anti-establishment rejection of 'politics as usual' (Bhambra, 2017). However, both votes were more strongly affected by the status anxieties of the relatively better-off. While the outcome of the UK's EU referendum has been blamed on the working class in the deindustrialised north of England, most people who voted Leave lived in the more-advantaged south, with 59% of Leavers coming from the middle classes (just 24% of the lowest two social classes voted Leave) (Dorling, 2016). There was also no association between voting Leave and 'working class' self-identification (Antonucci et al., 2017: 225). Middle-class Leavers were 'crucial' to the final result because the middle class constituted two-thirds of all those who voted, partly because 21 million of those eligible to vote did not take part in the referendum, with those not voting coming disproportionately from less-advantaged groups (Dorling, 2016). Although the most disadvantaged Britons do express anti-establishment nationalist views, it is economically advantaged white Britons who are more likely to express racist views as part of an 'imperial nationalist' stance (Flemmen and Savage, 2017), and the Brexit vote has been connected to 'imperial nostalgia' among this group (Dorling and Tomlinson, 2019).

A similar argument emerges about the American presidential election, where, as Bhambra (2017: S216) notes, 'it was middle class communities that overwhelmingly shifted to Trump in 2016 and were largely responsible for his victory' (Igielnik and Kochhar, 2016) with 'the swing to Trump . . . carried not so much by the white working-class vote, but the vote of the white middle class, including college educated white people'. In the United States, there is 'little evidence' that economic dislocation and marginality were significantly related to voters switching to Trump (Reny, Collingwood and Valenzuela, 2019), and the 'economic anxiety' of the changing financial situation had little impact on candidate preference; instead, voting for Trump was much better related to *racial* status anxiety related to white Americans' sense of a threat to their dominant group status (Mutz, 2018), with measures of voters' racism correlated much more closely with support for Trump than economic dissatisfaction (Schaffner, MacWilliams and Nteta, 2018).

The impact of patterns of inequality on people's sense of inequality is clearly complex, and to understand it we must also look at how subjective inequality is shaped within the broader context of nationalism, racial inequalities and how both global inequalities and national politics have been shaped by colonialism. Critics point out that renewed public concern about inequality only emerged when inequality rose in the *Global North*, while the mainstream analysis of social inequality has often neglected the enormous socio-economic inequalities between the Global North and Global South (Bashi Treitler and Boatcă, 2016: 160). This is an argument about the restricted vision of analysts, with a 'methodological nationalism inherent in the conventional analysis of social inequalities' in which the nation-state is 'the most common unit of analysis of inequality studies' while most dynamics of global inequalities 'go unnoticed' (Ibid.). The social analysis of inequality has often adopted a methodological nationalism which sees redistributive state policies, democratic participation and education within national borders as the 'best hope for achieving justice' (Weiß, 2017: 1318; Bashi Treitler and Boatcă, 2016: 164). But nation-states 'territorialize' struggles over inequality by limiting questions of equity and justice to the citizens of a bounded political community, 'drastically' limiting the obligations of justice across borders (Fraser, 2008: 401) which institutes birth-right citizenship and national borders as a major principle of global inequality (Weiß, 2017: 1320).

It has been suggested that attempts to address inequality within nation-states do little to reduce global inequality (Brankovic, 2016), while others argue that a focus on inequality reduction within national borders tends to overgeneralise from Western European experience and erase non-Western, non-European and non-white experiences (Bashi Treitler and Boatcă, 2016: 160). Bashi Treitler and Boatcă argue that we must move beyond the analysis of national income inequalities within borders to 'a broader understanding' of the history of global power relations, which recognises how 'ascriptive hierarchies of race, gender, caste, and national citizenship' are bound up with 'colonial conquest, enslavement, and labour migrations' as long-standing features of capitalism and the production of patterns of global inequality (Ibid.: 160, 159). This, of course, raises a fundamental question of how we should conceptualise 'inequality'.

A SENSE OF WHAT KIND OF INEQUALITY?

In thinking about subjective inequality, we must consider the different meanings of 'inequality' itself. 'Inequality' for many people means the unequal distribution of *economic* resources or opportunities, and this has certainly been the main focus of recent public debates. Yet inequalities in resources raise a broader set of questions about the social relations of inequality, since resource inequalities are inextricably bound up with social hierarchies, inequalities in safety and security and unequal autonomy, dignity and respect. Therborn (2013: 48–49) argues that inequality affects people as *organisms* (susceptible to pain, suffering and death), as *persons* (selves living in social contexts of meaning and emotion) and as social *actors* (striving towards goals). So inequality can be experienced as *vital inequality*, through unequal bodily life-chances; as *existential inequality*, through the unequal allocation of autonomy, freedom and dignity and rights to respect and self-development; and as *resource inequality*, through unequal opportunities to act (Ibid.).

> Inequality is a violation of human dignity; it is a denial of the possibility for everybody's human capabilities to develop. It takes many forms, and it has many effects: premature death, ill-health, humiliation, subjection, discrimination, exclusion from knowledge or from mainstream social life, poverty, powerlessness, stress, insecurity, anxiety, lack of self-confidence and of pride in oneself, and exclusion from opportunities and life-chances. Inequality, then, is not just about the size of our wallets. It is a socio-cultural order which (for most of us) reduces our capabilities to function as human beings, our health, our self-respect, our sense of self, as well as our resources to act and participate in the world. (Therborn, 2013: 1)

Inequality is never just a question of economic distribution but always entails relations of power, domination and subordination and hierarchies of respect, standing and accountability. To explore people's sense of inequality, we must examine all these aspects. Certainly *struggles* against inequality are usually not just focused on questions of economic distribution but also make 'an assertion of the basic moral equality of human beings', seeking 'a society in which all citizens meet each other face to face with mutual respect and cooperation' (Anderson, 2014: 259). Of course, struggles against inequality may be more focused on 'maldistribution' (economic inequality), misrecognition (status inequality) or misrepresentation and 'voicelessness' (political inequality) (Fraser, 2008), so how struggles are framed and organised is also a key question.

We must also recognise that too often the analysis of inequality 'conflates or ignores intragroup differences', an 'elision' that misses the intersections of different dimensions of inequality and discrimination (Crenshaw, 1991: 12420; 1989) and which fails to grasp how it is the 'interlocking' nature of these different dimensions which 'creates the conditions of our lives' (Combahee River Collective, 1983: 210). Too central a focus on the economic or class aspects of inequality risks marginalising gendered, racialised and sexualised inequalities, making one set of social inequalities visible while invisibilising others. So in thinking about *subjec-*

tive inequality, we must focus not just on 'class' but also on how the experience of 'gender', 'racial' and 'ethnic' inequalities are rendered into practical categories of understanding, examining how (and why) such practical categories take shape and how they are deployed in different contexts. As Hacking (2002: 113) argues, 'numerous kinds of human beings and human acts come into being hand in hand with our invention of the ways to name them', and I take the stance that our accounts of the social world and our place in it cannot be understood as straightforward descriptions, reflections or recognitions of an underlying reality, nor just as discursive frameworks, but rather are better understood as modes of practical engagement and intervention (and so, also, ways of constituting new kinds of relations and entities, partly as a result of these accounts).

In this book, I view 'inequality' as encompassing the array of unequal social relations which entail questions of subordination, unequal opportunity and uneven status, autonomy and constraint within practical social arrangements. However, reflecting the pragmatist approach of this book, I adopt a sceptical stance to generic concepts of 'inequality', 'social structure' or 'power' unanchored from concrete social arrangements and reject the reification of social arrangements into an 'objective' reality which exists at a different level from people's practical activities and social relations. As I argue in Chapter 7, people certainly do experience social arrangements as external, objective and constraining, but this is the constraint of the social relations required to enable practical activity. It is only once we understand how shared practices are collectively sustained (and constrained) that we can see why people develop a 'realistic' sense of what is possible and so often 'go along' with practices they do not necessarily commit to or support. Such constraint is not just a product of power relations or inequality but is also a feature of the collective steering of all social practices, and we can only fully understand the enduring character of power relations or inequality once we understand how this collective steering of practices operates.

To set out this argument, I draw on accounts of social life influenced by a distinctive set of philosophical accounts: chiefly classical pragmatism (Dewey, 1922, 1938; Mead, 1934) but also phenomenology (Schütz, 1962, 1964) and ordinary language philosophy (Wittgenstein, 1953). I focus on those approaches which most show this philosophical influence: interactionism, ethnomethodology, later theories of social practices and actor-network theory (ANT) as well as some more avowedly pragmatist analysts. In such approaches, social structures, economic markets, organisations, institutions, rules and social codes are seen as the continuous accomplishment of practical interaction, with an emphasis on the continual active work of social ordering and sense-producing that people must engage in to anchor and coordinate social relations. It is people's routine, often unnoticed activities which constitute and sustain orderly social arrangements, enable and transmit coordinated practices and impose a range of practical constraints on each other. Some degree of constraint is a condition of shared practice, because people must actively monitor, coordinate and align their practices. So while shared practice does depend on shared dispositions, and on people being able to view their actions from the viewpoint, and expectations, of others, it also depends on public, institutionalised methods of coordination and sanctioning.

The mundane work that facilitates collective practical action—an ongoing stream of accounting, anchoring, aligning, coordinating, assembling and sanctioning activities—is *constitutive* of conventions, rules, institutions and organisations and produces our sense of the external and constraining world to which we adjust our actions—and which, in so adjusting, we help to reproduce. Of course, practices are already pre-structured and steered through the objects and material arrangements which are an integral part of them, and this material aspect to social arrangements also works to frame our view of the world as it steers our practices. As a result, people's understanding of their situation—and so their 'sense of inequality'—is not just inside their heads but is also materially embodied in 'worldly phenomena, skills, equipment, institutions' (Rouse, 2002: 79). Our sense of groups, institutions, organisations and social structures as durable, external and constraining entities and 'real' social objects results from the constant work of interactive ordering that occurs within practical action and also from the socio-material arrangements and artefacts which also serve to steer practices and coordinate and stabilise social arrangements.

This is not to deny the role of power or social structure, coercion or symbolic legitimation in shaping social practices but rather to offer a different account of how they work. A focus on the co-constitution and collective steering of social life is sometimes seen as a consensual view of social arrangements. But this is more a question of people 'recognising' and adjusting to the socially ordered context they negotiate (and so help constitute). People 'reconstitute the system of shared practices by drawing upon it as a set of resources in the course of living their lives' (Barnes, 2001: 25–26). If we adopt a minimalist view of 'power' as being constituted through social alignments—in which a dominant agent can only exercise power over someone if enough other agents' actions are appropriately aligned with that of the dominant agent (Wartenburg, 1990; Rouse, 2001)—then power relations are sustained not just through the actions of the dominant but also by the accommodating actions of many other ordinary people. The typical explanation of this accommodation (or acquiescence) sees it as either the result of coercion or consent (whether genuinely self-interested or manipulated). However, people 'go along' with social arrangements for a great variety of reasons often based less in consent or coercion than in more mundane processes of everyday practical constraint and pragmatic conformity to the collective steering of practices. Too great an emphasis on people's knowledge or consent in reproducing social arrangements overestimates the degree of control that most people have over the situations that they find themselves in.

There are significant consequences of such an argument not only for how we think about inequality but also for how we view subjective inequality. Subjective inequality becomes more central to the production of unequal relations, not as a question of true or false consciousness but through constitutive acts of recognition. Many analysts focus on how well people's subjective sense of inequality approximates to 'objective' reality in order to assess why their understandings might be limited or distorted. However, a pragmatist focus emphasises the *constitutive* role of people's sense of inequality and requires us to recognise how the social world is 'managed, maintained, and acted upon' through people's ordinary accounts and descriptions (Heritage, 1984: 179, 137). Such accounts are less a reflection of, or on, people's situation and more a form of practical engagement and intervention within it. It is people's accounts and descriptions which help make their own and others' actions intelligible and which enable coordinated practice. Because people's activities must always be rendered visibly 'witnessable' and 'accountable' to each other, we always organise our actions in ways which routinely take into account how our actions might be seen and how others may react to or judge us.

The implication is that all relations of inequality are 'social constructs' in one sense and, in much the same manner, in terms of the way understandings of inequalities become embedded into the practical organisation and expectations around social arrangements. But such collectively held, materially embedded and publicly visible expectations are a matter of very real practical constraint which cannot just be 'thought away'. People's sense of social inequalities and their adjustments to them in their practices are—collectively—constitutive of such inequalities. This is not a question of people simply imposing meaning, though, because our sense of social arrangements is primarily related to our practical participation in the world: to the investigations in which we must engage in order to deal with people, events and circumstances and to our success and failures in our dealings (Quéré and Terzi, 2014: 111–14).

Throughout this book I critically interrogate the idea that inequalities persist because people's sense of inequality is somehow masked or naturalised. The book starts with an initial focus on everyday understandings of inequalities of income and wealth, because economic inequality is often seen as the most naturalised. The resurgent public debate about the negative consequences of inequality since the 2008 financial crisis has largely framed it in economic terms. Popular discourses of economic inequality raise questions of desert, merit, effort and worth, with such inequalities sometimes seen as legitimately achieved or natural. I take such public discourses and their everyday framings as the point of entry for analysis. However, it is also the case that arguments of 'naturalisation' have been central to accounts of the subjectivities of class inequality. Some argue that the popular emphasis on questions of merit and desert in social success means that class inequality is the most successfully 'naturalised' inequality, compared to relations of racial and gender inequality, where identity politics have been better mobilised to counter such inequalities as illegitimately ascribed (Sayer, 2005b). Leaving to one side which relations of inequality are really the most naturalised (since my argument is that they are all very incompletely naturalised), it is certainly class analysis which has placed the greatest emphasis on processes of symbolic legitimation, hegemony or misrecognition, with prominent and extended debates on how class inequalities come to be individualised or seen as part of the inevitable order of things. In Chapters 2 and 3, I therefore first focus on arguments about the naturalisation of *economic* inequality in order to examine the strengths—but also, crucially, the weaknesses—of such accounts in their most extended form.

While theorists of gender and race have been less enamoured with theories of the naturalisation of inequalities than class analysts, they too have engaged with such questions. Chapters 3 and 4 examine how people's sense of these intersecting dimensions of inequality challenge, qualify and curtail accounts of naturalisation, and Chapters 4, 5 and 6 explore how the limits to naturalisation create the space for struggles for recognition, protest and everyday 'insubordination' and subversion—against a range of inequalities and forms of domination. Work on the symbolic legitimation of class, race and gender inequalities indicates that such inequalities are never wholly naturalised by the members of subordinate groups, because such naturalisation constitutes the environment of expectation and judgement within which they are forced to manoeuvre. Members of subordinate groups often recognise—all too clearly—the arbitrary nature of privilege and disadvantage but must still negotiate environments in which their disadvantage is individualised and naturalised by others. There is a fundamental tension in arguments of naturalisation, therefore, which argue that it is people's misrecognition of inequality which serves to reproduce it but founds this in processes which rest on subordinates' recognition of, and adaptation to, such arrangements. This tension is sometimes resolved by an emphasis on people's tacit and pre-reflexive 'recognition' of inequality, where it is argued that because social environments are practically experienced as taken for granted and self-evident, people therefore also see them as inevitable and unchangeable. However, work on protest and everyday nonconformity and subversion shows that while unequal social arrangements *are* often experienced as taken-as-given features of our environment, this does not mean they are naturalised as inevitable and, depending on people's practical capacity for action, nor does it preclude dissent or social challenge.

Arguments about the naturalisation of unequal social arrangements often adopt a Global North focus, with processes of symbolic legitimation and naturalisation identified as the characteristic mode of domination undertaken in the liberal democracies of the Global North (Gramsci, 1971; Bourdieu, 1990a, 1998b). The methodological nationalism found in the analysis of social inequalities is also apparent in research on the subjectivities of inequality. It is generally argued that Northern liberal democracies have shifted away from repression or coercion to 'complex domination', with more 'managerial' or 'disciplinary' modes of regulation (Boltanski, 2011; Foucault, 1979). Coercive forms of domination are usually seen as less effectively naturalised than more 'hegemonic' forms, with many analysts arguing that coercion undermines symbolic legitimation. But the suggestion also seems to be that societies of the Global North have moved to more complex and sophisticated forms of power than brute force, where power relations are better disguised, and so people's consent to their subordination can be manufactured. However, this division between authoritarian and liberal democratic societies not only underplays the extent to which coercion, or its threat, remains a powerful organising force in liberal democratic societies but also understates the extent of dissent and protest that occurs in both liberal democratic and more authoritarian contexts.

Because research on subjective inequality is often focused on the Global North or on subjectivities within specific countries, we have a patchwork understanding of how inequality is experienced and perceived in different ways across some parts of the globe, with a marked lack of work on everyday understandings of global inequalities. The uneven and sometimes limited approach to place and context found in these different approaches demands a more plural and connected programme of research on the subjectivities of inequality which focuses on the central importance of the social contexts and the range of practical constraints which shape people's sense of inequality. Such a focus is necessary because everyday understandings of inequality are always practical categories of situated intervention. This book examines a range of work on the subjectivities of inequality, from both Global North and Global South, which indicates that neither symbolic legitimation nor coercion offer sufficient explanation of why disadvantaged people mostly—but not always—put up with unequal social arrangements or domination.

Instead I argue that we must look more broadly at how people become bound into situated social arrangements to examine how people's practical engagements within collective social practices provide a wider array of obligations, commitments and constraints which both underwrites conformity but also shapes people's ability to engage in dissent. However, in one respect, methodological nationalism (or rather methodological localism) makes more sense in work on subjective inequality, because people are generally more aware of—and more exercised by—'local' inequalities in their own lives and social contexts. Because people develop their sense of inequality in relation to their situated practical concerns and immediate milieu, this gives them a very particular viewpoint on inequality and can limit their grasp of its scale or distort their sense of their place within it. Many accounts focus on the restricted visions that people have of inequality; however, the most frequent explanation of this argues that people do not just have restricted points of view but rather their understandings are systematically distorted as part of the symbolic legitimation of such arrangements. Undoubtedly, there is considerable symbolic legitimation of inequality—but there are also significant limits to the reach and effectiveness of such legitimation.

THE PROBLEM OF SUBJECTIVE INEQUALITY AND THE LIMITS OF SYMBOLIC LEGITIMATION

For many analysts there is a 'problem' with people's sense of inequality. Research on subjective inequality frequently highlights the restricted or distorted nature of people's responses to inequalities, with the 'acquiescence' of disadvantaged groups the most troubling aspect of this. The problem is why a subordinate group seems 'to accept or at least to consent to' a system 'that is manifestly against its interests when it is not obliged to by the direct application of coercion or the fear of its application', with the answer most often seen to lie in 'a dominant or hegemonic ideology' which 'operates to conceal or misrepresent aspects of social relations that, if apprehended directly, would be damaging to dominant elites' (Scott, 1990: 71–72). As Scott notes, such accounts work on the assumption that subordinate groups are indeed relatively quiescent, relatively disadvantaged and not coerced, and, as this book shows, not all of these assumptions are well founded. However, solutions to the problem of 'acquiescence' usually focus on distortions in people's understandings of inequality, where it is argued that 'the lack of agitation for change on the part of the deprived has to be based upon either a moral consensus or upon some form of ignorance of true social processes', with people's understandings of inequality 'either limited or fragmented or false' (Stewart, Prandy and Blackburn, 1980: 143–44).

Various theories argue that inequality is legitimated through processes which misrepresent, disguise or naturalise ordinary people's grasp of its real nature, with such ideological 'misrecognition' seen as key to the reproduction of inequality. Early accounts emerged to explain the failure of the Western working classes to overthrow capitalism but also their acquiescence to authoritarian, fascist regimes (Gramsci, 1971; Adorno and Horkheimer, 1993; Adorno, 1991), and there have been multiple subsequent versions. While most commonly used in the analysis of class inequalities in democracies, such arguments have also been applied to racial and gender inequalities and to authoritarian and coercive contexts, as I explore in Chapters 3, 5 and 6. This book can only scratch the surface of the wide array of theories of symbolic legitimation and is more focused on empirical applications of such arguments; however, it is worth rehearsing some key analytical themes.

Many accounts show the influence of Marx's (2000 [1859]: 425) discussion of how people's understanding of their situation is ideologically shaped by capitalism. As Eagleton (1991: 83–84) notes, Marx's use of the term 'ideology' variously refers to 'illusory' beliefs which distract people 'from their actual social conditions', 'ideas which directly express the material interests of the dominant social class' and which promote its rule or 'the conceptual forms in which the class struggle as a whole is fought out' (Ibid.: 84). Accounts of symbolic legitimation are dominated by these first two meanings of ideology and also by a fourth aspect—naturalisation—which emerges in Marx's (1990 [1867]) account of commodity fetishism. Here the social relations of production disappear from view as human creations and instead take on the appearance of external, objective forces which control people. This is a process of mystification in which the 'real workings of society' become 'veiled and occluded', where it 'is no longer easy to grasp' society as a 'totality' and in which social relations acquire a 'spurious air of naturalness and inevitability' which makes them seem no longer 'humanly alterable' (Eagleton, 1991: 84). As Eagleton (Ibid.: 85, original emphasis) notes, this account of naturalisation goes beyond an argument of 'distorted perception', because commodities do not just '*appear* to exercise a tyrannical sway over social relations . . . they actually do', with ideology 'anchored in the day-to-day economic operations of the capitalist system'. This theme—of how particular beliefs and expectations become embedded in collective practices which then take on a constraining force—is one I shall explore throughout the book.

While Marx set out various ways in which distorted understandings become embedded within people's practices, he nonetheless believed that capitalism was creating practical conditions of collective labour that would enable the working class to better realise their commonality and strength and to act upon their shared interests. Most industrial societies have not experienced this revolutionary class conflict as Marx envisioned, so a succession of later theories focus on how symbolic legitimation forges the 'quiescence' of the masses as a much more stable and enduring feature of relations of inequality. Scott identifies 'thick' and 'thin' versions of such arguments, with the 'thick' version arguing that subordinate groups come 'to believe actively in the values that explain and justify their subordination', so making claims for the production of *consent*, while the 'thin' version maintains only that subordinate groups become convinced 'that the social order in which they live is natural and inevitable', so producing *resignation* (Scott, 1990: 72). But claims about 'resignation' are also sometimes 'thickened up' by an emphasis on how such resignation is also part of people's pre-reflective practical sense, in which unequal social arrangements become so taken for granted and self-evident that they disappear from view, with considerable slippage between claims of consent and claims of resignation.

The Frankfurt School's description of the culture industries (Adorno and Horkheimer, 1993; Adorno, 1991) provides an argument about consent in which subordinated groups are 'bought off' by the gratifications of consumer culture. Commodified popular culture generates false needs so that people become 'subdued' by culture as 'defrauded masses' who not only 'unresistingly succumb to whatever is proffered to them' but also come to support 'the ideology by which they are enslaved' (Adorno and Horkheimer, 1993: 115, 100, 123; Adorno, 1991: 106). Gramsci's more nuanced account sees the capitalist state defended by the 'trenches' of civil society which secure the 'spontaneous' consent of the masses through a process of cultural hegemony (1971: 12). The institutions of civil society promote the worldview of the dominant class into a popular 'common sense' which comes to be shared by subordinate groups. Hegemony is not just a question of belief, however, since as Eagleton (1991: 115) notes, Gramsci's account of hegemony makes a 'crucial transition' from ideology 'as "systems of ideas" to ideology as lived, habitual social practice' encompassing the 'unconscious, inarticulate dimensions of social experience'. This practical and tacit experience of inequality is seen as a particularly pernicious form of incorporation into the system, since it makes inequality harder to recognise or challenge. For Bourdieu (1977: 471), for example, it is people's practical, embodied 'sense' of the world which contributes to their domination, because their 'practical sense' of things is shaped by (unequal) conditions of existence. This is not a theory of false *consciousness* but rather an account of how symbolic domination 'operates through the unconscious manipulation of the body' (Bourdieu, 1992: 115).

> Practical belief is not a 'state of mind', still less a kind of arbitrary adherence to a set of instituted dogmas and doctrines ('beliefs'), but rather a state of the body. Doxa is the relationship of immediate adherence that is established in practice between a habitus and the field to which it is attuned, the pre-verbal taking-for-granted of the world that flows from practical sense. (Bourdieu, 1990a: 69)

This doxic 'practical sense' means the domination imposed on marginalised individuals becomes taken for granted in a manner which not only 'conceal[s] power relations' (Bourdieu, 1993a: 12) and produces in the dominated a 'natural' sense of limits but also means dominant values become internalised (Bourdieu, 1977: 77). 'Internalisation' occurs as the less advantaged negotiate unequal social relations, because their defensive adjustments to their situation distort and constrain their aspirations and sense of self-worth.

Bourdieu's account represents one of the 'thicker' versions of the symbolic legitimation argument, and such versions are often steeped in a profound pessimism about the possibilities of resisting inequality and domination. Bourdieu (1977: 114), for example, believes 'the capacity for resistance, as a capacity of consciousness' is 'overestimated' because 'people living in poor condition . . . are prepared to accept much more than we would have believed', and 'there are many things people accept without knowing'. Here the importance of doxa to practical activity makes resistance 'more difficult, since it is something you absorb like air, something you don't feel pressured by; it is everywhere and nowhere, and to escape from that is very difficult' (Bourdieu, 1992b: 115).

Yet people do dissent and protest, mobilise and organise and, as Chapters 4, 5 and 6 indicate, rather more often than such accounts often suggest. The difficulty is that symbolic legitimation tends to be presented as rather *too* overwhelming and powerful a force. Too often a dominant ideology is presented 'as impenetrable' (Willis, 1977: 175) so that 'it is difficult to explain how social change could ever originate from below' and, perhaps most damagingly, such theories do 'not allow for the degree of social conflict and protest that actually occurs' (Scott, 1990: 78). Accounts focused on the stable reproduction of inequality are always in danger of being awkwardly wrong-footed by events, but too often theorists have found themselves more fatalistic and pessimistic than the people they analyse.

Many analysts concede significant limits to the naturalisation and internalisation of inequality, not least because, as Chapters 2, 3 and 4 show, the penetration of symbolic legitimation is often uneven, incomplete and contested, takes stronger hold among the dominant than among the less advantaged and does not prevent substantial amounts of discontent or dissent. Accounts of symbolic legitimation are invariably qualified because they must identify cracks in the system where such dissent and contestation can arise. For Bourdieu, for example, disruptions in the adjustment between habitus and field can generate greater critical reflexivity, while for Gramsci, hegemonic 'common sense' always contains 'a healthy nucleus of good sense', derived from practical experience, which can become 'if only within narrow limits, a critical conception' (Gramsci, 1971: 348, 333–34).[6] However, conceding too much discontent potentially undermines accounts of symbolic legitimation, and so it is often argued that the discontent that does emerge is limited or ultimately self-defeating.

Therefore, even though they 'may be thoroughly disaffected', the argument is that 'normally most people find it difficult, if not impossible, to translate the outlook implicit in their experience into a conception of the world that will directly challenge the hegemonic culture' (Lears, 1985: 569). From this perspective, symbolic legitimation may not prevent discontent, but it still props up inequality by dissipating and misdirecting that discontent into attempts at assimilation, divisive sectional struggles and 'defence and survival mechanism[s]' (Bourdieu, 1992a: 96), none of which really challenge the system. And the argument often turns to the *affective* nature of symbolic legitimation, where people's 'sense' of inequality is more a question of the embodied dispositions and emotions produced by subordination, in self-restricting choices and feelings of shame, resignation and despair. But this move creates its own problems because, as Chapter 4 examines, while subordination does often produce a sense of humiliation and despair, it also sparks anger, indignation and struggles for greater recognition, respect and dignity. Work on the affective experience of inequality also shows the limits to the naturalisation of inequality.

THE LIMITS OF NATURALISATION

As Chapters 3 and 4 show, subordinate groups cannot avoid being judged against the values and practices of dominant groups and so often struggle to avoid internalising at least some of the values which position them as inferior, limiting not just their 'realistic' sense of the possible but also their sense of self-worth and empowerment. However, this represents a very incomplete and limited version of 'naturalisation', because such subordinating judgements and expectations are also a powerful force generating critique and dissent, embedded in the intersubjective aspects of everyday experience in which forms of reflexive monitoring, moral evaluation and affective commitments are routine aspects of social life. Work on people's affective and normative responses to inequality shows that people show a much greater ability to develop values and moral principles in opposition to dominant values than is sometimes suggested. As a result there is also a greater capacity for reflexivity and critique of social arrangements than models of symbolic legitimation typically allow.

One reason why this is possible, and why there are significant limits to the 'tacit' naturalisation of inequality, is because subordinates must have a reflexive, calculative and affective grasp of their subordination in order to be able to navigate dominant values and practices. Subordinate groups are forced to adjust and monitor how they behave in relation to dominant values and practices, because they must structure their actions in expectation of the likely responses and sanctions that may result. So the naturalisation of privilege can never be wholly 'invisibilised' to the members of subordinate groups precisely because such naturalisation constitutes the environment of expectation, judgement and sanction within which they are forced to manoeuvre. This does not deny the force of dominant practices and values on people's lives but argues that they take effect by forming the 'known' environment which people must negotiate and to which they adjust their practices. Because we must 'recognise' social arrangements as 'what they are' in order to organise our activities, we adjust our actions accordingly and, regardless of our opinion about such arrangements, in so adjusting we often help to reproduce them. This, ironically, locates the persistence of unequal social arrangements not in people's 'misrecognition' of them but rather in their processes of 'recognition'.

Of course, for some analysts, to recognise social arrangements as 'what they are' and to take them as a 'fact of life' is itself a form of symbolic legitimation, the 'thin' form of naturalisation in which people's resignation about inequality limits their capacity to challenge or resist. In these 'thinner' versions of naturalisation, subordinates do not necessarily swallow legitimating ideologies wholesale and can still be discontented. However, if they see inequality as a 'fact of life', part of the inevitable order of things, this makes them resigned to their fate. As Scott notes:

> The thin theory ... makes far less grandiose claims for the ideological grip of ruling elites. What ideological domination does accomplish, according to this version, is to define for subordinate groups what is realistic and not realistic and to drive certain aspirations and grievances into the realm of the impossible, of idle dreams. By persuading underclasses that their position, their life-chances, their tribulations are unalterable and inevitable, such a limited hegemony can produce the behavioural results of consent without necessarily changing people's values. (Scott, 1990: 74)

Scott regards the 'thin' version as more defensible, and certainly, as this book shows, there is considerable evidence that people do often feel resigned about inequality and that they frequently make a 'realistic' adjustment to the limits of their circumstances. But the identification of this as 'naturalisation' partly depends on just how realistic we consider people's 'realistic' adjustment to be.

People's awareness of inequality is generally framed in terms of its immediate practical relevance to their lives, as they tend to focus on those aspects of their social location which they feel can be changed, with most structures of inequality seen as beyond this scope. But while people always have partial, situated perspectives on their social world shaped by their practical engagements with it, these practical engagements vary enormously. Whether such engagements produce perspectives on the immediate situation or its wider connections depends on the practical activity in question. And while disadvantaged groups do often feel that they cannot do much to change wider social arrangements, they are not entirely mistaken in this. An emphasis on the naturalisation of social arrangements implies that if people could only recognise the real nature of their subordination then its constraint would be undermined. But this places undue weight on symbolic power in maintaining inequality and treats subordination and powerlessness as a matter of perception or 'practical sense', neglecting the role of economic clout, coercion and other forms of constraint in maintaining inequalities. Domination 'can operate on many occasions more through compliance or brute force than through tacit consent' as power relations 'can be clearly understood and still not contested where individuals do not see viable alternatives without tremendous risks' (Swartz, 1997: 220–21).

As Chapter 5 indicates, social movement research shows that disadvantaged groups *are* often resigned to their situation so that, in order to mobilise, they must develop a sense that change is possible. But such work also shows that people's resignation rests in 'objective' conditions of powerlessness and constraint which must shift in order for people to be able to act. So if aggrieved people feel that they cannot change their situation quite often this is because they really cannot, or at least they face formidable obstacles. The capacity for practical challenge depends on resources and collective organisation which the disadvantaged often lack, and it also entails significant risk. Such work provides a powerful set of reasons for why people put up with inequality, but reasons founded less in symbolic legitimation than in practical conditions of powerlessness and constraint. And this constraint is not just a feature of power relations but also of the practical arrangements of people's everyday lives, in which the difficulties of mobilisation are not only a question of the risks of repression if people do mobilise but also of the constraints of the daily routines and obligations that keep people within unequal arrangements, regardless of their critical awareness or dissent.

However, while people are often highly constrained, protest and resistance does still occur, even among the most deprived and disadvantaged. Work on social movements shows that 'collective refusal'—noncompliance and disruption in everyday social arenas—provides collective resources which enable protest and dissent for even the most powerless and deprived. The daily routines and obligations of people's lives do constrain them, but the ability to defy expectation, to break the rules and to withhold the cooperation on which social life depends bestows a power that arises from disrupting the mutual dependence which underpins collective social arrangements. Actualising such power is difficult, though, because in collective refusal people must disrupt their own lives and risk repercussion. But as Chapter 6 shows, there are other forms of 'refusal' much less visible which emerge through more mundane and disorganised practices of noncompliance and misbehaviour. Work on mundane forms of 'everyday' resistance argues that accounts of symbolic legitimation and naturalisation have too readily been taken in by people's *public* performance of acquiescence, failing to recognise that beneath the surface of people's compliance there is still widespread discontent. Even apparently 'compliant' social practices can express 'mundane' or 'unexceptional' forms of dissent, through everyday acts of nonconformism, concealed subversion and 'bending the rules'. This dissent is often concealed because subordinates have a vested interest in avoiding open displays of insubordination: it may more often be expressed through recalcitrance, insubordination and misbehaviour than by organised confrontation; nonetheless, such dissent shows that inequality is far from 'naturalised'.

But if subversion, misbehaviour and dissent are really so widespread, this returns us to the question of why relations of inequality and domination are still so persistent. One obvious conclusion—a central argument of this book—is that relations of inequality and subordination can be reproduced without symbolic legitimation and despite people's dissent, through various processes of practical constraint. However, many analysts resist this conclusion. Some, for example, see mundane resistance as survival or coping mechanisms which help people to put up with controlling social environments but which also allow that control to continue. This returns us to the 'thin' theory of naturalisation, where people's local acts of 'letting off steam' do not change their acceptance of the inevitability of wider arrangements. Others concede that rule-breaking is commonplace but argue that this does not represent 'resistance' but simply practices of self-help or self-organisation.

Regardless of whether nonconformity represents resistance or just corner-cutting self-help, such manoeuvrings show that people do not straightforwardly naturalise their social arrangements. If dignity, self-determination or a decent life can only be achieved by deliberately flouting the rules, this is scarcely an endorsement of the authorities or acquiescence to the status quo. The point here is that people are doing what they can to change their situation. Collective social arrangements *are* often experienced as taken-as-given features of our environment, but this does not mean they are naturalised as inevitable or unchangeable. Any form of social convention that is widely institutionalised is likely to become 'self-evident' simply by virtue of its pervasiveness in our everyday affairs. But as Chapter 6 indicates, insubordination, noncompliance and strategic re-interpretation of the rules are commonplace, not just in authoritarian contexts but also in the supposedly naturalised environments of 'symbolic legitimation'. And regardless of whether such deviations represent resistance, misbehaviour or just corner-cutting modifications for the purposes of self-help, they show that people do not straightforwardly naturalise their social arrangements. Rather, people constantly seek to adapt their circumstances as they find them to their own practical purposes, but their ability to do so depends on the situational constraints they encounter.

However, as Chapter 7 explores, we must also think more broadly about the nature of the constraint which shapes compliance and dissent. After all, if the scale of everyday dissent, recalcitrance, resistance and protest is a problem for theories of symbolic legitimation, it also poses a problem for explanations based on constraint. Even in authoritarian and repressive conditions, the most disadvantaged and disempowered do resist and sometimes even seize opportunities to challenge the system. So we need to rethink the complex nature of social constraint in which such constraint is not just a product of power relations, coercion or inequality but is also a feature of the collective steering of all social practices. People are not wrong if they feel their social relations are external and constraining because social relations are collectively ordered practices, encountered as features of a 'known' and 'external' socio-material environment, and are generally experienced as constraining socio-material conventions and routines which people must pragmatically negotiate. If we feel constraint in collective practices, this is not just imposed on us by the dominant but also represents the constraint of the many other ordinary people whose routines and conventions form our social-material environment, shape our expectations and accountability and constrain our room for manoeuvre. But the collective steering of social practices is also key to understanding how dissent, resistance and protest emerge. It is only by understanding constraint as a feature of *social* relations, and not just *power* relations, that we can understand how the practical and transformative capacities of collective action can take shape.

NOTES

1. Classical pragmatism did not place a central influence on questions of power and inequality, but it has been a significant influence on race and gender theory (West, 1989; Fraser, 1994; Hill Collins, 2012). However, one of the most important, but underexplored, contributions that classical pragmatism has to offer is to the analysis of subjective inequality, and it is this analytical contribution on which this book is focused.

2. Or enforcement through international bodies like the IMF and World Bank.

3. Deregulation of labour and product markets, restrictions on trade unions, financialisation, more regressive taxation and retrenchment of the welfare state.

4. Looking at how voting, representation in government, the ability to set political agendas and the ability to influence and implement political decisions varies by socio-economic position.

5. How access to justice, property rights, freedom of movement and freedom from forced labour vary by socio-economic position.

6. This is the reason why hegemony must always be backed by state coercive power 'which "legally" enforces discipline on those who do not "consent" either actively or passively' (Gramsci, 1971: 12).

TWO
Attitudes to Inequality

One way to explore people's sense of inequality is to examine *attitudes* to inequality using surveys which examine the extent to which people 'perceive existing inequality . . . as "too large"' (Lübker, 2004: 92). Inequalities of income and wealth are inextricably entangled with other dimensions of inequality, but the initial focus of this book is on everyday understandings of economic inequalities. Public debates have increasingly focused on the negative consequences of rising inequality, and in these debates inequality is framed largely in economic terms. I take that framing as the point of entry for analysis. In considering work on attitudes, it is also important to bear in mind that it adopts a particular focus. Richer nations in the Global North were for many years over-represented in internationally aligned survey data sets (Lübker, 2004: 93), which has skewed the focus of debates to 'developed' nations and their welfare policies. There is also limited work on everyday understandings of *global* inequalities (as opposed to understandings of national inequality across the globe) (Ibid.). Such research also tends to explore the subjectivities of inequality in a quite abstract and general way. Nonetheless, cross-national survey research across the globe reveals considerable complexities in ordinary people's perspectives on inequality and social justice and shows that high inequality does not automatically trigger discontent.

Various theories predict that high and rising inequality *should* have important political outcomes, creating pressures for 'income redistribution (in democracies)' or inciting 'revolution and other political violence (in non-democracies)', but such theories 'have proved hard to substantiate empirically', and the relationship between public attitudes and public policy or political action is complex (Gimpelson and Treisman, 2017: 2–3).[1] As Chapter 1 shows, high inequality in a society can create political disengagement, particularly among the less advantaged. So while some look to attitudes to 'provide a window into citizens' expectations about inequality' that can shed light on a 'driving force shaping social policy' (Sachweh and Olafsdottir, 2012: 150), we must be wary of assuming that national attitudes shape political action. Nonetheless, attitudes data does show the *potential* level of support for mobilisation against inequality.

However, there is not a straightforward relationship between 'objective' levels of inequality and discontent. Partly this is because in examining people's sense of *inequality*, we are actually exploring judgements of *inequity*:

> inequity refers to a subjective judgment that the actual pattern of distribution of resources differs from the ideal or preferred pattern . . . it is a sense of inequity, not objective levels of inequality *per se*, that can provide the basis for discontent and even political challenges. If individuals think that existing differentials and income gaps are suitable or even necessary, such gaps will not generate anger. (Whyte, 2011: 280)

Opinions about inequality depend not only on what levels of inequality people *perceive* and how much they regard as *acceptable* but also on whether they think it has been *fairly generated* (Janmaat, 2013: 359). This complexity helps explain some of the surprising patterns repeatedly identified in survey research where, for example, more unequal countries often show *greater* tolerance for inequality and where sharp increases in inequality are sometimes associated with increasing tolerance to inequality, declining support for redistribution and more negative views about the poor. There is disagreement on these patterns related to questions of measurement and which countries are compared (Dallinger, 2010; Kerr, 2011; Medgyesi, 2013; Jæger, 2013), but if we are looking for popular support for a greater political focus on tackling inequality, then the picture from attitudes data looks mixed. Yet while responses are complicated by judgements of fairness, by questions of prosperity and growth and by often very 'local' points of view, attitudes research does show that most people *are* concerned about high inequality and would like to live in more egalitarian societies.

One common argument is that people's attitudes are not just complex but also inconsistent. Certainly, they often contradict analysts' *expectations* about how inequality should shape attitudes. People's attitudes are 'not always where one would expect them to be and the patterns they follow are sometimes surprising' (Svallfors, 2006: 165), with many noting their 'paradoxical' (Svallfors, 2006: 165; Bamfield and Horton, 2009; Carriero, 2016: 133; Whyte, 2016: 2; Mijs, 2019), 'complex' (Osberg and Smeeding, 2006), 'puzzling' (Janmaat, 2013: 375) or 'contradictory' (Ibid.: 375; Hudson et al., 2016a: 238) nature. These puzzling contradictions are partly a problem of methodology. International public surveys using standardised questions sometimes struggle to unpack people's contextual understandings of justice, fairness or the meanings of inequality. People's interpretation of survey questions on 'income inequality' or 'poverty' often diverge quite significantly from that of the experts who designed the questions (Orton and Rowlingson, 2007: xi, 8), for example. Beliefs about 'inequality' may be 'affected by whether it is conceptualized as a relationship between the rich and poor, the rich and the middle class, the 1 percent and the 99 percent, whites and blacks, or men and women' (McCall, 2013: 229). And because research on attitudes has been 'occupied with opinions toward specific policies or broad normative ideals' (such as equity or redistribution), 'less is known about how the public perceives inequality and what kind of inequality they are willing to tolerate' (Sachweh and Olafsdottir, 2012: 149; Bamfield and Horton, 2009; McCall, 2014).

While an increasingly sophisticated body of research on people's attitudes to inequality has been facilitated by internationally aligned public opinion surveys,[2] views on inequality are 'multidimensional', and it is 'challenging to obtain a clear picture' of research in the field (Janmaat, 2013: 357–58). We can also wonder about how meaningful people's responses to questions about national-level inequality are. Reflecting its level of analysis, such research sometimes lacks a sense of social context and can seem divorced from the everyday practical concerns of the people surveyed—concerns which might help make better sense of their attitudes and perceptions. So in an attempt to situate attitudes in context, this chapter also takes a closer look at how people view inequality within three nations: China, the United States and Britain.

Context is important because attitudes to inequality are better explained by different inequality regimes (broadly understood) rather than vice versa (Holmwood, 2014: 611; Trump, 2017; Schröder, 2017). This is because people's attitudes are shaped by—and 'realistically' adjusted to—the contexts of inequality that they find themselves in. But as this chapter shows, people are generally more aware of—and more exercised by—'local' inequalities in their own lives and social contexts. This raises a central question of how people's frame of reference shapes their viewpoint on inequality. If people develop their sense of inequality in relation to their situated practical concerns and immediate milieu, this can limit their grasp of the scale of inequality. People certainly do underestimate levels of inequality and have a poor sense of their own place in the distribution of incomes, and their attitudes are better related to their often inaccurate *perceptions* of inequality. If people systematically misperceive inequality, then increasing economic inequality may not lead to greater pressures for equality and redistribution. For some (Mijs, 2019), the key 'paradox' of inequality is that increasing inequality has not fuelled growing popular concern about it, with those living in more unequal societies showing no greater concern than those in more egalitarian societies. As Mijs notes (Ibid.: 1–2), the explanations for this paradox—in which it is variously argued that people are unaware of the extent of inequality in their country, or that living in an unequal society increases tolerance of inequality because people adjust to it, or else that people associate increasing inequality with fair meritocratic processes—are all explanations founded on how living within a structure of inequality itself shapes what people come to see and think about it.

However, this must be understood as a feature of how people make sense of inequality in terms of how it affects their own ordinary concerns and practical activities. Certainly, people's perceptions of inequality are affected by institutional regimes or cultural factors in their society, which affect not only the *visibility* of societal inequality but also the *acceptability* of redistribution and welfare systems. Attitudes and perceptions are also influenced by the framing of these issues in political and media debates, and I consider the role of public discourse in the British and American contexts. But while people do misperceive and underestimate inequality, we should not overstate the extent or significance of this. As McCall argues, people's awareness of inequality is 'accurate and critical enough' (2013: 167) for them to prefer markedly lower levels of inequality. Attitudes and perceptions about inequality are often restricted by people's 'local' situated viewing points, but this is a consequence of how people's knowledge and values are generated within their ongoing practical experiences and concerns. People do care about high inequality, though their concerns and point of view are strongly shaped by how it affects their own daily lives and opportunities and those of the people around them.

TOLERATING INEQUALITY?

Cross-national survey research shows that, in every country surveyed, a clear majority of people 'agree' or 'strongly agree' that inequality in their own country is 'too high', with only a small percentage (on average around 7%) 'strongly disagreeing' (Lübker, 2004; Hadler, 2005; Osberg and Smeeding, 2006; Janmaat, 2013). There is cross-national variation in the *strength* of dissatisfaction with inequality, but everywhere we look there is a 'generalized preference for "greater equality"', and most people in most societies desire a more egalitarian social structure (Osberg and Smeeding, 2006: 453; Evans and Kelley, 2017). Levels of agreement that inequality is too high range from the very high levels (above 95%) found in Eastern European countries as well as Portugal and Brazil to the mid-range (75–85% agreement) found in Western European countries like Britain, France and Austria, with the lowest levels (65–67%) found in Cyprus, the Philippines, Switzerland and the United States (Lübker, 2004; Osberg and Smeeding, 2006).

Here we see the puzzle that countries with extremely high levels of inequality often show the least concern about it (Larsen, 2016). A slightly less abstract question, on income inequality between occupations, asks people what they think specific jobs[3] *do actually pay* and what they think they *should* be paid. The gap between people's estimates of what jobs 'do pay' compared to what they 'should be paid' indicates how people perceive inequality relative to their norms of 'fair' income inequality (Osberg and Smeeding, 2006: 459). While some level of earnings inequality is seen as justified ('should earn' inequality), there is always a significant gap between people's estimates of what jobs 'do earn' versus what they 'should earn' so that 'in every country, in every year, the average respondent thinks there should be less inequality than he or she thinks actually exists' (Ibid.: 460; Kiatpongsan and Norton, 2016).

In every country studied, most people want less inequality and believe a significant amount of the inequality that they see is unfair. Since people generally significantly underestimate actual levels of inequality (particularly at the top of the range), the real distance from what most think would be 'fair inequality' is actually even greater. But there is lower support for redistribution. In an analysis of 31 countries, around two-thirds of individuals agreed with the view that governments *do* have a responsibility to reduce the income difference between people with high incomes and those with low incomes—only around 16.5% disagreed (Lübker, 2004: 113). Countries with high support rates for redistribution also have the highest approval rates for progressive taxes.[4] Canada, the United States and New Zealand showed the lowest support, though even in these countries around two-thirds agreed that people with high incomes should pay tax at higher rates (Ibid.: 117). However, in one of the 'paradoxes' of attitudes to inequality, levels of agreement for redistribution are always lower than levels of agreement that inequality is 'too high'.

In another 'paradox', it is not the most unequal countries which have the most negative attitudes to inequality. When we look *within* a country, it is generally the less advantaged—people dependent on welfare receipts, the poor, the least well educated, those in lower social classes, with the lowest incomes or in the most precarious jobs—who are most likely to view inequality negatively and most in favour of state welfare intervention and higher public spending (Roex, Huijts and Sieben, 2019; Larsen, 2016; Lübker, 2004; Hadler, 2005; Svallfors, 2006). Self-interest models propose that 'individuals who are more exposed to social risks' have a greater incentive to support redistribution, so *countries* should also vary in this way (Jæger, 2013: 151). The more unequal a country, the higher the proportion of people who would benefit from greater equality, which *should* produce greater support for redistribution (Meltzer and Richard, 1981). But many cross-national studies show an inconsistent or weak relationship between 'objective' levels of income inequality in a country (measured using the Gini coefficient[5]) and either egalitarian attitudes or support for redistribution.

There is a stronger relationship with the prosperity of a country, as measured by GDP (Dallinger, 2010), as people in *richer* countries seem to be more tolerant of inequality and less supportive of redistribution. But richer countries are often the most unequal. For some analysts, while material self-interest explains people's attitudes *within* a country, it does not explain why some countries show greater tolerance for inequality than others. In fact, even predictions of how rising inequality in a country should affect self-interest vary according to different theories (Medgyesi, 2013: 3), with some predicting that people will dislike rising inequality if their own relative position deteriorates (Meltzer and Richard, 1981), while others suggest that people will accept rising inequality if they think it will improve their *future* situation (Hirschman and Rothschild, 1973). Much comparative analysis has therefore turned instead to the cultural or institutional aspects of national contexts to explain cross-national variation in attitudes, either using a welfare regimes approach or looking for other factors that might shape values, such as 'cultural or religious traditions or historical experiences' (Medgyesi, 2013: 2).

Inequality is more tolerated in 'liberal' welfare regimes, like the United States, than in the more expansive welfare regimes found in Western Europe, for example. But there is considerable regional variation, with the British more accepting of differences between rich and poor than people in the social democratic welfare regime of Sweden. One suggestion is that more redistributive regimes actively shape people's values and social interests in institutional 'feedback loops' (Pierson, 1993: 621; Skocpol and Amenta, 1986). A related issue is how the different 'reach' of welfare regimes affects both the visibility and acceptability of redistribution (Carriero, 2016), as more targeted regimes (such as the UK) develop a narrower basis for social support than universalist regimes, where more people benefit. Van Oorschot (2002) found strong support for social security contributions in the Netherlands, which he connects to its comprehensive welfare system in which 90% of respondents had received benefits themselves, expected to or had a family member receiving benefits. Lübker (2004, 2007) argues that it is only after controlling for different types of welfare regimes that we can identify a cross-national correlation between levels of 'objective' inequality and attitudes to inequality. But others identify variation within countries of the same regime 'type' (with lower support for redistribution in West Germany[6] compared to France or Austria) as well as similar support levels in countries from different types (as in the cases of Germany and Norway, where 'support for further redistribution is almost as low as in liberal countries') (Dallinger, 2010: 337, 340). On this basis, regimes are 'only partly homogeneous "worlds of social policy preferences"' (Ibid.: 340), although this also reflects disagreement about how best to classify different welfare regimes (Jæger, 2009).

The question of how national context affects the relationship between inequality and attitudes is complex, as we can see when we look at the former state-socialist countries of Eastern Europe. These experienced rapid increases in inequality in their shift from communist to market economies from the 1990s on. On the one hand, people became more accepting of income inequality between designated occupations.[7] In 1987, Central Eastern Europeans preferred less income inequality across selected jobs, but by 1999 they accepted 'substantially more income inequality than most Westerners' (Kelley and Evans, 1993; Kelley and Zagorski, 2005: 352). On the other hand, when asked a different question (whether inequality is 'too large'), people in these economies had higher agreement rates (over 90%) than those in many Western European countries (and were more likely to 'strongly agree') (Lübker, 2004: 97). As Janmaat argues (2013: 375), it seems 'contradictory that the degree of income inequality believed to be legitimate has risen steeply in the East [of Europe] while at the same time people in this region have become more sceptical about the extent to which existing incomes reflect meritocratic principles and are more disapproving of the degree of existing inequality in their country than people in the West'.

By 2009, however, attitude differences between post-communist countries and market economies on whether inequalities are 'too large' had reduced (Medgyesi, 2013). But clearly, questions of fairness also shape attitudes to inequality, with people in post-socialist economies showing very strong agreement that unequal outcomes are the result of 'nepotism' or 'the actions of the rich and powerful'. So an aversion to inequality in post-socialist countries is tied to people's concerns about fairness, in which inequality of opportunity drives attitudes towards overall inequality (Cojocaru, 2014: 590). We can further explore how market economies reshape attitudes to inequality by looking more closely at attitudes in national context in another 'transition' economy: China. The Chinese case shows that questions of fairness and opportunity are very significant when people assess levels of inequality, but it also shows the highly situated and practical character of people's understandings of inequality.

ATTITUDES IN CONTEXT: WHY DON'T THE CHINESE CARE ABOUT RISING INEQUALITY?

From 1978 on, communist China experienced a dramatic increase in inequality[8] from the Maoist[9] era, the result of market reforms aimed (successfully) at producing rapid economic growth. There are fears—from both commentators and the Chinese leadership—that the Chinese are angry about increasing inequality, creating a 'social volcano scenario' of potential unrest (Whyte, 2011: 275, 276). There are good reasons for this fear, since the 'entire system of distribution of centrally planned socialism' was replaced 'by market-oriented institutions, and . . . forms of wealth and privilege that the revolution set out to destroy . . . returned with a vengeance' while the 'downsides of capitalism' also returned, with 'unemployment, inflation, loss of health insurance, bankruptcy, and confiscations of housing and farmland in shady development deals' (Whyte, 2011: 275).[10] But fears of rising anger are not borne out by survey evidence on attitudes (Whyte, 2010a, 2010b, 2011, 2016; Whyte and Han, 2009). The Chinese are critical of certain aspects of inequalities in China (71.7% thought national income gaps were too large) but more generally express 'acceptance or approval rather than anger over current inequalities' (Whyte, 2011: 277, 278):

> Most respondents thought that differences in ability are an important factor explaining who is rich (69.5 percent) versus who is poor (61.3 percent), whereas the unfairness of the economic system was stressed by many fewer respondents—only 27 percent thought that such unfairness has a large influence on who is rich, and 21 percent stressed this explanation of who is poor. Only 29.5 percent of respondents favoured redistribution from the rich to the poor, and only 33.8 percent advocated setting a maximum limit on individual incomes. (Whyte, 2011: 278)

Not only is there apparently little discontent about rocketing inequality in China[11]; there is also the 'puzzle' (Whyte, 2011) of why more disadvantaged groups (such as poorer rural residents) are the most positive while the more advantaged (urban residents, the well educated, and communist party members) are more critical and more likely to want greater redistribution (Ibid.: 279).

One obvious answer to these questions rests in the success of the Chinese economic reforms in generating spectacular, sustained growth which, while very unequally shared, has still created dramatic improvements in standards of living and possession of consumer goods for many in China. With such dramatic improvements, it is perhaps unsurprising that Chinese attitudes indicate a 'predominantly optimistic expectation that the rising tide of economic development will lift all boats, even if not at the same pace' (Whyte, 2010b: 307). Another answer is that—partly in fear of unrest—from the late 1990s, the Chinese leadership introduced significant policy changes to create a fragmented but reasonably extensive welfare system based on social insurance, extending social protection and tackling the worst elements of rural poverty (Ringen and Ngok, 2013; Hong and Kongshøj, 2013; Whyte, 2011: 276).

But for Whyte, another answer to the puzzle is that many aspects of China's current inequalities are seen as fair and based on individual effort and ability. In China, there are high levels of agreement with the idea that poverty is the result of a lack of ability, low education or a lack of effort (rather than bad luck, discrimination, unequal opportunities or an unfair economic system) (Whyte, 2010b: 308–10). Whyte argues that this must be understood in contrast to the policies of the Maoist era, which, while promoting a particular vision of equality, also created sharp divisions in rights and resources between urban and rural areas under the restrictive *hukou* system.[12] The features of current inequalities to which people object most strongly 'have their roots in the socialist era (such as special treatment of officials and discrimination against those who lack urban *hukou*), rather than being products of the market reforms' (Whyte, 2011: 278). Whyte argues that it is comparisons to the Maoist era, which was widely seen as unfair, which explain why Chinese people see the increased inequality produced by the reforms as broadly fair (or, at least, fairer). This also explains why more disadvantaged groups, especially rural ones, 'have more positive attitudes . . . than their more advantaged fellow citizens', because the former have gained most from the changed policies to rural China (Ibid.: 284).

The basis of comparison through which people assess inequality is very significant. This also underpins the influence of reference groups on Chinese attitudes to inequality. Chinese people, on average, feel that their situation is better than that of the family they grew up in (Larsen, 2016). People partly base their sense of inequality on comparisons to their immediate milieu of family, neighbours and co-workers, and Whyte's data suggests it is local inequalities in people's immediate milieu which really matter to them. For example, when people responded to questions about why some people are poor while others are rich, 'they tended to focus on the rich and poor people in their own immediate environment, rather than on invisible or dimly perceived rich and poor people in other parts of China' (Whyte, 2010b: 310). However, workplaces and neighbourhoods are typically segregated along lines of inequality, so people will generally see less inequality in their locality. For example, while 71.7% of Chinese people thought that the *national* income gap was too large,[13] this fell to 31% when considering *neighbourhood* income inequality (Ibid.). Han's (2012: 937) analysis of Chinese people's satisfaction with their living standards found that rural people were 'more likely to identify with fellow rural hukou holders' as their reference group, and even though they were 'aware of the tremendous disadvantages that they suffer compared with their urban counterparts' they did not 'take urban citizens as a relevant reference point' in assessing their situation. If 'what matters most to individuals is how they see themselves compared to various local reference groups, rather than the entire nation, then it would appear that most respondents consider the inequalities around them to be acceptable' (Whyte, 2010b: 310).

Whyte argues that most people are not discontented with inequalities in China. However, there are some difficulties with this conclusion related to the limitations of national attitudes data. As Madsen (2011: 967) notes, surveys of what Chinese people *say* about inequality find limited discontent, but studies of social movements have examined what people *do* in China, and they tell a different story. Social movements are not representative of all citizens, but Chinese social movements show rising levels of protest against injustice since the 1990s, with a rapid increase in disruptive collective protests, such as strikes, sit-ins, factory occupations and confrontations with police (Cai, 2010; Yan, 2013; Liu and Shi, 2017). The dismantling of the Maoist 'iron rice bowl' system resulted in increased poverty and loss of various social protections, while education, healthcare and housing became widely unaffordable. Ringen and Ngok argue that the 'resulting misery gave rise to widespread and serious social unrest, including strike actions, throughout the country during the late 1980s and 1990s, on a regime-threatening scale beyond what has generally been recognized outside of China' (2013: 7). It was concerns about this unrest that led to the reintroduction of welfare protections and action to reduce rural poverty. How does this square with Whyte's attitudes data?

Whyte (2010b: 305) acknowledges the wave of protests that have buffeted China but argues that they are not driven by popular anger against inequality *per se* but rather are linked to specific local grievances about corruption and procedural injustice. Such protests have generally not targeted the rule of the central Communist Party, a legacy of the brutally suppressed 1989 Tiananmen Square democracy protests (Yan, 2013; Liu and Shi, 2017). Protest in China mostly comes from 'aggrieved citizens who have suffered economic losses and who demand concrete and practical rights for unfair and unjust treatments', with protests focused on local issues and targeted specifically at local authorities and corrupt officials (Yan, 2013: 342), on the 'cadres, managers and bosses who flaunt their opulence while many workers go unpaid . . . because people suspect foul play and unfair advantages as the real causes of wealth' (Wong, 2004: 166). These protestors are 'not motivated by abstract conceptions of social justice, but by concretely experienced injustice' and 'do not usually object to broad patterns of inequality but to people using their power to take away something that rightfully belongs to them' (Madsen, 2011: 968–69).

A major wave of protests was provoked by land confiscations, home demolitions, factory lay-offs, food contamination scandals or pollution caused by unscrupulous manufacturers (Cai, 2010; Yan, 2013; Liu and Shi, 2017; Lora-Wainwright, 2017). But is national inequality disconnected from local injustices? People may not be angry about high levels of national inequality in the abstract, but rising inequality is itself a serious threat to local political accountability and procedural justice because of the possibilities it creates for undue influence and corruption—precisely the factors shaping discontent and protest in China. While Chinese people do see meritocratic processes as important for getting ahead, there is also a widespread perception that cronyism and corruption are important influences too (He and Reynolds, 2017). A note of caution is also required. Chinese attitudes to inequality seem strongly affected by two decades of spectacular growth, but China's economy has noticeably slowed, potentially seeding more discontent, as 'slumping demand, frequent lay-offs, factory relocations and shutdowns have triggered wildcat strikes and disruptive protests over wages, jobs and social protection' (Liu and Shi , 2017: 355).

OPPORTUNITY, FAIRNESS AND ATTITUDES TO INEQUALITY

In China, people seem willing to tolerate high national inequality if they think it results fairly from hard work or if they feel their own opportunities and prosperity have improved (though this is also affected by their focus on local inequalities and by the limited practical possibilities for challenging state-level policies). But if we look cross-nationally, to what extent are popular attitudes to inequality shaped by beliefs about fairness and opportunity? As Chapter 1 notes, inequality is sometimes presented as a necessary evil, either as essential for growth (increasing prosperity for all) or else as necessary to encourage hard work (also good for growth and related to widely held beliefs that people should be fairly rewarded for their efforts). Because of the complexity in the relationship between a country's level of inequality and levels of dissatisfaction with it, one line of inquiry is to explore how attitudes to inequality are related to economic conditions more broadly, such as a country's prosperity, or else to the neo-liberal values (such as meritocracy) emphasised in capitalist market economies.

The ISSP asks whether people think inequality is the result of social injustice or is necessary for prosperity.[14] Significantly, everywhere we find *lower* levels of agreement with the instrumental statement that 'large differences in income are necessary for prosperity' than with social injustice statements that 'inequality exists because it benefits the rich and powerful' or that 'knowing the right people' is important for getting ahead (Osberg and Smeeding, 2006: 455). Conversely, people's agreement with the statement that 'large differences in income are necessary for [a country's] prosperity' is greatest in countries where people are 'less concerned about income differences' (Lübker, 2004: 98[15] ; Hadler, 2005). An emphasis on meritocratic principles in a society may generate more individualist understandings of inequality, the view that people 'get what they deserve and deserve what they get' (Lerner, 1980: vii–viii). This relates to the perceived fairness of inequality, and people do seem prepared to tolerate higher levels of inequality if they think it is generated fairly. Attitudes to *redistribution* are also shaped by beliefs about 'why people get ahead in society' (Linos and West, 2003: 393)—the perceived fairness or unfairness of opportunities for advancement. People are more likely to support redistribution if they think society is unfair, less so if they perceive good opportunities for advancement (Luo, 1998; Fong, 2001; Funk, 2000; Linos and West, 2003; Alesina and Giuliano, 2011; Kim et al., 2018). Linos and West (2003) also suggest that the relative importance that people assign to structural as opposed to individual factors in determining social mobility affects attitudes to redistribution, with those emphasising individual explanations showing less support.[16]

The more inequalities are seen as 'deserved', the less frequently they are seen as 'too large' (Duru-Bellat and Tenret, 2012: 245). Duru-Bellat and Tenret's (2012) analysis of perceived meritocracy[17] in 26 countries indicates that both *perceptions* about whether a society is actually meritocratic and *support* for meritocratic principles are greater in more unequal societies. For some, this suggests that very unequal societies develop a meritocratic ideology which legitimises inequalities (Huber and Form, 1973; Mijs, 2019). However, at the individual level, just under a third of participants to the ISSP survey agreed that people in their country were appropriately rewarded for their efforts, with individuals 'more sceptical about the prevalence of meritocracy than . . . expected' (Duru-Bellat and Tenret, 2012: 231–32). In most societies, people perceive that *both* meritocratic and nonmeritocratic processes influence opportunities, though with significant variation in emphasis between countries. Inhabitants of Eastern European post-socialist economies were particularly sceptical that their country was meritocratic, unlike North Americans and Australians,[18] who were 'more likely to believe that merit is rewarded', while Western Europe was inconsistent, with the French more sceptical than West Germans (Ibid.).

For Duru-Bellat and Tenret, these 'rather large between-country differences challenge the assumption of a universal belief in a just world or at least of a universal perception that inequality is deserved' (2012: 231–32). A country's objective level of social inequality (as measured by the Gini coefficient) was only weakly correlated with people's perception of meritocracy (with no correlation for most Western European countries) (Ibid.: 238). A country's *prosperity* (measured by GDP) seemed to be a more important factor, with people in richer countries more likely to see inequality in their country as meritocratic. There was also a positive correlation between 'perceptions of justice for oneself and for one's own country', as people who had 'a strong belief in the fairness of their own salary' were more likely to believe that people more generally were fairly rewarded (Duru-Bellat and Tenret, 2012: 238, 233–34).

ATTITUDES IN CONTEXT: THE 'AMERICAN DREAM' IN THE LAND OF INEQUITABLE OPPORTUNITY

Cross-national research suggests that people are more willing to accept higher inequality if they perceive that opportunity (whether in terms of meritocratic opportunities or growth/prosperity) is still widely available. In societies where meritocratic perceptions are more prevalent, higher-level groups show more tolerance of inequality, but people are also more polarised in their attitudes, with lower social groups showing greater dissatisfaction (Roex et al., 2019). Are beliefs in opportunity and concerns about inequality in opposition? This type of argument has been used to explain American 'exceptionalism'—the question of why the United States has extremely high income inequality yet Americans express higher tolerance for inequality, and lower support for redistribution, than other nations. Explanations often turn to the 'American dream' and Americans' belief that there are good opportunities for everyone. Certainly, over 90% of Americans believe that hard work is essential/very important in getting ahead, a level which, as McCall (2016: 423) notes, is 'greater than the median among advanced industrial countries, which is nonetheless quite high itself at 73%'.

Yet—partly because so many Americans share this 'bootstraps' notion of opportunity—beliefs about the importance of hard work for getting ahead 'have no discernible impact whatsoever on beliefs about income inequality' *within* the United States, so 'it is grossly misleading' to see such beliefs about hard work as 'an indicator of tolerant beliefs about income inequality' (McCall, 2013: 152–53). McCall insists there is a difference between *principles* (most Americans place great importance on the value of hard work) and *practice* (they also recognise that social barriers to opportunity are important), and their agreement with the statement that there is 'the opportunity for a person in this nation to get ahead by working hard' has been steadily falling since 2001 (2016: 425). Structural versus individual explanations of inequality are often presented as opposing principles, yet cross-national data shows most people recognise that *both* structural and individual factors affect success. Among Americans, 60% believe that 'both hard work and at least one of the factors unrelated to individual initiative are essential or very important for getting ahead. Less than a third think that only hard work is essential or very important' (McCall, 2013: 154; He and Reynolds, 2017). And compared to other nations, 'Americans are generally as or more likely to believe in the role of social factors in getting ahead, such as having well-educated parents, coming from a wealthy family, and knowing the right people' (McCall, 2016: 423–24).

McCall's analysis of 'variation in beliefs among individual Americans' over time, from 1987 to 2012, shows firstly, that Americans have desired less inequality for decades, and secondly, that they have become most concerned about inequality 'in times of *inequitable* growth, that is at times when they saw the rich as prospering while opportunities for good jobs, fair pay and high quality education were restricted for everyone else' (2013: frontispiece, original emphasis; 2016; McCall et al., 2017). Americans became more critical of inequality at times when it was 'perceived as benefiting the rich at the expense of the rest of Americans' (McCall, 2013: frontispiece). So concerns about opportunity may actually increase dissatisfaction with inequality. While Americans' concern about inequality grew during the period, this was 'not in a steadily upward direction as might be expected if mounting dissatisfaction simply corresponded to growing awareness and opposition to inequality as it escalated'. Instead, there was a swell of opposition to inequality during the 1990s, which fell back during the 2000s (though to a higher level than in 1987), then another peak in 2012. These peaks of concern about inequality were correlated to 'perceptions of the negative *consequences* of inequality—its practical impact on economic opportunity—rather than with perceptions of the *level* of inequality itself' (2016: 427–28). Overall, concerns about *both* inequality and opportunity rose substantially, with concerns about inequality even increasing 'at a time when Americans assessed the US economy as performing well' (Ibid.: 424). This, McCall argues (2013: xiii; McCall et al., 2017), shows many Americans are attuned to the distributional nature of growth and not just to growth alone.

Researchers have sometimes concluded that Americans are not concerned about inequality because they place faith in the United States as the land of opportunity. But McCall rejects the assumption that strong beliefs about opportunity create tolerance for inequality. She argues that beliefs about inequality and opportunity have multiple dimensions to them, and we must go beyond seeing them as oppositional. Americans *are* strongly concerned about equal opportunities, but this means more to them than just the role of 'individual hard work in getting ahead' ('bootstraps opportunity') as they are also concerned about 'the availability of jobs, the assurance of fair pay, and the equal treatment of individuals from different class backgrounds' as central components of a 'full-opportunity society' (2013: 8). Americans 'have a much more encompassing understanding of what opportunity means, and how it can be unfairly restricted, than is commonly thought', which means that they 'sometimes construe income inequality as *itself* a restriction of economic opportunity', with this occurring 'when everyone does not appear to be benefiting from economic growth or suffering from economic troubles' (Ibid.).

So Americans' concerns about inequality arise from their sense that inequality itself is restricting opportunities. However, Americans also express lower support for redistribution than many other nations. How can we square this with their concerns about inequality? McCall argues that if we 'dig deeper into views', we can see that American concerns about income inequality are 'best understood as fears of narrowing opportunities' in which 'greater labor market opportunities are the ultimate goal' (2013: 7). Americans' views about income inequality are rooted in *labour market opportunities*, so it is 'education, jobs, and fair pay, rather than progressive taxes and other government social policies' which are 'the outcomes that those Americans increasingly concerned about inequality wish to see' (Ibid.: xiii). American attitudes to inequality result from a very practical focus on how inequality affects the availability of good jobs which are fairly paid. This emphasis on labour market opportunities, she argues, resolves the paradox of why Americans express lower levels of enthusiasm for welfare state policies and yet still yearn for a more equitable society.

However, understandings of equity and the distribution of opportunities also depend on feelings of social entitlement and the relative social standing that people feel they *deserve*. This again raises questions about the selective basis on which people make social comparisons when assessing inequality so that objective levels of inequality are not straightforwardly related to social discontent. We can see this in the complex factors affecting voting in the United States in the 2016 presidential election of Donald Trump. Media debate has sometimes presented Donald Trump's victory as a reaction against neo-liberal policies and rising inequality, the electoral response of a post-industrial white working class 'left behind' by the declining opportunities created by free trade and factory closures, who feel government elites have become corrupt or unresponsive to ordinary people (Gusterson, 2017: 210). But while Trump did win the majority of both white and non-college-educated voters, the characterisation of this heterogeneous group as a left-behind 'working class' is problematic (Walley, 2017; Gusterson, 2017). Trump won the majority of votes among those earning over $50,000 a year, while the majority of those earning *less* voted for Clinton (Henley, 2016), while exit polls from the primaries show Trump voters earnt on average $72,000 a year, well above the US median yearly income of $56,000 (Walley, 2017: 232).

Hochschild (2016) has referred to the 'red state paradox', in which the poorest American states often receive more in federal subsidies than they generate in taxes, and yet the people in these states tend to elect Republicans espousing low tax and small-government policies. Hochschild argues that these apparently self-defeating choices reflect a sense among white voters in poor Republican-leaning states that the federal government does not represent their interests, expressing a sense not only that they have not got what they deserved but also that they have experienced other groups—black and Hispanic Americans—'cutting in line'. However, the poorest people in the poorest states are generally not white, and the 'left-behind' white Republicans that Hochschild studied were actually middle class (Bhambra, 2017). As Chapter 1 notes, economic dislocation and marginality were not significantly related to voters switching to Trump (Reny, Collingwood and Valenzuela, 2019), with 'economic anxiety' or 'economic distress' having little impact on candidate preference (Mutz, 2018; Oberhauser, Krier and Kusow, 2019). Instead voting for Trump was much better related to *racial* status anxiety related to white Americans' sense of a threat to their dominant group status (Mutz, 2018), with measures of voters' racism correlated much more closely with support for Trump than economic dissatisfaction (Schaffner, MacWilliams and Nteta, 2018).

So how inequalities are perceived and framed is a very significant question. McCall and Davidoff (2017: S49) point out that in American politics, neither of the major political parties have typically addressed the 'class' dimension of inequality 'explicitly, or at least not in a way that is historically and culturally resonant', with a failure to make 'economic and political arguments that address economic and political needs and aspirations as directly as possible'. Instead, as Bhambra (2017: S225) notes, the United States has long been organised around *race* as the primary category of differentiation.

McCall and Orloff (2017: S37) argue that the multidimensional nature of inequality, and the multiplicity of people's interests and identities, mean that we must reject the idea that we can 'read off' people's interests, aspirations and values from their economic or demographic characteristics, as if such interests were 'objective and transparent'. Hence, people's identifications are 'politically mediated and constructed' (Ibid.: S37), but this returns us to the question of how well people perceive and understand inequality and what factors shape their point of view.

THE MISPERCEPTION OF INEQUALITY?

Attitudes to inequality are not straightforwardly related to 'objective' levels of inequality. In fact, people in the most unequal countries tend to tolerate more inequality (Schröder, 2017; Mijs, 2019). For some analysts, this means we must focus instead on how values and beliefs (such as beliefs in opportunity) shape attitudes. But most studies have tended to use cross-sectional comparisons of how attitudes vary with levels of inequality (comparing countries with higher and lower levels of inequality), with fewer studies analysing the impact of changes in inequality *over time* (Medgyesi, 2013: 7). Studies that do examine change over time have found that rising inequality *is* generally associated with an increasing agreement that it is 'too large' (e.g., Lübker, 2004; Kerr, 2011; Medgyesi, 2013).[19] In European countries, people also express stronger support for *redistribution* as inequality rises (Finseraas, 2009; Pontusson and Rueda, 2010; Jæger, 2013); however, the relationship is complicated as 'high economic growth decreases the demand for redistribution, while high income inequality increases this demand' (Jæger, 2013: 160).

Furthermore, when asked about what they think is a fair level of inequality (so when they are not asked about their opinions on change), 'those living in unequal societies are more supportive of inequality than are people living in equal societies', which suggests people's views of acceptable inequality are 'realistically' bounded by the actual level of actual inequality in their country (Curtis and Andersen, 2015: 6). And it is not just the level of inequality or economic growth which affects attitudes but also how people feel that inequality affects the distribution of opportunities (McCall, 2013). However, studies of change over time suggest that a shift in a country's inequality has to be very *significant* for it to affect attitudes. Medgyesi (2013: 22) found that when inequality is on the rise, the agreement with the statement that 'inequalities are too large' also increases—but the size of the effect is relatively small, 'since a huge increase is needed in the Gini index to modify societal judgment about the level of inequality to a significant extent'. Hence, if the shift has to be very significant to shape people's attitudes, the question of just how well people perceive national inequality and what shapes those perceptions is raised.

It is commonly argued that people have a relatively poor sense of the actual extent of inequality in their country. From this perspective, 'uncertainty and misperception' about levels of inequality are 'widespread', with ordinary people knowing 'little about the extent of income inequality in their societies, its rate and direction of change, and where they fit into the distribution' (Gimpelson and Treisman, 2017: 1). Kiatponsan and Norton (2014) found that respondents in 40 countries underestimated the extent of inequality between CEOs and unskilled workers, with most people holding 'incorrect perceptions of inequality in their country' (Hauser and Norton, 2017: 22; Gimpelson and Treisman, 2017; Niehues, 2014; Keller, Medgyesi and Toth, 2010; Cruces, Perez-Truglia and Tetaz, 2013; Verme, 2014; Chambers, Swan and Heesacker, 2014). Take perceptions of the income gap. The ISSP asks respondents how much they think employees in five occupations (from unskilled factory worker to CEO of a large national corporation) earn, but respondents' estimates are generally well out. In the Philippines, a general practice doctor earned about $5,500, but Filipino respondents guessed $144,000. South Africans thought a typical CEO earned $77,000, but the average across 56 major South African companies was $1.7 million (Gimpelson and Treisman, 2017: 10). The British Social Attitudes Survey found that British people grossly underestimated the income gap between top and bottom incomes (they thought it *was* 12:1, and *should be* 6:1, when in fact it was 42:1) (Bromley, 2003). Many European respondents also 'think poverty is either much higher or lower than it is' (Gimpelson and Treisman, 2017: 11).

People also have a poor sense of their own relative position within their society. Evans and Kelley (2004: 3) found a 'pronounced tendency to see oneself as being in the middle of the social hierarchy' with very few people placing themselves at the top or bottom. This sense of a 'middling' social position holds true for 'the well-educated, the poorly educated, and those in-between', and in every country studied—from 'the impoverished Philippines to wealthy Sweden; in long established capitalist economies and under Communism and its aftermath in Eastern Europe' (Ibid.: 18, 17). Subjective social location *is* related to people's objective circumstances—for example, the more educated tend to place themselves a little higher in the hierarchy. A country's overall economic condition also matters. People in *richer* countries place themselves higher (on average) in their national social hierarchy than people in poorer ones, while people in countries with high unemployment feel lower down the social scale than those in equally rich countries with lower levels of unemployment (Ibid.).

Evans and Kelley (2004: 25) suggest prosperity influences subjective social location by giving people the feeling of having more opportunities, in the sense that a 'rising tide lifts all boats', while high unemployment makes everyone (not just the unemployed) feel less secure. But the 'objectively' poor also tend not to place themselves at the bottom of the hierarchy. In the Philippines, those with the lowest education—Filipino elementary school graduates, who are 'poor people in a poor country with great inequalities'—still placed themselves closer to the middle of society, with only 13% seeing themselves in the bottom stratum (Ibid.: 25). Cross-nationally, Gimpelson and Treisman found few people receiving targeted income benefits thought they belonged at the bottom of the national distribution: most located themselves above the bottom fifth (2017: 16). Even those who said they had 'gone without enough food to eat'[20] 'nevertheless placed themselves in the top six of ten income groups' (Ibid.). At the other end of the scale, 'many respondents who were almost certainly among the wealthiest in their country thought their incomes below average' (Ibid.).

But is it really surprising that people are pretty poor judges of the scale of inequality in their society, and of their own relative social position within it, given 'how hard it is to estimate distributions of income and property—for skilled professionals, let alone statistically unsophisticated citizens' (Gimpelson and Treisman, 2017: 4)? And is it really surprising that the staggering scale of economic inequality is beyond most people's imaginations? In the United States in 2017, for example, just three individuals—Bill Gates, Warren Buffett and Jeff Bezos—collectively held more wealth than the bottom 50% of the US population (a total of 160 million people), while one in five US households had zero or negative net worth (Collins and Hoxie, 2017: 1). Inequality on this scale is difficult for anyone to grasp. Gimpelson and Treisman (2017: 1) suggest that theories of the political impact of inequality 'need to be reframed as theories about effects of *perceived* inequality' as it is the perceived level of inequality which correlates with the belief that it is too high (Niehues, 2014; Brunori, 2016). Similarly, it is people's *perception* of being socially mobile (rather than their actual mobility) that results in greater approval for levels of inequality (Kelley and Kelley, 2009; Engelhardt and Wagener, 2014). And the 'demand for redistribution appears to vary not with actual inequality but the perception of it' (Gimpelson and Treisman, 2017: 23; Niehues, 2014; Engelhardt and Wagener, 2014; Keller et al., 2010). For example, a study of China, Japan, South Korea and Taiwan found *perceived* levels of economic inequality positively associated with attitudes towards redistribution (Kim et al., 2018).[21]

What shapes people's perceptions? One reason why attitudes to inequality only correspond loosely to actual inequality levels may be because people focus on the more *visible* aspects of inequalities (Keller et al., 2010: 7). Cross-nationally, people's (in)tolerance of inequality is better correlated with the rate and severity of poverty than conventional measures of inequality (Ibid.: 7–8), perhaps because poverty is a closer proxy to what people associate with 'inequality', but also because it is more visible. But we must also consider how perceptions are shaped and *how and why* people develop a view of broader social circumstances. A country's prosperity and unemployment level also affect perceptions of inequality by shaping people's sense of personal opportunities or insecurity and reflecting their practical focus on how inequality affects them. A similar emphasis on the practical and situated character of people's grasp of inequality can be seen in the argument that 'reference group effects' cause people to misjudge inequality and their own relative position. The argument here is that people base their sense of social inequality on their immediate milieu. However, inequality is baked into such social arrangements. If people assess their relative location in terms of the people around them, the 'tendency for one's spouse and friends to be similar to oneself in education, occupational status and income' also means a 'tendency to perceive everyone as similar to oneself' (Evans, Kelley and Kolosi, 1992: 465; Kelley and Evans, 2017; Evans and Kelley, 2017). Cruces and colleagues' (2013) Argentinian study found systematic biases in people's evaluation of their relative income position (with poorer individuals overestimating and richer individuals underestimating it), which they connect to reference group processes. The bias in people's perceptions was significantly correlated with an individual's relative income rank within their local neighbourhood (a proxy of reference group processes, as neighbourhoods are strongly segregated by income), while respondents with friends from heterogeneous social backgrounds were less prone to such biases (Ibid.: 101).

Peer groups are generally quite homogenous, so the limited nature of people's 'reference-group' comparisons restricts perceptions of the scale of inequality (Kelley and Evans, 1995, 2017). Nonetheless, objective circumstances (income and education, the prosperity of the nation and the national level of unemployment) do still influence subjective location, but they are 'muted' by reference-group effects (Evans and Kelley, 2004: 1; 2017). Similarly, studies examining how income variation in neighbourhoods shapes *attitudes* to inequality show that people living alongside others of the same income level are more likely to hold meritocratic beliefs, while those living in more mixed-income neighbourhoods are more aware of the structural factors affecting success (Mijs, 2019: 5; Merolla, Hunt and Serpe, 2011; Newman, Johnston and Lown, 2015).

In the United States, for example, those who live alongside people from different income backgrounds in their neighbourhood perceive larger income gaps and are more favourable to action on the issue compared to those who do not get this daily exposure to income diversity where they live (Minkoff and Lyons, 2017). Those who perceive higher levels of wage inequality are both more likely to think this is shaped by nonmeritocratic principles and more likely to see inequality as negative (Kuhn, 2019). Conversely, higher-status people tend to see their societies as more egalitarian than low-status people (Evans and Kelley, 2017). As Mijs (2019: 6) argues, income inequality only 'becomes economic reality when it affects affluent and poor people's wages and employment' and only 'becomes social reality when it impacts the social and spatial environment in which the rich and poor lead their lives'. However, growing income inequality has a segregative effect, creating 'greater spatial and social distance between the wealthy and the poor', who increasingly live lives in different neighbourhoods and institutions with less interaction 'across income, wealth and racial fault lines' (Ibid.: 6–7). For Mijs (Ibid.), this explains why people in highly unequal societies believe they are meritocratic because 'inequality creates the social conditions for its legitimation':

> Unequal societies are marked by greater social distance, such that the rich and poor develop an understanding of society and their own place in it from a position of socioeconomic insulation. As a result, people in more unequal societies underestimate the extent of inequality and the role of structural advantages or barriers that help or hurt them. (Mijs, 2019: 7)

But while people do misperceive economic inequality, we should not overstate the extent or significance of this. People's underestimation of inequality does not prevent majorities—in every country surveyed—from thinking that it is too high. This is certainly true in the United States (Norton and Ariely, 2013; Franks and Scherr, 2019). McCall (2013, 2016; McCall et al., 2017) is sceptical about what she calls the 'ignorance thesis'. She rejects the idea that Americans are ignorant about inequality but also the idea that if only they 'knew how extreme inequality is, they would object to it in greater numbers' (Ibid.). She argues that Americans' awareness of inequality is 'accurate and critical enough' 'to underwrite elevated concerns about inequality', noting that 'Americans are dissatisfied with pay disparities' and that 'this dissatisfaction grew dramatically over the 2000s' (2013: 167). Over two-thirds of Americans feel CEOs are overpaid, and Americans are also 'generally aware' of the rise in executive pay, the stagnation of worker pay and the widening of pay disparities (McCall, 2016: 423–24; McCall and Chin, 2013). People do 'significantly understate' the dramatic increase in earnings inequality, but the earnings ratio they desire is 'still remarkably low—4:1 in 2000 and 7:1 in 2010' (2016: 423–24.). Because Americans' preferred level of inequality is *already* so low, it is 'unlikely that preferences for less inequality would be substantially altered by a more accurate appraisal of the scale of executive pay' (Ibid.).

There does remain a question of perception, however. As we have already seen, McCall argues that the peaks in Americans' concern about inequality fluctuated in line with their concerns about the inequitable nature of growth. But what shaped that sense of inequitable growth? McCall suggests that people partly gain their sense of national inequality from the media. Her analysis of the media coverage of inequality shows that in the United States, public attitudes changed in line with the nature of that coverage. She argues (2013: xiii) that 'the media, far from posing solely as an apologist for the rich and rising inequality, often document the tilt of inequitable growth toward the rich, and did so especially in the recovery from the early 1990s' recession' (precisely when attitudes changed). So while Americans hold quite sophisticated views on inequality (with their concerns about rising economic inequality centred on how it might compromise equality of opportunity), these were more influenced by trends in media coverage than by the level or trend in objective inequality in the United States. On this basis, she argues that Americans are 'both more and less clued in' about inequality than much research suggests (Ibid.). They are less clued in because they are 'in the dark as to how to address the problem of inequality', although McCall attributes this 'more to a lack of political leadership than to ignorance' (Ibid.). But this raises the more general question of how political debates and media coverage shape the public awareness of inequality and its solutions. In Britain, such debates seem to have shaped increasingly negative attitudes to the poor and to redistributive policies. However, the British case again demonstrates the complex nature of social attitudes, because while it does show the force of negative public discourses, it also shows that we cannot dismiss the effects of concrete social conditions on attitudes.

ATTITUDES IN CONTEXT: HAVE NEGATIVE PUBLIC DISCOURSES UNDERMINED BRITONS' SUPPORT FOR REDISTRIBUTION?

In Britain, sharp increases in inequality have been associated with an increased tolerance to certain aspects of inequality as well as declining support for redistribution. One prominent explanation for this points to the influence of political and media debates which present an increasingly negative view of the poor and welfare recipients as 'scroungers' (Taylor-Gooby, 2013: 35; Tyler, 2013; Jensen and Tyler, 2015). Inequality in Britain rose markedly from 1979,[22] but since the mid-1980s, survey data shows falling support for redistribution, a hardening of attitudes to welfare benefits as well as increasingly negative views of the poor and benefits recipients (Baumberg, 2014; Taylor-Gooby and Taylor, 2015). This trend continued after the global financial crisis of 2008–2009, a time of fiscal austerity, economic recession then stagnation, falling real incomes and, after 2010, steep cuts in public services in Britain. It has long been argued that there is a 'thermostat effect' which sees attitudes to welfare fluctuating in reaction to changing social conditions (with people more likely to agree that public spending should be cut after a period of high spending, or having more favourable views on unemployment benefits when the unemployment rate rises) (Wlezien, 1995; Curtice, 2010). But some argue that the influence of negative public discourses about the poor and welfare mean that British people's views have become detached from social conditions so that even big increases in inequality and poverty create no reaction.

Taylor-Gooby and Taylor (2015: 93) argue that the 'thermostat effect' has become 'weaker in recent years', with a long-term decline in support in Britain for spending on public services in general and on welfare in particular. In 1989, 61% agreed that the government should spend more on welfare—but by 2009, in the midst of a major economic crisis, this figure was just 27% (Ibid.: 77–78). We can also see a hardening of attitudes towards spending on unemployment benefits. In 1996, 33% thought more should be spent on this benefit compared to just 16% in 2016 (Curtice, 2016). And it is 'striking' that attitudes were so unsympathetic during 'the most severe and long-lasting recession in living memory, five years of a government intent on reducing welfare expenditure and an increase in poverty among working age people with no children' (Taylor-Gooby and Taylor, 2015: 93). Jensen and Tyler (2015: 484, original emphasis; Jensen, 2014) argue that while in previous recessions 'public support *for* welfare provisions increased as poverty and hardship became visible in everyday lives', during the most recent recession there has been 'growing public support for *cuts* to state welfare programmes'.

Jensen and Tyler (2015: 474, 480) suggest 'an anti-welfare common sense' has emerged in Britain generated by political and media discourses which identify an 'undeserving poor', fuelling 'public hostilities towards populations imagined to be a parasitical drain on resources'. Hills (2015) and Taylor-Gooby (2013) identify widespread public 'myths' about welfare in Britain, particularly the false assumption of a divide between people who benefit from the welfare state ('skivers') and people who pay into it ('strivers'). Media analysis indicates increasingly negative representations of welfare claimants, with a high proportion of the coverage on benefit fraud (Baumberg et al., 2012: 43). Since 2008, there has also been increasing media focus on claimants' nonreciprocity (i.e., not paying back into the system) and lack of effort, with an emphasis on 'large families on benefits, bad parenting, antisocial behaviour, people who have never worked or haven't worked for a long time' (Ibid.). Investigating the extent to which the public accepts these 'myths', Baumberg Geiger (2018) found low levels of understanding of the benefits system. People overestimated public expenditure on unemployment benefits compared to pensions, overestimated the proportion of unemployed, believed out-of-work benefit claims had risen in the past 15 years (they had actually fallen significantly) and significantly overestimated benefit fraud (Ibid.). Skewed media debates may also explain why the public believes that fraud is higher *nationally* than it is in their local area—with 'a disconnect between the local, concrete experience of benefit fraud and the national rhetoric, perhaps because the preponderance of media coverage may have served to reinforce the sense that there is a large group of people somewhere in the country . . . who are fraudulently claiming' (Baumberg Geiger et al., 2017: 21).

The British have expressed increasingly negative attitudes about certain welfare benefits and the poor since the 1980s. Before 2008, during a period of economic growth, there were widely held beliefs that poverty was either inevitable or an individual's own fault as well as limited awareness of UK poverty, with many feeling that 'real poverty' did not exist in Britain (Castell and Thompson, 2007). For most, 'the default associations with poverty related to developing countries' and 'to images of malnourished "third world" children' or when pressed to consider Britain, 'a bygone age of Dickensian squalor' (Ibid.: 10). Even after a long period of recession and austerity policies (when around one in five people in working households said their own household was struggling financially, and almost two-thirds agreed that 'there is quite a lot of poverty' in Britain), there was still widespread concern about welfare benefits, with 54% agreeing that 'most unemployed people could find a job if they really wanted one', 57% thinking that unemployment benefits 'discourage people from finding paid work', while 77% agreed that 'large numbers of people falsely claim benefits' (Baumberg, 2014: 12, 6). Such benefit stigma is related to judgements of the 'deservingness' of welfare recipients and whether people think claimants will make a future contribution into the welfare system (Baumberg et al., 2012: 12). People overestimate the proportion of long-term benefit claims (Ibid.: 27), with most (wrongly) thinking claimants will not pay back into the system in the future.

Negative attitudes to the poor and welfare recipients may explain why British people's desire for lower inequality is not matched by a similar level of support for redistribution. Attitudes to redistribution are also related to judgements of 'deservingness' and of social contribution, and redistribution is much less popular when it is framed as providing welfare benefits for the poor (Rowlingson, Orton and Taylor, 2010). Support for reducing the income gap 'drops dramatically' when support for 'the poor' through the benefits system is mentioned (Ibid.: 9). While 57% agreed that 'it is the responsibility of the government to reduce the differences in income between people with high incomes and those with low incomes', only 27% agreed that 'the government should spend more on welfare benefits for the poor even if it leads to higher taxes' (Ibid.). People's concern about the income gap coexisted with a widespread belief that some inequalities were fairly deserved (Bamfield and Horton, 2009). High incomes were supported if people felt they were merited on the basis of performance or social contribution. Many people supported the idea of progressive tax and benefit systems but were not persuaded by abstract arguments for greater equality, instead preferring arguments framed in terms of fairer rewards for effort and contribution (Ibid.).

This might seem to offer bleak prospects for redistribution and for the future of the welfare state in Britain. But we must be cautious about such a conclusion. Firstly, we should not dismiss the effects of concrete social conditions on attitudes too quickly. By 2017, there were signs that, after seven years of severe cuts in public spending, the 'thermostat' effect on attitudes was still in operation (Curtice, 2017), with declining support for cutting public expenditures and increased support for more spending on public services. In 2017, 60% thought the government should increase taxes and spend more, the highest level of support in 15 years, with support almost doubling from 2010 (the start of austerity policies) (Kelley, Warhurst and Wishart, 2018). Over half of people (56%) agreed that 'cutting welfare benefits would damage too many people's lives' (Ibid.). Table 1 shows the fluctuation in some attitudes to welfare benefits from 1987 up to 2016. Attitudes to unemployed people remained negative (though this is at a time of high employment levels [Cribb et al., 2018]), but there was a sharp drop in people agreeing that 'people receiving social security don't really deserve any help' or that most people on the dole are 'fiddling'.

Such fluctuations suggest that public attitudes to poverty and welfare are still connected to perceptions of changing economic circumstances (Hall, Leary and Greevy, 2014: 11) and not just shaped by welfare discourses. Before 2008, after long-term economic stability in the UK (and low levels of unemployment), the public felt there was 'no excuse for

Table 2.1. Attitudes towards People Receiving Welfare Benefits: Selected Years, 1987–2016. British Social Attitudes Survey data, sources: Pearce and Taylor, 2012, table 2.4: 45, and Geiger et al., 2017, table A2: 26.

% agreeing with statement:	1987	2004	2012	2016
Many people who get social security don't really deserve any help	31	39	35	21
Most unemployed people could find a job if they really wanted one	41	69	54	56
Most people on the dole are fiddling in one way or another	32	41	37	22

poverty', believing that opportunities existed for those willing to take them and that if people were poor this was 'the result of bad choices and wrong priorities, and therefore not a subject for public help' (Castell and Thompson, 2007: vi). However, after the financial crisis of 2008–2009 and prolonged economic stagnation, and with severe reductions in public spending from 2010 on, more difficult economic circumstances 'encouraged some to reconsider both who might be affected by poverty and what its causes are' (Hall et al., 2014: 13).

Nor is it the case that British people see only negative aspects to welfare and redistribution, with considerable complexity to their attitudes. There is a 'strong streak of fatalism' around inequality (76% of people agreed that 'large differences in people's incomes are inevitable whether we like them or not'), but a substantial number (52%) think inequality is unfair (Rowlingson et al., 2010). A majority see a positive side to inequality, in giving people an incentive to work (61%), but only 27% see it as necessary for Britain's prosperity, and there is considerable support for higher taxes on the rich and for lower taxes for those on low incomes (Ibid.). And support for specific redistributive *policies* is greater than support for the concept of 'redistribution' or government help for 'the poor', as people are more likely to support policies which are *implicitly* redistributive (Ibid.). Echoing McCall's (2013) American research, there is strong support for policies to promote more equality of opportunity, such as better education and training but also fairer pay and better jobs. In 2017, there was strong support for a minimum standard of living for everyone, with 71% wanting an increase in the minimum wage and 77% feeling that employers should pay a wage that covers the basic cost of living (Kelley et al., 2018). The British are also very strongly attached to collective welfare provision in institutional form, such as the National Health Service or the state provision of education and pensions (Pearce and Taylor, 2012). And while levels of support for redistribution are not particularly high, neither are levels of opposition since a substantial minority (28%) 'sit on the fence', neither supporting nor opposing redistribution (Rowlingson et al., 2010).

While it is true that political and media debates have presented an increasingly pejorative view of welfare, if we place British attitudes in wider context, we can see that welfare 'myths' and negative attitudes to the poor also occur at times and in places where the welfare state is more generous, so it is by no means certain that such attitudes do undermine support for welfare principles (Baumberg Geiger and Meuleman, 2016; Hudson et al., 2016a, 2016b). It is often assumed that British attitudes to welfare were much more positive in the 1950s and 1960s, in the 'golden age' of the welfare state. But knowledge of public attitudes in Britain largely relies on one survey series, the British Social Attitudes Survey, which has run since 1982. Hudson and colleagues (2016a: 231) argue that we need a clearer sense of what attitudes were like before 1982, because the 1980s saw exceptionally high unemployment in Britain combined with extensive spending cuts, which means—with the 'thermostat' effect in mind—that 1982 may present a misleading baseline, when positive attitudes to welfare were at a peak. Using diverse survey evidence from the 1940s onwards, Hudson, Lunt and colleagues (2016a: 231; 2016b) show negative attitudes also existed during the 'golden age' of the welfare state, followed by 'a clear upturn in support for the welfare state in the 1980s'. So viewed from a longer perspective, 'rather than attitudes having hardened since the post-war period they have, instead, fluctuated over time' (2016a: 232):

> Widely held pejorative attitudes to welfare have long co-existed alongside widely held positive attitudes to welfare, including during the 'golden age of the welfare state'. A strong hierarchy of preferences around social spending has always persisted almost throughout the period being examined. Health is overwhelmingly the most popular area, with education and pensions also typically high in the list of social spending priorities. Support for working age cash benefits, particularly for the unemployed, tends to be lower than support for services. There does appear to be a moralistic tone reflected in much of the data . . . [with] very clear notions of there being distinct groups of 'deserving' and 'undeserving' poor. (Hudson et al., 2016a: 238)

And when British attitudes are examined cross-nationally, the problem is '*not* that negative attitudes exist, nor that there is little support for claimants who are seen to be undeserving, nor even that there is ambivalence about the benefits system' because 'all of these' seem to be 'universal' (Baumberg Geiger and Meuleman, 2016: 301). In Europe, people typically express both negative and positive perceptions of the welfare state (Reeskens and Van Oorschot, 2013), with substantial negative attitudes even in the relatively generous welfare systems of Scandinavia (between 29% and 43% of Scandinavians agree that social benefits/services make people lazy, and 32–51% agree that many people manage to obtain benefits/services to which they are not entitled) (Reeskens and Van Oorschot, 2016: 299). Van Oorschot and colleagues (2012: 181, 192) found that in all European countries the public saw both negative and positive consequences to the welfare state,[23] with the perception of negative consequences higher in countries with greater welfare expenditures. However, in most countries people had 'a clearer eye for the positive social than for negative economic and moral consequences', which they argue is 'a remarkable outcome, given that usually, the negative welfare state consequences dominate media portrayal and public debates' (Ibid.: 181, 185). The exceptions were Hungary, Slovakia and the UK, where people saw the negative consequences of the welfare state as outweighing the positive ones.

In the case of the UK, the perceived negative consequences outweighed the positive only slightly: over 50% of Britons were convinced of the positive social consequences of the welfare state, with the proportion perceiving negative consequences only a few percentage points higher (Van Oorschot et al., 2012: 188). In contrast, in the more generous Nordic social democratic welfare regimes, the positive consequences of welfare are emphasised much more strongly (Ibid.). It seems that 'a higher spending welfare state promotes its social legitimacy by stimulating in people the idea that it is doing a good job, more than that it arouses their worries about its effect on the economy and morals' (Ibid.: 194). The reasons for this are complex. It does relate to media coverage, as stories about benefits in Britain are split between the positive and negative, while stories in the Scandinavian press are usually more positive (Baumberg Geiger and Meuleman, 2016: 301–2). But it also relates to the nature of welfare state provision—and the targeted or 'selective' nature of the British welfare state—since 'the extent to which welfare state institutions divide people into "them" and "us" plays a key role in shaping public attitudes to "welfare"' as selective systems are 'more likely to foster negative attitudes and less likely to foster positive attitudes' (Hudson, Patrick and Wincup, 2016: 218). In Britain, the declining universality of the welfare system may explain why some attitudes are so negative, and it is certainly the most universal benefits (the NHS, for example) which remain the most popular.

BEYOND PUBLIC OPINION

There are 'quite remarkable' differences in attitudes to inequality and redistribution between countries (Lübker, 2004: 113), differences which do not straightforwardly reflect 'objective' levels of inequality. Other national social conditions or values (a country's prosperity, the generosity of its welfare regime, its level of corruption, how public discourses emphasise meritocracy, as well as the distributional effects of growth) all affect people's perceptions of how much inequality there is and their sense of how fair it is. There *is* widespread concern about inequality, but support for redistribution is complicated by ideas of fairness, contribution and 'deservingness' that often sit alongside negative views of the poor and of welfare benefits. Survey research on 'lay normative beliefs about economic justice' suggests that people often use different kinds of moral reasoning, endorsing 'humanitarian arguments for redistribution to those in dire need' but also contributive principles 'that everyone should contribute what they can' as well as support 'for a desert based justification . . . according to which effort and merit in contribution are seen to deserve higher rewards' (Sayer, 2009: 13; Gomberg, 2007). Reflecting these different kinds of moral reasoning, attitudes to inequality and ideas of 'deservingness' or the appropriate role of state-funded interventions show considerable complexity. Attitudes to welfare benefits systems, for example, are characterised by 'ambivalence' so that 'even when the benefits system is generous and popular, many people still have some concerns', with negative views about the 'undeserving' poor or of redistributive welfare more generally (Baumberg Geiger and Meuleman, 2016: 301).

Attitudes research often struggles to locate the situated practical engagements which shape people's understandings and most often focuses on whether public attitudes indicate support for particular political and welfare policies. But the impact of public attitudes on social policy is 'often weaker than imagined' and 'rarely decisive in shaping policy decisions' (Hudson et al., 2016: 218). As a result, more attention should be directed 'upstream', to the 'attitudes and perspectives of "elites" in the media, in politics or in other positions of power', in order to assess how these influence and frame 'both policy making and the dominant narrative and discourses around "welfare"' (Ibid.: 221). However, as Hudson and colleagues also argue, since 'widespread pejorative attitudes to welfare' can be observed even in the most popular welfare states as well as during the 'golden era of welfare state expansion', this suggests such attitudes 'need not be a barrier to expanding social policy provision now' (2016a: 238).

Levels of objective inequality are not straightforwardly related to social discontent. In this chapter I have argued that this is because people's attitudes and perceptions are shaped by—and 'realistically' adjusted to— the contexts of inequality in which people find themselves and which they must daily navigate. The views on inequality elicited in surveys offer us one perspective on understandings of inequality, but a necessarily abstract one. When such research does take context and milieu into account, it becomes clear that people are much more aware of how inequality affects their immediate situation and practical concerns. Questions of fairness and opportunity are very significant when people assess levels of inequality, but this, I argue, reflects the highly situated and pragmatic character of how understandings of inequality are formed, with people's attitudes shaped by a very practical focus on how inequality affects their own prospects and endeavours, and with an emphasis on such opportunities as the availability of good jobs which are fairly paid or good access to education and healthcare. I have also argued that the basis of comparison through which people assess inequality is very significant. Such comparisons are often made on a very selective and restrictive basis so that people often underestimate levels of inequality and have a poor sense of their own place in the distribution of incomes. Attitudes are generally better related to *perceptions* of inequality. This is partly a question of how living within a structure of inequality itself shapes what people come to see of it. People's perceptions of inequality are affected by institutional regimes and political and media debates which affect not only the visibility but also the acceptability of inequality. But it is because people also develop their sense of inequality in relation to their own practical concerns that they are generally more aware of, and more concerned by, 'local' inequalities in their own lives and immediate milieu. So again, we must see attitudes and misperceptions as practically generated, emerging within the everyday concerns of people as they daily negotiate local contexts which are shaped by inequality.

As a result, people *do* have a restricted point of view on inequality. However, while some look to these limited or distorted understandings to explain the persistence of inequalities, a notion of caution is required. Because while people do underestimate economic inequality, their preferred levels of inequality would still mean a massive reduction in its scale. And while views of redistribution and social welfare are shaped by often negative public discourses, they also remain tied to changing economic circumstances. Situated and partial viewpoints on inequality must be understood in terms of how people *acquire* their sense of inequality, through various kinds of everyday endeavours, where knowledge is generated as a means to practically navigate given situations.

For others, of course, people's restricted viewpoints and 'realistic' assessments of inequality reflect symbolic domination. Sayer (2011), for example, suggests that in assessing perceptions of fairness and opportunity, survey research sometimes takes the legitimacy of unequal positions too readily for granted. He argues that we need a more critical understanding of how people think about economic justice, which recognises how this is 'already shaped' by a highly unequal division of labour which is 'normalized and naturalized' (2011: 12). Hence, the next chapter turns to critically examine the argument that if people 'misrecognise' inequality, this is because ideological processes of symbolic domination disguise, legitimate and naturalise unequal social arrangements.

NOTES

1. The cross-sectional association between income inequality and redistribution among OECD countries seems to show more unequal countries engage in *less* redistribution. Though if we look beyond cross-sectional analysis, 'countries that have experienced greater increases in market inequality also exhibit larger increases in redistribution' (Kenworthy and Pontusson, 2005: 450).

2. Such as the International Social Survey Programme [ISSP] and the European Values Study/World Values Survey [EVS/WVS].

3. In the 1999 ISSP, questions were asked about what specific jobs do pay and what they should pay, with the question asked about jobs including skilled factory worker, doctor in general practice, chairperson of a large national company, lawyer, shop assistant, owner/manager of a large factory, judge in the country's highest court, unskilled worker and cabinet minister.

4. For example, at least 80% of respondents in Brazil, Bulgaria, Hungary, Portugal and the Russian Federation agreed that people with high incomes should pay a larger/much larger share of their income in taxes (Lübker, 2004: 117).

5. The Gini index is a standard measure of income inequality ranging on a scale from 0 (when everybody has an identical income) to 1 (when all income goes to only one person).

6. Although East and West Germany were unified in 1990, the analysis of attitudes often distinguishes the two to consider whether their different historical legacies still shape attitudes and values.

7. The question in which people are asked what they think specific jobs should be paid.

8. In 1981, the Gini coefficient of national income inequality in China was 0.29, a relatively low level, but by 2002 it had risen to 0.45 (Whyte, 2011). The World Bank considers a Gini coefficient above 0.40 as severe income inequality. It is argued that the Chinese National Bureau of Statistics understates the level of economic inequality, with suggestions that fear of public unrest even led China to withhold estimates of Gini coefficients when inequality surpassed the U.S. level (Riskin, 2014). The estimated Gini coefficient for family income in China is now in the range of 0.53–0.55 (compared with 0.45 in the United States in 2010) (Xie and Zhou, 2014: 6928).

9. Under Mao's state socialism, communist rule collectivised agriculture and the state organised production.

10. Prior to the reforms, social protection and welfare benefits were organised through collectivised work units, with guaranteed access to jobs or land (though rural workers received markedly fewer benefits and rights) (Ringen and Ngok, 2013: 7). These social protections were lost under the market reforms.

11. Whyte argues that, cross-nationally, the Chinese are more positive than people in post-socialist societies in Eastern Europe, and for some questions 'even more positive' than countries such as Japan and the United States (2011: 278–79).

12. Under the *hukou* system, citizens are registered in either a rural or urban *hukou* (residential area), with tight residency and internal migration restrictions for rural citizens. Whyte (2011) argues that, under Mao, peasant farmers were essentially tied to the land with little chance of changing their status, and those with urban *hukou* status received substantially more benefits. The *hukou* system was significantly relaxed under the market reforms, though key elements remain and major inequalities continue between urban and rural areas.

13. Combining respondents who thought the income gap was 'somewhat large' and 'too large' from Table 11.1a, Whyte, 2010b: 306.

14. Asking for levels of agreement with three statements: 'Knowing the right people—how important is that for getting ahead in life?', 'Inequality continues to exist because it benefits the rich and powerful' and 'Large differences in income are necessary for [country's] prosperity'.

15. The exceptions were Brazil, Chile and the Philippines, all showing very high agreement with the statement that inequality is necessary for prosperity but also strong agreement with the statement that income inequality is too large. Lübker (2004: 97–98) suggests that people in these countries seem to 'consider inequality as a regrettable but somehow necessary evil'.

16. More marked in the United States and Australia than in Norway and Germany, however, which Linos and West connect to the different welfare regimes in these countries.

17. Using two questions: 'Would you say that in your country, people are rewarded for their efforts?' and "Would you say that in your country, people are rewarded for their skills?'

18. Under 10% of Bulgarians, Slovakians and Russians believed people in their countries were rewarded appropriately for their efforts and skills (perceived meritocracy) compared to more than 50% in the United States and Australia (Duru-Bellat and Tenret, 2012: 231).

19. However, Kerr found that increasing objective inequality also increases people's preferred earnings ratio (in this survey question the ratio of the preferred earnings of a doctor compared to an unskilled worker), indicating that people accept some but not all elements of rising inequality.

20. In an analysis of the 2010–14 WVS.

21. In addition, the level of perceived inequality of opportunity (or the extent to which outcomes are seen as unfair or corrupt) also affected attitudes towards redistribution, although only in China and Korea (Ibid.: 34).

22. The United Kingdom is the most unequal European country in the OECD group—only the United States, Turkey and Mexico are more unequal. Income inequality has steadily increased since the 1980s (Atkinson and Salverda, 2009), with the Gini index rising from 0.23 in 1978 to 0.35 in 2001 and fluctuating around this level since.

23. Measured by levels of agreement with statements of (five) negative consequences (social benefits/services place too great a strain on the economy, cost businesses too much in taxes/charges, make people lazy, make people less willing to care for one another, make people less willing to look after themselves/family) compared to levels of agreement with three positive consequences (preventing widespread poverty, leading to a more equal society, making it easier to combine work and family).

THREE
Misrecognising Inequality

A range of empirical work on people's attitudes to economic inequalities argues that their responses are restricted, constrained by their social location or 'paradoxical', with significant misperception of the scale of inequality. I now consider arguments that these misperceptions and contradictions are in fact *systematically distorted* understandings, or 'misrecognitions'[1] of inequality. There are two versions of this claim: accounts which suggest that people's sense of inequality is restricted by their focus on their immediate milieu and practical concerns, and accounts which emphasise the role of ideology, symbolic domination or hegemony in naturalising and legitimising inequality. Research on relative deprivation argues that people understand 'inequality' in terms of the practical arrangements of their own lives, so that they typically establish their relative social position by comparing themselves to people in their everyday lives. But inequality structures everyday lives, so such comparisons are usually to people in *similar* social positions. For some analysts, this masks the scale of inequality and explains the relative lack of discontent about it.

One way of looking at this sees it as a 'non-ideological component of false consciousness', in which 'practical experience' shapes 'awareness or non-awareness of crucial aspects of the social order', constituting a 'boundary to perception' (Levy, 1991: 62, 63). This may be 'non-ideologically' produced, but it is still seen as 'false consciousness'. There are two potential criticisms of this reading, which go in quite different directions. The first is a pragmatist criticism, in which the limits of knowledge are seen in relation to its situated practical character rather than as false consciousness *per se*. From this perspective, people's views and understandings of inequality inevitably vary depending on their particular practical engagements and are shaped by their practical capacities for action. I shall return to this argument throughout the book.

The second criticism, the focus of the latter half of this chapter, argues by contrast that processes of *symbolic domination* distort understandings of inequality. In these accounts, people do not just have restricted points of view on the structures of inequality they inhabit but are also embedded in relations of domination and subordination, with distortions in their understandings part of the symbolic legitimation of such arrangements. While most prominent as explanations of the stable reproduction of class inequality (Gramsci, 1971; Bourdieu, 1984), related claims have been made in classic arguments about gender and racialised inequalities, though, as we shall see, with significant variation (Fanon, 1986; Hall, 1986; hooks, 2003; Bordo, 1993). As the chapter progresses, I consider increasingly extended claims about the misrecognition of inequality, in work which suggests that it does not just generate compliance with domination but actually prevents people from recognising that they *are* dominated. However, strong versions of the misrecognition argument are hard to sustain. The difficulty of representing legitimating ideologies as so seamless and effective is that it is hard to see how critique or social challenge can ever emerge (Willis, 1977: 175; 1983: 121). Yet empirical studies show the penetration of symbolic legitimation is often uneven, incomplete and contested, takes stronger hold among the dominant than among the less advantaged and does not prevent discontent or dissent.

In accounts of the 'misrecognition' of inequality, the ideas which become dominant in society are ideologies which legitimate the interests of dominant groups. So when structural inequality is 'misrecognised' in terms of individual attributes, privilege becomes 'naturalised', with disadvantage individualised into a personal failing. It is generally claimed that legitimating ideologies of inequality become accepted by both dominant and subordinate groups; however, the focus of analysis is on their acceptance by *subordinate* groups—because holding such views not only works against their interests, stops them challenging their situation, but also means accepting that they are somehow inferior or deficient. In 'thinner' versions of the naturalisation argument, subordinates do not necessarily swallow legitimating ideologies wholesale and can still be discontented and see their situation as unfair. But if they think inequality is a 'fact of life', part of the inevitable order of things, this makes them resigned to their lot.

Stronger versions of the argument suggest that inequality becomes 'internalised', so that as less advantaged people negotiate unequal social relations, their defensive adjustments to their situation distort and constrain their aspirations and sense of self-worth. This represents a particularly pernicious form of the legitimation of inequality, where dominated groups come to accept at least some of the values which position them as inferior. Accounts of 'symbolic violence' or the 'internalization of inferiority' provide powerful arguments of the 'hidden injuries' of inequality (Sennett and Cobb, 1977), in which the experience of subordination becomes incorporated into people's corporeal and affective 'sense' of the world, shaping how they value themselves and others and constraining self-esteem and empowerment. And there are even stronger versions in which unequal social relations become so embodied into people's pre-reflective 'practical sense' of their world that this limits what people can envisage or voice about the unequal worlds in which they live. Here dominated groups not only adjust to their situation but also come to 'make a virtue of necessity . . . and to love the inevitable' (Bourdieu, 1977: 77).

There is considerable variation in the degree to which analysts see subordinated groups incorporating dominant values or in the extent to which symbolic legitimation obscures relations of domination or suppresses discontent. Most concede significant limits to the misrecognition of inequality. Strong accounts of 'misrecognition' are often pessimistic about the possibilities for effective challenge to inequality or resistance to domination. Pessimism is not necessarily a fault—there may be good grounds for it, given the persistence of inequalities. A common criticism however is that such accounts cannot adequately explain the level of social conflict and protest that actually occurs (Scott, 1990: 78). Arguments of symbolic domination are generally stronger when explaining how inequality becomes naturalised and legitimated than in setting out how dissent, critical consciousness or resistance manage to emerge. Disadvantaged and subordinated groups do challenge and resist their situation, though, and sometimes even overturn naturalised forms of domination. So analysts invariably qualify their accounts by identifying cracks in the system of legitimation where contestation can arise. But if symbolic legitimation does not prevent discontent, suffering or even dissent, why does inequality persist?

One possible implication—a key argument of this book—is that the obdurate and durable nature of inequality has less to do with symbolic legitimation and 'misrecognition' than many analysts have imagined. Unsurprisingly, this is not the conclusion drawn by theorists of misrecognition. Instead, one frequent argument is that while misrecognition may not prevent discontent, it does dissipate and misdirect it—into shame, attempts at assimilation or divisive sectional struggles. Others suggest that some dissent and insubordination actually perpetuates domination by allowing people to 'manage' subordination or 'let off steam' so that more fundamental challenges to the system never emerge. This represents a fall-back to 'thinner' accounts in which the naturalisation of inequality operates by producing resignation and fatalism. The suggestion here seems to be that a truly critical 'recognition' of relations of inequality only really emerges in dissent which is capable of changing the structure of inequality rather than dissent which is simply aimed at improving someone's situation. This sets a high bar for critical consciousness or meaningful dissent and identifies people's 'misrecognition' of their situation by comparison to the analyst's own structural assessment. However, a simpler pragmatist point of view focuses on how people's understandings of their situation are shaped by their practical engagements and capacities for action. This sees sectional struggles and 'letting off steam' activities rather differently, as the practical strategies of constrained people doing what they feel they can under the circumstances. People are not necessarily deluded if they feel a certain resignation about wider social relations being resistant to change, because collective challenge is both hard to achieve and risky. But people do sometimes seize opportunities to challenge the system, and overcoming resignation is often a question of the practical capacities for collective action.

RESTRICTED VIEWPOINTS?

Analysts have long been puzzled by the 'apparently general acceptance by the majority of the population of considerable levels of social and economic inequality' (Pahl, Rose and Spencer, 2007: 1). Theories of relative deprivation offer one explanation of this 'quiescence', arguing that people make narrow social comparisons and so develop a restricted sense of inequality. Inequality 'necessarily invites us to examine the advantages of different groups or different individuals and to assess these advantages relative to one another' (Marshall and Swift, 1996: 376), so comparison matters for people's subjective sense of inequality. But *which* comparisons establish people's sense of their relative social position and wider inequalities? As Chapter 2 indicates, people often compare with proximate membership groups (neighbours, friends, etc.), but they can also compare to themselves at earlier points in time, to earlier generations or to more socially distant groups, including those featured in the mass media (Runciman, 1966; Rose, 2006). However, it is not so much that people are *unaware* of wider inequalities but rather that they assess these in terms of their immediate salience to their own lives. Research on relative deprivation suggests that people locate questions of inequality within very pragmatic concerns about the practical arrangements of their everyday lives and their own biography, in which their focus on structural inequality is as a 'fact of life', a feature of their environment which must be negotiated and managed.

Runciman's (1966: 286) account of the restricted nature of reference group comparison starts from the now familiar premise that levels of objective inequality do not straightforwardly produce discontent. Instead, people's sense of inequality is better related to how their social expectations and assessments of deservingness and injustice emerge from comparisons between reference groups. People feel relatively deprived if they think their situation is worse than others they identify and compare with—that is, via comparison to groups they think *should* be in the same situation (Ragnarsdottir, Bernburg and Olafsdottir, 2013: 758). The manual workers in Runciman's study compared themselves to friends, family, work colleagues and neighbours—groups within a relatively short range of inequality. Inequality 'sorts' the people in workplaces, neighbourhoods and social networks, so such comparisons are typically to people in similar social positions. For Runciman, this explains why most people do not feel deprived. Of course, such comparison can work the other way, fuelling resentment if people's sense that they are entitled to greater advantages than another group is undermined.

Chapters 1 and 2 have already discussed the 2016 American presidential election, where voting for Donald Trump was shaped by the racial 'status anxiety' of white Americans, who felt a sense of a threat to their dominant group status (Mutz, 2018). White Americans voting for Trump felt a relative loss of privilege compared to black Americans (Bhambra, 2016), with voters' measures of racism correlated much more closely with support for Trump than their levels of economic discontent (Schaffner, MacWilliams and Nteta, 2018). Harris (1993: 1713) argues that in the United States 'the set of assumptions, privileges, and benefits that accompany the status of being white' have become part of the 'settled expectations of whiteness', in which white Americans' relative advantage over African Americans is seen as the 'psychological wages of whiteness' (DuBois, 1935). Support for radical right-wing parties (such as UKIP, the BNP and the Tea Party) is also associated with the 'nostalgic deprivation' of white groups who feel that their own social group has become less central or important over time (Gest et al., 2018: 1712). Such comparisons over time are about the perceived loss of status relative to a group's sense of what they think their standing *should be*.

However, change over time in affluent, consumption-oriented societies is often associated with a *restricted* sense of inequality and discontent, because people making temporal comparisons often develop a sense that 'now' is better than 'then'. The suggestion here is that many people's lives are, materially at least, better than their parents' or grandparents'; so in comparing across generations or even their own lifetimes, people generally experience a sense of social *improvement*, personally and more generally (Payne, 1992; Pahl et al., 2007). This helps explain why people are more accepting of inequality in prosperous societies. Of course, if *most* people are better off, the relative inequalities between them remain unchanged. But people are 'better able to compare, and are more likely to be conscious of, the differences between how they themselves have fared in life and the achievements of others from the same neighbourhoods and schools' (Roberts, 2001: 199), so people are more likely to focus on how a 'rising tide lifts all boats'.

As Rose (2006: 3) notes, some analysts wonder if the growth of social media, reality television and lifestyle programs has 'expanded horizons' beyond 'the small worlds in which we live our lives'. However, British research (Pahl et al., 2007: iii) found little evidence of this. There was an *awareness* of the scale of inequalities in society and of other, very different lifestyles, but this did not create a sense of relative deprivation or discontent, because they were not seen as relevant to people's own lives. Where people were aware of others doing very much better, this tended to be in relation to celebrities whose lavish lifestyles 'were seen as "unreal"' and 'far removed from their own', so respondents saw '"no point" making any comparisons' and 'were not openly resentful' (Ibid.: 11). People could always 'think of others less fortunate than themselves' and 'felt lucky compared to people living in squalor, in run down areas' (Ibid.). There was little 'serious resentment' because people compared to those they knew well 'who lived in a similar area to them and had a similar life style' (Ibid.: 17–18). People felt 'relative contentment' because they were 'concentrating on their own and their family's welfare' and felt they were 'doing better than their parents or than they themselves had done at an earlier point in their lives' (Ibid.: 12, 0).

Such findings of 'relative contentment' are at odds with other work on the hidden injuries and resentments of inequality understood as relations of domination and subordination (Sennett and Cobb, 1972; Bourdieu, 1984; Skeggs, 1997) which I discuss later. First, however, there is the question, raised in Chapter 2, of the way attitudes to inequality are shaped by people's sense of *prospective* opportunity. Work on temporal comparison suggests that over time people see change for the better. But times can change for the worse too. Do periods of economic crisis, austerity or recession provoke a heightened sense of economic grievance and injustice? Some suggest, for example, that revolutions are most likely to occur when a prolonged period of growth is 'followed by a short period of sharp reversal', when expectations about the future are dashed (Davies, 1962: 5). Here discontent is seen to emerge from the comparison between what people expect to get and what they actually get. The 2008–2009 global economic crisis provided just such conditions, as in many countries the economic crash abruptly stalled a prolonged period of prosperity and growth, leading to recession, austerity policies and declining living standards. However, as the British and Icelandic cases show, while abrupt social changes, such as economic crises, do affect subjective deprivation and perceived injustice, they do so in a complicated fashion.

The 2008–2009 economic crisis hit Iceland particularly hard, coming after a period of sustained (but debt-fuelled) growth and affluence. The country's banking system collapsed, the economy plunged into recession and public trust in the politicians who had overseen the financial bubble plummeted (Bernburg, 2016; Oddsson and Bernburg, 2018). Yet the effect on Icelandic people's sense of relative deprivation and subjective injustice was muted. Ragnarsdottir and colleagues' study (2013: 770) found that most people saw a reduction in their standard of living, but this had only 'modest overall effects' on their sense of subjective injustice[2] and 'no overall effect on anger'. People's sense of relative deprivation was modified by their comparisons to others (evaluating whether the crisis had harmed them more than others) and to their expected future outcomes (Ibid.: 756). There was a greater sense of subjective injustice and anger among those with negative expectations for the future but no effect on those with positive expectations (Ibid.: 770). Those who felt the crisis *had* harmed them more than others felt greater injustice and anger, but there were 'no effects' for those who believed that the crisis had affected them less (Ibid.). Most Icelanders seemed to feel they were all in the same boat:

> When there is a widespread perception that most people have been hit hard by a crisis, most individuals may tend to accept their economic loss because they think that others have been hit at least just as badly . . . apparently producing a weak overall effect of perceived reduction in standard of living on subjective injustice and anger. Ironically, a widespread perception of despair creates a social context where even a large drop in the standard of living has only a small overall effect on individual distress. (Ragnarsdottir et al., 2013: 771)

Nonetheless, there were widespread social protests (the 'Kitchen Revolution'[3]) about the role of political cronyism and government nepotism in the 2008–2009 economic crash, which resulted in the fall of the government in 2009. Following further protests, the people voted in a referendum to ignore bank-friendly policies backed by the IMF, choosing instead to default on the debts created by the banks, and despite going against neo-liberal economic advice, 'the economy bounced back in part *because* the government did not have to repay debts' (Gorringe and Rafanell, 2015: 8, original emphasis). Of course, the protests only led to the fall of a government, not the fall of capitalism, but Icelanders who saw political connections (i.e., nepotism and corruption) as important structural barriers to opportunity in Iceland reported significantly more subjective status injustice than others[4] (Oddsson and Bernburg, 2018: 289–92).

Why did concerns about political connections feature so prominently in Icelanders' sense of injustice when class, race and wealth did not? Oddson and Bernburg (Ibid.: 287, 294) argue that this depends on what becomes 'defined as social problems in a given social context', a process in which the 'media, as well as political and social movement actors . . . frame certain opportunity barriers as important social problems, while ignoring others'. In Iceland, some structural barriers receive much more attention than others. The crash and the Kitchen Revolution made political connections a prominent public social issue in Iceland, whereas class, race and wealth have not received similar attention (Ibid.). In support of this conclusion, Oddsson and Bernburg point to how a belief in *gender* as a structural barrier is also tied to a greater sense of status injustice. Why? Because the feminist movement has played a very prominent role in public campaigns and policy interventions on gender equality in Iceland, which helps to 'explain why beliefs in gender-related barriers significantly influence status justice evaluations' (Ibid.: 294).

People's sense of inequality is framed by their milieu, but in a complicated manner. A parallel argument emerges in Irwin's (2015: 256; 2018) study of subjective inequality among British people during the depths of recession after the global economic crisis. Irwin (2015: 265) found heightened concerns about inequality and the entrenchment of disadvantage, 'with wide reference to increasing costs of living and employment insecurity, experiences of constraint, and risk, and hardship for the least advantaged'. However, this was qualified by temporal comparisons to when people were growing up. So while many 'were struggling with costs of living, notably rising food, energy and fuel prices, and some with unemployment' nevertheless 'the less advantaged participants in this study typically felt better off than their parents' (Ibid.: 270). However, Irwin found that it was not so much that 'proximate' reference group comparison gave people a restricted viewpoint—since her participants showed a keen awareness of wider structural inequality and change over time—but rather that structural constraint was situated within very practical, pragmatic concerns about how it affected their own situation and how it could be managed or improved. Irwin's (2018: 218; 2015: 271) sample gave 'very rich, nuanced and diverse accounts of broader social arrangements, and changes in the structure of opportunity as it has impacted on them', but such 'comparisons appear to be most relevant in referencing very immediate alternative possibilities' so that people perceive their positioning in society very practically. This 'does not mean that people do not relate their experiences to wider structural and economic processes'; however, in their viewpoint on these structural shifts, people's focus was on how they managed them and sought to make changes in their own lives (2015: 277).

The fact that people focus on their immediate practical concerns and take relations of inequality as 'given' is sometimes seen as a 'non-ideological component' of false consciousness (Levy, 1991: 62). But others see more ideological processes at work. For example, the idea put forward by many politicians that 'there is no alternative' to policies of austerity, or the view that inequalities are somehow inevitable, are for many analysts ideologies which serve to legitimate inequalities, limiting those unhappy with their lot to resigned or fatalistic responses. Nor can reference group processes be entirely divorced from questions of ideology. Bourdieu (1984) argues that temporal comparisons reflect symbolic domination, because when dominated groups 'compare their present conditions with their past' they 'are exposed to the illusion that they only have to wait in order to receive advantages which, in reality, they will only obtain by struggle', and their 'frustrated expectations' 'do not necessarily threaten the survival of the system' (Ibid.: 164). The frustrated expectations of subordinate groups simply mean they accept the values of the dominant class in a competitive 'struggle to keep up', implicitly accepting 'the legitimacy of the goals pursued by those whom they pursue' (Ibid.: 147, 165). As Sayer (2011: 13) notes, the argument here is that dominated classes 'struggle for position, but not to change the nature and structure of positions themselves'. The implication seems to be that people must not only struggle with their own inequality but with inequality itself. This is such a large task that it is hardly surprising that people are often resigned or fatalistic.

Irwin (2015: 271) argues that 'in day to day experiences and perceptions, people tend to take the social world in which they move, and the configuration of opportunity and constraint, as effectively given'. Her participants focused on those aspects of social location that they felt could be changed, with most structures of inequality seen as beyond this scope. However, while most people may adopt a pragmatic focus on manoeuvring within their milieu, this does not prevent dissent, and the discontented do sometimes seize avenues for social challenge. As the Icelandic case shows, if political resources are available, then dissent can lead to effective social struggle. And even when such resources may be lacking, the most deprived and disadvantaged do sometimes revolt. In 2011, for example, a series of riots erupted in many British cities, the result not just of austerity and material deprivation but also the result of the stigma and discrimination directed at poor and minoritised groups (Slater, 2011: 107; Tyler, 2013). Tyler (Ibid.: 204, 12) argues that for people with a sense of no prospects and with few viable political avenues for recognition, rioting was the only way to show their anger and exercise political agency. I shall explore these issues further in Chapter 4, but, for now, it is worth flagging that inequality and subordination do not always lead to resignation and despair but instead sometimes spark anger, indignation and social struggle.

Of course, indignation is often the result of being treated with indignity. If inequality becomes internalised as *personal* failure or success, it becomes not simply a question of unequal incomes or position but also unequal worth, dignity and respect. Surveys of people's subjective sense of social location show a pronounced tendency for people to place themselves in the middle of social hierarchies, with this pattern often explained by reference group effects. But inequality raises questions about the relative worth of individuals, making matters of inequality morally charged. For some analysts, if people have a distorted 'middling' sense of their own social position, this is more a reflection of them seeking to avoid the moral degradation and shame that inequality generates, where the increasingly individualised experience of inequality leads people to place themselves in a 'middling' social position to deflect the continuing power of class to 'judge', shame and position people in negative ways (Savage, Bagnall and Longhurst, 2001; Skeggs, 1997, 2004; Savage et al., 2001a; Sayer, 2005).

Pascale (2007: 82) similarly argues that middle-class identities in the United States are 'produced and naturalized in ways that are unrelated to economic circumstances', through common-sense discourses of class in which 'talk about "being middle-class"' often refers to a particular kind of person (the 'ordinary joe') 'rather than . . . a particular level of income or assets'. Pascale argues that this naturalisation occurs in both media and everyday discourse. For example, discourse analysis of popular legal dramas on American TV shows that the representation of the wealthy professional central characters focuses on how 'their membership in a professional class provides a particular set of collegial relationships' but does not emphasise the significant economic benefits, with socioeconomic class 'represented through personalities, not through particular kinds of opportunities, activities, or possessions' (Ibid.: 86). Pascale argues that the everyday discourses through which ordinary people articulate class identities also 'disorganize' and efface the 'presence and meaning of social and economic capital' in their class situation. This is partly a feature of how 'the routine nature of daily life leads most people to think of themselves as average' (Ibid.: 84) but also reflects the way in which people understand class 'as a social judgment', which functions 'not just as an evaluation of economic resources, but of their self' (Ibid.: 94). As a result, people's talk about class often 'systematically hides from view the cultural, social, and economic conditions that structure access to jobs, income, and wealth', because they instead seek to assert 'the primary importance of a "me" that stands apart from one's economic conditions' (Ibid.: 95).

Reference group processes and processes of symbolic legitimation are not easily disentangled. Pahl and colleagues' (2007: iii, 12) respondents did have a focus on their immediate milieu, which helped shape their view of themselves as middling '"ordinary, hard-working families"', but they were also 'reluctant to make comparisons that were detrimental to their sense of self-worth or to admit that—in a consumer society—their own lifestyle was somehow inadequate'. Such responses, many analysts suggest, are a direct consequence of neo-liberal, meritocratic discourses which produce an individualised understanding of inequality, which 'functions as an ideological myth to *obscure* economic and social inequalities' and to encourage self-blame for disadvantage (Littler, 2013: 55, original emphasis).

INDIVIDUALISING INEQUALITY

Questions of fairness, effort and contribution matter for how people view inequality, often encapsulated in the idea of meritocracy. Meritocratic principles are enshrined in the idea that 'whatever our social position at birth, society ought to facilitate the means for "talent" to "rise to the top"', with meritocracy often presented as the best solution to inequality in neo-liberal economies (Littler, 2013: 52). Cross-national evidence, presented in Chapter 2, indicates that the more inequalities are seen as 'deserved' the less likely they are to be seen as 'too large'. In more unequal societies, people are more likely to endorse meritocratic values and to perceive their society as meritocratic, which some see as the product of a 'dominant ideology' legitimating inequality in neo-liberal capitalist societies (Mijs, 2019; Huber and Form, 1973). The belief that inequality is the product of meritocratic processes both naturalises inequality (with inequality seen as the inevitable result of unequal abilities) and legitimates it (where, if inequality reflects effort, it is seen as deserved). This is seen as a hegemonic process, where meritocratic principles which are presented as being in everyone's interests really justify the interests of the privileged.

Certainly, meritocratic principles are widely endorsed. Young (1958) conceived a fully meritocratic society as dystopian,[5] but its contemporary use in popular discourse and policy debate presents 'meritocracy' almost entirely positively (Littler, 2013, 2017). As McNamee and Miller (2004: paras. 1–2) note, meritocracy is the idea that 'you get out of the system what you put into it'. But meritocratic explanations overstate the individual components of inequality while greatly underestimating the structural components (such as inheritance, unequal educational opportunity, the changing structure of job opportunities, discrimination) (Ibid.). So meritocracy is a distorting and legitimating 'myth' of how people are rewarded, because the impact of merit on economic outcomes is 'vastly overestimated', not least because the 'highly skewed distribution of economic outcomes' is 'quite in excess of any reasonable distribution of merit' (Ibid.: paras 2, 5). Sayer (2011: 13) notes that meritocratic discourses wrongly assume 'that because success in getting a good job and upward social mobility are possible for some individuals, success must be possible for all individuals simultaneously'. As McNamee and Miller (2004: para 15) point out, in the United States higher education has expanded while job growth has disproportionately been in the low-wage service sector, so the economy 'is not producing as many high-powered jobs as the society is producing highly qualified people to fill them'. Similarly, structural job shortages common in deindustrialised local labour markets make it impossible for many jobseekers to find employment; however, neo-liberal governments 'have avoided acknowledging this and have chosen instead to hold the unemployed responsible for their unemployment' (Sayer, 2012: 584–85).

By focusing on the competition for jobs, the structure of the labour market is simply taken as given, with little attention to the very unequal structuring of jobs into poor and good kinds of work. This is a form of 'contributive injustice' (Gomberg, 2016) in which a highly 'unequal division of labour limits what some people can do and hence the extent to which they can develop their own abilities and find fulfilment, respect and self-esteem' (Sayer, 2011: 17). For Sayer (2011: 9; 2012: 586), the way in which the unequal division of labour constrains what people are allowed to contribute 'is at least as important as what they get in terms of resources'; however, 'most people—including social scientists—do not even notice it in the wider formal economy, where it is institutionalized and naturalized'. So differences in the 'quantity and quality of work that people are able or expected to do in the wider division of labour in the formal economy are thoroughly naturalised and rarely seen as problematic—and this, despite the fact that they have such a profound effect on people's lives' (Sayer, 2011: 10).

Popular and policy discourses of meritocracy naturalise inequality because they emphasise 'equality of opportunity' on individualised terms, where 'the act of addressing inequality becomes "responsibilized" as an individual's moral meritocratic task', making the individual personally responsible for his or her success or failure (Littler, 2013: 64, 65). This justifies the success of the privileged and is 'a key means through which plutocracy is endorsed by stealth within contemporary neoliberal culture' (Littler, 2013: 54, 52). Meritocratic beliefs are most heavily endorsed by economic elites in what is generally seen as a justification of their own privilege. However, less privileged groups generally show more scepticism about whether society is meritocratic. Wealthy or elite groups frequently emphasise their hard work and effort as the secret to their success (Khan and Jerolmack, 2013; Power, Allouch and Brown, 2016; Sherman, 2017; Kantola and Kuusela, 2018), and cultural elites similarly emphasise their talent. The cultural sector in Britain has very marked structural inequalities in access, with over-representation of people from professional or managerial occupational backgrounds and under-representation of women and ethnic minorities (Taylor and O'Brien, 2017; O'Brien et al., 2016; Oakley et al., 2017). Yet 'almost everyone' in the sector believes 'hard work, talent, and ambition are essential to getting ahead, while class, gender, ethnicity, and coming from a wealthy family are not' (Taylor and O'Brien, 2017: 44). But it is those in the *most privileged positions* who have 'the strongest belief in meritocracy', not only 'more likely to ascribe success to talent' but also 'more likely to deny the relationship between success and structural factors' (Ibid.: 40, 27–28, 44).[6] It is the worst rewarded and most precariously employed workers who are the 'most aware of structural inequality' and how it constrains access to the sector (Ibid.: 27; McRobbie, 2015).

As Littler (2013: 69, original emphasis) notes, in accounts of prominent business leaders there is a rhetoric of 'hard work' as the basis of social mobility and success, despite the 'swathe of research proving that *inheriting opportunity* in the form of finance and social connections is by far more important a factor'. For example, wealthy Finnish entrepreneurs stressed their own hard work, risk-taking and persistence while at the same time labelling the less well off as 'lazy', 'unproductive' or 'low-initiative' (Kantola and Kuusela, 2018). Despite being in the top 0.1% of earners and coming from middle-class backgrounds, this elite group still saw themselves as 'ordinary blokes' from 'humble backgrounds'. Of course, such self-serving stances may also reflect reference group effects, with elite groups often segregated residentially and socially and more likely to work for and interact with the super-rich (Hecht, 2017; Dorling, 2014; Mijs, 2019). While most people have a poor sense of the scale of inequality and their place within it, this is particularly so for richer people. For example, around 70% of Swedes underestimate their relative income position, believing they are poorer relative to others than they actually are, but people on lower incomes have a much more accurate sense of their relative situation (Karadja, Mollerstrom and Seim, 2017).

Research on attitudes to poverty and inequality among elites in a range of countries—Brazil (Reis, 2005), the Philippines (Clarke and Sison, 2005), Bangladesh (Hossain and Moore, 2005), Haiti (Ribeiro Thomaz, 2005) and South Africa (Kalati and Manor, 2005)—shows elites in the Global South also adopt meritocratic beliefs by consistently focusing on education as the key policy solution to poverty. These elites adopt individualised perspectives on inequality, perceiving poverty to be the result of the 'backward', fatalistic and unenterprising attitudes of the poor while also endorsing an orthodox economic view that economic development can be facilitated by improving 'human resources' through education and training (Moore and Hossain, 2005: 204–5).[7] Building schools is their preferred way of tackling poverty, one which does not challenge their own privilege.

Critics of the meritocracy 'myth' see it as a misrecognition of how inequality is generated, because when social inequalities are individualised the structural advantages of dominant groups disappear from view in explanations which focus on their superior effort, ability or drive, while the disadvantage and exclusion of subordinate groups becomes a question of inherent inferiority. But how widely does this misrecognition of structural processes of inequality and domination extend? For some (Khan and Jerolmack, 2013), privileged groups endorse meritocracy in sometimes cynical fashion, rhetorically emphasising 'hard work' as a way of fending off potential criticism. Bourdieu, by contrast, sees meritocratic discourses as not only the means by which members of the dominant class produce a 'justification of the social order that they dominate' but also as 'what causes the dominant class to feel justified in being dominant: they feel themselves to be *essentially* superior' (Bourdieu, 1993a: 177, original emphasis).

Certainly, higher-class, richer and more highly educated individuals seem to have the strongest beliefs in meritocracy, being not only more likely to believe that their *own* position is merited but also more likely to believe that the disadvantage of *others* is also merited, as well as being more likely to discount structural barriers to opportunity than other groups. McCall and Chin (2013: 17) found that 'only 1 percent of the top one percent in America believes that coming from a wealthy family is very important for getting ahead, whereas 20 to 30 percent of the public believe this', and 'only a quarter of the top one percent believes that having well-educated parents is very important, whereas nearly half of Americans think so'. There is widespread endorsement for meritocratic principles, but the penetration of meritocratic ideologies is still partial and uneven.

It is certainly the case, as Chapter 2 shows, that if people perceive good opportunities for advancement and prosperity, they will tolerate higher levels of inequality. Nevertheless, such research indicates that people generally recognise that inequality is caused by *both* individual and structural factors. People in (highly unequal) liberal welfare regimes (such as the United States or Australia) are more likely to emphasise individual factors (Linos and West, 2003), but even in the land of the 'American dream', just over 50% agreed that their society was meritocratic, with a substantial proportion disagreeing (Duru-Bellat and Tenret, 2012: 231–32). Cross-nationally, the more privileged (with greater income and education) are most likely to see society as meritocratic[8] (as are people who see their own pay as fair), but the less privileged are less likely to do so (and women are less likely than men) (Duru Bellat and Tenret, 2012). It is less advantaged groups who show the greatest awareness of the structural factors affecting inequality (McCall and Chin, 2013; Edmiston, 2017; Taylor and O'Brien, 2017; Duru-Bellat and Tenret, 2012).

This suggests that we must qualify our notion of meritocracy as a dominant ideology (Oddsson and Bernburg, 2018; Larsen, 2016) or at least as a dominant ideology that explains the persistence of inequality. The trouble is that plenty of people recognise structural barriers to opportunity yet still put up with inequality. Take the Icelandic case. The Icelandic economic crisis certainly had muted effects on most Icelanders' sense of anger or 'subjective injustice' (Ragnarsdottir et al., 2013; Oddsson and Bernburg, 2018), but this does not seem to be explained by a belief in meritocracy, since substantial proportions recognised a range of structural inequalities in 'getting ahead' in Iceland (such as 'knowing the right people', 'having political ties', 'coming from a rich family' and 'a person's gender').[9] However, even if less advantaged groups are more sceptical of the ideologies which legitimate inequality, it is hard to escape their damaging consequences in a society in which many others do. The normalisation of the advantage of privileged groups means subordinate groups are often forced to negotiate environments in which they are exceptionalised, encountering expectations which both exclude and judge them.

NORMALISING INEQUALITY

For Bourdieu (1993a: 177), ideas of meritocracy represent the 'misrecognition' of class inequality by *both* dominant and dominated groups, in which the advantage of dominant groups is not only legitimated but also becomes 'normalised' as a taken-for-granted feature of social life. Savage (2003: 540, 536), for example, suggests that increasingly in neo-liberal economies the individualisation of inequality has led to the emergence of the middle class as the 'universal–particular class', the class 'around which an increasing range of practices are regarded as universally "normal", "good" and "appropriate"', and where 'those who live up to middle class norms see themselves as "normal" people while those who do not see themselves (and are seen by the powerful) as individual failures'. The argument is that when privilege is individualised it becomes 'invisibilised'. Similar arguments about the normalisation of inequality have been made in relation not only to class but also to race and gender divisions, with the suggestion that 'ideological hegemony operates in the assumptions that we make about life and the things we accept as natural' in which relations of power 'become naturalized through commonsense' (Pascale, 2007: 5).

Drawing on an ethnomethodological conceptualisation of common sense (understood as the procedures by which ordinary people make sense of and negotiate the situations they encounter), Pascale (2007: 2, 4) argues that in the United States there is a naturalised common sense about race, gender and class inequalities which operates through broad shared cultural assumptions about 'apparently routine matters of social difference'. Such assumptions are mundanely and repetitively drawn upon by people as sense-making procedures about the social landscapes they find themselves in and which they enact in 'unreflexive daily practices that reinforce the value people place on their own lives and the lives of others' (Ibid.: 5). Pascale argues that the routine production of race, gender and class inequalities in daily life occurs through people's common-sense 'knowledge' about race, gender and class differences in their social world, which presents such differences as 'self-evident and familiar', as 'something that everyone can and should recognize' (Ibid.: 4, 5). However, such assumptions normalise the situation of dominant social groups by rendering them unmarked, while marking, and so problematising, subordinate groups.

Common sense 'leads us to believe that we simply see what is there to be seen—to believe that we are observers of an objective social world', but by routinely and repetitively acting on such common-sense knowledge, we help to constitute that world and its inequalities (Pascale, 2007: 24). While common sense makes us 'believe that accounts describe an objective social world, it is through our accounts that we produce a sense of what is true, relevant, and meaningful' (Ibid.: 27). So, for example, common sense about race in the United States 'constitutes people as accountable members of racialized groups' with race understood as both self-evident and meaningful, so that the 'the ability to recognize race' is rendered 'not only unproblematic but a routine competence expected of all people' (Ibid.: 24). However, there is an asymmetry in this reporting and accountability of race which helps to constitute racial dominance. The race of white people is not rendered reportable or accountable. Pascale's analysis of U.S. television programmes and newspaper reporting, for example, found that whiteness took on an 'unmarked' character, with whiteness 'produced as a "normal" or ordinary way of being, both through the overwhelming presence of white people and through the way that whiteness consistently passed without remark' (2007: 34). These representational practices 'produced whiteness as the daily context on which racial issues may be overlaid' (Ibid.: 33). The 'unmarked' nature of whiteness constructs whiteness 'not as a racial category, per se, but rather as a kind of "normalcy," an invisible centre from which "difference" can be measured' and so a process which 'produces and maintains white racial dominance' (Ibid.: 30–31). So the 'power of whiteness—for white people—works through virtue of its invisibility, through the ability of commonsense to erase the presence and meaning of white racial identities' and which also produces 'all other racial identities as apparently inherently meaningful . . . through practices that withhold ordinariness from people who are "not white"' (Ibid.: 35). This means that

> whiteness emerges as the space against which racial categories gain meaning and visibility. In hegemonic U.S. culture, whiteness comes to stand as the 'ordinary' way of being human . . . Since discourse constitutes subjugated subjectivities by marking 'difference' from an unspoken hegemonic centre, the visible processes that mark or name what they point to always constitute subjects as 'others'. (Pascale, 2007: 33)

Similarly, the 'self-evident' common-sense linkage of gender with sexual desire 'means that in daily life heterosexuality need not be named—it is an unmarked category in talk and representation. Concomitantly, non-hegemonic sexualities must be produced as marked categories' (Ibid.: 63).

Such arguments, as important as their insights are, require qualification: the normalisation of privilege can never be wholly 'invisibilised' or naturalised to the members of subordinate groups, because such normalisation constitutes the environment of expectation and judgement within which they are forced to manoeuvre. This is not to deny the force of dominant practices and values on people's lives but rather to offer a different explanation of how they take their force, through how they form the 'known' environment which people must negotiate and to which they adjust their practices. But the damaging effects of individualised or naturalised understandings of inequality occur even when disadvantaged groups do not fully accept them. So while the members of subordinate groups often recognise the arbitrary nature of privilege, they must still negotiate environments in which their disadvantage is individualised and naturalised by others.

Take accounts of the normalisation of racialised inequality, which operates through the taken-for-granted nature of white privilege. Here whiteness is a location of structural advantage, but one existing within 'cultural practices that are usually unmarked and unnamed' (Frankenberg, 2000: 447). The naturalised nature of white privilege is such that 'in Western representation whites are overwhelmingly and disproportionately dominant, have the central and elaborated roles, and above all are placed as the norm, the ordinary, the standard' (Dyer, 2000: 541). The taken-for-granted nature of 'whiteness' means that white privilege takes on the status of 'seeming normativity . . . structured invisibility' (Frankenberg, 2000: 451, 452). People of colour often very clearly recognise the normalisation of white privilege and struggle against it. But when white people not only dominate more privileged positions (in politics, the labour market, the cultural sector) but are also placed as the 'norm' in such positions, the consequence is that people who are not white become constructed as abnormal and exceptional in them, as 'bodies out of place'. Ahmed (2007: 149, 156) argues that whiteness creates 'institutional habits' which shape how racialised bodies '"take up" space, and what they "can do"', which profoundly affects the 'experiences of inhabiting a white world as a non-white body'. Public spaces 'take shape through the habitual actions of bodies' and become 'orientated "around" whiteness, insofar as whiteness is not seen', but the effects of this 'institutional whiteness' 'makes non-white bodies feel uncomfortable, exposed, visible, different, when they take up this space' (Ibid.: 157).

Puwar (2004) similarly argues that spaces of authority are marked by masculinity as well as by whiteness, and so they produce female and/or racialised bodies as 'bodies out of place'. As Ahmed notes (Ibid.: 160), the same processes can be identified in accounts of working-class mobility into the middle class (Skeggs, 2003), where people 'can move up only by approximating the habitus of the white bourgeois body'. And normalisation also produces *self-exclusion*. Skeggs's (1997; 2009: 37) study of British white working-class women found that they 'were constantly subject to negative value judgements about their futures and pasts, behaviour, intelligence, taste, bodies and sexuality, to such an extent that it shaped their spatial sense of entitlement, engagement and limited where they did or did not want to go, how they felt they could or could not "be"'. For example, 'when they entered "posh shops" they were acutely aware of the way they were being read and judged by others', a process of being 'looked down on' to which they felt continually subject (Skeggs, 2009: 37). While 'subject to the judgmental gaze of middle-class institutions and authority', these women were 'fully aware of how cultural distinction and classification work in the interests of the powerful—legitimating inequalities so that privilege cannot be contested' (Skeggs, 2012: 283). However, in a defensive response, they 'learnt not to enter certain social spaces for fear of contempt, misrecognition, and negative judgment' (Ibid.: 280). Skeggs argues that this 'is not just about individualized social encounters but how through repetition and performativity total social relations are shaped', where institutions 'make people feel they *should not* belong' (Ibid., original emphasis).

Where the privilege of dominant groups is naturalised and normalised, subordinate groups must constantly negotiate the view, widespread in popular culture, that their disadvantage is somehow deserved. In such circumstances they may struggle to avoid internalising the stigma of disadvantage. Individualised explanations for inequality often result in very negative, moralising views of the poor and welfare recipients. We can see why privileged groups might endorse individualised understandings of inequality, because this is a self-serving ideology. But studies of people living in poverty or on welfare benefits show they often *share* pejorative views of poverty, so that ideological discourses about the 'undeserving poor' 'are not simply a "top-down" rhetoric of the powerful' (Shildrick and McDonald, 2013: 299–300; Seccombe, James and Walters, 1998; Patrick, 2016; Pemberton et al., 2016). Poor people often feel 'pressure to dissociate themselves from the shame and stigma of being identified as "the poor"' (Shildrick and McDonald, 2013: 301), engaging in moral condemnation of 'the poor' while simultaneously differentiating their own situation. Such activities can be seen as a form of 'defensive othering' (Schwalbe et al., 2000) in which members of a stigmatised group attempt to resist and distance themselves from that stigma. However, when the members of such groups 'seek safety or advantage by othering those in their own group, the belief system that supports the dominant group's claim to superiority is reinforced' and 'subordinate solidarity is undermined' (Ibid.: 425–26).

Shildrick and McDonald's (2013: 286) study of poor people living in severe hardship found that they denied they were 'poor', were doubtful there was 'real' poverty in Britain, and when they did identify other groups as 'poor', saw them as undeserving scroungers. American women receiving welfare payments similarly drew on 'individualising' and 'victim-blaming' theories to explain *other* women's reliance on the welfare system while distinguishing their own situation as very different (Seccombe et al., 1998: 849). Given the stigma of poverty, it is unsurprising that poor people 'make strenuous efforts to demarcate themselves' from the 'undeserving poor' (Pemberton et al., 2016: 29–30). But why do they share this view of an undeserving poor? To explain why stigmatising views of poverty become accepted by welfare recipients, 'even if it contradicts their own self-interest', Seccombe and colleagues (1998: 861–62) argue that people draw on a hegemonic 'common sense' to understand questions of inequality and poverty, a common sense in which 'the contradictions inherent in the interests of the dominant and subordinate groups are ignored'. They fail 'to see the shared political nature of their problems' because they 'internalize the common-sense ideology that a need for welfare represents a personal inadequacy, rather than a weakness or contradiction within the social structure' (Ibid.: 862). Similarly, for Shildrick and McDonald, individualised 'heavily ideological accounts of poverty' are prominent among poor people while a sense of class solidarity or social structural explanation is rare, which they connect to a decline in working-class institutions (such as trade unions), suggesting that 'ruling ideas' 'take hold more easily in the context of a diminishing politicized, working-class consciousness' (2013: 301).

However, many analysts also note that the penetration of individualising ideologies is uneven, with the empirical picture a complicated one. So while individualised explanations of poverty *do* shape the 'practices, attitudes and language of people experiencing poverty', such explanations are also 'actively resisted and rejected' (Pemberton et al., 2016: 22). 'Surprisingly', 'given the power of neoliberalism to project on to individuals a sense of responsibility for their own fate', poor people generally do not engage in *self-blame*; rather blame is projected onto others (Shildrick and McDonald, 2013: 301).

While poor people tend to draw on individualising theories to explain *others'* reliance on the welfare system, they do recognise the structural factors affecting their *own* situation (Shildrick and McDonald, 2013: 301) and when explaining their own situation blamed social structure or the welfare system (Seccombe et al., 1998: 849). The people in Pemberton and colleagues' study experienced 'no difficulties connecting their immediate circumstances to broader structural contexts' (2016: 29–30) and were 'conscious of the structural factors that shaped their lives', such as high rates of unemployment, a low-wage economy and rising costs of living. But they responded in 'complex and contradictory' ways to discourses of 'the poor' as 'scroungers': resisting its application to their own lives but still using it to judge others and going 'to considerable lengths to distance themselves from the "poor"' (Ibid.: 32–34). Pemberton and colleagues (Ibid.; 22) see these complex responses as a form of Gramscian (1971) 'contradictory consciousness', where people's understanding of their situation contains a mixture of a practically derived 'good sense', with a critical recognition of structural constraints, but also an individualising hegemonic 'common sense', drawn from dominant worldviews. However, the critical elements of 'good sense' were generally too fragmentary to fully challenge hegemonic common sense, and the defensive efforts of people on low incomes to distance themselves from the stigma associated with 'the poor' ultimately served to reinforce the public stigma of being poor. For those 'living on the margins of social inclusion, the labels "undeserving" or "feckless" must . . . be avoided at all costs'; however, their demarcation strategies 'lend currency to these ideas insofar as they contribute to wider "common-sense" positions concerning "the poor"' (Pemberton et al., 2016: 34–35). As a result, it was hard to avoid 'internalizing messages that suggest that poverty is rooted in choice, personal failure and dependency', with many developing 'injuriously low levels of self-esteem and personal confidence' (Ibid.: 32). Here we see the hidden injuries of internalised inequality.

INTERNALISING INEQUALITY

It has been argued that all systems of inequality are 'maintained and reproduced, in part, through their internalization by the oppressed' (Pyke, 2010: 552). Because subordinate groups are forced to adjust and monitor how they behave in relation to dominant values, they come to internalise at least some of the values which position them as inferior. This is understood as an embodied, affective process in which subordination shapes the self, affecting not just people's 'realistic' sense of what is 'possible' but also, as they must daily negotiate their negative valuation by dominant groups, damaging their sense of dignity, self-worth and empowerment. Analysts vary in the degree to which they see subordinate groups incorporating dominant values as well as in the extent to which they think such processes serve to conceal relations of domination and suppress discontent. Nonetheless, most agree that it is impossible to experience subordination without having to negotiate judgements of inferiority in ways which bleed into the self.

Arguments of the 'internalization of inferiority' focus on how the daily negotiation of the prejudices of dominant groups can result in 'self-hatred' and 'feelings of inferiority, resignation, isolation, powerlessness' among subordinates (Pheterson, 1986: 146). Accounts of colonialism and racial subordination offer powerful versions of this argument. Here the defensive adaptations people of colour are forced to make when negotiating racial domination can negatively shape their view of themselves and of what is possible for them, helping to perpetuate their situation. hooks, for example, argues that black Americans must 'live with the shadow of the cultural negatives' in a white-dominated society 'that routinely assaults black Americans' self-esteem' and where they 'daily receive the message' that 'to be black is to be inferior, subordinate, and seen as a threat to be subdued or eliminated' (2003: 138, 161). The inability to 'shape how we see ourselves and how others see us is one of the major blows to collective self-esteem', for without self-esteem people 'feel powerless. They feel they can only be victims' (Ibid.: xii).

This can result in internalised racism: 'the "subjection" of the victims of racism to the mystifications of the very racist ideology which imprison and define them', with these 'hidden injuries of racism' identified as one of 'the subtle mechanisms that sustain white privilege' (Hall, 1986: 27; Pyke, 2010: 551). hooks (2003: 162) sees internalised racism as 'a feature of black life in the United States from the very first moment black people found that white people would reward them, be kinder to them, like them better, if they showed a higher regard for whiteness than blackness'. She identifies the most obvious example of this in 'shame about appearance, skin color, body shape, and hair texture', where many black Americans have 'passively accepted and condoned' a 'color caste hierarchy' where lighter skins are seen as superior, resulting in internal hierarchies and 'shaming on the basis of skin color' (Ibid.: 37). Such internalisations, she argues, are corrosive for black people's self-esteem, empowerment and group solidarity.

Processes of symbolic domination are sometimes presented as a more sophisticated and effective form of control than coercion (Gramsci, 1971; Bourdieu, 1990a, 1998b). But Fanon (1986, 1967a, 1967b) provides an influential account of the internalisation of inequality even under brutal repression in his analysis of French colonialism (in the Antilles and Algeria). Fanon insists that the coercive nature of colonialism[10] must also be understood as a form of ideological domination, as it 'is not possible to enslave men without logically making them inferior', and so colonisers racialise the people they dispossess as 'natural' inferiors to legitimate colonial domination (1967a: 169). These racist ideologies become internalised by the colonised as they 'work their way into one's mind and shape one's view of the world and of the group to which one belongs' (1986a: 118). This is because colonial subalterns cannot escape the colonisers' constructions 'that one is a Negro to the degree to which one is wicked, sloppy, malicious, instinctual' and where it is only possible to become closer to a 'real human being' by becoming 'proportionately whiter' (1986: 118, 18).

Fanon (1986: 110) emphasises the phenomenological, embodied nature of this process, where self-awareness is always bound up in seeing oneself through the negative gaze of the (white) other. This 'inferiorization' produces a form of 'colonized mentality', generating 'fear, inferiority complexes, trepidation, servility, despair [and] abasement'[11] in black colonial subjects in an 'internalization' or 'epidermalization' of inferiority (1986: 9, 13). The result is destructive and divisive forms of hierarchical 'Negrophobia'[12] between people of colour as well as self-serving attempts at assimilation into white society (1986; 1967a: 47). These are defensive adaptations to subjugation, but in so adapting people reproduce the racial hierarchy which judges them as deficient, while the fear, shame and self-contempt such racist ideologies generates keep colonial subjects divided and subjugated.

A related argument about the internalisation of inequality emerges in accounts of how subordinate groups 'realistically' limit their hopes and aspirations. In developing a self-limiting sense of what is appropriate and possible for people in their position, subordinate groups reproduce that position in a kind of self-fulfilling prophecy. For example, the capability approach to social justice (Sen, 1985) suggests that people's adaptation to structures of inequality often limits their aspirations and desires. The problem of 'adaptive preferences' emerges in a process of 'realistic' adjustment:

> Our mental reactions to what we actually get and what we can sensibly expect to get may frequently involve compromises with a harsh reality. The destitute thrown into beggary, the vulnerable landless labourer precariously surviving at the edge of subsistence, the overworked domestic servant working round the clock, the subdued and subjugated housewife reconciled to her role and her fate, all tend to come to terms with their respective predicaments. (Sen, 1985: 21–22)

A more embodied account of dominated groups 'realistically' adjusting their expectations emerges in Bourdieu's concept of the habitus. Bourdieu (1977: 166) argues that people generally operate with a practical and tacit 'sense' of the world, acting on the basis of embodied dispositions rather than conscious calculation. But we develop this practical sense from the conditions of our upbringing, so 'society' becomes 'written into the body', producing classed 'social instincts' for how to behave which generally work conservatively, leading to self-limiting tastes and aspirations (Bourdieu, 1990a). Dominated groups develop 'a sense of limits, a practical anticipation of objective limits acquired by experience of objective limits, a "sense of one's place" which leads one to exclude oneself from the goods, persons, places and so forth from which one is excluded' (Bourdieu, 1984: 466–7, 471). As people 'realistically' adjust to inequality, they may not feel they can do any better. This, ironically, seems to locate the reproduction of unequal social arrangements not in people's 'misrecognition' of them but rather in their processes of 'recognition'. Because we must 'recognise' social arrangements as 'what they are' in order to organise our activities, we adjust our actions accordingly, and, regardless of our opinion about such arrangements, in so adjusting we help to reproduce them. But in such arguments, the identification of 'naturalisation' depends on just how realistic we consider people's 'realistic' adjustment to their circumstances.

However, there is a stronger version of the argument, in which subordinate groups not only feel they cannot do any better under the circumstances but also come to feel that they do not *want or deserve* any better. This is the claim made in more extended arguments about the internalisation of inequality, exemplified in accounts of 'symbolic violence'. Symbolic violence occurs when dominated groups come to accept the values of the dominant classes as legitimate, with this violence '*exercised upon a social agent with his or her complicity*' (Bourdieu and Wacquant, 1992: 167, original emphasis). Here it is not just that dominated groups respond 'realistically' to their situation (and thus unintentionally reproduce it); they also learn to 'love' these limits (1984: 244). Disadvantaged groups not only become 'resigned' to the idea that a practice 'is not for the likes of us'; their 'awareness of impossibility and of prohibition' goes further to become the internalisation of limits so that 'one *prohibits oneself*' from valuing such activities (Bourdieu, 1990c: 16–17, original emphasis). Dominated groups develop the 'taste of necessity', learning to only value what they can have. Not only is there a naturalisation of the 'established order' but dominated groups come 'to refuse what is anyway refused and to love the inevitable' (1977: 164, 77).

This account goes much further in the extent to which dominated groups are said to internalise dominant ideologies and values, where 'adapting to a dominated position implies a form of acceptance of domination' through a 'sense of incompetence, failure or culture unworthiness' (Bourdieu, 1984: 386), and where

> the further you go down the social scale the more they believe in natural talent or gifts—the more they believe that those who are successful are naturally endowed with intellectual capacities. And the more they accept their own exclusion, the more they believe they are stupid, the more they say 'Yes, I was no good at English, I was no good at French, I was no good at mathematics'. It doesn't mean that the dominated individuals tolerate everything; but they assent to much more than we believe and much more than they know. (Bourdieu, 1992b: 114)

As Lawler (2011: 1424) notes, Bourdieu sees symbolic violence not only in class relations where all classes 'agree that the middle classes are more intelligent, more capable of running the country, more deserving of higher pay', but also gender relations where 'both men and women agree that women are weaker, less intelligent, more unreliable'. Indeed, Bourdieu (1992a: 115) suggests that gender relations are 'the paradigm case of the operation of symbolic violence', where male domination 'operates in a . . . subtle manner—through language, through the body, through attitudes toward things which are below the level of consciousness'. Feminist writers have similarly emphasised that gender inequality operates as an embodied process of naturalisation. For example, Bordo (1993: 189) argues that traditional Western sexist ideology justifies 'a culture which subordinates women's desires to those of men, sexualises and commodifies women's bodies, and offers them little other opportunity for social or personal power', but this is naturalised by arguments which suggest this state of affairs simply reflects women's 'feminine nature'. However, this is not just a process of the imposition of a dominant group's values but also occurs through recognition of wider gender expectations which produces 'individual self-surveillance and self-correction to norms' (Ibid.: 191). Bordo (1993: 186, 197), adopting a more Foucauldian variant of this type of argument, notes that 'female subjectivity is normalized and subordinated by the everyday bodily requirements and vulnerabilities of "femininity"'; as women cannot avoid being judged and valued on their appearance, they must adjust their behaviour to negotiate such judgements, which are also 'strongly racially, ethnically and heterosexually inflected'. There is a naturalisation of a dominant group's standards as the norm. So, for example, the 'images of beauty, power and success which dominate in US culture are generated out of Anglo-Saxon identifications and preferences and . . . are globally influential through the mass media', but these images act as the 'standard against which other women will measure, judge, discipline and "correct" themselves' (Ibid.: 196–97).

There is a tension in accounts of naturalisation which describe the 'misrecognition' of inequality but which often seem to rest on subordinates' 'recognition' of, and adjustment to, such arrangements. For Bourdieu, this tension is resolved through an emphasis on the nonreflexive doxic acceptance of inequality, in which social environments are practically and tacitly experienced, as 'natural', inevitable and self-evident. Here symbolic violence is 'a more effective, and in this sense more brutal, means of oppression' than coercion, because its effectiveness rests in people's 'pre-verbal taking-for-granted' of the world, because 'that which goes without saying' also 'therefore goes unquestioned' (Bourdieu, 1992a: 115; 1990: 68). It is on this basis that Bourdieu is pessimistic about people developing a critical consciousness of their situation. He suggests it is generally only when habitus is dissonant with field that the 'taken-for-granted' nature of the world is thrown into question and individuals can develop a 'heightened awareness' of their environment. But such disjunctures are presented as relatively rare because of the conservative choices of the habitus. Critical reflexivity can also be generated by crisis moments. For example, in something of a rapprochement with theories of relative deprivation, Bourdieu argues that 'an abrupt slump in objective chances relative to subjective aspirations is likely to produce a break in the tacit acceptance which the dominated classes—now abruptly excluded from the race . . . previously granted to the dominant goals, and so to make possible a genuine inversion of values' (1984: 168). Nevertheless, while crisis is 'a necessary condition for a questioning of doxa', it is 'not in itself a sufficient condition for the production of a critical discourse' (Ibid.: 169).

Chapter 1 introduced Scott's (1990) distinction between 'thick' and 'thin' versions of theories of hegemony and symbolic domination, and both versions can be seen in the arguments discussed in this chapter. The 'thin' version argues that symbolic domination 'achieves compliance by convincing subordinate groups that the social order in which they live is natural and inevitable', producing resignation or fatalism among dominated groups (Ibid.: 72). However, Scott argues that there is a tendency to 'take this more defensible notion of hegemony and, as it were, to fatten it up' by arguing 'that what is conceived as inevitable becomes, by that fact, just. Necessity becomes virtue' (Ibid.: 76). The 'thick' version sees symbolic domination persuading 'subordinate groups to believe actively in the values that explain and justify their subordination' (Ibid.: 72). Bourdieu's (1992b: 115) account of symbolic violence represents one of the 'thickest' of such theories, since he argues that symbolic domination operates through 'the unconscious manipulation of the body', with the force of doxa so effectively naturalising inequality that it severely restricts people's capacity to even recognise their situation as domination. However, analysts of symbolic domination and misrecognition themselves vary considerably in the degree to which they see subordinated groups incorporating dominant values. Nor do they agree on the extent to which symbolic domination actually manages to conceal relations of domination, suppress discontent or prevent critical consciousness. I now consider how analysts of symbolic domination and misrecognition themselves assess the *limits* of misrecognition.

THE LIMITS OF MISRECOGNITION

An emphasis on 'the naturalization of ideas' has the strength of allowing examination of the 'unconscious mechanisms' of inequality (Eagleton, 1992: 113). But Eagleton argues that Bourdieu's emphasis on the doxic naturalisation of inequality as 'that which is beyond question' is overextended, leaving insufficient room for 'dissent, criticism and opposition' (Ibid.: 114). Lawler (2011: 1425) notes that 'aside from exegesis, symbolic violence has only relatively rarely been taken up and used in any extended way by other analysts', with critics arguing that 'Bourdieu overemphasises the efficacy of symbolic violence' and overstates the extent to which 'dominated groups really take the point of view of the dominated' (Ibid.). Eagleton sees a danger in 'overstressing the naturalizing function of ideology or doxa', because people can be 'critical, even ... sceptical, of those values and beliefs, and nevertheless continue to conform to them' so that it is 'too simple to claim that all symbolic violence or ideology is actually naturalized' (1992: 113–14).

Coercive forms of domination are usually seen as less effectively naturalised than more 'hegemonic' forms, with many analysts arguing that coercion undermines symbolic legitimation. Fanon, for example, argues that colonial ideological domination is never fully effective, since notions of a superior 'white civilisation' are so compromised by the brutality of colonialism and the 'violence with which the supremacy of white values is affirmed' (1967a: 33). Colonial racist ideologies are a form of 'mystification' which subjugates colonial subjects by generating divisive feelings of fear and shame, but in the context of decolonial revolutionary struggles[13] the question of how colonial subjects are able to 'decipher' colonialism is key. Fanon argues that colonial ideologies take uneven hold, with groups least co-opted into the colonial system (peasants and the people of the 'shanty towns') more likely to rebel. But he also identifies intrinsic limits to the effectiveness of racist colonial ideologies, since 'it is evident that what parcels out the world . . . is the fact of . . . belonging to a given race' so colonialism never fully masks its 'human realities' (1967a: 30–31). Theories of legitimation must be 'stretched' in the colonial context, because colonialism is distinguished by racialised coercion, where a 'foreign governing race' has 'imposed rule by means of guns and machines' (Ibid.: 31). Because they must constantly be on guard not to step out of line, 'the muscles of the colonized are always tensed', and 'deep down the colonized subject acknowledges no authority', being 'dominated but not domesticated' and 'made to feel inferior, but by no means convinced of his inferiority' (1967a: 16).

hooks, too, sees the naturalisation of American white supremacy as incomplete and historically variable. The same black Americans 'who passively accepted the internalization of the color caste system' 'resisted the notion that they were inferior based on intellectual capability' and 'utterly rebelled' against this ideology (2003: 40). It 'was not internalized' because 'the great majority of black folks saw themselves as victims of unfortunate circumstance, believing that if they had the same opportunity as their white counterparts they would demonstrate intellectual equality' (Ibid.: 39). And subjugation sometimes enhances rather than diminishes a dominated group's critical awareness because of the vigilance required by subordinated groups. In the United States, under slavery or Jim Crow segregation 'the everyday survival of black people demanded that they develop basic skills of critical thinking' because during 'the long period of racial apartheid black folk had to be critically vigilant to be always aware of how the system that was exploiting and oppressing them worked and as aware of what needed to be done to intervene in this system' (2003: 70). hooks argues that the gaining of civil rights and greater economic prosperity led many black Americans to relax this critical vigilance. However, she also notes the importance of collective struggle in weakening the hold of symbolic domination because such protest challenges the internalisation of inferiority—arguing that 'when mass-based protest against racism was strong, black people felt psychologically stronger' (Ibid.: 150), because 'militant antiracist political struggles placed the issue of self-esteem for black folks on the agenda' (Ibid.: 2).

For Bourdieu, the effectiveness of symbolic violence does not rest 'in mystified consciousnesses that only need to be enlightened' but rather in embodied dispositions 'attuned to the structure of domination of which they are the product' (Bourdieu, 2001: 41). However, even a highly naturalised, embodied inequality like gender domination—which Bourdieu sees as paradigmatic of 'naturalised' symbolic violence—is challenged and resisted. Bordo (1993: 182, original emphasis) argues that we must be wary of over-emphasising the idea of 'resistance' to naturalised inequalities, noting that in relation to gender, '"normalization" is still the *dominant* order of the day', 'especially with regard to the politics of *women's* bodies'. Nonetheless, Bordo points to the significance of the feminist movement in creating a politics of women's bodies, and producing a 'demystification of the naturalness and political innocence of gender', as part of a 'general challenge to cultural consciousness which began in the late 1960s', through demonstrations, manifestos and consciousness-raising sessions (Ibid.: 180–81). Bordo also argues, for example, that the rising number of women who seek plastic surgery such as breast augmentation 'are not "cultural dopes"' but are rather 'all too conscious of the system of values and rewards that they are responding to and perpetuating' (Ibid.: 188).

Here again is the suggestion that it is people's awareness of their subordination that unintentionally helps to reproduce it, as people structure their practices in expectation of the likely rewards or sanctions that may result. And in line with Eagleton's (1992: 114) argument that there are different kinds of legitimation, ranging from the internalisation of ruling ideas to a more pragmatic or sceptical acceptance, feminist analysts also point out how ambivalently or ironically women often inhabit '"feminine" positions' in which they 'simultaneously accept and refuse their location' (Lawler, 2011: 1425; Skeggs, 1997; Butler, 1999).

It has been argued that symbolic violence, as the method of domination undertaken in liberal democracies when 'brutal exploitation is impossible', is actually more effective than coercion because it is an 'invisible form of violence' (Bourdieu, 1977: 192). But for critics this overstates the importance of symbolic legitimation in maintaining domination: not only neglecting the role of economic constraint, coercion or threat as features of unequal class relations in liberal democracies (Swartz, 1997) but also understating the extent of dissent and protest that does occur. It is hard to sustain arguments of symbolic domination or hegemony without substantial qualification, because there are higher levels of discontent, resistance and awareness of structural inequality than we would expect if symbolic domination really did secure consent to subordination. Often, the explanation then turns from the manufacturing of consent to the steering of dissent into self-defeating forms. So while symbolic domination may not prevent discontent (indeed it produces it), this only results in limited forms of dissent and adaptation—in strategies of coping or letting off steam, or at best, sectional and divisive struggles.

Bourdieu makes perhaps the strongest claims about dominated groups' incorporation of dominant values, seeing doxa as generally producing unconscious conformity to subordination. This does not prevent discontent, but Bourdieu argues that such discontent is restricted in nature. While the 'doxic attitude means bodily submission, unconscious submission', 'pain comes from the fact that one internalizes silent suffering, which may find bodily expression, in the form of self-hatred, self-punishment' (1992a: 121). Here the suffering of subordinate groups turns inwards, though Bourdieu (2000: 161; Bourdieu, Accardo and Ferguson, 1999: 511) also acknowledges that 'occupants of precarious positions' can be 'extraordinary "practical analysts" . . . constrained, in order to live or to survive, to practice a kind of self-analysis, which often gives them access to the objective contradictions which have them in their grasp'. So suffering can turn outwards, leading to the 'rejection' of 'submissiveness and docility' among 'the least integrated in the economic and social order' (Bourdieu, 1992a: 95). However, such 'transgressions' are limited—primarily a way of 'resigning oneself to a world with no way out, dominated by poverty and the law of the jungle, discrimination and violence' (Ibid.: 96). Such discontent generally only results in 'defence and survival mechanism[s]' which are difficult to sustain, as transgressors 'come to know only too well the cost of revolt' (Ibid.: 96). Bourdieu also argues that the 'poses and postures of bravado (e.g., *vis a vis* authority and especially the police) can coexist with a deep-seated conformism regarding everything concerning hierarchies' (Ibid.: 96). Here true critical recognition can only emerge in dissent which is capable of challenging domination and changing the structure of inequality (rather than dissent aimed simply at improving people's situation).

For Eagleton, there is a 'danger of accepting too quickly the idea that people do legitimate prevailing forms of power', since there are 'different kinds of legitimation, all the way from an absolute internalization of ruling ideas to a more pragmatic or sceptical acceptance' (1992: 114). Some suggest that the compliant demeanour of subjugated groups is often only a *public performance* of deference, strongly shaped by how the dominant group 'would wish things to appear' (Scott, 1990: 5)—an argument examined in Chapter 6. In acknowledging that the grasp of naturalising ideologies is uneven and partial, analysts often focus on how the discontent and suffering of subordinate groups becomes dissipated—in shame, attempts at assimilation or divisive sectional struggles, which never really pose a fundamental challenge to the system. But to mount an effective challenge to structural arrangements requires considerable collective effort, so is it surprising that people often feel resignation or fatalism about inequality? For Bourdieu, the limited nature of dissent reflects 'an adherence to the relations of order which . . . are accepted as self-evident' and represents symbolic domination where the most 'implacable' form of 'hidden persuasion' is the one exerted 'by the *order of things*' (Bourdieu, 1998a: 471; Bourdieu and Wacquant, 2002: 168, original emphasis). But is this really 'misrecognition'?

In this chapter I have adopted a sceptical approach to theories of symbolic legitimation and misrecognition, particularly to those more extended versions which suggest that naturalisation prevents subordinate groups even recognising their domination. It is hard to sustain such arguments without significant qualification, because the penetration of symbolic legitimation is uneven, incomplete and contested, takes stronger hold among the dominant than the less-advantaged and does not prevent discontent or dissent. And in fact, most accounts of symbolic legitimation do veer into substantial qualification, with analysts conceding that dominant ideologies do not prevent discontent but instead misdirect it into self-defeating forms—into shame, attempts at assimilation, letting-off-steam activities or divisive sectional struggles. However, to acknowledge this is to concede sharp limits to the 'naturalisation' of social arrangement.

Legitimating ideologies undoubtedly produce hidden injuries and adjustment to limits, but these take their force from people's recognition of their subordination and occur even when subordinate groups are sceptical of dominant ideologies and recognise the arbitrary nature of privilege. It is hard to escape the stigma of inequality because subordinates must negotiate environments in which they are exceptionalised and their disadvantage individualised and stigmatised by others. There is a fundamental tension in arguments of naturalisation, therefore, which argue that it is people's misrecognition of inequality which serves to reproduce it but found this in processes which rest on subordinates' recognition of, and adaptation to, such arrangements. This tension is sometimes resolved by a fall-back to 'thinner' accounts of the naturalisation of inequality, which focus on the nonreflexive 'recognition' of inequality, where the practical and tacit experience of social environments as inevitable or self-evident works to produce resignation and fatalism among subordinates regardless of their discontent. Such claims are on stronger ground, because people's focus on structural inequality does often construct it as a 'fact of life', a given feature of their environment which must be negotiated and managed. However, our apprehension of features of our environment as given or self-evident depends on our practical engagements and capacities for action and does not preclude more reflexive, critical understandings or indeed dissent (as I explore further in Chapter 7). Nor is a certain resignation about changing features of our environment necessarily a form of misrecognition.

Irwin argues that people 'are more sophisticated analysts of social process, and of their own situatedness within the wider social structure, than often thought' (2018: 211), displaying a pretty good grasp of the interplay of structural and individual factors in shaping social outcomes. But while people are *aware* of structural inequality, she argues that they assess it in terms of its immediate practical relevance to their lives, focusing on those aspects of their social location which they feel can be changed, with most structures of inequality seen as beyond this scope (Irwin, 2015: 271). People reflect 'on their social position within quite conservative and proximally relevant understandings of how things might be otherwise', which 'points towards the perceived-as-given structure of social arrangements' in which people's evaluation of their position reflects 'circumscribed, proximally relevant and realistic ideas of how things might be improved' (Ibid.: 277–78). For others, of course, the 'perceived-as-given structure of social arrangements' is still symbolic domination, the 'thin' form of naturalisation in which people's resignation about inequality as a 'fact of life' limits their capacity to challenge or resist. However, the identification of this as 'misrecognition' depends on just how realistic we consider these adjustments to be.

While disadvantaged groups do often feel that they cannot do much to change wider social arrangements, they are not entirely mistaken in this. Collective challenge is difficult, and as I explore in later chapters, the capacity for practical challenge depends on resources and collective organisation which the disadvantaged often lack and also entails significant risk. In these accounts the explanation for why people put up with inequality is less a question of naturalisation than one of various kinds of practical constraint. But people do sometimes seize opportunities to challenge the system, and overcoming resignation is often a question of the practical capacities for collective action. So it is not at all clear that people's practical viewpoints and their resignation about inequality actually prevent challenge, critique or resistance.

In later chapters, I consider arguments that dissent, critique and resistance are more widespread than many analysts have acknowledged, arguments which again indicate that the naturalisation of inequality is only ever partial. As Chapter 4 explores, the experience of subordination does often create feelings of shame and degradation among subordinated groups, but this does not always result in resignation or despair. The experience of subordination is also bound up with anger and indignation, sometimes resulting in collective struggles. And collective protest movements not only help to raise the self-esteem of subordinate groups but also overturn resignation by offering practical avenues for challenge to social arrangements. So while it is true, as Irwin (2015: 271) argues, that 'people tend to take the social world in which they move, and the configuration of opportunity and constraint, as effectively given', the extent of discontent and dissent in social life suggests that people only take the social world as effectively given *for now*.

NOTES

1. The next chapter considers another type of 'misrecognition', where inequality entails the denial of 'recognition' (rights, dignity and respect) to marginalised groups (Honneth, 1995).
2. Measured by the questions 'Do you ever get angry or frustrated due to your status in the society?' and 'Overall, do you feel that your current status in the society is just or unjust?'.
3. So called, because the protestors banged pots and pans.
4. While beliefs about opportunity barriers caused by class origin, social ties and race had no significant effects on subjective status injustice in the study (Oddsson and Bernburg, 2018).
5. Because if social positions are determined solely by ability, this does not eradicate inequality but simply creates a new form of it which amounts to a caste system, with no hope —beyond revolution—for those at the bottom of society, as their fates are fixed.
6. This reinforces inequality, because if the group responsible for hiring and promotion believe 'the current process is meritocratic, it is unlikely that this process will change, and patterns of inequality reflected in the sector will persist' (Taylor and O'Brien, 2017: 40).
7. Elites in these nations were also sceptical about the state's capacity to reduce poverty and so focused on education, as they still had faith in their government's ability to construct schools (Ibid.).
8. That is, agreeing that people in their countries are rewarded appropriately for their efforts and skills.
9. So 41% thought 'having a rich family' was important for getting ahead, 49% felt this way about political connections and 81% said that 'knowing the right people' was important (Oddsson and Bernburg, 2018).
10. His work draws on his experiences as a psychiatrist in Algeria, where he was required to treat the psychological ailments of both the French soldiers who conducted torture against the anti-colonial resistance as well as the Algerian torture victims.
11. Fanon is quoting the poet, author and politician Cesaire.
12. Fanon argues that this can be seen in the way Antilleans under colonialism construct themselves as more 'civilized', 'that is, closer to the White man' than Africans, and racial hierarchies develop between different groups along lines of colourism (1986: 26, 110).
13. Fanon took part in the Algerian war of independence.

FOUR
Affective Inequality

Many analysts focus on the naturalisation of inequalities but most concede considerable limits to this, so the argument then turns to the *affective* nature of symbolic legitimation, in which people's 'sense' of inequality becomes less a question of critical awareness and more a question of the embodied dispositions and emotions produced by subordination, in self-restricting choices and feelings of shame, resignation and despair. But inequality and subordination do not always lead to resignation and despair. This chapter reconsiders the affective dimension to inequality, examining accounts which focus on how inequalities spark dissent, anger, indignation and struggles for greater recognition, respect and dignity. These accounts place a much greater emphasis on people's ability to develop values and moral principles in opposition to dominant values, on people's 'ordinary' capacity for reflexivity and critique of social arrangements and therefore on people's ability to challenge and resist domination. These differences are all predicated on a greater focus on how affect is shaped by lay normativity and intersubjective social relations. But in opening up a greater space for critique, dissent and struggle, we still have to explain how subordination persists, so accounts increasingly turn to the difficulties of dissent and how it is often stifled, not only by dominant groups but also by the everyday practical constraints on social struggle.

All social relations involve affect, for 'every time we meet somebody we experience the encounter through different emotional responses such as disgust, horror, fear, anxiety, dignity, gravitas, pleasure, warmth, kindness'—affects which fundamentally shape people's subjectivity, their feelings of constraint or entitlement, their capacity to inhabit different social spaces and their agency (Skeggs, 2012: 280). The dual nature of the affective experience of inequality is emphasised, where suffering, disrespect and stigmatisation are bound up with control and conformity but are also powerful forces *generating* dissent and struggle. In framing inequalities in terms of affect, the focus of analysis is not just on unequal economic resources but also unequal access to dignity and recognition, in struggles operating across gender, racial and class inequalities and disenfranchisement. For Honneth (1995), all social struggle arises from the denial of *recognition*, when people are refused the social bases for self-confidence, self-esteem and self-respect in processes of exclusion and insult. Social struggle emerges from 'disrespect', a term which includes humiliation, degradation, insult, disenfranchisement or physical assault (Anderson, 1995: viii). But such struggles only make sense in relation to normative principles and commitments, where what motivates people 'to call the prevailing social order into question and to engage in practical resistance is the moral conviction that, with respect to their own situations or particularities, the recognition principles considered legitimate are incorrectly or inadequately applied' (Honneth, 2003: 157).

Many of these accounts take issue with notions of symbolic domination, in particular Bourdieu's account of the doxic 'incorporation' of structures of inequality. Bourdieu acknowledges the 'positional suffering' that derives from a lack of respect but argues that resistance is impossible while 'stigmatized groups . . . claim the stigma as the basis for their identity' (Bourdieu, Accardo and Ferguson, 1999: 913; Bourdieu, 1992a: 95). By contrast, others see social struggle proceeding *through* subjugated groups embracing and reclaiming their stigma (Boltanski, 2011; Honneth, 1995; Tyler, 2013, 2018). There are also attempts to recuperate critical capacity as a more routine feature of social practice. A common criticism of the doxic nature of 'practical understanding' is that this model does not 'adequately equip practical agents with reflective and critical abilities', making it impossible to explain how they can initiate 'transformative processes, or . . . succeed in enlisting the cooperation of other agents in transforming social identities and conditions' (Bohman, 1998: 143). Even sympathetic commentators concede that Bourdieu's framework curtails the 'life of the mind', underestimating the degree to which agents can stand back from their milieu and reflect critically, making resistance 'hard to understand' (Sayer, 2005b: 23, 32). Some analysts simply attempt to insert greater reflexivity into the Bourdieusian framework, but others place greater emphasis on lay normativity as a self-conscious feature of subjectivity (Sayer, 2005a, 2005b; Boltanski, 2011).

A recurrent argument is that reflexivity must be understood in relation to the normative aspects of everyday experience, in which moral evaluation, affective commitments and forms of 'justification work' are routine aspects of social life (Boltanski, 2011, 2012; Sayer, 2005a, 2005b; Honneth, 1995). Here normative principles are not mere rationalisations of self-interest but reflect genuine values and commitments expressing more general claims to legitimacy. For Sayer (1999, 2005a, 2005b), dissent and resistance must be understood in terms of people's moral and ethical values, which have a strong affective component. Sayer suggests that analysts too often adopt a reductive approach to lay normativity, emphasising how it is influenced by social position, but he argues that we cannot understand morality 'unless we recognize that it also spills out beyond such divisions and sometimes ignores them', which is why moral sentiments underpin resistance as well as conformity (2005a: 951). People draw on alternative sources of value and moral principles to dominant values to evaluate their situation (Skeggs, 2011, 2014; Boltanski, 2011; Sayer, 1999, 2005a, 2005b). Boltanski (2011) argues that accounts of symbolic domination misjudge the extent to which people are blinkered about power relations and underestimate people's critical abilities, but he also links this to the way such models overstate the extent to which people incorporate dominant norms, failing to acknowledge the *plural* nature of forms of value, legitimation and justification. Consequently, such theories overemphasise the 'implacable' character of domination and make it 'hard to differentiate different degrees of subjection and to understand how actors can open up roads to liberation, if only by establishing necessarily local *temporary zones of autonomy*' (Ibid.: 46, original emphasis). Acknowledging the normative dimension of social life helps explain how people can 'challenge the necessity of a social order' (Ibid.).

For Sayer, moral judgements are not solely an expression of self-interest because 'morality is primarily about relations to others, about how people should treat one another in ways conducive to well-being . . . whether you are honest or deceitful, generous or selfish, respectful or contemptuous' (2005a: 951–52). So dominant values are not always the values of the dominant (Sayer, 2005b). This raises another important theme: the intersubjective basis not only of normative principles and affect but also subjectivity and reflexivity (Honneth, 1995; Boltanski, 2011; Sayer, 1999, 2005a, 2005b). Moral evaluations do not neatly correlate with social divisions because 'moral understandings underpin all kinds of social interaction' (Sayer, 2005a: 952). Honneth similarly argues that dignity and self-respect only emerge intersubjectively, through our being granted reciprocal recognition from others that we also recognise.

Some analysts (Honneth) make explicit reference to Mead's (1934) account of intersubjectivity; in other cases (Boltanski, Sayer), there is a Mead-adjacent argument. Regardless, Mead's account of the social self is useful for thinking through the interrelationships between reflexivity and critique, affect and normativity, identified in this chapter. For Mead, both the formation of the social self and coordinated action depend on taking on the attitude of the 'other' and governing our conduct accordingly. This helps explain how subordinate groups come to internalise at least some of the values which position them as inferior. As Shott (1979: 1323) notes, certain emotions—guilt, shame, embarrassment, pride, vanity and empathy—occur through 'putting oneself in another's position and taking that person's perspective'. It is because 'people can view themselves as others do' that 'social control can operate in terms of self-criticism' (Ibid.: 1324–25). Shame, for example, 'is provoked by the realization that others (or the generalized other) consider one's self deficient' (Ibid.: 1325). But taking on the attitudes of others also results in an 'objectification' and evaluation of the self, which is the basis for both reflective self-consciousness and social critique (Mead, 1934: 225, 197). And the social self (and notions of acceptable conduct) occur through identification with a complex *range* of different others (Ibid.: 156–57). As we shall see, many of the analysts discussed here see the ability to draw on alternative and competing normative principles as central to dissent and critique.

This chapter considers a range of qualifications and departures from accounts of symbolic domination and naturalisation, all creating a greater analytical space for reflexivity and dissent, struggle and resistance. For some, it is a matter of arguing that habitus/field disjunctures, and so reflexivity, are relatively commonplace (McNay, 1999; Friedman, 2016; Ingram, Abrahams and Ingram, 2013). For others (Skeggs, 2011, 2014), it is about recognising the existence of alternative value formations beyond the dominant values of capitalism and the limits in the extent to which the logic of capital is internalised. Alternatively (Sayer, 2005a, 2005b), it is about acknowledging that moral evaluation and critique are central to social life, with such evaluation often based on genuine commitments and values rather than just self-interest. For others (Boltanski, 2011), it is about recognising that plural and competing criteria of evaluation make acts of justification and 'ordinary denunciation' routine features of everyday life. And for some (Honneth, 1995; Lamont et al., 2016; Tyler, 2013), it is a question of how disrespect, stigma and abjectification violate people's sense of self in ways which provoke anger and resistance.

At the same time, in acknowledging that dissent, critical capacities and alternative sources of value are widespread, we must also recognise their limits. As Rafanell and Gorringe (2010: 604–5) note, it is the need to explain the durable nature of inequality that leads so many to argue that the dominated 'internalize existing social rules and come to see them as natural'. But if critique, dissent and struggle are widespread, how is it that inequalities endure? One common response is to argue that such dissent is often nullified by processes of incorporation and subversion, suggesting that symbolic domination is more successful when counteracting dissent than in preventing it from arising in the first place. However, there is also an increasing emphasis on the practical constraints and difficulties that confront people who dissent. So this shift to emphasise people's critical capacities, ethical dispositions and moral judgements represents a move away from symbolic domination as an explanation of the reproduction of inequality towards arguments focused more on the constraints, compulsion and sanctions that keep people within unequal arrangements, regardless of their critical awareness or dissent.

REFLEXIVITY, LAY NORMATIVITY AND AFFECT

Let us first consider the question of reflexivity. Bourdieu argues that the habitus tends to produce unconscious conformity to subordination, as objective structures become bodily incorporated. Critics argue that in countering 'overly rationalised approaches' Bourdieu *over*-corrects and is in danger of 'denying or marginalizing the life of the mind' (Sayer, 2005b: 29). Some analysts attempt to insert more reflexivity into the model, but for others reflexivity is ultimately a question of the role of normative principles, moral evaluation and emotion in social practice. For Sayer, moral evaluation is a 'common feature of everyday life', since people 'frequently evaluate each other and themselves on moral grounds' in processes of 'mutual and self-monitoring' and 'often have to confront moral dilemmas' (1999: 413). So while much behaviour has a 'bodily, habitual character', taking proper account of actors' normative judgements raises 'a much more conscious aspect of subjectivity' central to the experience of inequality—emotion (Sayer, 1999: 404; 2005b: 35–36). From this perspective, we acquire embodied 'ethical dispositions, virtue and vices' through our routine practices with others, in which the 'activation of these dispositions has an emotional aspect, evident in sentiments such as gratitude, benevolence, compassion, anger, bitterness, guilt and shame' (Ibid.: 42–43). Only by acknowledging the 'normative orientation of the habitus' can we see how 'resistance can be intrinsic to the formation of the habitus' (Ibid.: 23). Such approaches locate the question of reflexivity within a broader account of the affective and normative basis of social action.

However, a greater focus on reflexivity *is* required. A common criticism of Bourdieu is that his emphasis on the 'adaptation of the habitus to circumstances . . . exaggerates actors' compliance with their position and makes resistance appear to be an anomalous form of behaviour occasioned only by special circumstances' (Sayer, 2005b: 23). Attempts to insert more 'everyday' critical reflexivity into this framework argue that such 'special circumstances'—disruptions between habitus and field—are actually pretty routine. McNay, for example, argues that gender reflexivity emerges through relatively frequent mismatches between gender habitus and fields, 'resulting in ambiguities and dissonances . . . in the way that men and women occupy masculine and feminine positions' (1999: 107). Others (Ingram, 2011; Abrahams and Ingram, 2013; Ingram and Abrahams, 2015; Friedman, 2015) suggest that the reflexive 'torn habitus' (which results from field crossing) is commonplace. Bourdieu (2000: 160) argues that field-crossing results in a divided habitus which provokes reflexivity, because people 'forced to keep watch on themselves and consciously correct the "first movements" of a habitus that generates inappropriate or misplaced behaviours' must reflect on 'that which, for others is taken for granted' (Ibid.: 163). Bourdieu sees this as the exception to a more general rule of restricted reflexivity, because he believes that the habitus 'tends to protect itself' from such 'crises by providing itself with a milieu to which it as pre-adapted as possible' (1990a: 61). However, Bourdieu underestimates the extent of social mobility and so fails to see that 'the experience of 'being "between two worlds"' is relatively frequent, providing a 'unique capacity for reflexivity and self-analysis' (Friedman, 2016: 145). For Bourdieu, a torn habitus is negative because it results in a less effective adaptation to field, creating unease, anxiety and uncertainty (Bourdieu et al., 1999: 511). However, Ingram and Abrahams (2015; Ingram, 2011; Abrahams and Ingram, 2013; 2.4) argue that holding 'a unique position between two fields' not only generates greater reflexivity but, through people creating 'their own differently structured space', also opens up 'a space of new cultural possibilities'.

Others look beyond field-crossing to argue that critical reflexivity also emerges from the plural nature of what people value. For Skeggs (2011; 2014: 14), conventional models of symbolic domination do not accord enough space to what falls 'beyond the logic of capital', or to how people develop 'values beyond [capitalist] value'. She argues that the most disadvantaged groups hold values 'generated *in opposition to* the logic of capital, against an instrumental "dog eat dog world"' (Skeggs and Loveday, 2012: original emphasis), raising serious questions about the extent to which there is an 'internalization of the logic of capital' (Skeggs, 2014: 14). For example, McKenzie's (2015) account of life on a poor working-class council estate shows that those living there experienced a stigmatised devaluing of their position as a welfare-dependent 'under-class' and 'were acutely aware of being 'looked down on' and 'disrespected' (Ibid.: 204). These 'stigmatised readings' generated shame, in an internalisation of the disrespect encountered, but they also generated anger and frustration and led the people on the estate to seek alternative sources of value in their strong sense of community support and their pride in 'getting by' (Ibid.: 206, 200). Skeggs argues that 'defence against denigration' is one of the main ways in which subjectivity is produced for marginalised groups (2012: 280), with such defences producing alternative sources of value. These are not just struggles against economic constraint but also '*against* unjustifiable judgment and authority and *for* dignified relationality' in which expressions of 'anger, bitterness and resentment' are responses to being 'misrecognized as valueless and judged unjustly by those considered undeserving of authority' (Skeggs and Loveday, 2012: 472, 483–4, original emphasis). It is through 'non-utilitarian affects of care, loyalty and affection' that people find 'other routes to valuing each other outside the circuits of exchange that demand a value-return' (Skeggs, 2011: 504)—which also provides a basis for resistance:

> Those designated as improper do not internalize the norms as has been presumed ... They occupy spaces not completely colonized by capital,

calculation and conservativism. We see this in the protests against capital's logic, environmental struggles, the occupy movement and small-scale local responses to support people (e.g., food banks, creative solutions to the bedroom tax by Unite, etc.). These represent the expression of values beyond value. (Skeggs, 2014: 15)

However, the affective nature of class relations also reflects *shared* values. Sayer argues that people on low incomes are not disadvantaged 'primarily because others fail to value their identity and misrecognize and undervalue their cultural goods, or indeed because they are stigmatized' but rather because they 'lack the means to live in ways which they, as well as others, value' (2005a: 947). Class inequalities 'mean that the "social bases of respect" in terms of access to valued ways of living are unequally distributed' so 'shame is likely to be endemic to the experience of class', but without at 'least partial cross-class agreement on the valuation of ways of life and behaviour, there would be little reason for class-related shame, or concern about respectability' (Sayer, 2005a: 954–55). Shame, for Sayer, does not just result from 'external disapproval' since failing to act or live in a way 'which one does not care about need not provoke shame', so 'the stronger the commonality of values, the greater the possibilities for shaming'. Sayer here argues that dominant values 'are not necessarily identical to the values of the dominant', as people hold values not just 'because they have been conditioned into believing them . . . but because they probably rightly judge them to be important for their well-being' (2005b: 955, 958–59). Shame is an emotion 'often associated with class', but while it is 'deeply social in that it is a response to the imagined or actual views of others' it is 'only if we have certain expectations of ourselves and our society that we can be shamed' (Sayer, 2005a: 954).

From Sayer's perspective, dissent and resistance are not simply a question of reflexivity but also of how the habitus includes ethical dispositions 'which, when activated, produce moral emotions' (2005b: 42). So we must acknowledge the significance not just of mundane reflexivity but also of 'normative orientations, emotions and commitments' (Sayer, 2005b: 51–52). Bourdieu's focus on the 'evaluative character' of social behaviour primarily analyses this in strategic terms, a consequence of his 'interest- and power-based model of social life' (Ibid.: 42). But people also 'value others and their conduct in terms of their goodness or propriety' (Ibid.: 42). So while the feelings associated with class (such as envy, resentment, compassion, contempt, shame and pride) 'are *evaluative* responses to particular properties of class inequalities and relations' they also reflect more general normative principles and moral values (2005a: 950, original emphasis). This more general aspect of normative principles allows them to be deployed as levers of social critique. The moral dimension of lay normativity is concerned with 'matters of how people should treat others and be treated by them, which of course is crucial for their subjective and objective well-being', and this 'includes but goes beyond matters of justice and fairness, to relations of recognition, care and friendship, and it implies a conception of the good life' (Ibid.: 951).

For Sayer (2005b: 39–40), people 'invest emotionally in certain things not merely for the rewards but because they come to see them as valuable in themselves', and so we must recognise that the people or practices that 'matter most to actors are not merely things which they happen to like or prefer but things in terms of which their identities are formed and to which they are committed, sometimes to the extent that they will pursue them against their self-interest'. Sayer therefore advocates the concept of 'commitment' over the Bourdieusian concept of *illusio* (where people are 'invested' and 'taken in' by the game), because *illusio* presents such investments 'as egotistical, instrumental, involving competitive, reward-seeking behaviour' (Ibid.: 40). By contrast, 'commitment' 'implies a stronger and more serious attachment, one that has an emotional dimension and involves objects, practices, others and relationships which we *care* about' (Ibid.: original emphasis). It is because of these commitments and emotional investments that our relationship to the world 'is not simply one of accommodation or becoming skilled in its games' but also one of 'wanting the world and its games to be different' (Ibid.: 35). People may become habituated to working in an organisation, for example:

> yet while they certainly have a feel for the game they can still experience conflict between how they feel they ought to act and are allowed to act, and between how they feel they ought to be treated and are treated. They may feel that they are struggling to maintain their integrity in the face of pressures from others, be they fellow workers, clients, or managers relaying budget pressures or government directives. . . . The identities and commitments which are being challenged are invested in consciously and normatively, and not just through habituation. They are not simply about power and resources, but over what is considered to be good. (Sayer, 2005b: 41–42)

Sayer (1999: 412) argues that analysts too often adopt a reductionist view of moral actions, seeing them as 'arbitrary norms backed up by sanctions' and simply reflecting social position or self-interest. This overlooks the possibility of their 'internal normative force grounded in what is good or bad for us and others' (Ibid.). People's ethical dispositions and beliefs do relate to their social location and interests, but moral behaviour and evaluation also 'vary *independently* of divisions such as those of class, "race", gender, or age' and are based on 'reflection and engagement with different ideas' (Sayer, 2005b: 47, 49, 47, original emphasis). It is the 'reciprocal character of relations with others' which produces 'not only a generalising tendency' in ethical beliefs but also a concern with consistency, fairness and integrity which underpins critique (2005b: 48). Certainly, principles of lay normativity can be 'overridden by sectional interests and inequalities'; nonetheless 'the strength of the ideal of fairness is even evident in spurious appeals to it by the dominant, which show a realization of the need at least to appear to be fair in their dealings with the subordinate if they are not to lose legitimacy' (Ibid.: 48). So although it may be 'incompletely carried through', moral thought has a 'generalising moment which can cross the boundaries between social groups; indeed, it is to this that we owe our ability to criticise inequalities' (Ibid.: 50). Here criticism—'of domination, unfairness, hypocrisy and inconsistency'—*depends upon* the existence of moral norms with a more general legitimacy (Ibid., original emphasis). Moral values are intersubjectively generated, and their generalising character derives from

> the ongoing mutual and self-monitoring that occurs in everyday interactions with others, imagining what our behaviour implies for others and how it will be viewed by others, and generalizing from one kind of moral experience to other situations which seem similar. In monitoring our own conduct according to its effects and the responses of others in different social situations we develop a complex set of ethical (and sometimes unethical) dispositions, partly subconsciously and partly through reflection and repeated practice. Of course, moral beliefs may sometimes endorse inequalities and relations of deference and condescension, but they also embody notions of fairness and conceptions of the good which can prompt resistance to domination. Moral systems usually have internal inconsistencies which can be exploited, for example by applying a norm of fairness which is common in one kind of practice to another where it is lacking. To imagine that morality was *never* indifferent to social divisions would be to imply that people only ever act with 'double standards', never consistently . . . but some degree of consistency is intrinsic to morality insofar as it refers to people with similar capacities for flourishing and suffering, and often lay criticisms of inequalities appeal to these. (Sayer,[1] 2005a: 951–52)

THE NORMATIVE BASIS OF 'ORDINARY' CRITIQUE

Analysts who qualify accounts of symbolic domination are often reluctant to 'throw the baby out with the bathwater', and seek to retain an emphasis on people as embodied, dispositional beings (Sayer, 2005b: 51, 52). Others make a more decisive break, adopting a more rationalist stance on critique. One such departure is Boltanski's (2011) attack on Bourdieusian 'critical sociology'. Boltanski (2011: 20, original emphasis) argues that in critical sociology, 'domination' becomes overextended into a notion of 'symbolic violence' in which 'actors are dominated without knowing it', a process explained by 'the *illusions* that blind them and appeals to the notion of the unconscious'. But this creates major explanatory problems. Trying to 'explain virtually all . . . behaviour by the internalization of dominant norms' places too much weight on the dispositions of actors 'at the expense of the properties inscribed in the situations into which they are plunged' (Ibid.: 20). And for Boltanski, arguing that people's behaviour is in accordance with innate dispositions makes it impossible to account for 'the disputes actors engage in' (Ibid.: 20–21). It treats actors 'as deceived beings or as if they were "cultural dopes"' in which their critical capacities are underestimated or ignored[2] (Ibid.: 20).

> If we want to take seriously the claims of actors when they denounce social injustice, criticize power relationships or unveil their foes' hidden motives, we must conceive of them as endowed with an ability to differentiate legitimate and illegitimate ways of rendering criticism and justifications. It is, more precisely, this competence which characterizes the ordinary sense of justice which people implement in their disputes.
> (Boltanski and Thévenot, 1999: 364)

The space for critique is provided by the plural criteria of justification which govern social institutions (with no single axis of domination or legitimation) where people can draw on competing regimes of evaluation and justification for their actions. Boltanski and collaborators examine the critical capacities of actors and their 'ordinary denunciations' of injustice, focusing on how people justify themselves in the face of critique, the disagreements that emerge over the legitimacy of social practices and how people resolve disputes using different principles of justification (Boltanski and Thévenot, 2006; Boltanski and Chiapello, 2007; Boltanski, 2011, 2012). In this framework, the social world 'does not appear as a place of a domination suffered passively and unconsciously but more like a space intersected by a multitude of disputes, critiques, disagreements and attempts to produce fragile local agreements' (Jagd, 2011: 345–46). Here the exercise of 'ordinary' critical competences is a routine feature of social life. This reflects the normative character of social interaction, in which individuals must justify (or be able to justify) their actions to each other, appealing to legitimate principles of action which they hope will command respect or agreement (Boltanski and Thévenot, 2006). People engage in confrontation when their sense of justice is affronted, with such interventions not simply strategic but instead drawing on arguments that claim a more general validity.

The human 'capacity for criticism' becomes 'visible in the daily occurrence of disputes over criteria for justification' which display the 'ordinary sense of justice' used by actors when reaching agreements in daily struggles (Boltanski and Thévenot, 1999: 359; Boltanski, 2011: 27–29). Refusing to see such justifications as merely forms of the legitimation of power, Boltanski argues that 'overarching theories of domination tend to reduce all asymmetries to one basic symmetry (depending on the case, social class, sex, ethnicity, etc.)', which ignores 'the disseminated nature of power' and the 'pluralistic character of the modes of assessment and attachments operative in social life' (2011: 47). It is this plural nature of justification which enables critique and dissent and makes the exercise of 'critical capacity' both widespread and routine.

A variety of 'orders of worth' provide different principles of justification and evaluation (Boltanski and Thévenot, 2006).[3] Particular orders are more associated with certain domains than others, but not exclusively so, coexisting in the same social space:

> There is no direct and stable relation between specific principles and specific institutional contexts (the state, the market, the family, etc.). Rather, different modalities of justification can be pertinent in one and the same institutional context, e.g., when a worker claims her rights as a citizen in a place, the factory, where she wasn't expected to; and one mode of justification can be equally pertinent in different institutional contexts, e.g., when I claim that being an equal member of society does not only have effects in the political domain, but also in the educational system. (Celikates, 2006: 31)

The plural nature of orders of worth 'enables agents to distance themselves critically from a situation and to put the justifications offered into question by referring to another regime of justification' (Boltanski and Thévenot, 1999: 366). Since different criteria can apply to the same social situation, disputes frequently arise from people appealing to different principles of evaluation, and social spheres are shaped and reshaped by such disputes. Public spheres are here conceived as 'discursive realms shaped by open debates between different "orders of value", and by a ceaseless undertaking of "tests"' which can 'confirm or undermine the legitimacy of a given set of normative arrangements and practices' (Susen, 2014a: 13). Such tests can 'challenge the confirmed representations of reality' (Boltanski, 2011: 106) by pointing out illegitimate applications of justifications or by identifying 'inconsistencies between the logics governing different tests in different spheres of reality' (Ibid.: 107). So some disputes can be understood as disagreements about whether the values accepted in a social world have been violated in practice ('reality tests'), a form of internal critique where practices are criticised for not living up to their own ideals.[4]

But a more radical form of critique ('existential tests') occurs in disputes about which mode of justification should apply, where there is the possibility of changing the principles by which practices can be legitimately organised and assessed. These are denunciations which derive from the affective experience of injustice, from the 'lived experience' of suffering, humiliation or shame (or, more positively, from transgression when it affords a greater sense of authenticity)' (Boltanski, 2011: 107) which appeal to external principles of legitimacy. Existential tests seek to publicise previously private experiences of 'contempt and denial' and to challenge the 'generally accepted relations between symbolic forms and states of affairs' by 'casting doubt on the universal character of confirmed relations' (Ibid.: 108–9).

> To arrive at a better appreciation of what I mean by existential tests, think of the tests *in themselves* experienced by homosexuals, forced for centuries into a quasi-clandestine existence, and faced with insult and opprobrium, whose experience was initially conveyed in literary, dramatic or pictorial works, before taking a collective form paving the way for a movement that could claim public recognition for what had become a *collective*. This gradual recognition (which is far from being complete) went hand-in-hand with a change in the contours of reality and the establishment of tests *for self*—more precisely, reality tests—enabling objectification of the injury, which makes it possible, for example, to establish a crime of homophobia in law. (Boltanski, 2011: 108, original emphasis)

Disputes may be on unequal terms, but outcomes are never predetermined and processes of justification are never simply an 'ideological smokescreen', because 'they exert discursively negotiated constraints upon systems of domination' (Susen, 2014a: 13). As Lemieux (2014: 159) notes, Boltanski believes disputes can result in emancipatory social change with 'discursive processes of intersubjective argumentation . . . one of the driving forces underlying material and symbolic processes of social transformation'. Even in disputes based 'on very asymmetrical relations, a minimal amount of uncertainty prevails' which 'permeates the "real" worth of each protagonist' and 'leaves room for subversion' and 'even for the genuine transformation of power relations' (Ibid.). For Boltanski, capitalism is characterised by a continual series of 'tests' over the legitimacy of institutional practices, and the responsiveness of post-industrial capitalism to such tests can be seen in the shift to a 'new spirit' of capitalism—characterised by a move away from monolithic, hierarchical bureaucratic and factory systems to network forms of organisation, semi-autonomous work groups and flatter management structures (Boltanski and Chiapello, 2007). Arguing from the French case, Boltanski and Chiapello suggest that this shift was a response to protests by workers and intellectuals in the 1960s, products of an 'artistic critique' (the demand for liberation and the rejection of inauthenticity) and a 'social critique' (the refusal of egoism and the response to suffering). These critiques were incorporated into the 'new spirit' of capitalism, ultimately as a way of defusing such challenges and maintaining the legitimacy of the capitalism system, but nonetheless institutionalising critique and tests of legitimacy within the system.

Some see Boltanski's emphasis on the routine nature of critical capacity as producing an unduly rationalist view of social practices (Susen, 2014b). Boltanski presents a social world characterised by everyday justification work, disputes, ordinary denunciations and tests of legitimacy. But if such critique is really so widespread and effective, why do inequality and injustice persist? This is a recurrent problem in accounts which open up a greater space for critical reflexivity, dissent and struggle, and a question to which I shall return.

SUFFERING, ABJECTION AND SOCIAL STRUGGLE

A rather different account of critique emerges in work on recognition and abjection, which places central emphasis on the affective dimension of dissent and struggle. For Honneth, for example, it is social disrespect which leads to struggle and conflict, where 'being ashamed or enraged, feeling hurt and indignant', results in the realisation 'that one is being illegitimately denied social recognition' (1995: 135–36). Honneth argues that human flourishing depends on the development of self-confidence, self-esteem and self-respect (or dignity). This is another intersubjective account of moral values, drawing on Mead (1934), which argues that the integrity of people depends on the reciprocal receipt of approval or recognition from others (Honneth, 1995, 1992: 189). Self-confidence, self-esteem and self-respect 'can only be acquired and maintained intersubjectively, through being granted recognition by others whom one also recognises', which means the conditions for self-realisation are 'dependent on the establishment of relations of mutual recognition', that is through relations of love, legal relations (rights) and relations of solidarity (Anderson, 1995: xi). As Ohlström notes (2011: 207), Honneth argues that when 'social relations of recognition fail to live up to this standard of reciprocity—that is, when they are skewed, subordinating some to others—those being subordinated perceive themselves as disrespected', and these feelings of disrespect 'then spark and fuel struggles for recognition, aimed at creating or restoring the necessary conditions of reciprocity'. Insults to dignity and recognition are insults to the social self, so critique and dissent are *built into* relations of inequality:

> When individuals who see themselves as victims of moral maltreatment describe themselves, they assign a dominant role to categories that, as with 'insult' or 'degradation,' are related to forms of disrespect, to the denial of recognition. Negative concepts of this kind are used to characterize a form of behavior that does not represent an injustice solely because it constrains the subjects in their freedom for action or does them harm. Rather, such behavior is injurious because it impairs these persons in their positive understanding of self—an understanding acquired by intersubjective means. There can be no meaningful use whatsoever of the concepts of 'disrespect' or 'insult' were it not for the implicit reference to a subject's claim to be granted recognition by others. (Honneth, 1992: 188–89)

Honneth argues that the affective experience of disrespect provides the basis for social critique and struggle but, like Sayer and Boltanski, locates such affect within more general normative principles, seeing a 'moral logic' to all social conflicts. Social struggle results from 'moral feelings of indignation, rather than pre-given interests', where the 'motives for social resistance and rebellion are formed in the context of moral experiences stemming from the violation of deeply rooted expectations regarding recognition' (1995: 161, 163).

> In the context of the emotional responses associated with shame, the experience of being disrespected can become the motivational impulse for a struggle for recognition. For it is only by regaining the possibility of active conduct that individuals can dispel the state of emotional tension into which they are forced as a result of humiliation. But what makes it possible for the praxis thus opened up to take the form of political resistance is the opportunity for moral insight inherent in these negative emotions, as their cognitive content. It is only because human subjects are incapable of reacting in emotionally neutral ways to social injuries—as exemplified by physical abuse, the denial of rights, and denigration—that the normative patterns of mutual recognition found in the social lifeworld have any chance of being realised. For each of the negative emotional reactions that accompany the experience of having one's claims to recognition disregarded holds out the possibility that the injustice done to one will cognitively disclose itself and become a motive for political resistance. (Honneth, 1995: 138)

Are struggles for equality always struggles for recognition, however? Honneth (2003: 114, 157, original emphasis) sees capitalism as primarily an ordering of recognition, arguing that 'even distributional injustices must be understood as the institutional expression of social disrespect— or, better said, of unjustified relations of recognition', where what motivates people 'to call the prevailing social order in question and to engage in practical resistance is the *moral* conviction that, with respect to their own situations or particularities, the recognition principles considered legitimate are incorrectly or inadequately applied'. Others (Fraser, 2001; Fraser and Honneth, 2003) see different dimensions to social injustice and inequality, arguing that social practices (and struggle) must be assessed in terms of *both* distribution and recognition.

For Fraser, injustice is not always the product of misrecognition, as in the case 'of the skilled white male industrial worker who becomes unemployed due to a factory closing resulting from a speculative corporate merger' (2001: 29). Here, 'the injustice of maldistribution has little to do with misrecognition' but rather is a consequence of profit accumulation, in which 'economic mechanisms that are relatively decoupled from structures of prestige and that operate in a relatively impersonal way . . . impede parity of participation in social life' (Ibid.). Conversely, the injustice of an 'African-American Wall Street banker who cannot get a taxi to pick him up' goes 'beyond the distribution of rights and goods' to 'institutionalized patterns of cultural value' and how these 'impede parity of participation in social life' (Fraser, 2001: 28). Both sides concede that recognition is intertwined with redistribution, however. As Sayer (2005b: 960) argues, recognition of others is also 'partly conditional upon behaviour and achievements, and these depend on access to valued goods and practices'. Struggles for respect must also challenge distributional inequalities in access to such valued goods and practices because such inequalities 'render equality of conditional recognition impossible' (Sayer, 2005a: 960). For Sayer (2005b: 959), struggles for recognition depend on 'more equality of access to the social bases of respect and self-respect', with both Fraser (2003) and Sayer arguing that there can be 'no recognition without redistribution'.

Such debates offer relatively abstract understandings of struggles for social justice. For some, the literature on recognition is too generalised, failing to consider the practical process of 'how non-elite individuals from stigmatized groups cope with the challenge of creating equality' and the role of wider social conditions and 'universalism and multiculturalism (or particularism) in this process' (Lamont and Mizrachi, 2012: 370). By contrast, Lamont and colleagues (2016) offer a detailed comparative analysis of the discriminatory experiences of diverse groups (African Americans, black Brazilians and Arab Palestinian citizens of Israel, as well as Israeli Ethiopian Jews and Mizrahi [Sephardic] Jews) to examine the different practical strategies by which stigmatised groups respond to 'assaults on their worth' and struggle to 'get respect'. As an examination of the 'phenomenology of experiences of ethnoracial exclusion' (Lamont et al., 2016: 7), the aim is to explore 'the micro-politics of recognition' as this emerges from 'subjective experiences of categorical exclusion' (Koenig, 2017: 1263) in processes of discrimination and stigmatisation.[5] Lamont and collaborators show 'assaults on worth' are more widespread than incidents of discrimination, with minoritised groups experiencing stigmatisation on a daily basis. For example, African Americans refer to 'incidents that led them to feel a "defilement of the self"', seeing themselves as 'over-scrutinised, overlooked, underappreciated, misunderstood and disrespected' (Fleming, Lamont and Welburn, 2012: 404). Lamont (2016: np) argues that such experiences affect people just as deeply as being deprived of resources, pointing to the daily 'wear and tear that comes with living as the non-member of the dominant group' where 'dealing with this kind of challenge and assault on your worth all the time takes a toll'.

However, the aim is not just to explore 'society from the perspective of marginalized groups' but rather to examine how everyday practices can be 'social sites for the transformation of social hierarchies' in which the 'choices made in everyday life form the politics of small things' (Lamont and Mizrachi, 2012: 367). Members of stigmatised groups adopt a range of different strategies to try to deal with stigmatisation, racism and discrimination. For example, some seek to minimise conflict and circumvent racial stereotypes by emphasising their competence, intelligence or respectability (as in the case of African Americans wearing Gucci to go shopping), while others find it easier to ignore racism or use humour to deflate it, choosing to 'pick their battles' selectively. Some assert the moral worth or even superiority of their own cultural group over the dominant group; while others directly confront racism through legal challenges or by engaging in collective protest. But there are systematic differences in the strategies stigmatised groups adopt. Lamont and colleagues (2016) found Arab Palestinians more frequently remained silent due to resignation and cynicism, African Americans were more likely to confront stigmatisation, while Ethiopian Jews and Mizrahim in Israel tended to downplay their exclusion. These very different group responses were enabled—but also significantly constrained—'by the broader context in which these individuals find themselves' (Lamont et al., 2016: 3), a theme to which I shall return.

Another account of the emancipatory dimension of social suffering, even in the face of significant control and coercion, is provided by Tyler (2013, 2018), who sees a dual aspect to stigmatisation—binding people in place but also provoking them to rise up. Stigma is an effective mechanism of social control; nonetheless, stigmatised groups can and do 'refuse and revolt against the disenfranchising effects' of their stigmatisation and seek to 'reconstitute themselves not only as citizens with rights, but as *subjects of value*' (Ibid.: 214, original emphasis). Tyler (2018) extends Goffman's (1963: 139) account of stigma as 'a means of formal social control', departing from his focus on how people manage this process to instead examine stigma as a form of power. Tyler (2018; Tyler and Slater, 2018: 732, original emphasis) focuses on stigma as a 'political apparatus' with the production of stigma analysed in terms of 'the motives of *institutions* and *states* within a broader political economy of neoliberal capitalist accumulation'.

Tyler argues that neo-liberal governments operate through the 'daily, pervasive production and mediation of stigma', which does the 'dirty ideological work of neoliberalism', channelling 'public anxieties and hostilities . . . towards those groups within the population, such as the unemployed, homeless people, welfare recipients, irregular migrants, disabled people, ill and elderly populations who are imagined to be a parasitical drain upon scarce resources' (2013: 210–11, 11). Stigmatisation deflects the real causes of people's fears and anxieties, with 'refugees transformed into bogus asylum seekers, unemployed young people into feckless chavs, people with disabilities into welfare cheats' (Ibid.: 9). Tyler shows greater sympathy for models of symbolic domination than many of the theorists discussed in this chapter. She argues, for example, that neo-liberal democracies function 'through the generation of consent via fear and anxiety', in which the ability to govern depends not only on people's economic insecurity and labour precarity but also on the deliberate stoking of people's anxieties and fears, about their economic situation but also 'about border controls and terror threats' (Ibid.: 8–9). Here 'psychic anxiety' becomes 'a mode of (self-) governance', as 'crises are generated, or, as in the case of the current economic crisis . . . exploited by governments' to 'procure public consent' (Ibid.: 9, 11). But while processes of stigma do '"get inside" people—instructing, correcting, regulating and shaping subjectivities', they also produce 'practices of resistance in which revolting subjects engage to survive stigma and disenfranchisement' (Ibid.: 214).

Extending Kristeva's (1982) psychoanalytical concept of abjection[6] to a form of governmentality, Tyler (Ibid.: 38, 21) links stigmatisation to abjection as a 'mechanism of governance through aversion', a 'violent exclusionary force' which strips people of their 'dignity and reproduce[s] them as dehumanized waste, the disposable dregs and refuse of social life'. Echoing the accounts in Chapter 3, Tyler notes that disgust is 'also experienced and lived by those constituted as disgusting' (Ibid.: 26). People do internalise the stigmatising social judgements made about them, taking affective form in shame and self-disgust. But on the other hand, because abjection is *'lived*, as a form of exclusion and humiliation', this creates the 'capacity to trouble' such symbolic and material violence (Ibid.: 42, 47, original emphasis). Tyler (Ibid.: 157, 44) points out that 'people are never identical to the categorical versions of themselves that circulate in the public sphere' and 'often actively reject' stigma, so there is always 'potential within abjection for political agency and resistance' (Ibid.: 157, 44).

Tyler quotes Sayad's (2006: 173) argument that 'the primary form of revolt against stigmatization . . . consists in reclaiming the stigma, which then becomes an emblem [of resistance]' (cited in Tyler, 2018: 759), giving the example of the struggles of black Americans against Jim Crow segregation in the 1960s. Black activists intentionally broke the rules of segregation (for example, sitting in 'whites only' seats at lunch counters and on buses) and in so doing 'provoked violent forms of stigmatization' and retaliation (Ibid.: 759). This was a deliberate strategy to make the daily humiliations and brutality of white supremacy more publicly visible (Ibid.). For Tyler, what 'is of interest' is 'not only how stigma is lived and managed but how it is refused, reworked and resisted by those whom it abjects', in struggles for dignity and recognition which 'remediate' stigma (Ibid.). In such resistance, the 'common refrain' is people's 'insistence that *they are human*' so that resistance emerges from abjectification, from being 'tortured by words, images, policies and mechanisms of policing and control which continuously produce you as less than human' (Ibid.: 213, original emphasis). Tyler (2013: 3) argues that a series of 'revolts by disenfranchised populations' in Britain,[7] including the 2011 riots, exemplify 'the dual meanings of "abjection" and "revolt"': showing how minoritised populations are 'configured as revolting and become subject to control, stigma and censure' but also showing how people 'resist, reconfigure and revolt against their abject subjectification' (Tyler, 2013: 3–4). The 2011 riots, for example, were the result of the stigma directed at the poor, with the rioters reacting not just to 'material conditions of deprivation' but also to 'the denial of dignity' (Slater, 2011: 107). Tyler argues that 'for many of the rioters it was their sense of being invisible, of being stigmatized, of having no future prospects, which motivated their disorderly behaviour. They wanted to be seen and heard' (2013: 204).

THE LIMITS TO DISSENT—DISARMING CRITIQUE

I have explored a series of arguments which substantially qualify the arguments of symbolic domination and misrecognition discussed in Chapter 3. All see the affective, bodily experience of inequality and subordination as generating not just shame and stigma but also anger and indignation, dissent and struggle. But if anger, indignation, the awareness of injustice and dissent are so widespread, why does inequality and domination persist? If critical capacities, dissent and struggle are widespread (and, as this and later chapters show, there is support for such a claim), then relations of inequality and subordination can be reproduced without widespread consent or misrecognition, as people often understand their situation reasonably well, dissent to it and yet lack the capacity to change it. But what stops them? One common explanation for how inequalities persist in the face of dissent and struggle is the suggestion that dissent often becomes nullified in processes of incorporation and subversion. Here symbolic domination remerges into explanations, but as a force disarming dissent rather than preventing it from arising in the first place.

Boltanski, for example, having started from a position setting out the transformative nature of everyday critique later moves to focus on how critique becomes institutionalised and defanged by regimes of domination. For Boltanski, contemporary 'democratic-capitalist' societies are characterised by 'complex domination', as managerial regulation and the rule of experts replaces coercion, with an 'incorporation of critique' into these systems (2011: 127). In earlier work, this institutionalisation of critique was characterised positively, indicating the creative, adaptive nature of capitalism, its multiple sites of power and value and its openness to dispute and challenge (albeit for instrumental purposes) (Boltanski and Chiapello, 2007). But capitalist institutions survive as forms of domination despite the prevalence of critique. Boltanski explains this by arguing that the incorporation of critique within the 'managerial mode of domination' defuses and subverts it. The move to a 'new spirit' of capitalism is in fact a hegemonic shift:

> The key ingredients of this 'new spirit'—such as 'initiative', 'creativity', 'imagination', 'transparency', 'commitment', 'openness', 'dialogue',

and 'team work' — provide capitalist forms of domination not only with systemic elasticity and adaptability, but also with an unprecedented degree of ideological legitimacy. As a consequence, capitalism is now widely perceived as the only — viable and acceptable — game in town — that is, as the hegemonic mode of production almost everywhere in the world. (Susen, 2014b: 195)

The institutionalisation of critique not only legitimates complex domination but ironically offers 'less purchase to critique than a regime of repression' (Boltanski, 2011: 128). Boltanski identifies several ways in which critique is 'disarmed'. One is a process of 'domination by change' in 'neo-managerialist' institutions, where the key mode of justification becomes instrumental efficiency, creating an audit culture (management through targets and metrics) in which tests and benchmarks proliferate (Ibid.: 129). Here the principle of efficiency overrides other normative principles, 'with contemporary leaders claiming they have no option but to listen to the advice of experts' restricting the 'space for meaningful conversation and debate about the role of normative values in guiding policy' (Stones, 2014: 222). In domination by change, the 'incessant character of change in test formats undermines the possibility of radical critique' for 'no sooner have the dominated grasped the putative values of legitimation embedded within the relevant tests than the test are altered once again', which 'subverts the formulation of critique, creating a sense of dissonance and powerlessness' (Ibid.: 213).

Critique is not wholly disarmed, however. Boltanski argues that one type of critique — 'existential tests' — resists institutionalisation. As denunciations which derive from the affective experience of injustice, and the 'lived experience' of suffering and humiliation, 'existential tests' appeal to principles of legitimacy from outside the institution and so are less easily institutionalised. However, there is a catch. The effectiveness of such denunciations depends on whether they can be connected with a collective 'capable of corroborating their complaint and offering it backing', and so claimed as injustices 'capable of general validity'. Unless existential tests are framed collectively, they are in 'danger of being dismissed as "subjective" concerns or the product of individual deficiencies' (2011: 34–37):

> They are often called 'subjective', which makes it possible, when the one who experiences them seeks to share them with others, to deny their reality, disqualify them, or ridicule them (e.g., it can then be said of someone who expresses the way an injustice or humiliation has affected her that she is overly 'sensitive' that she has 'misunderstood', even that she is 'paranoid' etc. (Boltanski, 2011: 108)

In a reprise of some of the accounts in Chapter 3, Boltanski emphasises the ways in which 'dissatisfaction and suffering are individualised' so that complaints can be 'all too easily dismissed as lack of mettle' or 'pathologized as instances of mental fragility' (Stones, 2014: 216–17).

In arguing that complex domination perseveres because people's critical capacities become institutionalised and disarmed, Boltanski places a central emphasis on critical capacity as key to whether domination is sustained or undermined. Susen (2014b: 197) argues that Boltanski therefore fails to break with the 'rationalist straitjacket' that prevents analysts 'from understanding that self-enlightenment is a necessary but not sufficient condition for human emancipation'. Boltanski 'remains caught up in the tradition of mainstream theories of domination in conceiving of the subject's rational and critical capacities as the motor of emancipatory social processes' (Susen, 2014b: 197). As Stones (2014: 227, 228) argues, too often Boltanski seems to treat people's powerlessness as 'a matter of perception', failing 'to position actors adequately within the fullness of their strategic context' and thus to address 'the extent to which identifiable, situated groups have the power to effect particular outcomes'.

Honneth, by contrast, places rather more emphasis on the strategic context and the collective resources available to those who struggle for respect. Turning the experience of hurt or shame into a 'moral-political conviction' depends on the 'cultural-political environment' and whether social movements can emerge to help transform the experience of disrespect into a 'source of motivation for acts of political resistance' (1995: 138–39). Here social movements 'play a crucial role in showing this disrespect to be typical of an entire group of people, thereby helping to establish the cultural conditions for resistance and revolt' (Anderson, 1995: xix). This shift into political resistance partly hinges on highlighting the 'social causes of individual injuries', turning experiences of disrespect that have been 'fragmented' and 'coped with privately' into the 'moral motives for a collective "struggle for recognition"' (Ibid.: 163–64). However, a collective resistance is needed as the practical instrument for asserting such claims. The argument that people from marginalised groups often lack the symbolic legitimacy to make their complaints stick is a recurrent one. As Skeggs (2012: 281) notes, 'even if the working class feel anger, resentment, and hate, it is unlikely that their expression of these emotions will be given legitimacy through access to symbolic power—they are more likely to be criminalized for their expression', because 'justifiable responses to inequality are often read as a problematic pathology of the person who expresses them'. But the availability of collective resources, such as social movements, can transform the meaning of individual troubles into social injustices—however, the poor and disadvantaged often lack these practical resources.

Tyler (2013) makes both points in her analysis of the aftermath to the 2011 British riots. The rioters were swiftly characterised by press and politicians as workshy, violent criminals, with 'the abject conceptual and perceptual frame of the underclass . . . deployed as a means of both explaining and containing the meaning of the riots as an "apolitical" event' (Ibid.: 17). The depiction of the rioters as a criminal underclass reframed and undermined their struggle. As a result, 'the rioters became the abjects they had been told they were, and in so doing confirmed the consensus that they were the product of their own, and their families' "chaos and dysfunctionality"' (Ibid.: 204–5). For Tyler, what *'matters most'* is 'often not events of protest or resistance themselves, many of which barely register within the public domain or are quickly forgotten or suppressed, but rather the *storying* of revolts—and the forms of aesthetics this affects' (Ibid.: 12–13, original emphasis). Tyler here emphasises 'the *mediation* of resistance, the reframing of events' (Ibid.: 12). But she also notes that disenfranchised and abjectified populations are also severely practically constrained, with no 'escape' from their situation and few viable political resources for struggles for recognition. Indeed it is precisely the absence of other routes to recognition which 'moves many "failed citizens" and non-citizens to revolt' (2013: 12). Tyler argues that in many countries 'people's capacity to protest effectively . . . has been eroded' while there is often 'effectively no mainstream political opposition' to the neo-liberal governmentality which has 'fractured communities, decomposed the fabric of social life and (re)constituted nineteenth-century levels of economic inequalities', resulting in a 'dramatic collapse of trust in political, civic and judicial institutions and processes' (Ibid.). As a result, it is often only 'through revolt . . . that political agency is exercised, even while demands for recognition often lead to further cycles of punishment and capture' (Ibid.: 12).

A similar argument—of the role of structural constraints and social resources in shaping people's struggles for recognition—is made by Lamont and colleagues (2016) in their explanation of how groups respond in very different ways to discrimination and stigmatisation. Lamont and colleagues' study shows systematic differences (both within and across national contexts) in how groups react to 'assaults on worth', because 'cultural and structural contexts enable and constrain individual and group responses', showing the importance of 'national contexts and national ideologies and definitions of the situation in shaping responses to stigmatization' (Lamont and Mizrachi, 2012: 366). Responses to assaults on worth depend on a variety of factors, including the degree of collective identity among the groups, the differing national histories of intergroup conflict and the diverse national ideologies and cultural repertoires that people in the different countries can draw upon.

Lamont and colleagues (2016: 87–88) argue, for example, that African Americans adopt more confrontational responses to stigma because the United States has a legal culture backed by civil rights acts, which produces a 'culture of litigation' in which 'it is legitimate to stand up for oneself when facing racial slights'. Brazilian and Israeli groups, by contrast, show less confidence in their legal system, and since states vary widely in their 'culturally responsive policies' toward minority groups' this affects 'the extent to which groups direct their efforts toward specific institutions when claiming recognition and rights' (Lamont and Mizrachi, 2012: 370–71). African Americans were more likely to 'name' racism, which, for Lamont and colleagues, reflects how the civil rights movement created more readily available cultural scripts about group discrimination in the United States compared to Israel and Brazil. A high proportion (80%) of the Brazilian respondents reported stigmatisation but were more likely to deflect or ignore such incidents, more hesitant to say they had experienced racism and preferred redistributive over identity-based policies to address their situation. This connects not only to lower trust in the legal system in Brazil but also to weaker levels of racial identification, as national ideologies of Brazilian 'racial democracy' and 'racial mixing' have resulted in a greater emphasis on questions of class redistribution rather than racial injustice. It also relates to 'a relative lack of institutionalized repertoires' for racial identification in Brazil, such as those 'made broadly available by the Civil Rights Movement in the United States' (Lamont et al., 2016: 142). Israeli Palestinians showed a strong faith in collective mobilisation; however, they often avoided confrontation to stigmatisation, with their responses strongly shaped by 'a sense of inevitability and cynicism' because they felt there was little they could do to improve their recognition (Ibid.: 280–81). So broader social conditions and national contexts 'make it more likely that members of groups will draw on some rather than other strategies available in their cultural toolkits' and 'make various kinds of rhetorics more or less readily available to social actors' (Lamont and Mizrachi, 2012: 368).

In later chapters, I consider work which focuses much more centrally on the practical constraints to dissent and social challenge. This work identifies formidable risks and constraints to mobilisation, protest and resistance, and provides a powerful set of reasons for why inequality persists, but reasons founded in practical conditions of powerlessness and constraint rather than in symbolic domination or the naturalisation of social arrangements. The focus here is not just on struggle against powerful agents of the state or capitalism but also on forms of dissent and noncompliance which challenge the constraints of normative codes, dominant social arrangements and accepted ways of life. As subsequent chapters argue, this also raises questions about the constraining and enabling force of all shared practices, constraints which extend beyond relations of inequality, power or domination but which help to explain their persistence. However, I first examine a final set of arguments about the affective nature of inequality which explores this very set of issues. Here the argument is that both consent and dissent to social arrangements depend on interpersonal processes of mutual monitoring and social sanctioning within shared practices.

AFFECTIVE SANCTIONING

In Rafanel and Gorringe's (2010) account of affective sanctioning, unequal social relations are maintained by the constraining force of shared practices, underpinned by interpersonal sanctioning mechanisms of both a negative and positive kind. But it is people's *awareness* of their subordination that helps to reproduce it, as subordinates must always structure their practices in expectation and calculation of the likely sanctions that may result. As a result, embodied practices 'often reproduce domination', but such practices are not 'unconscious and pre-discursive' but rather 'dispositional, routinized activity, *constantly reinforced* by the practices, beliefs and mutual monitoring of a collective' (Ibid.: 615, original emphasis). To engage in any practice, people must take account of, and act in accord with, the expectations of the people that they encounter in given social situations. However, for Rafanell and Gorringe, this is not just a question of a dispositional internalisation but also a question of the reflexive reinforcements experienced within concrete networks of specific others in given situations.

Drawing on the work of Barnes (1988), Rafanell and Gorringe offer an 'interactionist understanding' of both acquiescence and challenge to subordination which analyses the 'micro dynamics of everyday practices between dominant and dominated' (2010: 606, 618). The 'contested, rather than internalized, nature of subordination' is revealed in 'the ubiquitous presence of social sanctions' (Gorringe and Rafanell, 2007: 108), which show that people always test the constraints of collective practices. This is because the collective pressures and sanctions on people's actions are also contingent and situational. People act on the basis of their knowledge of what will be accepted, and of what they can get away with, and this partly depends on the nature of the groups within which practices occur (Bottero, 2010). So while subordinates' knowledge of their situation, and the likely repercussions to their actions, often result in 'unwilling collusion', this collusion is always provisional and contingent (Gorringe and Rafanell, 2007).

Rafanel and Gorringe (2010: 605) argue that most accounts of power relations 'unwittingly reify power as an external force which determines how individuals act in any given situation', failing to recognise 'the central role that all individuals play in creating regimes of power'. By contrast, Rafanell and Gorringe argue that the embodied and affective nature of unequal relations requires us to recognise that 'it is interactions between conscious individuals (both power-holders and subjects) that underpin social structures', with the social structural world 'conceived not as external and guiding individuals' practices but rather as constituted and maintained by the activity of people from the ground' (Ibid.: 605, 618). Here, affective social sanctioning mechanisms are not only a ubiquitous feature of social life but are 'profoundly implicated in the constitution of collective phenomena' (Rafanell, 2013: 186; 2007: 69). Such sanctioning goes well beyond power relations since it helps constitute all social relations (even egalitarian ones). Rafanell argues that pride and shame are central to the regulation of social life, as conformity to group norms is 'rewarded with appreciation and dissent is punished with the withdrawal of respect, respectively generating pride or shame in individuals' (Rafanell, 2013: 197). Because all practices are shaped by the mutual susceptibility and accountability of people within collectives, this explains how relations of subordination are reproduced but also how they 'are inherently mutable and always susceptible to change' (Rafanel and Gorringe, 2010: 605). People's actions always occur

> against a background of collectively shared knowledge and mutual influence. Individual practices are always subject to negative and positive social sanctioning by other group members. This results in the adoption of uniform collective practices that become so normalized that they *by-pass*, but do not preclude, conscious reflection. On the other hand, the constraining force of the collective equally explains resistance; when resistance is organized, such social sanctions can work to create solidarity within a rebellious group and help to co-ordinate their actions. (Rafanel and Gorringe, 2010: 606, original emphasis)

Rafanell and Gorringe (2010; Gorringe and Rafanell, 2007; Gorringe, 2005) refer to caste relations in India to illustrate their arguments, arguing that neither symbolic domination nor the naturalisation of inequality can explain *both* the durability of caste relations *and* the emergence of Dalit[8] resistance and activism. To explain both acquiescence and challenge to caste relations requires an 'understanding of the daily processes by which caste is continuously reconstituted rather than internalized at an early age' (Gorringe and Rafanell, 2007: 106–7). Rafanell and Gorringe reject conventional depictions of caste, which present it as an enduring hierarchical social structure 'so naturalized as to impinge upon people's self-definitions and identities', where 'each caste knows its place' in a system seen as 'consensual and permanent' (Ibid.: 615). They point out that caste relations exhibit 'a multitude of conflicts' and constraints, with the lowly position of Dalits 'defined as much (if not more) by dependence and their role as labourers as by the ritual tasks assigned to them', and with this dependence enforced by various practical constraints rather than ideological acquiescence (Ibid.: 616). Dalits are 'not in consensus with caste values' and 'many refuse to perform, or challenge, the roles assigned to them', with 'the power of dominant castes . . . continuously created and reinforced by a variety of "sanctioning" mechanisms' (Ibid.: 616).

The caste system is certainly embodied and affective, inspiring 'feelings of revulsion or unworthiness that hinder social change and constitute hierarchical social identities' (Gorringe and Rafanell, 2007: 108). And caste inequalities are 'etched into the social fabric' by codes of conduct governing 'modes of address, attire and physical positioning that carry most force in isolated villages' (Ibid.: 103). For example, Dalits 'cannot wear shoes in higher caste streets', must 'drink from separate receptacles' and 'often still cannot cycle through high caste areas, spit in the streets, use the drinking water wells frequented by higher castes or sit on benches in the common areas of the village' (Ibid.). The body is 'not merely a *symbol* of caste difference' but 'the means by which such differences are constituted, perceived and subjectively experienced' (Ibid.: 105):

> Social interactions between Dalits and caste Hindus emphasize the inferiority of the former. On the approach of a locally dominant caste member, village Dalits assume a hunched posture, take their towel off their shoulders and tie it round their waist (or tuck it under their arm), lean forward and raise one or both hands in greeting. When conversing with higher castes their hands are held behind their backs or to their sides and their heads remain inclined. In sum, they pay exaggerated forms of respect, which are expressed non-verbally through bodily positioning. They usually stand apart from the higher castes, and will not enter their houses but call out to the householder from the backdoor using idioms and dialects that accentuate their social status. (Gorringe and Rafanell, 2007: 103)

However, such embodied responses only make sense for individuals 'who are constantly reminded of their social status' (Rafanell and Gorringe, 2010: 618.) Rafanell and Gorringe note that Dalits have been killed 'for "presuming" to walk down a high-caste street in western clothing', but such coercive strategies would 'not be necessary if the subordinate groups did not engage in permanent acts of challenge to the status quo' (2010: 618). Caste structures are initiated through early socialisation which certainly gives rise to dispositions to act, but these 'are maintained by monitoring individuals' activity and punishing transgressions' with the 'contested, rather than internalized, nature of subordination' revealed in 'the ubiquitous presence of social sanctions' (Gorringe and Rafanell, 2007: 108). The body 'is the medium through which caste is manifested', but this is not a wholly dispositional process because 'caste bodies are constantly monitored and disciplined' (Ibid.: 107). Indeed, dispositional activity cannot occur without 'permanent reinforcement, permeated by the calculative and conscious activity of individuals' and rarely remains unmodified (Rafanel and Gorringe, 2010: 615).

So while power mechanisms dictate what Dalits 'can and can't do, and thus, repeatedly condition them to accept their status', caste relations 'are neither set in stone nor non-negotiable, but emerge in and through interaction' (Gorringe and Rafanell, 2007: 109). While Dalits remove their shoes 'as a matter of routine', this 'does not mean that they cannot question such behaviour' (Ibid.). Because norms operate as shared practices, collectively reinforced, this generates expectations of behaviour in given situations which people must always take account of, but this only ensures conformity on a calculative and contingent basis. Such expectations operate through the accountability that agents demand of each other, but such accountability also means that people sometimes resist expectation, through their ability to provide plausible and intelligible narratives of what they are doing (Barnes, 2000). Gorringe and Rafanell illustrate this with the example of Athai, an elderly Paraiyar (an untouchable caste in Tamilnadu), describing her negotiation of the prohibition on wearing shoes in public:

> When I used to go to market . . . I would be told to take my shoes off, but I never did. I can't walk without my chappals! So I walked along the market street with my chappals on—The shop keeper said: 'What are you?' I asked 'Does who or what I am affect the colour of my money?' Then they said 'you are not supposed to wear slippers on this road', so I said; 'I'm a Puliyamma [a low, but touchable, caste in Tamilnadu] I can wear them, are you going to serve me or do I have to return to the bus?' (Athai, quoted in Rafanel and Gorringe, 2010: 617)

For Rafanel and Gorringe, this illustrates 'the critical importance of shared knowledge to a system of domination'—here both parties 'know the rules of caste conduct but do not know each other's place within the system. The shop-keeper may suspect that Athai is untouchable due to her clothes, language or mannerisms, but does not know enough to deny her his services or create a scene by insisting that she remove her slippers' (2010: 617). Two key points follow: that 'caste distinctions crystallize because they operate at the level of continuous *collective* reinforcement' but also that such reinforcement happens precisely because caste distinctions are 'not permanently incorporated pre-discursive individual dispositions' (2010: 617, original emphasis). Caste-based patterns of behaviour 'become the norm because they are lived and performed on a daily basis', and the performative, interactional basis to relations of subordination helps to explain not just the durability but also the 'unstable nature of caste identity' (Gorringe and Rafanell, 2007: 108).

In this chapter I have explored the argument that people have a much greater ability to develop values and moral principles in opposition to dominant values than many accounts of symbolic legitimation presume. We can see three aspects to this basis for dissent: deriving from the plural basis of value and legitimacy; from people's 'ordinary' capacity for critical reflexivity about social arrangements; but also from how suffering, disrespect and stigmatisation represent powerful affective forces generating dissent and struggle. All three aspects reflect the normative dimension of everyday experience, in which moral evaluation, affective commitments and emotional investments and forms of 'justification work' are routine aspects of social life, bound up in the intersubjective nature of social relations. Both the formation of the social self and coordinated social practice depend on ongoing processes of mutual and self-monitoring, in which we must always anticipate how our behaviour will be viewed and in which we monitor our conduct according to how it affects others. Of course, such adjustments are often driven by self-interest and people's location within relations of inequality, but there is also a reciprocal and normative character to social interaction and an expectation of some degree of mutual recognition, which underpins notions of fairness, consistency and dignity.

The normative character of social interaction means that individuals must be able to justify their actions to each other, appealing to different principles of legitimate action which they hope will command agreement or respect. So accounting practices, 'justification work' and ordinary disputes over justice are a routine feature of social life. Because insults to dignity and recognition are insults to the social self, this means that shame and anger, dissent and critique are *built into* relations of inequality. And because coordinated social practice requires us to take into account how a complex range of social others will view us and respond, we acquire embodied, habitual ethical dispositions through our routine practices with others. But these dispositions also represent ethical commitments and investments with a strongly emotional, self-conscious and often critical aspect.

What are the consequences of such arguments for how we view people's sense of inequality? If we see moral evaluation, affective commitments and forms of 'justification work' as everyday features of intersubjective social relations, this helps us to understand anger, scepticism and dissent to legitimating ideologies as intrinsic features of unequal relations, which can sometimes generate significant levels of recalcitrance, resistance and protest. But if anger and critique, dissent and struggle, are really so widespread, how is it that inequalities endure? The implication is that the obdurate and persistent nature of unequal social relations has less to do with symbolic legitimation and people's restricted sense of inequality than many analysts have imagined. Subordinates' compliance with the status quo is often less a question of consent, or internalised dispositions, and more a question of the various practical constraints binding people into unequal arrangements. Such constraint is not just a question of coercion but also of the obligations, commitments and sanctions of shared practices.

Rafanel and Gorringe's account of affective sanctioning presents collective practices as underpinned by mutual susceptibility and by reflexive, calculative processes of mutual monitoring, sanctioning and adjustment. This represents a different perspective on how dominant practices take their force, through how they form a 'known' environment of expectations and sanctions to which people must adjust, or at least take account of, in their own practices. The persistence of unequal relations is located not in people's 'misrecognition' of them but rather in their processes of *recognition*. We must 'recognise' social arrangements as 'what they are' in order to organise our activities and avoid likely sanctions, and as we adjust our actions accordingly we help to reproduce these arrangements. Sayer (2005b: 955) qualifies the idea of affective sanctioning as a wholly external constraining force within social practices, arguing, for example, that shame can produce 'either conformity or resistance, but we cannot make sense of this if we reduce it to no more than a product of fear of external disapproval'. He reiterates the significance of the internal normative dispositions and commitments which sometimes make us resist external pressures, arguing, for example, that 'the anti-racist who keeps silent when others make racist remarks is likely to feel shame for conforming instead of resisting' (Ibid.). On this basis, without our normative commitments 'it is hard to see why we would ever want to resist and how we would ever be shamed, because we would simply "go with the flow", accepting whatever the pressures of the moment required' (Ibid.).

The fact that we sometimes do not 'go with the flow' shows the significance of the ethical dispositions and moral values which also emerge from our routine practices with, and mutual susceptibility to, others. But our ability to swim against the tide also depends on our practical capacities for action. And our ethical dispositions also emerge through forms of collective life, through monitoring the effects of our conduct on a range of social others, and are never wholly pre-reflexive. This raises a fundamental question of how the constraints and obligations, commitments and sanctions, of shared practices help to perpetuate — but also sometimes undermine — unequal arrangements. I now turn to examine one aspect of this question by exploring the different ways in which those who dissent from social arrangements experience practical constraints which make protest and resistance difficult and risky. However, while people are often highly constrained, protest and resistance still occur, so we must also reconsider the nature of this constraint.

NOTES

1. Sayer draws on the work of Archer (2000) and Smith (1984) to make this argument, though it is also homologous to Mead's account. This perhaps reflects Sayer's endorsement of a critical realist ontology at odds with Mead's pragmatist stance.

2. Boltanski also argues that if actors are framed as 'dopes', the question remains how the truth will be revealed to them. He suggests critical sociology assumes an 'asymmetry between deceived actors and a sociologist capable — and, it would appear from some formulations, the only one capable — of revealing the truth of the social conditions to them', a stance which overestimates 'the power of sociology as science' and invests it 'with the overweening power of being the main discourse of truth on the social world' (Ibid.: 21). As Lawler (2011: 1425) neatly summarises: 'if symbolic violence is so naturalized, so legitimated that we fail to see its workings as violence, how

is Bourdieu (or any other analyst) able to see through it?'—a theme to which I return in Chapters 7 and 8.

3. The six orders of worth are the civic order (reflecting the principle of collective interest), the market order (the principle of price/profit), the order of inspiration (creativity), the order of fame (renown), the industrial order (efficiency/productivity) and the domestic order (the principle of reputation/trust).

4. For example, in claims that recruitment practices are not based legitimately on the potential efficiency of applicants but rather on illegitimate preferences for family connections or people with a preferred racial or gender identity.

5. Where discrimination refers to being denied resources, while stigmatization entails being assigned low status and experiencing 'assaults on worth' in which people experience 'disrespect and their dignity, honour, relative status or sense of self' is challenged'—not only 'when one is insulted, receives poor services, is excluded from informal networks . . . is the victim of physical assault, or is threatened physically' but also 'where one is stereotyped as poor, uneducated, or dangerous, or where one is misunderstood or underestimated' or 'ignored and overlooked' (Lamont et al., 2016: 6, 7).

6. The casting out and radical exclusion of the 'other' through processes of horror, bodily disgust and aversion.

7. Other revolts examined include the protests of people in migrant detention centres, the 'ongoing resistance of Gypsies and Travellers to eviction from their land and homes' and 'protests by disability activists against the erosion of welfare support systems' (Tyler, 2013: 3).

8. 'Dalit' (meaning 'broken, ground-down, downtrodden, or oppressed') is a self-chosen political name adopted by groups who fall outside the traditional Hindu caste system in India. They traditionally performed manual jobs regarded as 'dirty' or 'unclean' and were previously known as Untouchables or Harijans.

FIVE
Protesting Inequality

We can certainly see processes which legitimate inequality, but disadvantaged and subordinated groups do challenge and resist their situation. In fact, the last 10 years have seen an upsurge in protest across the globe — so I now turn to consider research on protest and mobilisation. Echoing the arguments previously examined in this book, work in social movement studies (SMS) shows a far from straightforward relationship between inequality, discontent and social protest — but presents an alternative set of arguments about why this is the case, focusing on the practical constraints on mobilisation and social challenge. The protest examined in this research entangles grievances not only over material inequity and hardship but also over inequalities in rights, recognition, autonomy and dignity, in a range of mobilisations (including workers' and poor people's movements, civil rights movements, gender, race equality and sexuality-based activism, alter-globalisation movements and lifestyle and 'prefigurative' movements).

Research into social movements, perhaps unsurprisingly, does not spend much time on questions of naturalisation or symbolic domination. While class analysts have expended considerable effort explaining the lack of popular mobilisation against class inequalities, research on social movements is instead focused on how protest movements come about. Accounts of hegemony and symbolic domination do crop up, but normally in relation to how they shape protest rather than prevent it. However, social movement research does show that inequalities cannot, by themselves, explain why social protest occurs because, as analysts repeatedly observe, grievance and anger are more widespread than protest, so 'the question to be answered is not so much whether people who engage in protest are aggrieved, but whether aggrieved people engage in protest' (Van Stekelenburg and Klandermans, 2013: 887). Much analysis starts from the premise that people with shared grievances often fail to act collectively in pursuit of their interests, [1] so the focus is on the particular conditions which enable protest. But in setting out the conditions necessary for mobilisation, analysts also identify a formidable set of constraints on action. Protest and mobilisation, it seems, is hard, with participation difficult and risky, and attempts to mobilise people must overcome widespread perceptions of the difficulty of effecting real change.

This latter issue—that people are pessimistic about the prospects for change—does return us to questions of symbolic domination and the naturalisation of inequality. Here social movement research engages with the 'thin' version of theories of symbolic legitimation, in which it is not so much that disadvantaged people *consent* to their fate but rather that they are often *resigned* to it, feeling it is 'unalterable and inevitable' (Scott, 1990: 74). Work in social movement theory is less concerned with the ideological basis for this than on the processes of 'cognitive liberation' by which people come to see their situation as changeable (McAdam, 1982). But echoing the arguments of Chapter 4, such cognitive shifts also depend on the availability of practical avenues for social challenge. Social movements mobilise people by creating alternative forms of collective agency which construct inequality as injustice, framing it not just as unfair but also as *practically preventable*. Gamson (1992a; 1995: 89–90) argues that to mobilise, people must not only have an affective sense of injustice—the moral indignation necessary for collective action, aimed at those responsible for 'bringing about harm and suffering'—but also a 'sense that change is possible', with both 'a consciousness of human agents whose policies or practices must be changed and a "we" who will help to bring about change' (Ibid.). Such work also sees people's resignation as partly based in 'objective' conditions of powerlessness and constraint, which must shift in order for people to be able to act. So if people feel that they cannot change their situation, quite often this is because they really cannot, or at least have formidable obstacles to overcome.

In such work there is a recurrent argument: that there are good reasons why discontented people do not protest, because mobilisation is difficult and dangerous and particularly so for the poor and powerless. This is not just a question of the risks of repression if people do mobilise but also of the constraints of the daily routines and obligations of people's lives. Often, the only effective exercise of protest for the disadvantaged comes from 'collective refusal' and disruption, but such disruption also jeopardises the daily activities by which people sustain their lives. Yet people do mobilise and protest. How is this possible when it is so difficult? From one perspective, mobilisation occurs under exceptional situations of social or economic crisis, when elites become more assailable, when people's everyday lives are already disrupted and where shifting external conditions create new spaces for demands to be heard and a changed sense that social change is possible. But the emergence of protest depends not just on external 'objective' conditions but also on processes of 'grievance construction' and cultural framing, in which people must come to believe that real change is possible, so social movements are also engaged in a struggle over the meanings that people attach to their situation.

Work in the area has a heavy focus on organised movements and contentious politics targeted at the state or other powerful agents, with protest and dissent understood as 'collective, organized efforts at social change' (Edwards, 2014: 2). This focus is selective, with the rise of social movements and their repertoires of protest (strikes, demonstrations, occupations, etc.) linked to the emergence of democratic governments guaranteeing rights of assembly and free expression (Tilly, 2004, 2008). This model of mobilisation often applies poorly to more repressive or authoritarian contexts, where public, organised protest is forbidden or much more risky. Yet protest does occur in authoritarian societies, and coercion is only part of the explanation of why people put up with unjust or unequal conditions. Much SMS analysis is Northern-centric, using movements in Southern societies as, at best, 'laboratories for testing the theories which were developed in the North' (Fadaee, 2016: 2). Yet the uniqueness and complexity of Southern social movements challenges many theoretical assumptions in SMS, since—as the history of mobilisation against colonialism shows—'in many instances social movements and struggles in the South are characterised by a much larger scale and function in much more challenging circumstances' (Fadaee, 2016: 1). However, even in countries with guaranteed rights of protest, the 'brutal fact of routine, institutionalized liberal democratic politics is that the interests of the poor are largely ignored until and unless a sudden and dire crisis catapults the poor into the streets' (Scott, 2012: 14, 19). In both Global North and South, analysts looking at protest and mobilisation are examining how people advance contentious claims not addressed by conventional political processes and where authorities may be unresponsive or hostile.

Because grievance is seen as widespread, it recedes into the background of much social movement analysis, with a comparative neglect of more mundane forms of dissent and noncompliance, or of how people manage discontent and grievance in their everyday lives. Indeed, in a theme repeated from Chapter 3, mundane forms of noncompliance are sometimes seen as a barrier to mobilisation, allowing people to 'let off steam' rather than challenge the system. But such mundane forms of discontent and dissent are important, not only in their own right, as I argue in later chapters, but also for understanding protest and mobilisation. Dissent and protest can occur even in the most coercive and unequal contexts, with social movement research showing the transformative power of 'collective refusal', in which people refuse to comply with social rules and expectations in everyday arenas (Piven, 2008; Piven and Cloward, 2005; Bayat, 2013).

Understanding the force of this requires a different way of thinking about power and the collective resources which enable social challenge, protest and dissent. The 'power' of dominant agents is constituted through keeping other agents' actions appropriately aligned, and the withdrawal of the cooperative interdependence which underpins all social arrangements disrupts such alignments and represents a source of collective resources and leverage for even the most deprived or subjugated (Piven, 2008; Piven and Cloward, 2005). However, as Holloway (2010: 159) notes, SMS has focused rather narrowly on organised movements, yet such movements merely represent 'the smoke rising from the volcano' of more widespread discontent, nonconformity and disruption. Holloway argues that we must explore the connection between organised protest and more everyday acts of subversion, noncompliance and 'inarticulate non-subordination' to identify 'the substratum of negativity which, though generally invisible, can flare up in moments of acute social tension' (Ibid.: 159–60). So this chapter and the next also consider other forms of discontent and dissent, such as social 'non-movements' (the 'collective action of non-collective actors' [Bayat, 2013: 1]) and the 'everyday' forms of resistance more typically employed under authoritarian regimes (Scott, 1989, 1990).

FAILURE TO ACT IN THE FACE OF GRIEVANCE

We might expect unequal and unjust social conditions to give rise to social protest, but, reiterating a now familiar theme in this book, social movement research shows this is often not the case: 'It is a gross mistake to assume that any kind of malignant or harmful social condition or arrangement in a society becomes automatically a social problem for that society. The pages of history are replete with instances of dire social conditions unnoticed and unattended in the societies in which they occurred' (Blumer, 1971: 302).

Of course, dire social conditions are not unnoticed by the people at the sharp end of them, but the key issue is how troubling situations become constructed as *public problems*, with such problems not simply 'a set of objective arrangements' but rather the product of 'collective definition' (Blumer, 1971: 298). An adverse situation must not only become identified as a 'social problem' but also 'acquire a necessary degree of respectability' entitling it to a public hearing, otherwise it may be dismissed as part of the 'accepted order of things' or 'the shouting of questionable or subversive elements of society' (Ibid.: 303–5).

Blumer argues that a sense of grievance emerges when people's *expectations* of their situation come into question and their practical experience of the world becomes interrupted. Theories of relative deprivation offer a related way of thinking about how grievance leads to protest. In work on mobilisation (Gurr, 1970), the argument is that people come to feel frustration or anger when their expectations are disappointed (through unexpected hardship, or when rising expectations are no longer met by improved conditions), so it is the grievances which emerge through a sense of relative deprivation (rather than objective conditions of hardship *per se*) which prompt unrest and protest. However, while this is a plausible way of thinking about the link between social conditions and protest, it is not well supported by research. Edwards (2014: 16) notes that social problems and grievances are 'far more widespread than instances of protest', and a series of studies indicate that hardship, relative deprivation and grievance cannot—by themselves—explain protest. As Edwards (Ibid.: 16, original emphasis) notes, 'the experience of deprivation, levels of anger and frustration, and people's beliefs and attitudes, could not account for why they participated in protest events, like riots, civil rights marches, and student demonstrations because many of those who *did not* participate shared the same characteristics—they were equally as deprived, equally as upset about it, and often shared attitudes and beliefs in common with those who did participate'. The idea that people are more likely to mobilise when their expectations are disrupted and their routines become unpredictable *is* a recurrent theme in SMS (Snow et al., 1998) but in terms of how interruptions to people's practical routines undermine some of the everyday obligations and constraints which hinder protest.

Since 'grievances abound while protest does not', the question is 'why do some aggrieved people become mobilized, while others do not?' (Van Stekelenburg and Klandermans, 2013: 888–89). One possible answer is the 'free rider' problem of collective action (Olson, 1965: 2), the idea that individuals will not participate in collective actions designed to secure public goods if they can still secure the benefits without participating, catching a 'free ride' on other people's efforts,[2] and a significant strand of social movement theory has explored the conditions under which movement organisations are able to resolve the 'free rider' problem. But protest is not just a question of free choice nor equally available to all (Piven and Cloward, 1979). For other analysts, the failure to protest is not a general problem of rational action but rather a feature of power relations and the obligations of everyday life, which constrain the disadvantaged and provide restricted opportunities for collective defiance.

> Sharp inequality has been constant, but rebellion infrequent. However hard their lot may be, people usually remain acquiescent, conforming to the accustomed patterns of daily life in their community, and believing those patterns to be both inevitable and just ... most of the time people conform to the institutional arrangements which enmesh them, which regulate the rewards and penalties of daily life, and which ap-

pear to be the only reality. Those for whom the rewards are most meagre, who are the most oppressed by inequality, are also acquiescent. Sometimes they are the most acquiescent, for they have little defence against the penalties that can be imposed for defiance. Moreover, at most times and in most places . . . the poor are led to believe that their destitution is deserved, and that the riches and power that others command are also deserved. (Piven and Cloward, 1979: 6)

Piven and Cloward advance an argument comparatively rare in social movement research about symbolic domination and naturalisation. But they also insist that disadvantage is *objectively* constraining on mobilisation, as the poor lack the resources for formal organisation and are the most vulnerable to repression if they do mobilise. Chapters 2 and 3 indicate that people typically understand 'inequality' in terms of the practical arrangements of their own lives. Piven and Cloward also note that peoples' grievances are generally focused on concrete, local and specific targets rather than abstract social systems. In one sense this might seem as if people have a limited understanding of their plight, but from a more pragmatist perspective it reflects people's very practical concerns and their restricted capacity to act:

> People experience deprivation and oppression within a concrete setting, not as the end product of large and abstract processes, and it is the concrete experiences that moulds their discontent into specific grievances against specific targets. Workers experience the factory, the speeding rhythm of the assembly line, the foreman, the spies and the guards, the owner and the paycheck. They do not experience monopoly capitalism. People on relief experience the shabby waiting rooms, the overseer or the caseworker, and the dole. They do not experience American social welfare policy. Tenants experience the leaking ceilings and cold radiators, and they recognize the landlord. They do not recognize the banking, real estate, and construction systems. No small wonder, therefore, when the poor rebel they so often rebel against the overseer of the poor, or the slumlord, or the middling merchant, and not against the banks or the governing elites to whom the overseer, the slumlord, and the merchant also defer. In other words, it is the daily experience of people that shapes their grievances, establishes the measure of the demands, and points out the targets of their anger. (Piven and Cloward, 1979: 20–21)

Piven and Cloward argue that the deck is so stacked against the disadvantaged that it is only really under exceptional circumstances that they can mobilise. In explorations of just how people do manage to mobilise there is a divide between 'a dominant, structural approach that emphasizes economic resources, political structures, formal organizations, and social networks' and a 'cultural or constructionist tradition, drawn partly from symbolic interactionism, which focuses on frames, identities, meanings and emotions' (Goodwin and Jasper, 2004a: vii). However, both sets of approaches emphasise that mobilisation entails people overcoming different kinds of constraint.

THE CONDITIONS FOR MOBILISATION: FROM RESOURCES TO INTERDEPENDENT POWER

Approaches which focus on the role of resources in mobilisation start from the premise of a 'constancy of discontent' in society (McAdam, McCarthy and Zald, 1988) and so focus on the conditions which enable the discontented to be mobilised. The assumption is that there is 'always enough discontent in any society to supply the grass-roots support for a movement', but a movement can only emerge if it is 'effectively organized' and has the necessary resources (McCarthy and Zald, 1977: 1215). These include activists with the personal resources and incentives to offset the costs and risks of activism. This emphasis on enabling resources means that deprivation and grievance become background issues, and McCarthy and Zald distinguish 'social movements' (the more general 'preferences for change' that exist within a society) from 'social movement organizations' (the groups that pursue those preferences). People will only act on their preferences for change if there are organisations with the right resources and leadership to mobilise them, with pre-existing organisations or networks often providing vehicles for mobilisation. For example, in the United States in the 1960s, Southern black churches and black colleges played an important role in the civil rights movement, providing organisational resources, supportive community networks and spaces of association relatively free from white control (Morris, 1984; McAdam, 1982). Similarly, in the civil rights 'Freedom Schools' (McAdam and Paulsen, 1993),[3] what distinguished those who volunteered from those who did not was the presence of supportive friends and relatives and connections to those already participating. Here the bonds of obligation and accountability found in networks—particularly tight-knit ones— provide not only organisational resources but also the support, solidarity and threat of social sanctions (such as social shaming) required to counter the risks of protest and keep people engaged (Crossley, 2002).

This is a very 'top-down' view of protest focused on organisations, resources and activists. Yet there are also more spontaneous, disruptive forms of protest (Piven and Cloward, 1991). If existing organisation is a precondition for mobilisation, how do we explain the emergence of 'bottom-up' grassroots organisations? Furthermore, while dense networks can nourish and protect the 'nonmainstream' values often associated with protest movements, they can also work to enforce conformity and prevent mobilisation (Krinsky and Crossley, 2014: 7). For Piven and Cloward, outlining 'similarities between the structure of everyday life and the structure of protest is not an explanation of why people sometimes live their everyday lives and other times join in collective defiance' (1991: 435). They argue that since poor people generally lack the resources for formal organised protest, they must protest differently: through spontaneous, disruptive tactics, such as civil disobedience, riots and noncompliance with the demands of authorities—all of which amount to a 'collective refusal'. However, the risks of this noncompliance are 'profound', not just because people can expect repressive responses but also because it disrupts 'the very activities that members themselves need to sustain their accustomed lives' (Flacks, 2004: 141–42).

Piven and Cloward reiterate the general theme of social movement studies that 'only under exceptional circumstances will the lower classes become defiant', but they reframe it as *'only under exceptional conditions are the lower classes afforded the socially determined opportunity to press for their own class interests'* (1979: 7, original emphasis). Here the reason why people do not rise up against inequality is the social relations which constrain them, preventing them from mobilising and punishing them when they do. Protest is 'not a matter of free choice; it is not freely available to all groups at all times, and much of the time it is not available to lower-class groups at all' (Ibid.: 3). Even when protest is possible, 'the forms it must take, and the impact it can have are all delimited by the social structure in ways which usually diminish its extent and diminish its force' (Ibid.).

Flacks (1988; 2004: 149) distinguishes 'resistance' movements, where people seek to defend their accustomed way of life, from 'liberation' movements, where people seek instead to overthrow it. 'Liberatory perspectives' emerge among those 'who share a condition of subordination, disadvantage, or stigma over which they have little or no individual control' (such as race, ethnicity, gender, sexuality, disability), and where such subordination is 'regarded in the dominant culture as a normal, taken-for-granted feature of everyday life' (Flacks, 2004: 149). Liberation means challenging this taken-for-granted subordination. Here we see an echo of the arguments about symbolic domination discussed in Chapter 3, but—also echoing the frequent qualification of such models—this subordination is never entirely doxic:

> Those who are so subordinated have typically accommodated to the situation for generations, seeming to reproduce in their own conformity the conditions of their oppression. Such public accommodation, however, has usually been accompanied by more subterranean expressions of opposition. Such expressions are typically made symbolically—through song and language, religion and story, and a variety of covert resistances. Out of such cultures of protest emerge forms of collective identification and a recognition of shared fate and destiny. (Flacks, 2004: 149)

I explore these more subterranean expressions of opposition further in Chapter 6, in work which argues that people's 'public face' of conformity is often a response to power relations rather than actual consent or naturalisation. However, reiterating a theme from Chapter 3, Flacks argues that having to adapt to the dominant practices that perpetuate their stigmatisation and subordination has debilitating effects on the subordinated, so liberation movements must not only seek a 'cultural transformation in the wider society', they must also seek to combat the devaluing of subordinate groups by 'consciousness raising' exercises, 'encouraging forms of self-assertion and self-esteem previously unavailable' (2004: 149–50). This entails collective refusals and transgressions of codes of public conduct (for example, not riding at the back of the bus, not following codes for acceptable 'feminine' behaviour, not being closeted). 'Liberation' movements are fundamentally disruptive to participants' everyday lives, as they attempt to 'renegotiate power relations in close-up institutional settings and face-to-face encounters', by acts of 'non-compliance and nonconformity within the context of "private", "personal", and everyday domains' (Ibid.: 150). But how is such disruption possible for the powerless and subjugated?

One explanation argues that changing times create more fertile conditions for disruption. For example, McAdam (1982) argues that the gains of the civil rights movement were facilitated by shifting political opportunities[4] in the United States which, at least for a time, altered the power imbalance between the movement and the white establishment. For Piven and Cloward, 'extraordinary disturbances in the larger society are required to transform the poor from apathy to hope, from quiescence to indignation' because the 'quiescence' of the poor 'is enforced by institutional life', by the daily routines, obligations and social sanctions which constrain people (1979: 14). During wars or economic crises, protest movements are better able to extract concessions from elites, but the real significance of such disturbances is that they 'destroy the structures and routines of daily life', weakening 'the regulatory capacities of these structures' (Ibid.: 10–11). The ordinary routines of social life constrain protest (since people have families to feed, jobs to keep, obligations to uphold), but if their lives are *already* disrupted, then people have less to lose. However, a change in perspective is also required with a transformation 'of consciousness and behaviour' as people 'who are ordinarily fatalistic' and believe existing arrangements are 'inevitable' must develop 'a new sense of efficacy' so that those who 'ordinarily consider themselves helpless come to believe that they have some capacity to alter their lot'. These shifts 'do not arise during ordinary periods' but only 'when large-scale changes undermine political stability', because such disruption gives the poor hope, makes 'insurgency possible in the first place' and renders political leaders more vulnerable (Ibid.: 28).

But just as significantly, a focus on the 'collective refusal' of noncompliance in everyday social arenas presents a different way of thinking about power and the collective resources which enable social challenge, protest and dissent. If the power of the dominant rests on keeping the actions of other agents in appropriate alignment (Wartenburg, 1990; Rouse, 2001), then power relations are sustained not just through the actions of the dominant but also by the accommodating actions of many other ordinary people. So the interdependence which underpins all social arrangements, including the most iniquitous, can be a source of power for even the most deprived or subjugated. Much work on social movements adopts a fairly conventional 'distributional' view of power, in which power comes from the command of authority and material resources. However, for Piven and Cloward, 'if the distribution of power simply reflected other structural inequalities, then political challenges from below would always be without effect' (2005: 38). They identify another kind of power 'based not on resources, things, or attributes, but rooted in the social and cooperative relations in which people are enmeshed by virtue of group life' (Piven, 2008: 5). This 'interdependent power' arises from the 'networks of cooperative relations, more or less institutionalized' which are the basis of all social arrangements (Ibid.). This gives rise to power resources 'embedded in the pattern of expectation and cooperation that bind people together, even when all that is expected or required of particular people is their quiescence' (Piven and Cloward, 2005: 39). Because 'cooperation implies patterns of mutual dependence', *everyone* who is part of these systems of cooperation has 'potential power over others who depend on them' (Ibid.):

> Workers ... have potential power over capitalists because they staff the assembly lines on which production depends. In the same vein, landlords have power over their tenants because they own the fields the tenants till, but tenants have power over landlords because without their labor the fields are idle. State elites can invoke the authority of the law and the force of the troops, but they also depend on voting publics. Husbands and wives, priests and their parishioners, masters and slaves, all face this dynamic. Both sides of all these relations have the potential for exercising interdependent power, and at least in principle, the ability to exert power over others by withdrawing or threatening to withdraw from social cooperation. In fact, interdependent power is implicit in much of what we usually think about power from below. (Piven, 2008: 6)

From this point of view, there is potential power in the ability to disrupt the mutual dependence which underpins social life. Collective practices, however constrained, rest on patterns of mutual dependence, expectation and cooperation which provide resources for the exercise of the power that comes from disrupting such interdependence (Piven, 2008: 39, 5). The implication is that 'all of us have the capacity to change things' and that collective action 'can alter social structures even without taking power' (Gorringe and Rafanell, 2015: 1–2). This is a power that arises from defying expectation, from breaking the rules and withholding the cooperation on which institutions depend. However, the actualisation of such power is difficult, because people must disrupt their own lives and in doing so become subject to repercussion and sanction. So they must not only organise collectively to make their rule-breaking effective but also overcome the 'inhibiting effect of other relations' and find ways to endure the interruption of the cooperative relations 'on which they also depend' (Piven, 2008: 8). Breaking the rules is also difficult because rules 'reflect prevailing patterns of domination' (Piven and Cloward, 2005: 45). Rules and rule-making are not just about power, of course, because rules more generally 'secure people against the totally unexpected in social encounters' and 'make possible the tacit cooperation that underpins social life' (Piven and Cloward, 2005: 44). But rules typically reflect the interests of the powerful within institutions, though 'institutions also become sites of contention and the exercise of interdependent power' as 'people continue to pursue other ends than those promoted by the regimens of institutional life' (Piven, 2008: 5).

Moments of social crisis help people to exercise their interdependent power. But shifts in social conditions are only part of the story. Mobilisation also requires 'cognitive liberation', in which 'people must collectively define their situations as unjust *and* subject to change through group action ' (McAdam, 1982: 51, original emphasis). How people make sense of their situation is key to the question of action (and inaction), since expanding political opportunities 'only offer insurgents a certain objective "structural potential" for collective political action' — so we must also consider the subjective meanings people attach to their situation (Ibid.: 48). But how do people come to frame their situation as 'injustice' or see that the time is ripe for change?

FRAMING INJUSTICE AND THE CONSTRAINTS OF CULTURAL CODES

Movement analysts emphasise the ubiquity of discontent in society, so mobilisation requires 'a revision in the manner in which people look at some problematic condition or feature of their life, seeing it no longer as misfortune, but as an injustice' (Snow et al., 1986: 466). In social movement studies, how people construct (and reconstruct) their situation is most commonly handled through the analysis of 'framing', where frames are 'schemata of interpretation' (Goffman, 1974: 21) which 'organize experience and guide action' (Snow et al., 1986: 464). People know they have troubles, but what kind of troubles are they? Mobilisation requires a 'frame shift', where what was previously seen as an 'unfortunate' situation 'is now defined as inexcusable, unjust, or immoral' and, at the same time 'someone comes to be seen as to blame' (Ibid.). Such analysis looks at the 'interpretation of grievances' (Snow et al., 1986: 464–65, 466) and starts from the premise that social situations are indeterminate and variably understood, where people 'often misunderstand or experience considerable doubt and confusion about what it is that is going on and why'. Given 'the enormous variability in the subjective meanings people attach to their objective situations' (McAdam, 1982: 34), collective action frames work to clarify and direct those meanings, providing an interpretative framework 'intended to mobilize potential adherents . . . garner bystander support, and to demobilize antagonists' (Snow and Benford, 1988: 198).

A movement frame must provide 'answers and solutions to troublesome situations and dilemmas that resonate with the way in which they are experienced' (Snow et al., 1986: 477). This is not just a question of activists 'reaching' out to people who think similarly but also entails activists working to *transform* how situations are viewed (Benford and Snow, 2000: 614).[5] Another factor is 'counter-framing' by antagonists and powerful vested interests,[6] with framing a contested struggle over meaning. Zuo and Benford (1995) give an account of such framing struggles around the mass mobilisations by the Chinese democracy movement in 1989 (which ended with the Chinese state violently repressing the movement and the People's Army firing on crowds at Tiananmen Square). Zuo and Benford argue that activists were able to develop a resonant frame that change in a communist state was a realistic possibility by pointing to previous political reforms in the Soviet Union. The student activists anticipated that the state would try to counter-frame their activities as 'counter-revolutionary' 'upheaval', so they framed their own activities as 'reform' in line with accepted Chinese narratives of nationalism, community-mindedness and self-sacrifice. To match this rhetoric, activists adopted nonviolent direct action tactics, and their framing proved the successful one, as state counter-framings 'failed to sway the masses' and 'participation spread from a few hundred college students to millions of citizens', not least because of the 'perceived consistency between what the student activists asserted in their public framings and their behaviour at Tiananmen Square compared with the inconsistencies between what the state elites claimed and their actual policies' (Zuo and Benford, 1995: 131; Benford and Snow, 2000: 620). Of course, the Chinese state's resort to repression stopped the movement and shows the risks to mobilisation as well as the constraints on reframing activities.

People may be 'convinced of the desirability of changing a situation while gravely doubting the possibility of changing it' so it is necessary to create the sense that people can be 'agents of their own history' (Gamson, 1995: 89; Gamson and Meyer, 1996: 285). Work on framing suggests that resignation—people's sense that real change is impossible or that protest is futile or too risky—can be overcome by collective action framing which persuades people that change is not only 'urgent' and 'necessary' but also 'possible' (Ibid.). Partly this is achieved by identifying concrete targets to blame, such as corporations or government agencies, because the more abstract and impersonal the framing of a problem the less likely people are to mobilise.

> When impersonal and abstract forces are responsible for our suffering, we are taught to accept what cannot be changed and make the best of it. Anger is dampened by the unanswerable rhetorical question, Who says life is fair? . . . From the standpoint of those who wish to control or discourage the development of injustice frames, symbolic strategies should emphasize abstract targets that render human agency as invisible as possible. Reification helps to accomplish this by blaming actorless entities such as 'the system,' 'society,' and 'human nature'. (Gamson, 1995: 90, 91)

Of course, the conditions of people's daily lives *are* in many ways 'determined by abstract sociocultural forces that are largely invisible to them' (Gamson, 1995: 92), but critical views of 'the system' can lead to reification and encourage inaction, because 'systemic' problems may be seen as simply too big and overwhelming for people to solve. Injustice frames work to counter such paralysis. The anti- or alter-globalisation movement (which mobilises against neo-liberal economic globalisation), provides one example of this. Activists in the movement (a network of many different groups) protest against the way that deregulation of markets gives large multinational corporations an unprecedented degree of power, unfettered from local political control. Anti-globalisation activists argue that global corporations have pursued profit at the expense of workers' safety and rights, increasing levels of inequality and creating a global elite free from political accountability. One difficulty with this kind of diagnosis is that it presents the problem as one of unaccountable global processes and the disempowerment of local actors. The danger is that the nature and scale of the problem may make people feel that change is impossible and that any local action will be a drop in the (global) ocean.

Yet there *has* been extensive protest against globalisation. Activist groups endeavoured to identify concrete targets for action, seizing on opportunities created by the 2008 global financial crisis, caused by the high-risk financial speculations of banks and brokers. The Occupy movement targeted these groups, reframing the problem of class inequality as one of the inequality of global power between the 99% and the 1% (referring to the heavy concentration of wealth among the top 1%), using the slogan 'We are the 99%'. By focusing on the 1%, Occupy sought to create a concrete target to blame, focusing their protest action against financial elites, stock markets and global finance organisations like the World Trade Organization and the International Monetary Fund (Graeber, 2014; Glasius and Pleyers, 2013). Starting with the Occupy Wall Street protest in the New York financial district in 2011, the Occupy movement led to a wave of international protests and mobilisations. The emergence of anti-corporate, anti-globalisation movements was made possible by the resonance of connecting local injustices to global processes of neo-liberalism, which brought together a very diverse set of local grievances and inequalities under a broad umbrella (Pickerill et al., 2015). This umbrella framework was used to connect anti-capitalist, anti-corporate, pro-democracy, human rights, feminist, charity, church and NGO groups (groups with very different constituencies and agendas) into an international network of support, strengthening the hand of activists fighting local battles. However, frames are susceptible to very different interpretations and uses. We can see this in manoeuvres around 'anti-globalisation', where the term 'alter-globalisation' has increasingly been adopted by many left-wing activists in contrast to that of 'anti-globalisation', to distinguish their movement from right-wing, nationalist anti-globalisation movements (such as UKIP, Trumpism, the French National Front or the Greek Golden Dawn) who share their opposition to the ills of globalisation but who mobilise for the protection of the nation-state and employ anti-migrant rhetoric in so doing.

There are also limits to interpretation. 'Frame analysis' focuses on the self-conscious framing strategies of SMOs (and on how movements create new cultural meanings), but this comes at the expense of examining the pre-existing beliefs of recruits or a broader assessment of how struggles over meaning are constrained by wider systems of discourse, meaning and ideology (Jasper and Poulsen, 1995; Goodwin and Jasper, 2004b; Steinberg, 1998, 1999, 2002; Oliver and Johnston, 2000; Polletta, 2003). Part of the problem is that framing is often presented as a 'cultural' process, a question of the subjective interpretation of 'structure' understood in terms of objective and external constraints. But this neglects the constraints of culture and creates an 'excessive voluntarism' paying insufficient attention to how cultural meanings have 'structural characteristics independent of actors' control' (Steinberg, 2002: 210; 1998). For critics, people's sense of inequality and injustice is never just a question of how they subjectively interpret their circumstances, nor is mobilisation simply a question of the reframing activities of activists changing people's perspectives. Certainly, people's sense of their situation and the problems they face are very variably understood and framed, but this is not just a question of personal interpretation because 'traditions, principles, codes, and arrangements' are 'supra-individual and constrain individual action . . . they are ways of ordering reality' and so 'cannot easily be "thought away"' (Polletta, 2003: 101). Shared social arrangements and codes of meaning constrain individual interpretations and practices, as the cultural but also collectively organised, publicly visible and external 'environment' which we must always take account of in our activities. Culture is observable in linguistic practices, institutional rules, and social rituals rather than existing only in people's heads. This conception of culture puts us in a better position to grasp conceptually and empirically the generation of cultural but 'objective' opportunities—objective in the sense of prior to insurgents' interpretative activities . . . to grasp culture's durable character . . . and to identify political institutions' and processes' role in constituting grievances, identities, and goals. (Polletta, 2003: 100)

I return to the constraints (and affordances) of shared practices in later chapters, but, for now, my focus is on how such arguments indicate another constraint on mobilisation. Protest activity is an attempt to subvert dominant understandings of social arenas, but this 'is both facilitated and limited by the ways in which claims and alternative visions can be represented within a larger discursive field' (Steinberg, 1998: 740). Institutional contexts are shaped by dominant practices and codes of meaning which 'impose boundaries on the ways in which people understand and represent their lives', so 'challengers' in given arenas must develop their discursive repertoires against accepted codes of meaning greatly defined by 'powerholders' (Ibid.: 742). To illustrate these constraints, Steinberg gives the example of English textile workers in the early nineteenth century who engaged in a sustained series of strikes against increasingly powerful mill owners. The textile workers countered the mill owners' dominant rhetoric of political economy (which argued that market forces alone should determine workers' conditions, justifying lower wages) by drawing on broader discourses of national identity, religious virtue and family life in order to make counter-claims about how their labour should be valued. But by presenting themselves as the upholders of piety and respectable family life, the workers also constrained themselves, since the legitimacy of claims made on the basis of piety and good citizenship were undermined by threats against strike breakers or loom-breaking. They could only frame themselves as legitimate challengers as long as they remained 'deferential underlings' (Steinberg, 2002: 223). The creation of 'any discursive repertoire not only facilitates collective action; it imposes constraints on how challengers can construct their claims and legitimate their identities' (Ibid.: 224), and those who wish to change social arrangements must engage with the dominant discourses which already surround any sphere of activity. 'As challengers seek to transform existing meanings in discursive practices to articulate a sense of injustice, make claims, and establish alternative visions, they also remain bounded by the field and the genres within which they struggle . . . discursive resistance is always a dialogue with domination' (Steinberg, 2002: 213).

While any process of framing is constrained, it is also relational and dialogic. So while challengers 'often create oppositional discourses by borrowing from the discourses of those they oppose,' in protracted conflicts 'both dominant and challenging discourses can mix together' (Steinberg, 2002: 209). Powerful actors try to restrict the development of meanings hostile to their own, devaluing or marginalising antagonistic points of view (Steinberg, 2002: 213). However, the indeterminate, contested and 'multivocal' nature of discourse means there is always potential for resistance and subversion—a theme to which I return in Chapters 6 and 7.

A focus on the dominant cultural frames which shape and constrain collective arenas of practice also requires us to rethink just what it is that collective mobilisation opposes. Much work in the area focuses on organised movements targeted at powerful agents of the state or capitalism. But there are other 'movements'—loosely organised and sometimes not collectively organised at all—engaged in wider forms of countercultural practice. Much movement activity is aimed at creating 'another world', challenging cultural codes and accepted ways of life as part of much broader 'collective challenges to systems or structures of authority' (Snow, 2004: 11). Here the 'systems of authority' that are targeted are not just political systems but rather more general institutional, organisational, or cultural systems which function 'in a kind of Foucauldian fashion, to coordinate patterns of behaviour and orientation, typically among a fairly large number of people, such that the activities, orientations, identities and/or interpretations of one set of actors is subordinated to the directives, mandates, and perspectives and framings of another set of actors' (Ibid.: 13). As Death (2010: 235) notes, the influence of Foucault on studies of social movements and protest has been relatively slight, perhaps because Foucault 'is generally regarded as focusing more on the analysis of power and government than forms of resistance'.[7] However, this broader Foucauldian sense of challenge to dominant cultural codes (or counter-conduct) is the province of 'new', 'prefigurative' and 'lifestyle' social movements. These movements are engaged in countercultural projects to change the practices and minds of *everyone* in society, through various forms of direct action, and represent another approach to exercising the interdependent power of collective refusal. Such movements also raise questions about more mundane forms of dissent and noncompliance and of how people manage discontent in their everyday lives, questions which much social movement analysis has failed to address.

ANOTHER WORLD?

Work on 'new social movements' shifts the view of social movements as agents of 'political struggle' to agents of 'cultural struggle' (Edwards, 2014: 113). Theories of 'new social movements' (NSM) suggest that shifts in society have resulted in new kinds of struggle, not against material inequality but rather against the imposition of 'system' logics, in struggles for autonomy, self-determination and self-expression. Critics query whether these elements are really all that 'new' and reject the idea of a 'post-material' turn. But raising questions of cultural challenge and nonconformity does offer a different way of thinking about protest and collective action. Social movements can also be understood as 'counter-cultural spaces' in which 'excepting for a few visible moments of public protest, social movement activity can be "submerged"' and 'can involve individuals in constructing cultural alternatives, which, while not divorced from collective efforts at change, can involve them in carrying out collective actions "on their own"' (Edwards, 2014: 213). This raises the question of how social change can occur not just through 'contentious politics' but also through a 'DIY' approach, a 'micro' politics of direct action, social experimentation and the construction of new collective identities.

The NSMs emerging as significant forces from the 1960s (the civil rights movement, the antinuclear, students', women's liberation, gay liberation, disability rights and environmental movements) looked very different to older class-based movements, and NSM theory argued that these new movements were not 'seeking to gain political and economic concessions from institutional actors' but rather 'recognition for new identities and lifestyles' (Edwards, 2014: 117–18; Polletta and Jasper, 2001: 286). A series of European theorists argued that shifts in contemporary Western societies were changing the nature of conflict and mobilisation. Whether these shifts were to a 'postindustrial' 'programmed society' (Touraine, 1981), an 'information' society (Melucci, 1996), a 'network' society (Castells, 1997) or simply to a capitalism where 'system' had colonised 'lifeworld' (Habermas, 1981, 1987), the claim was that conflict was increasingly 'post-material'. This 'new' politics emerged from people feeling that they had lost autonomy and dignity, through the intrusion of regulation and market and instrumental rationalities into personal lives. For example, Melucci's (1996) 'information society' is characterised by affluence and increasing individualisation of experience but also greater pressures for conformity. People's lives must still be compatible with capitalism's drives, so social control is increasingly targeted at people's personal lives through 'dominant cultural codes', 'patterning people's thoughts, emotions and feelings' (Ibid.: 180) to be the aspirational, self-responsible capitalist subjects already encountered in Chapter 3. The NSMs focused on moral values, quality of life, individual self-realisation and struggles over identity and were not just a means to a political end, since the creation of the movement and its construction of cultural alternatives *was* the aim (Melucci, 1985: 800). Reflecting this, many of these movements were informally structured, based on loose networks or confederations of smaller groups, often explicitly rejecting formal hierarchies.

The idea of an epochal change to a 'post-material' society of 'cultural struggle' has a very Global-North, post-industrial focus. As Fadaee (2016: 5) notes, many countries in the Global South 'do not fit in the definition of Fordist-industrial or post-industrial societies' yet have still 'witnessed the emergence of rights-based and quality-of-life movements'. Analysis of such movements in the Global South indicates the limiting assumptions of much NSM theory. For example, Currier and Thomann's (2016) work on LGBTI movements in Côte d'Ivoire, Malawi, Namibia and South Africa argues that casting LGBTI movements as 'identity movements' diminishes the 'survival challenges that gender and sexual minorities encounter . . . [and] the profound daily struggles in which activists are engaged' (Ibid.: 88–9). Similarly, 'green' campaigns in the Global South often address pressing issues of material life-chances and subsistence in an 'environmentalism of the poor' (Guha, 2000; Martinez-Alier, 2002). And to further complicate the picture, in contexts like Iran and China where organised challenge to state authorities is restricted, 'quality of life' activism—such as environmental campaigns—can be safer ways of mobilising political dissent (Fadaee, 2012; Lora-Wainwright, 2017).

Critics also challenge the distinction between 'old' and 'new' social movements and reject the 'new times' assumptions underpinning NSM theory. Flacks (1988; 2004: 150) notes that 'liberation' movements (such as the civil rights movement) also attempt to renegotiate dominant social codes through acts of noncompliance and nonconformity in the 'private', 'personal' and 'everyday'—but such movements are neither 'new' nor 'post-material' in their concerns. Questions of material reward intrinsically raise questions of moral worth, dignity and social recognition (Fraser and Honneth, 2003; Sayer, 2005a, 2005b), so the 'cultural' and the 'material' are not distinct arenas of struggle. Long before the advent of 'advanced capitalism', class-based movements organised to resist threats to autonomy, self-determination and self-expression (Calhoun, 1993; Buechler, 1995). More prosaically, but most damaging to the idea of a 'post-material turn', from the 1990s a wave of 'even newer' or 'newer still' movements (Crossley, 2003; Touraine, 2002) emerged with a strong focus on material inequality. These 'newer' movements (the alter-globalisation movements and anti-corporate activism) often adopt the same 'rhizome' form as the NSMs (operating as anti-hierarchical, leaderless networks) and are similarly engaged in struggles to show that 'another world is possible' but with explicitly 'material' concerns, their struggle directed against the economic and power inequalities of capitalist society and global neoliberalism:

> Not only do global activists cite 'extremes of wealth and poverty' as one of their key concerns, but some of them actually are the Trade Unionists and socialists that new social movements theory had written off. In addition, one 'camp' within the movement adopts 'political'

claims-making rather than the 'cultural' strategies associated with new social movements. (Edwards, 2014: 179)

Nonetheless, NSM theory does focus attention on how mobilisation also represents a struggle over dominant social codes and conventions, in which 'movements also transform cultural representations, social norms—how groups see themselves and are seen by others' (Polletta and Jasper, 2001: 284). Here people are engaged in challenges to the cultural conventions not just of elites but also of other ordinary people. This not only raises questions of the power of rule-breaking and cultural innovation but also when social transgression becomes a political act.

Many of the 'even newer' social movements are 'prefigurative': creating experimental or 'alternative' social arrangements to actively 'live the change' they want to bring about, where the practices of the movement already embody 'those forms of social relations, decision-making, culture, and human experience that are the ultimate goal' (Boggs, 1977: 100). For the global justice, Occupy and anti-austerity movements, 'making decisions by consensus, decentralizing organization, and rotating leadership serves to model the radically democratic society that activists hope to bring into being' (Polletta and Hoban, 2016: 286). Prefigurative politics includes projects to establish 'moral communities' to counter 'the depersonalised, market and instrumental relationships' of contemporary society (Breines, 1982), through 'social experiments that both critique the status quo and offer alternatives'[8] (Cornish et al., 2016: 116). In constructing countercultural alternatives, such movements are engaged in a very large task. They are not challenging (or, at least, not *just* challenging) governments but rather dominant ways of living and thinking ('authority' in Snow's expanded Foucauldian sense).

The routines and obligations of everyday life create strong pressures for compliance and make 'collective refusal' hard, so prefigurative movements seek to create autonomous social settings or networks which lift some of these pressures, providing a countercultural space free, to some extent, from dominant arrangements (Polletta and Jasper, 2001). Such spaces enable alternative practices, oppositional identities and counter-hegemonic ideas. Whether they work by providing distance from the physical or ideological domination of the powerful (Morris, 1984; Hirsch, 1990) or by institutionalising alternative belief systems (Polletta, 1999), such sites shape the networks and activities of participants, helping to create countercultural 'social worlds' with alternative routines and obligations, in which nonmainstream values and innovation are reinforced and supported (Crossley and Ibrahim, 2011).

But when is nonconformity a movement? In prefiguration, participants 'act out a vision of a better world' (Epstein, 1991: 122). But Yates argues that we must distinguish prefiguration from 'countercultures, subcultures or other forms of idealistic or utopian grouping', because the act of 'building alternatives' is only prefiguration when activists seek to enlist wider constituencies (2015: 5, 18). It is fine to lead by example, but in prefiguration the intention is to make others follow. However, the question of when practices which swim against the tide cross the line into practices aimed at social transformation is a difficult one, as 'lifestyle movements' show. Lifestyle movements[9] 'actively promote a way of life as a primary means to foster social change', with participants also seeking 'to "be the change they wish to see in the world"', but through *individual* lifestyle change rather than through collective action, 'integrating movement values into relatively private individual actions' affecting the mundane aspects of daily living, such as 'consumption habits, leisure activities, eating and cooking, modes of dress, money management, transportation/travel, and water and energy consumption' (Haenfler, Johnson and Jones, 2012: 1, 13, 15, 6). Participants do aim to change the world, but through 'a morally coherent, personally gratifying lifestyle and identity' (Ibid.). This represents a highly individual and disaggregated form of movement activity, a form of 'doing collective action on your own', in which a movement becomes more of an 'imagined community' than a collectivity (Edwards, 2014: 143). Of course, if enough people take part, such activities *are* transformative. And if we shift our focus still further, to look at the dispersed but large-scale self-help rule-breaking practices of 'social non-movements' in the Global South (Bayat, 2013), we can see that collective refusal need not be all that organised nor explicitly aimed at social transformation and yet can still be profoundly transformative.

SOCIAL 'NONMOVEMENTS'

Accounts of 'social movements' have been dominated by examples and analysis from the Global North. Yet the conventional elements of 'social movements' which have been identified (organised claims-making against governments via public meetings and protest marches) are historically specific, emerging in Western Europe and North America after 1750 with the emergence of specific citizenship rights (Tilly, 2008). Critics argue that these models do not work well in other global settings (Scott, 1989; Deess, 1997; Bayat, 2013, 2016; Fadaee, 2016) and generalise too much from Western experience:

> In the global South we encounter somewhat different social settings and forces for change. Until recently, most of these postcolonial societies suffered (and still many suffer) from undemocratic states, unelected autocrats, military rulers, or life-long presidencies. A paradox of the contentious politics here is that while the undemocratic regimes become a prime target of dissent, organized and open opposition becomes painfully limited precisely because of the repressive policies of

these regimes. Secretive and underground movements were until recently a key feature of oppositional politics in the global South movements that usually assume quite different dynamics and modes of operation then those operating in the open and legally sanctioned environments. (Bayat, 2016: xxiii)

Bayat argues that where citizenship rights are restricted, or where authoritarian regimes show little tolerance for dissent, dissent must take a different form. Similar arguments have been made about dissent in the former state-socialist authoritarian regimes in Eastern Europe, such as the GDR (Deess, 1997), so this is not a simple division between the Global North and South. Fadaee (2016: 9) notes the range of regime types across the Global South but also that 'semi-democratic or authoritarian regimes' are 'not homogenous', suggesting a need to move beyond the 'dichotomy of liberal democracy vs. non-democracy in social movement analysis'. But despite their heterogeneity, most Southern societies have experienced colonialism, often resulting in different kinds of mobilisation for change compared to the Global North (Bayat, 2016). As Fadaee (2017: 48) notes, 'for a long period the most significant uprisings and social movements in most parts of the global South were anti-colonial movements in one way or another' and 'imperialism has to a large extent affected social movements and contentious politics in regions such as Latin America and the Middle East'. In many of these uprisings, dispossessed and marginalised groups mobilised not only against colonial domination but also against the nationalist elites who replaced colonial rule, through social movements which 'created a new discourse of entitlement' centred on 'subaltern groups and popular classes' who made claims 'both to dignified livelihoods and political recognition and participation' (Nilsen, 2016: 277).

Autocratic and repressive regimes limit the space for organised protest, but dissent and activism still occur within them. However, this dissent is sometimes underestimated or misunderstood because it does not fit the conventional pattern of organised protest movements. The failure to recognise alternative forms of activism and dissent left many Western analysts wrong-footed by events like the uprisings of the Arab Spring (2010–2014), which for some observers seemed inexplicable without conventional movement organisations leading the charge (Bayat, 2013: 3–4). Explaining this requires recognising 'social nonmovements' as 'distinct and unconventional forms of agency and activism' (Ibid.: 4). The product of people struggling to go about their everyday lives with dignity, 'nonmovements' involve people illegally helping themselves to the rights and resources (spaces to live and trade, to water, to electricity, to autonomy and self-expression) that they have been denied. The people involved in 'nonmovements' are not seeking civil rights or political change but rather are engaged in everyday individual infringements on rules and laws, producing piecemeal encroachments against what is allowed. But how do the powerless and disadvantaged—who lack the right or ability to protest—express their dissent?

For Bayat, the key question rests in how social conditions create spaces for certain kinds of dissent. Nonmovements emerge when organised protest is constrained but where 'informality in social, economic, and political life features prominently' and 'extra-legal practices tend to dominate large swaths of the state, economy and society' (Bayat, 2016: xxiii–xxiv). Such conditions in the Middle East, he argues, create 'many escapes, spaces, and uncontrolled holes—zones of relative freedom that can be filled and appropriated by ordinary actors' (2013: 28). This gives rise to social nonmovements, in which the urban poor engage in a disaggregated form of 'street politics' (Ibid.). Bayat argues that this is the prevalent form of activism not only in authoritarian states but also in 'soft states' that lack the capacity 'to impose full control' (Ibid.). Bayat identifies such social informality in many societies of the Global South, with 'significant implications for our understanding of the dynamics of social struggles (as well as compliance)' there (2016: xxiii–xxiv).

Bayat argues that 'for those urban subjects (such as the unemployed, housewives, and the "informal people") who structurally lack institutional power of disruption (such as going on strike), the "street" becomes the ultimate arena to communicate discontent' (2013: 21). Discontent is expressed in 'poor people building homes, getting piped water or phone lines, or spreading their merchandise out in the urban sidewalks' as well as 'the women striving to go to college, playing sports, working in public' and the young 'appearing how they like, listening to what they wish, and hanging out where they prefer' (Ibid.). These are the actions of dispersed, unorganised individuals engaged in 'quiet encroachments' on authorities and result from people's individual direct action to 'help themselves'. In doing so, people also defy authorities, but they seek redress not in '*extraordinary* deeds of mobilization and protestation' but instead through 'practices that are merged into, indeed part and parcel of, the ordinary practices of *everyday life*' (2013: 14, 20–21, original emphasis). Nonmovements are more resilient against repression than conventional movements precisely because they are embedded in the practices of everyday life. The state 'may be able . . . to abolish political parties, but cannot easily stop the normal flow of life in streets' (Ibid.: 21, 13).

Chapter 3 looked at arguments that people seeking to 'help themselves' can actually perpetuate domination by allowing them to 'let off steam' rather than engage in collective struggle. Bayat (2013: 21), by contrast, emphasises the transformative force of nonmovements through the impact of 'many people simultaneously doing similar, though contentious, things'. Although 'rarely guided' by recognisable leaderships or organisations, as the 'shared practices of large numbers of ordinary people' they can still 'trigger much social change' (Ibid.: 15). Encroachment can also become more organised mobilisation. When encroachers are confronted by authorities, their defence of their gains can become 'collective and audible' with 'epidemic potential' (Bayat, 2000: 547; 2013: 21). But even without organised mobilisation, nonmovements are a force for change simply through the sheer numbers of people engaging in the same kinds of subversive practices. The 'discreet and prolonged ways in which the poor struggle to survive and to better their lives by quietly impinging on the propertied and powerful, and on society at large' represents a 'protracted mobilization of millions of detached and dispersed individuals and families who strive to enhance their lives' (Ibid.: 15–16). Without formal leadership or organisation, these everyday encroachments 'have virtually transformed the large cities of the Middle East and by extension many developing countries, generating a substantial outdoor economy, new communities, and arenas of self-development in the urban landscapes' (Ibid.: 16).

Bayat's (2013) 'quiet encroachments' represent another version of the power of cooperative interdependence and collective refusal identified by Piven and Cloward (2005), though this time facilitated by informality in the civil sphere rather than by social or economic crisis. However, as Chapter 6 indicates, such encroachments are not exclusively the province of authoritarian regimes, 'soft' states or moments of crisis. Scott (2012) argues that people everywhere routinely push against rules through minor infringements, and he argues that such minor infringements can build, through tacit coordination (in which people partly base their behaviour on what others are doing and can get away with), into much more substantial renegotiations of the rules. For Scott (Ibid.: 13–14), 'tacit coordination and lawbreaking can mimic the effects of collective action without its inconveniences and dangers'. Of course, 'what people can get away with' depends on how rules are enforced and the degree to which everyday life is regulated. But this also depends on how the people around us behave, with strength in numbers (Ibid.). Even in the most authoritarian regime, a power that everyone disobeys is not a power, and when 'that belief evaporates—as it did across the Arab world in 2011, the consequences for despots can be catastrophic' (Gorringe and Rafanell, 2015: 10).

FROM PROTEST TO RESISTANCE

The mantra of work on social movements is that grievance is widespread but protest and mobilisation are not. As a result, the focus of analysis is on the factors enabling mobilisation, with grievance (and the social conditions under which people manage and express discontent more generally) slipping to the background. Even in work on how discontent is framed and constructed, the focus is on the framing strategies of activists and movement organisations at the expense of the pre-existing beliefs of recruits and the wider systems of meanings and practices within which both are located. This reflects a wider tendency in social movement studies to separate protest and mobilisation from everyday social practices and routines. Mobilisation and protest are typically presented as difficult and exceptional, costly and risky to organise, and so constituting a break with everyday life. Where there is examination of the connection between everyday social practices and protest, the focus is on how people's networks or organisational resources or disruptions to their everyday ways of life serve to facilitate mobilisation. But in examining how protest grows out of the social organisation which creates collective capacities, the focus has turned away from questions of how compliance, dissent and grievance emerge and are handled within the routine practices of everyday life, and the majority of social movement research 'neglects ordinary life until it has ceased being ordinary' (Deess, 1997: 208).

At first sight, this is entirely reasonable. Mobilisation is not routine, so it makes sense to focus on what is distinctive and exceptional about it. But if 'social movements' are the more general 'preferences for change' that exist in a society (as distinct from the organisations which pursue those preferences) (McCarthy and Zald, 1977), then it seems strange to restrict the study of preferences for change to processes of mobilisation and protest. Protest and dissent have become understood as 'collective, organized efforts at social change' (Edwards, 2014: 2), in which people are oriented towards 'making history' rather than 'making their everyday lives' (Flacks, 1976). But people do sometimes make history (if inadvertently) by making their everyday lives, as Bayat's (2013) work on 'nonmovements' shows. Movement research does address nonconformity and struggles for autonomy, but the emphasis is on countercultures and relatively sequestered sites: settings which provide a space free, to some extent, from 'dominant' arrangements. This remains a focus on nonmainstream practices and the social worlds of activists and—again—is primarily concerned with how such settings provide a resource for mobilisation and the diffusion of protest. Nonconformist practices only become a focus of interest when they actively seek to foster wider social change. But the dispersed practices through which people evade or resist dominant codes and seek greater resources, autonomy and dignity for themselves with no wider aim in view can—in the aggregate—have considerable consequences both for mobilisation but also for how social change can occur without mobilisation.

Work on social movements provides a very different answer to the question of why discontented and aggrieved people are more likely to acquiesce to their situation rather than mobilise against it. Such analysis indicates a range of reasons for why people put up with inequality, but reasons founded less in symbolic legitimation than in practical conditions of powerlessness and constraint. Social movement research shows that disadvantaged groups *are* often resigned to their situation and that, in order to mobilise, they must develop a sense that change is possible; but such work also shows that people's resignation rests in 'objective' conditions of constraint, which must shift in order for people to be able to act. The capacity for practical challenge depends on resources and collective organisation which the disadvantaged often lack, and also entails significant risk. So if aggrieved people feel that they cannot change their situation, quite often this is because they face daunting obstacles to change. Protest, as a result, is often focused on local and specific targets, with the daily experience of concrete settings shaping people's grievances and anger in ways which reflect their very practical concerns and restricted capacities to act. Nonetheless, the disadvantaged and deprived do manage to dissent, protest and mobilise, even in the most repressive contexts, and social movement research also shows the variety of enabling practical conditions which help make mobilisation possible.

To fully understand the practical possibilities for dissent and mobilisation, we must think more broadly about the nature of constraint, non-compliance and dissent. The constraints on protest are not just a question of coercion or repression but also of the routines, obligations and commitments of ordinary social life which keep people in the alignments which constitute unequal arrangements. But this constraint represents a form of mutual interdependence, and such interdependence offers a potential source of collective resources and leverage for even the most deprived, arising from the ability to disrupt the patterns of mutual dependence, expectation and cooperation which underpin collective social arrangements (Piven and Cloward, 2005). The power that exists in 'collective refusal' arises from defying expectation, from breaking the rules and withholding the cooperation on which collective arrangements depend. Of course, in collective refusal people must disrupt their own lives, often at considerable cost. Nevertheless, while these acts of rule-breaking and disruption may not fit the conventional pattern of organised protest movements, we should also not underestimate the scope of such refusal.

Too great a focus on organised mobilisation leads to a truncated view of the practices which produce social change, sidelining questions of how dissent emerges in people's everyday lives. Yet apparently 'compliant' social practices and routines can express 'mundane' or 'unexceptional' forms of dissent through everyday acts of nonconformism, concealed subversion and 'bending the rules'. Discussion of the social organisation of everyday life in repressive contexts, for example, has pointed to 'concealed' subversive ideas and practices operating within official (or dominant) spaces (Deess, 1997; Scott, 1990). Chapter 6 explores research on 'mundane' dissent, rule-breaking and misbehaviour, which asks us to think more closely about everyday activities which may not directly confront inequalities or power relations but which, for many analysts, are forms of 'everyday resistance' to inequality and domination. Scott (2012:

16–17) sees 'everyday' resistance as the most likely form taken under authoritarian rule, where those 'who are denied the usual means of public protest' often 'have no other recourse than foot-dragging, sabotage, poaching, theft, and, ultimately, revolt'. However, tacit dissent and subversion are not made obsolete by the 'freedoms of expression and assembly' of democratic citizens, not least because democracies are also underpinned by state force, and their concentration of wealth and privileged access to political influence means democracies are often marked more by their 'immobility than for facilitating major reforms' (Ibid.: 17). Work on mundane resistance indicates that it is very widespread and raises more general questions of the indeterminacy of practices, and rule-making and rule-breaking in the coordination of activities and the constitution of shared forms of life, issues which will be explored further in Chapters 6 and 7.

NOTES

1. In fact, in addressing why people often don't act in their collective interest, SMS has spent more time discussing the 'free rider problem' of collective action (a rational action model examining the costs and benefits to any collective action) (Olson, 1965: 2) than questions of symbolic domination.

2. Olson gives the example of workplace unions to explain this. Unions pursue 'public' or common goods for their members, using collective action to bring pressure on employers. But there are costs and risks to individuals from participating in union actions like strikes, so a cost-benefit analysis suggests individuals will not strike, instead seeking to 'free-ride' on others' efforts. Union action does, of course, take place, which Olson attributes to the additional selective incentives and pressures which unions provide for members (changing the individual's cost-benefit analysis).

3. Where civil rights activists led voter registration drives and taught classes aimed at increasing the political participation of school students.

4. Including a decline in lynchings in the American South (so mobilization carried fewer risks), a population shift to key urban areas (increasing black political influence) as well as the United States' international role during the Cold War (with civil rights presented as a means by which the federal government could assert the moral superiority of the United States).

5. Snow et al. (1986: 474–75) give the example of the American activist group Mothers Against Drunk Driving, whose campaign changed the meaning of fatalities in drunk driving incidents from 'unfortunate accidents' into 'inexcusable tragedies', reframing drunk driving as a crime demanding punishment.

6. A classic example is the antagonistic framings of abortion by 'pro-choice' and 'pro-life' activists, where the framing of the issue in terms of a woman's reproductive rights (the 'right to choose') has been attacked by opponents who provide a counter-frame of abortion in terms of the rights of the foetus (the 'right to life'). Both movements employ the master frame of 'rights' but to pursue opposing ends.

7. And as Death also notes, the governmentality literature 'tends to treat dissent and protest as an afterthought, or failure of government' with surprisingly little focus on such issues (2010: 235).

8. Such as workers' cooperatives, direct democracy initiatives, timebanks, eco-villages, community gardening, the open-source movement.

9. Including groups such as vegetarians, green lifestyle adopters, locavores, slow fooders and voluntary simplifiers (Haenfler et al., 2012: 13).

SIX
Resisting Inequality

Work on social movements shows that 'collective refusal'—noncompliance in everyday social arenas—provides collective resources which enable protest and dissent. This represents a source of collective resources and leverage that arises from defying expectation, breaking the rules and withholding social cooperation. Actualising the power of collective refusal is difficult, because the routines and obligations of everyday life create strong pressures for compliance, and in collective refusal people must disrupt their own lives and risk repercussion. But there are other forms of 'collective refusal' which are not all that organised and only tacitly collective. This chapter considers these more dispersed and disorganised acts of mundane noncompliance. Such misbehaviour may not explicitly confront unequal relations, but, for some, this still represents a form of covert 'resistance'. In this turn to focus on 'everyday' forms of resistance, unequal social arrangements are typically discussed as power relations and forms of domination.

As with the accounts of symbolic legitimation discussed earlier in this book, work on mundane resistance attempts to explain *the lack* of more explicit and organised opposition to domination. For example, in the 1970s and 1980s, anthropologists seeing the devastating effects of globalising capitalism on social life in rural areas in the Global South were puzzled that this rarely led to class-based mobilisation in such communities (Vincent, 1990: 403). But the absence of direct confrontation is not taken as a sign of acquiescence nor symbolic domination. Instead, the dearth of conventional collective action has shifted the focus to 'small-scale, local or ... individualistic' types of dissent, leading to a new paradigm of 'resistance' (Bayat, 2013: 41). Similarly, in organisational studies, the perception that post-industrial labour markets left 'little space for public and formalised contestation' (Spicer and Böhm, 2007: 1676) led to a greater focus 'on the interstitial spaces of organizational life as the place where resistance may be flourishing', with this shift occurring 'out of the recognition of decreased possibilities for collective, organized, and confrontational forms of worker resistance' (Mumby, 2005: 38–39). An emphasis on mundane forms of dissent moves beyond a simple dichotomy of people being *either* engaged in dissent and protest against inequalities *or* else subsumed in consent or acquiescence. It also raises the question, however, of when rule-breaking and recalcitrance become 'resistance'.

A focus on mundane, interstitial forms of resistance is often bound up with a rejection of the idea that a lack of organised confrontation is a sign of 'consent' or evidence that power relations produce 'docile subjects', with pioneering theorists of mundane resistance attacking a variety of theories which suggest that power and inequality are 'naturalised'. Accounts of symbolic domination and hegemony suggest that the most pernicious aspect of power relations is how they mask the nature of inequality and domination, generating a 'manipulated consent' in subordinate groups. Alternatively, work using Foucauldian notions of disciplinary power sees power working through systems of surveillance and discursive practices which define what is normal and acceptable, producing 'willing' and 'docile' subjects. Weaker versions of such arguments focus instead on the production of grudging but compliant resignation, in which people come to accept the unalterable nature of social arrangements. However, theorists of mundane resistance argue that such accounts too readily focus on the *appearance* of consent, docility or resignation, failing to recognise that beneath the surface of people's compliance there is still widespread discontent. Scott (1990) sees everyday resistance as a force that can check or transform the actions of the powerful but argues that this is often obscured by both parties: by subordinates because they have a vested interest in avoiding open displays of insubordination and by the powerful because they have a vested interest in maintaining an aura of authority and control. As a result, domination produces an 'official transcript' that provides 'convincing evidence of willing, even enthusiastic complicity' so that while 'power appears naturalized', this is merely an appearance which 'elites exert their influence to produce' and which 'ordinarily serves the immediate interests of subordinate groups to avoid discrediting' (Ibid.: 86–87). So while dissent is more often expressed through recalcitrance, insubordination and misbehaviour than by organised confrontation, nonetheless the argument is that it shows that inequality is far from 'naturalised'.

Some argue that Scott's argument best applies to authoritarian conditions of coercive domination where it is safest to hide resistance, suggesting that theories of symbolic domination still work well in less authoritarian democratic capitalist societies (Lukes, 2005). However, similar arguments of mundane resistance have emerged in cultural studies and in organisational studies in liberal democracies, in which managerial or disciplinary regulation (rather than repressive coercion) is the form of power being resisted (de Certeau, 1984; Ackroyd and Thompson, 1999). Such work makes some shared arguments. Firstly, there is the assertion that subversion, resistance and misbehaviour are a widespread, even endemic, feature of unequal social arrangements, but this is grossly underestimated by analysts who mistake the absence of open and organised confrontation for consent and acquiescence. Secondly, there is the suggestion that analysts who see consenting or 'docile subjects' have been taken in by the 'official' or dominant account of social arrangements. This represents a failure to recognise that power relations give subordinates good reason to act *as if* they consent (even when they do not) while also giving superordinates good reasons for acting *as if* their control is effective and consensual (even when it is not). Finally, it is argued that there are important limits to the ability of the powerful and privileged (or the dominant order) to control subordinates, or to shape their hearts and minds, so we should be cautious about seeing the strength and durability of inequality and power relations as resting in 'symbolic domination' or 'government of the soul'.

For many of the theorists considered in this chapter, it is the indeterminacy of any convention, code or regulation which creates limits to control and regulation, because there is always room for discretion, manoeuvre and reinterpretation. This indeterminacy creates space for nonconformism, dissent or misbehaviour, and the field of 'resistance studies' documents the widespread nature of everyday acts of subversion, misbehaviour and dissent. But if indeterminacy is endemic, and subversion, misbehaviour and dissent so widespread, why do inequality and domination still persist? In debates on resistance, there has been a substantial shift in understandings of 'power', with a move to a poststructural reading which locates 'resistance' as an inevitable, mutually implicated, aspect of power relations and in which 'power' is seen as an ineradicable feature of all social relations. This stance suggests that resistance can never transcend power relations, only rework them. However, even poststructural accounts see the potential for counter-conduct to effect the aim of 'not being governed quite so much' (Foucault, 2007b: 45) — so the question remains why stark inequalities are so durable in the face of dissent and resistance.

Accounts of mundane resistance argue that widespread practices of noncompliance show that inequality is far from 'naturalised'; yet critics express caution about seeing nonconforming or noncompliant behaviour as representing dissent to wider social arrangements or as opposition to power and authority, beyond very local and immediate concerns. In a theme repeated from previous chapters, the argument here is that much of what has been labelled as 'resistance' is in fact simply survival, self-help or corner-cutting strategies. Indeed, much rule-breaking behaviour in organisations is not undertaken as noncompliance but rather represents a flexible interpretation of how to apply rules. However, such 'encroachments', 'everyday modifications' and 'evasions' do have the potential to substantially transform wider social arrangements. If we are interested in the practical possibilities of social transformation and the nature of social conformity and control, then we need to look more broadly at both mundane resistance and everyday encroachments and evasions. In doing so, however, we need to focus not just on the constraints of power relations but also on the collective steering of social relations more generally.

EVERYDAY RESISTANCE AND INFRAPOLITICS

The concept of 'everyday resistance' aims to correct the tendency of social analysis to overlook 'the vital role of power relations in constraining [the] forms of resistance open to subordinate groups' (Scott, 1989: 54). For Scott, if we only focus on *organised* opposition to power as 'real resistance', then 'all that is being measured may be the level of repression that structures the available options' (Ibid.: 51). Here it is coercion that keeps subordinates aligned—publicly at least—to the actions of the dominant. But this does not mean that people simply passively accept or consent to their situation. Through his research on subaltern groups (beginning with peasant groups in South East Asia then extending this analysis more generally), Scott (1985, 1989, 1990) argues that there is widespread 'everyday resistance' among 'subordinate' or 'powerless' groups. However, this has been ignored or misinterpreted, because the activities in question fail to conform to the types of protest expected—or preferred—by analysts.

Most attention, Scott suggests (1989: 34; 1990), is 'concentrated on those forms of resistance which pose a declared threat to powerholders: social movements, dissident sects, revolutionary groups and other forms of publicly organized political opposition', but this misses the 'hidden transcript' of everyday forms of resistance. Scott argues that exploited people are constrained in their options, but this does not prevent them countering repressive domination—however, they must use 'quiet', ambiguous or disguised forms of resistance to do so, especially in situations where open confrontation is simply too risky. In 'pragmatic adaptation to the realities' of their lives, subalterns recognise 'limits that only the foolhardy would transgress' (Ibid.: 246, 247). Attention therefore needs to be refocused on 'everyday resistance' or 'infrapolitics' (1990: 184), which Scott characterises as 'weapons of the weak' (1985), a 'vast realm of political action . . . almost habitually overlooked' (1989: 33). Such 'everyday' forms of resistance occur in the 'prosaic but constant struggle between the peasantry and those who seek to extract labor, food, taxes, rents, and interest from them' in which most 'forms of this struggle stop well short of outright collective defiance' (1985: xvi).

Scott sees 'resistance' as 'any act(s)' by subordinates 'intended to mitigate or deny' the claims of superordinates or 'to advance their own claims' (1985: 290). The 'ordinary weapons' of 'relatively powerless groups' comprise practices such as 'foot dragging, dissimulation, desertion, false compliance, pilfering, feigned ignorance, slander, arson, sabotage'—activities which often 'represent a form of individual self-help', 'require little or no coordination or planning' and 'typically avoid any direct, symbolic confrontation with authority' (Ibid.: xvi). These are 'creeping incremental strategies which can be finely tuned to the opposition they encounter' and 'since they make no formal claims, offer a ready line-of-retreat through disavowal' (1989: 54). Scott argues that such forms of resistance have been 'absent or marginal to most accounts of class relations' precisely because the aim of such practices 'is to avoid notice and detection' (Ibid.: 34), often taking a disguised and ambiguous form to avoid open challenge—and open retaliation' (Ibid.: 54).

For Scott, such defiance, while muted or disguised, can still check the encroachments of the powerful on the powerless and lead to progressive social transformation. This is because acts of mundane resistance have 'aggregate consequences all out of proportion to their banality' (Scott, 1989: 34). To illustrate this, Scott gives the example of Malay peasants who resent paying the Zakat, the official Islamic tithe:

> It is collected inequitably and corruptly, the proceeds are sent to the provincial capital, and not a single poor person in the village has ever received any charity back from the religious authorities. Quietly and massively, the Malay peasantry has managed to nearly dismantle the tithe system so that only 15 percent of what is formally due is actually paid. There have been no tithe riots, demonstrations, protests, only a patient and effective nibbling in a multitude of ways: fraudulent declarations of the amount of land farmed, simple failures to declare land, underpayment, and delivery of paddy spoiled by moisture or contaminated with rocks and mud to increase its weight . . . neither the religious authorities nor the ruling party wishes to call public attention to this silent, effective defiance. To do so would, among other things, expose the tenuousness of government authority in the countryside and perhaps encourage other acts of insubordination. (Scott, 1990: 89)

Scott's account is a minority report in work on protest, which has tended to focus on organised social movements. Scott attempts to correct the undue privileging of organised or public resistance. But some critics suggest that, in turn, he is in danger of privileging everyday forms, as if subalterns were *only* capable of hidden resistance (Gutmann, 1993; Bayat, 2000). Gutmann, reflecting on debates in Latin American studies, argues that 'we must not overlook manifestations of organized resistance', since 'rebellions *do* occur, and resistance *does* become overt and aim for structural change. People still give their lives for these goals in Latin America every day' (1993: 75, 78, original emphasis). Scott does see everyday forms of resistance as able to 'achieve many, if not all, of the results aimed at by social movements' (1987: 422), which might seem to downplay the role of organised movements. But he also argues that paying attention to 'disguised or offstage' political acts helps to 'map a realm of possible dissent' 'that might, if conditions permitted, sustain more dramatic forms of rebellion' (1990: 20). Scott (1976: 4) does not pay much attention to how this transition might occur, however, focusing on 'the creation of social dynamite rather than its detonation'. Others, however, argue that we need to explore the relationship between hidden resistance and mobilised confrontation (Sivaramakrishnan, 2005a; Lilja et al., 2017; Baaz, Lilja and Vinthagen, 2017).

Some analysts do consider this relationship. As Chapter 5 indicates, Bayat (2000, 2013) sees the collective action of dispersed and unorganised actors as 'social nonmovements', quiet 'claims-making practices' which chiefly occur through people's direct action to 'help themselves' rather than through people intentionally exerting pressure on authorities and which, like Scott, he sees as 'un-articulated strategies' to limit the risks of mobilisation against repressive authorities. Bayat (2000, 2013), who prefers the term 'quiet encroachment' to that of 'everyday resistance', argues that while the advances of encroachment are made individually and gradually, there is always the potential for a shift into collective protest if encroachers are confronted by authorities. What Bayat has in mind here is the unrest and political mobilisation that has sometimes erupted in countries of the Middle East when the police crack down on unauthorised street vendors or when state authorities move to break up squatter camp encroachments on city boundaries. Social nonmovements are more about people improving their life-chances than about aiming at political reform, but if the opportunity presents itself, this dispersed activity can turn into more collective contention and organised mobilisation. The dispersed practices of nonmovements represent a submerged but powerful force for dissent which, Bayat argues, helped to facilitate the uprisings against authoritarian regimes in the Arab Spring (2010–2014).

Not all covert resistance is dispersed or unorganised, however. Egypt after the 2013 coup provides an example of more organised yet still hidden forms of contestation, which illustrates the point that while regimes of power structure the available options for resistance, they do not so much *eradicate* resistance as instead *channel* it (Scott, 1990; Mirshak, 2019a, 2019b). In Egypt, while the popular uprisings of 2011 succeeded in toppling the authoritarian regime of President Mubarak, in 2013 a military coup d'état saw the reimposition of an authoritarian form of semi-democratic rule under President Fattah al Sisi, characterised by restrictions on opposition parties, control over the media, prosecution of journalists and activists and a crackdown on the operation, registration and funding of civil society organisations (CSOs). However, resistance still occurs within this repressive context. Mirshak (Ibid.) draws on a more counter-hegemonic reading of Gramsci (1971) to suggest that hegemony and authoritarianism are never absolute and can always be challenged, though that challenge may have to proceed through covert resistance methods which are not overtly political or oppositional. Mirshak (Ibid.) argues that even repressive authoritarian systems seek some form of wider legitimacy, so al Sisi's regime still offers a limited space for civil society organisations (such as educational organisations, rights-based organisations and legal-support organisations) to operate. Within this limited space, many CSOs have adapted their activities, both to evade legal and extra-legal restrictions on registration and funding (by, for example, crowdfunding, registering as nonprofit organisations or legal firms or operating as unregistered initiatives) but also to pursue covert forms of resistance and contestation (for example, organised through activities such as readings groups, summer camps, cinema clubs or creating board games) which will not call the attention of the authorities. While not overtly political, these activities still allow many CSOs to advocate regime reform, defend human rights, challenge inequalities and provide critical political education (Ibid.).

Scott uses the concept of everyday resistance to reject notions of false consciousness and manipulated consent. He particularly attacks readings of the Gramscian concept of hegemony which sees subordinate groups as 'socialised into accepting a view of their interests as propagated from above' (Scott, 1990: 20). As Mirshak's (2019a, 2019b) work shows, Gramsci's work can also be used to explore the limits of hegemony and counter-hegemonic practices. But the central point still holds—we cannot assume that the absence of overt contestation means that there is no dissent or resistance. Scott argues that the 'public transcript' of power too often fools analysts into thinking that people's compliance means that they consent to their subordination. To assume this is to fail to look 'behind the official story' and to miss the 'hidden transcripts of power' which occur offstage and out of the sight of the powerful (1990: 5). If we just analyse the public transcript, we are 'likely to conclude that subordinate groups endorse the terms of their subordination and are willing, even enthusiastic, partners in that subordination', but public transcripts are strongly shaped by how the dominant group 'wish[es] things to appear', and it is in the interest of subordinates 'to produce a more or less credible performance, speaking the lines and making the gestures expected' (Ibid.). Scott argues that it is only by assessing the discrepancies between the hidden transcript and the public transcript that 'we can judge the impact of domination on public discourse' (Ibid.: 5, 6). Scott outlines numerous ways in which subordinate groups have been able to reverse or negate dominant ideologies, either by reinterpreting official values to carve out concessions from the dominant, by creating an alternative dissonant political culture in spaces outside the gaze of power or through hidden transcripts in which dissent is expressed but in disguised form (through gossip, mockery, double meaning and irony).

Scott does not doubt the existence of dominant ideologies, merely their *effectiveness* on subalterns. However, if dissent is typically covert, dispersed and disguised, there is a question of the extent to which not just the powerful but also other subordinates may assume there is wider consent (or at least little dissent) to social arrangements. Adnan's (2007) examination of the mobilisation of poor peasants in Daripalla, Bangladesh, in the parliamentary elections of 1986 offers another account of how covert resistance can become overt, which raises questions about how the visibility of dissent affects mobilisation. In Daripalla, cultures of dependency [1] meant that poor peasants often found covert forms of resistance safer; nonetheless, when an anti-establishment election candidate emerged, they switched to public support and mobilisation, successfully campaigning against the candidates of their powerful patrons. But their ability to overcome fear and transform 'deferential compliance into open disagreement' only came after seeing that 'support . . . was becoming increasingly infectious and *visible* among fellow poor peasants' (Ibid.: 204, original emphasis).

> Individuals picked up the courage to express their real preferences only after they saw others in similar positions doing the same, because the sense of collective participation made them feel safer when doing so. In other instances, the courage to show open defiance came from the strength of numbers and the collective bargaining power of the weak. (Adnan, 2007: 214)

Adnan (2007: 214) argues that the ability 'to cross a threshold of fear and insecurity' depends on a growing sense of shared dissent and collective efficacy, so that *others* showing increasing support becomes a mechanism of 'transmission' of resistance among the powerless. This emphasises the interactive nature of dissent and mobilisation, in which people's awareness of resistance can give rise to further resistance. This is not just a question of everyday resistance feeding the emergence of more organised confrontation however, as the transmission of resistance can also flow in the other direction, with collective mobilisations encouraging greater levels of everyday resistance (Lilja et al., 2017; Baaz et al., 2017). And we also must consider how strategies of resistance are shaped through the interaction between the weak and the powerful. In Daripalla, the strategies of peasant groups were also 'shaped by fluctuations in the nature and intensity of domination' (Adnan, 2007: 222), just as the 'strategies of domination used by powerful groups escalated from intimidation during the election campaign to use of violence and repression in its aftermath . . . [and] when the balance of forces shifted against them . . . they switched their strategy to one of conciliation and co-option' (Ibid.). So we must recognise 'flexibility and substitution in the strategies adopted by the weak and powerful' and consider 'the middle ground between everyday and exceptional forms of resistance' (Ibid.).

For Scott, the key issue is that the 'greater the power exercised over them and the closer the surveillance, the more incentive subordinates have to foster the impression of compliance, agreement, deference' (Scott, 1990: 89–90). Scott argues that subordinate classes are '*less* constrained at the level of thought and ideology, since they can in secluded settings speak with comparative safety, and *more* constrained at the level of political action and struggle, where the daily exercise of power sharply limits the options available to them' (Ibid.: 91, original emphasis). Scott therefore criticises the concept of hegemony for ignoring 'the extent to which most subordinate classes are able, on the basis of their daily material experience, to penetrate and demystify the prevailing ideology' (1985: 317, original emphasis). Arguing that we can only understand resistance and compliance in the context of 'real and anticipated coercion' (Ibid.: 244), he argues that the powerless are 'obliged to adopt a strategic pose in the presence of the powerful' (1990: xii). But Scott's analysis of everyday resistance typically focuses on 'extreme forms of domination — slavery, caste, serfdom, and jails' (Sivaramakrishnan, 2005b: 324), a world 'sharply divided between the powerful and the powerless' (Greenhouse, 2005: 357; Mitchell, 1990). Greenhouse argues that a sharp power binary is not essential to Scott's argument, but Lukes (2005: 130), who advocates a 'radical' notion of power similar to that of hegemony,[2] suggests arguments of everyday resistance only work in contexts characterised by 'overt coercion, compulsory appropriation and systematic degradation'.

The question here is whether the existence of everyday resistance in authoritarian contexts really undermines Gramsci's concept of hegemony, which was developed in relation to liberal democratic societies (Greenhouse, 2005: 359). Lukes argues that hegemony remains deeply relevant in situations where 'coercion is less overt or absent, and inequalities more opaque' (2005: 131). Again we see the suggestion that some societies (typically democracies in the Global North) have moved to more complex and sophisticated forms of power than brute force and where, since power relations are better disguised, people's consent to their subordination can be manufactured, in the hidden as well as the public transcript. But this division between authoritarian and liberal democratic societies often underplays the extent to which coercion, or its threat, remains a powerful organising force in liberal democratic societies. Nonetheless, it is generally argued that such societies have shifted away from repression or coercion to 'complex domination', with more 'managerial' or 'disciplinary' modes of regulation (Boltanski, 2011; Foucault, 1979). Does Scott's argument stand up in such contexts?

In fact, very similar arguments have been applied to contexts of 'complex domination', in situations of 'disciplinary' or 'managerial regulation'. Research on mundane resistance, often with a Global North focus, has grown within a range of fields, so much so that it can be argued that a new paradigm of 'resistance studies' has emerged (Johansson and Vinthagen, 2016; Bayat, 2000). However, this work often significantly departs from Scott's own formulation (Johansson and Vinthagen, 2016: 417). So before considering these adaptations, I look first at two examples of parallel arguments—in the fields of cultural studies and organisational studies—with considerable similarities to Scott's account of 'everyday resistance' but applied to (largely) nonrepressive situations of 'disciplinary' or 'managerial' regulation. These accounts—of the everyday 'tactics of the weak' (de Certeau, 1984) and organisational 'misbehaviour' (Ackroyd and Thompson, 1999)—make a similar argument: that noncompliant and subversive behaviour is widespread but neglected by analysts who have taken the 'official version' of situations at face value. One target for these authors is class-focused accounts of false consciousness and symbolic domination, but another target is Foucauldian-inspired accounts of disciplinary regulation. The argument is that both these frameworks (or, at least, particular interpretations of them) greatly overstate the extent to which inequalities and power relations generate either consent or docile subjects.

ANTI-DISCIPLINE AND 'TACTICS OF THE WEAK'

Based on an analysis of French society, de Certeau's work (1980, 1984) addresses the subtle, mundane ways in which ordinary people routinely resist systems of regulation from within, disrupting the logic of the established order. de Certeau attacks notions of the 'passive consumer' (found in Frankfurt theory critiques of capitalist consumption practices), which argue that mass production imposes a homogenised 'top-down' culture on consumers, creating false needs which bind people passively into capitalist consumption (Adorno, 1991; Adorno and Horkheimer, 1993). de Certeau refuses to see consumers as 'sheep progressively immobilized and "handled"', rejecting the idea that 'the public is moulded by the products imposed on it' (1984: 165, 166). He outlines the many ways in which people's everyday practices go 'beyond the limits that the determinants of the object set on its utilization' so that in acts of consumption (reading a book, watching a TV show, cooking) the consumer is always engaged in a creative process of 'making it one's own, appropriating or reappropriating it' (Ibid.: 98, 166). Here de Certeau distinguishes strategy from tactics. 'Strategy' refers to the actions of the powerful and to the control of the established or dominant order which shapes social spaces and sets systems of regulation. 'Tactics' by contrast are the 'art of the weak', the 'last resort' of the powerless, which 'must play on and with a terrain imposed on it' (Ibid.: 37). They are 'a manoeuvre "within the enemy's field of vision"' which make 'use of the cracks . . . in the surveillance of the proprietary powers' and so 'poaches' and 'creates surprises in them' (Ibid.).

> Innumerable ways of playing and foiling the other's game, that is, the space instituted by others, characterize the subtle, stubborn, resistant activity of groups which, since they lack their own space, have to get along in a network of already established forces and representations. People have to make do with what they have. In these combatants' stratagems, there is a certain art of placing one's blows, a pleasure in getting around the rules of a constraining space. We see the tactical and joyful dexterity of the mastery of a technique. (de Certeau, 1984: 18)

While focused on consumption practices, de Certeau makes the more general point that people's actions are never reducible to the established rules and structures within which they occur. On this basis, he criticises Bourdieu's account of the habitus as reductionist, downplaying the possibilities for tactical creativity and subversion which always remain open (de Certeau, 1984: 95–96). He argues that Bourdieu's theory throws a 'blanket' over tactics 'as if to put out their fire by certifying their amenability to socioeconomic rationality or as if to mourn their death by declaring them unconscious' and suggests Bourdieu's interpretation of practices in terms of field logics represents the same kind of symbolic imposition that Bourdieu attacks in the dominant symbolic order (Ibid.: 59). de Certeau also takes issue with Foucauldian accounts of disciplinary regulation for overstating the extent to which the 'grid of discipline' shapes and produces people's everyday practices.

For de Certeau, people inevitably find a *'way of using* imposed systems' (1984: 18, original emphasis), turning 'the actual order of things' 'to their own ends' (Ibid.: 26). In walking through a city, for example, the walker is constrained by the spatial order created by city planning which 'organizes an ensemble of possibilities (e.g., by a place in which one can move) and interdictions (e.g., by a wall that prevents one from going further)', but the walker always goes beyond the possibilities 'fixed by the constructed order', following shortcuts and detours, creating trajectories which follow 'their own logic in "the jungle of functionalist rationality"' (Ibid.: 98, xviii). For de Certeau, people's everyday practices always construct their own logic and space which escape the rules and boundaries embedded in regulatory systems, practices and cultural objects. He accepts that there has been an increasing disciplinary regulation of everyday life but insists that this is not the whole story, as people resist being reduced to the grid of discipline, and we can always identify 'cracks, glints, slippages, brainstorms within the established grids of a given system' (1980: 6).

de Certeau argues that because tactics are often 'miniscule and quotidian', analysts focused on a 'one-sided and obsessive' analysis of institutional mechanisms of regulation have simply been unable to see the practices which they think have been repressed (1980: 9). For de Certeau, resistance is endemic, but—echoing Scott's account of 'hidden transcripts'—such practices are 'tales of the unrecognised' and the 'murmurings of the everyday' (1984: 70). To properly recognise them, we must look beneath the surface of the established order in order 'to perceive and analyze the microbe-like operations proliferating within technocratic structures and deflecting their functioning by means of a multitude of "tactics" articulated in the details of everyday life' (Ibid.: xiv). Such an approach is made necessary by 'the clandestine forms taken by the dispersed, tactical, and make-shift creativity of groups or individuals already caught in the nets of "discipline"' (Ibid.: xiv–xv). But looking more carefully, we can identify a 'network of anti-discipline' in which people 'manipulate the mechanisms of discipline and conform to them only in order to evade them', employing 'innumerable practices' in order to 'reappropriate the space organized by techniques of sociocultural production' (Ibid.). The clandestine nature of tactics in de Certeau's account is less the consequence of coercive repression and more the result of people seeking to evade more mundane forms of regulation and constraint as best they can.

Because 'tactics' operate in the 'space of the other', de Certeau argues that they are opportunistic and operate in 'isolated actions' (1984: 37) as the 'guerrilla warfare of everyday life' (1980: 7). Tactics are ways of 'knowing how to get away with things' and are the victories of the weak over the strong ('whether the strength be that of powerful people or the violence of things or of an imposed order') (Ibid.: xix). de Certeau also suggests that everyday tactics not only *deflect* the gaze of power but can also *redefine* such spaces by deviating from rule-governed practices. So 'tactics of the weak' have the potential to reorganise the established order (Ibid.: 94–96). To illustrate this, de Certeau gives the workplace example of the practice of 'ripping off' (*la perruque*) in which workers use time at work for their own ends (e.g., writing a love letter on company time or 'borrowing' a lathe to make furniture for themselves), tricking the employer into thinking that they are officially on the job but subverting the rules of the space by turning a place of work into a space of enjoyment, for activities that are 'free, creative, and precisely not directed toward profit' (Ibid.: 25). de Certeau argues that there is a 'constant presence of these practices in the most ordered sphere of modern life' (Ibid.: 26) and that this way of 'using imposed systems'

> constitutes the resistance to the historical law of a state of affairs and its dogmatic legitimations. A practice of the order constructed by others redistributes its space; it creates at least a certain play in that order, a space for manoeuvres of unequal forces and for utopian points of reference. That is where the opacity of a 'popular' culture could be said to

manifest itself—a dark rock that resists all assimilation. (de Certeau, 1984: 18)

ORGANISATIONAL MISBEHAVIOUR

While de Certeau mainly focuses on cultural practices as 'tactics of the weak', similar forms of 'anti-discipline' have been observed in other social spheres, including the workplace. Reviewing a range of (largely Anglo-American) research in industrial sociology and organisational and labour process studies, Ackroyd and Thompson (1999; Thompson and Ackroyd, 1995) conclude that organisational 'misbehaviour' (defined as 'anything at work you are not supposed to do') (1999: 2) is endemic, continuous and 'incorrigible' to management efforts of control but—in a now familiar theme—argue that it is neglected and underestimated by analysts. This neglect is partly because post-industrial labour market shifts have resulted in a decline in more visible, 'expected' forms of worker recalcitrance (such as trade unions and organised industrial actions), leading some to assume that recalcitrance overall has declined. But Ackroyd and Thompson argue that such an assumption is false and can only be advanced because analysts have too readily accepted the 'official' version of how organisations work.

This intervention is partly aimed at organisational theory which suggests that the 'spaces' for employees to misbehave has declined with the introduction of new forms of workplace control and technical surveillance and new management discourses (such as human resource management and total quality management) which seem to create greater control over the identities of employees, constructing them as 'obedient bodies' (Mumby, 2005; Richards, 2008; Johansson and Vinthagen, 2016). As Mumby notes, while neo-Marxist research on organisations examined (certain kinds) of resistance to managerial regimes of control, these were interpreted as 'ultimately reaffirming the prevailing workplace hegemony', while Foucauldian-inspired studies similarly ascribed 'large amounts of agency to managerial forms of control and relatively little to the employees who struggle with them every day' (Mumby, 2005: 26, 27). For Ackroyd and Thompson, such analyses overestimate the effectiveness and control of managerial regimes, too often taking the 'official' version of organisational practices at face value and underestimating the agency, innovation and sheer bloody-mindedness of workers (Thompson and Ackroyd, 1995; Ackroyd and Thompson, 1999). They argue that it is necessary to look beyond the 'apparent consent' of workers to the formal organisation of capitalist employment and to explore the widespread misbehaviour occurring 'beneath the surface of the formal and consensual' (Thompson and Ackroyd, 1995: 615).

'Misbehaviour', for Ackroyd and Thompson, consists of 'non-compliant' or 'counter-productive' practices which deviate from the expected standards of conduct (as defined by management). A wide array of practices represent 'misbehaviour', including sabotage and vandalism, absenteeism, go-slows, time-wasting and 'soldiering', pilfering, bullying, harassment and sexual misconduct, rumour and gossip, practical joking, rituals and rites of passage, leisure practices conducted in work time, misuse of company equipment, whistleblowing, deceit and cover-ups, deliberate misinterpretation of official procedures, sarcastic counter-cultures and detached or cynical stances to management practices. The common element underlying these diverse 'misbehaviours' is that they all result from employees' attempts to assert their autonomy through informal self-organisation. As Edwards (2014: 215) notes, 'misbehaviour' is a concept that 'can only apply in a context of power inequalities in which there are attempts to direct behaviour as part of maintaining control . . . misbehaviour is about breaking the link between direction and expected response'. For Ackroyd and Thompson,

> people at work are not inert or passive. They actively engage with their work, developing identification with workmates and the activities they undertake. They adapt their conduct to what they experience . . . self-organization is active everywhere [and] continues to be of enormous importance to the experience of work and to the effect of management initiatives. People at work can and do make innovations in self-organization, both in response to what management does and independently. The behaviour of workgroups develops and produces new patterns of behaviour to which management, in its turn, often feels it has to respond. (Ackroyd and Thompson, 1999: 74)

Echoing Scott's argument of a 'hidden transcript', Ackroyd and Thompson present organisational misbehaviour as informally organised, generally not openly opposed to management practices and sometimes symbolically ambiguous. As such, it is often hidden from view. But too often in organisational research there has been a tendency to assume that the official, public face of the organisation (or what *should* happen) is what *actually* goes on in practice. This mistake is also made by managers. For Ackroyd and Thompson (1999: 74), workers' struggles for autonomy are 'often beyond the perception—not to mention the control—of management' so that 'managers often act unknowingly of existing patterns of self-organization' and that 'even when they do have some perception of what exists, this is usually far from being accurate and complete'. Even when managers *are* aware of misbehaviour, they are 'explicitly or implicitly involved in a recurrent cost-benefit analysis on whether, when and how to act much of the time' (1999: 81). For while management 'always seeks to regulate activity, other than in exceptional circumstances, it can only do so through a policy of partial accommodation of the self-organization of workgroups' (Ibid.: 87). Ackroyd and Thompson's review of organisational research indicates that the everyday functioning of organisations is heavily dependent on informal practices and worker self-organisation. As such, they see intrinsic limits to the extent of management knowledgeability and control. So even where management attempts to stamp out misbehaviour, 'employees innovate new forms of behaviour which exploit any weaknesses of managerial control' (1999: 96). As a result,

> the intensification of direct control does not lead to elimination of misbehaviour, merely to its deflection and adaptation. In fact it is typical for regimes to become locked into the perpetuation of particular forms of misbehaviour, and to promote and consolidate distinct (and often frankly resistive and uncooperative) ways of thinking and acting by employees. (Ackroyd and Thompson, 1999: 94)

Ackroyd and Thompson take issue with Foucauldian-influenced analyses of organisations which see workplace relations in terms of disciplinary power. They argue that such work is so focused on explaining how workers are controlled (as docile and useful bodies through the 'government of the soul') that it simply fails to see how workers resist such constraints and exercise agency. They are also critical of industrial sociology and labour process theory approaches which tend to frame misbehaviour as class resistance, seen through the lens of antagonistic capitalist relations. They are critical for several reasons. In addressing resistance as the product of capitalist pressures to transform work conditions for greater profit, labour process theory identifies inherent conflicts between workers and management but adopts a selective approach to workplace recalcitrance more generally. Ackroyd and Thompson argue that to focus only on the kinds of misbehaviour which can be seen as 'proto-class struggle' means ignoring less progressive forms of organisational misbehaviour — such as sexual or racial harassment or bullying. But viewing worker recalcitrance as only a 'rehearsal for class struggle' (1999: 52) not only misses the wider scale and scope of misbehaviour but also *fails to understand it on its own terms*. Misbehaviour 'should not be treated as a junior form of trade unionism or class struggle which should or will one day grow up. Misbehaviour is not an alternative to or better than these grown-up pursuits, it is just different, it is what it is and no more' (Ackroyd and Thompson, 1999: 164). It is never simply a response to managerial initiatives, since those misbehaving have their own aims and agendas, and their innovations often *prompt* managerial changes rather than simply reacting to them (Thompson and Ackroyd, 1995: 615).

Edwards (2014: 213) argues that the concept of misbehaviour can be a useful addition to understandings of social protest and social movements, not only because movement organisations have often employed tactics of misbehaviour as strategies of protest but also because behaviour that 'subverts the cultural pattern . . . rather than conforming to it, is the secret to changing the social order'. Edwards acknowledges that we need to distinguish noncompliance from resistance but suggests that it is 'only by separating out the "rebels" seemingly "without a cause" and the rebels with one' that we can 'explore the possibility of a relationship between the two' (Ibid.: 222). 'Misbehaviour', she argues, retains the assumption that misbehaviour can 'sometimes be a collective strategy used to express collective discontent, and/or employed in collective efforts towards social change' (Ibid.). Drawing on Goffman's (1967) concept of the 'situational impropriety' of 'everyday troublemakers', Edwards (2014: 232, 233) suggests that 'seemingly trivial acts of non-compliant behaviour (through body, dress, comportment, performance) in public situations can have destabilising effects' so that it is 'really in public realms that the everyday troublemaker realizes her potential to be the "destroyer of worlds"—at least symbolically'. However, the term 'misbehaviour' is not intended to replace the concept of 'resistance' but rather to focus on workplace recalcitrance *on its own terms* and to recognise a 'realm of workplace behaviour that should not be understood merely as a form or step towards what has become identified with the term resistance' (Ackroyd and Thompson, 1999: 163, 165). Nonetheless, in the proliferating work on resistance in organisations, 'many studies tend to equate misbehaviour with resistance' (Collinson and Ackroyd, 2005: 315).

WHAT ARE YOU RESISTING?

Scott, de Certeau and Ackroyd and Thompson all argued that mundane resistance had been neglected in social analysis. Partly in response to their interventions, this is no longer the case. 'Resistance' is a 'fashionable topic' across a range of disciplines and contexts of study (Hollander and Einwhoner, 2004: 533). For example, in cultural studies the focus of much work has been on how people creatively reappropriate 'imposed' cultural objects and trends, making them their own; in organisational studies 'the pendulum has swung more toward a focus on—perhaps even celebration of—possibilities for employee resistance' (Mumby, 2005: 21) while the form of political action most studied in peasant societies is that of everyday resistance (Kerkvliet, 2009). A paradigm of 'resistance studies' has also seen the theme of micro-resistance taken up in feminist and women's studies, queer studies, labour studies, identity politics, education, poststructural studies and studies of the urban subaltern (Bayat, 2000: 541; Mumby, 2005; Collinson and Ackroyd, 2005; Vinthagen and Johansson, 2013; Johansson and Vinthagen, 2016: 417; Lilja et al., 2017; Baaz et al., 2017). But what is striking is the diversity of understandings of 'resistance' on display. And just as strikingly, some of the concepts attacked in the initial debates (such as hegemony or disciplinary power) have re-emerged as tools for the analysis of resistance.

There is considerable disagreement about what it means to 'resist', with suggestions that the concept is used in an 'unfocused' way (Hollander and Einwhoner, 2004: 547; Johansson and Vinthagen, 2016: 417). Kerkvliet (2009) offers a definition of the common assumptions underlying work on resistance in peasant studies, a definition close to Scott's own:

> Resistance refers to what people do that shows disgust, anger, indignation or opposition to what they regard as unjust, unfair, illegal claims on them by people in higher, more powerful class and status positions or institutions. Stated positively, through their resistance, subordinate people struggle to affirm their claims to what they believe they are entitled to based on values and rights recognised by a significant proportion of other people similar to them. . . . Resistance involves intentionally contesting claims by people in superordinate positions or intentionally advancing claims at odds with what superiors want. Acts at the expense of other people who are in the same or similar boat is not resistance. (Kerkvliet, 2009: 233)

However, both of Kerkvliet's defining features—the intentionality and the upward orientation of 'resistance'—have been challenged or even abandoned in debates in other arenas. And an eclectic set of activities have been seen as 'resistance'. Scott, de Certeau and Ackroyd and Thompson adopted a deliberatively expansive strategy, arguing that if we look less restrictively, then the sheer extent of noncompliant and subversive practices becomes apparent, and it is much harder to argue that power is naturalised. Later work is similarly eclectic. Everything from revolutions to hairstyles, from poetry reading to armed struggle, has been described as 'resistance', with little consensus on definitions (Hollander and Einwhoner, 2004: 534; Bayat, 2000: 542). In the field of organisation studies, for example, Mumby notes that (in line with the poststructuralist perspective which has framed much research) there has been an increasing focus on workers' 'deployment of discursive strategies' to create resistant spaces against management, with examination of largely covert and nonconfrontational tactics such as irony, joking, 'bitching' and gossip, mimicry and parody, modes of dress, office graffiti and discursive distancing (Mumby, 2005: 32). More generally, there is no agreement as to whether 'resistance' has to be *intended* as resistance by the agents involved or whether it must be recognised as 'resistance' by targets or other observers (Hollander and Einwhoner, 2004: 544).

For critics, this eclecticism results in too broad a treatment of what it means to 'resist', with a risk of labelling too many expressions of difference, deviation or individuality as 'resistance' (Vinthagen and Johansson,

2013: 3, 17) or of confusing 'awareness about oppression with acts of resistance against it' (Bayat, 2013: 43).

> The fact that poor women sing songs about their plight or ridicule men in their private gatherings indicates their understanding of gender dynamics. This, however, does not mean that they are involved in acts of resistance . . . Such an understanding of 'resistance' fails to capture the extremely complex interplay of conflict and consent, ideas and action, operating within systems of power. (Bayat, 2013: 43)

Vinthagen and Johansson (2013, 16–17) argue that 'non-conventional' practices are not resistance if they lack the potential to affect power relations. But the difficulty here is that even the most banal practices of recalcitrance have this potential, because if enough people participate, there can be aggregate consequences out of all proportion to the individual actions themselves (Scott, 1989: 34; Bayat, 2013). Hollander and Einwhoner (2004: 544) argue that there *is* a consensus that resistance involves 'oppositional action of some kind', but this means our understanding of 'resistance' depends on *what* is being opposed and, for some, definitions of power (Lilja et al., 2017; Baaz et al., 2017).

Scott saw everyday resistance largely in terms of structural class antagonisms, whereas others adopt a more intersectional approach, rejecting a 'one-dimensional' notion of power 'fixated around a specific set of relations (such as relations of class, "race"/ethnicity or gender) or one type of conflict (for example, workers/capital)' which 'keeps one stuck with a one-dimensional, structural notion of resistance' (Johansson and Vinthagen, 2016: 424; Lilja et al., 2017; Baaz et al., 2017). This partly arises from arguments about the complexity of power relations, with multiple dimensions to inequality and domination that intersect but do not neatly align. But there is also an awareness that struggles for autonomy can adversely affect other subordinated groups. In organisational studies, for example, a series of studies note that the masculinist 'shop-floor cultures' of white male workers, which resisted management control by forging solidarity and enforcing informal rules, also often excluded or demeaned women or people of colour (Richards, 2008; Mumby, 2009).

Kerkvliet's insistence that acts of subversion that occur at the expense of other subordinates should not be seen as 'resistance' begins to look like an insistence on the moral high ground of resistance which is not easily maintained. Many writers reject 'dichotomizing resisters and dominators' because to do so 'ignores the fact that there are multiple systems of hierarchy' and 'individuals can be simultaneously powerful and powerless within different systems' (Hollander and Einwhoner, 2004: 550). Johansson and Vinthagen (2016: 423) argue that 'resistance does not necessarily need to be progressive' since agents of resistance 'often simultaneously promote power-loaded discourses' and people are always 'both the subject and the object of power' (Vinthagen and Johansson, 2013: 13).

The 'internal politics of subaltern groups' means we must acknowledge the possibility of 'domination within domination', rejecting a 'unidimensional' perspective on resistance and domination (Chin and Mittelman, 1997: 32).

These debates show an increasing adoption of poststructural conceptions of the nature of power and domination. Scott operates with a structural, neo-Marxist view of power and attacks Gramscian notions of hegemony, while de Certeau and Ackroyd and Thompson criticise Foucauldian-inspired accounts of disciplinary power. Yet later work on 'resistance' has adopted Gramscian notions of (counter-) hegemony or — more frequently — has taken a poststructural turn and adopted Foucauldian approaches to power. It may, at first sight, be surprising to find Gramsci and Foucault on *both* sides of the argument about resistance, but this is partly due to varying interpretations, in which different elements of the author's work have received emphasis at different points in the debate.[3] The use of Gramsci in resistance studies has tended to draw more on his concept of *counter*-hegemony than earlier accounts, while those adopting Foucault have been more focused on his statement that 'where there is power there is resistance' (Foucault, 1976: 95). As Bayat notes, it was partly the upsurge of poststructuralism 'which rendered micro-politics and "everyday resistance" a popular perspective' as Foucault's 'decentered' notion of power offers 'a key theoretical backing for micro-politics and thus the "resistance" paradigm' (Bayat, 2000: 541).

However, this poststructuralist, Foucauldian turn gives a different emphasis to what it means to 'resist'. Foucault (1982: 789) views 'power' as productive as well as constraining, shaping and directing people's action by 'inciting, inducing, seducing' rather than simply being a question of coercion or repression. Because power is 'everywhere' and 'comes from everywhere', there can never be a society without power relations and, unlike more structural accounts, power is not seen as something that can be eradicated by resistance (Foucault, 1976). Foucault sees power relations as 'agonistic', always producing resistance and struggle, since at the 'heart of the power relationship, and constantly provoking it, are the recalcitrance of the will and the intransigence of freedom' (1982: 790). For him, 'there is no power without potential refusal or revolt', and power always gives rise to a 'struggle against the processes implemented for conducting others' (2000: 324; 2007a: 201), what he calls 'counter-conduct'. But the aim of such counter-conduct is not the removal of all government but rather 'the will not to be governed thusly, like that, by these people, at this price' (Foucault, 2007b: 75). For Foucault, power as governmentality[4] is always linked to a continual search for 'how not to be governed *like that*, by that, in the name of those principles, with such and such an objective in mind and by means of such procedures, not like that, not for that, not by them' (Ibid.: 44, original emphasis), or, more simply, 'not being governed quite so much' (Ibid.: 45).

In poststructural accounts of 'resistance', 'power' and 'resistance' are always mutually implicated and constituted as struggles over subjectivity and identity (Lilja et al., 2017; Baaz et al., 2017). This represents an emphasis on 'the inevitability of resistance and its expression in everyday life', where people resist the constraints 'that flow from established social categories used to label and subject individuals to others' notions of who they are and should be' (Simi and Futrell, 2009: 90). Similarly, in organisational studies,

> while Marxist, class-based analyses situate the impetus for resistance within the inherent structural antagonisms of capitalist relations of production, discourse-based, poststructuralist approaches possess no such foundational mechanism. Instead, resistance is framed as a form of identity work; that is, social actors engage with organizational discourses as a means of securing a stable sense of identity . . . [and] self-formation becomes the primary impetus for resistance. (Mumby, 2009: 35)

This very different way of framing 'resistance' is not without its critics. The conventional objection to Foucault's approach is that if there is nothing beyond power, there is also no possibility of emancipation. For Ackroyd and Thompson (1999: 157), if 'power is everywhere . . . the impression can be given that it is a force from which there can never be any escape'. Bayat's (2013: 44) concern is that the 'decentered' notions of power found in much poststructuralist work on 'resistance' fail to properly recognise that power circulates 'unevenly', and 'in some places it is far weightier, more concentrated and "thicker"'. As a result, Bayat argues, the 'resistance' literature leaves little room for the analysis of the state and underestimates the extent of state power. But these limitations are not necessarily intrinsic to poststructural accounts of resistance since, as Foucault noted, 'to say that there cannot be a society without power relations is not to say . . . that those which are established are necessary' (1982: 791–92). Resistance, as counter-conduct, can still *change* power relations even if it cannot emancipate people from power altogether. Nonetheless, these criticisms raise some important concerns. If 'resistance' is everywhere, an endemic and ubiquitous feature of social arrangements, how is it that entrenched and severe forms of inequality and domination still persist? For sceptics, even if there is widespread subversion (or counter-conduct), it has not been too effective in the aim of being governed less or governed differently.

RESISTANCE, RESISTANCE EVERYWHERE?

For critics, work on 'resistance' reads too much into the ordinary practices of agents, wrongly interpreting them as acts of defiance, grouping too many activities under the label of 'resistance' and overestimating and even romanticising such practices. There are a series of overlapping objections: that an awareness, and dislike, of domination or inequality is not the same as 'resistance' to it, that many activities labelled as 'resistance' have little impact on inequalities (and can actually reinforce them) and, finally, that many activities labelled as 'resistance' are not intended as such but rather arise from the many ways in which people ignore or reinterpret the rules to cut corners and strategically manoeuvre their way through social arrangements. These concerns raise two questions: about the role of *intention* in how we understand resistance (is an act only 'resistance' if someone intends to oppose power relations?) but also about potential *effectiveness* (is an act only 'resistance' if it can transform power relations?).

The question of effectiveness is a significant one, because some commentators suggest many acts of 'resistance' pose no real challenge to power relations and, in fact, by preventing a real crisis, may help to prop them up. This theme—of the limited nature of subversion which only helps people to manage but not transform their situation—has already been encountered in Chapter 3. For Bayat (2000: 544–45), some activities interpreted as resistance 'may actually contribute to the stability and legitimacy of the state', and he suggests that the resistance literature too often 'confuses what one might consider as coping strategies' and 'effective subversion' of domination. Scott's critics also suggest that much 'everyday resistance' represents 'letting off steam' mechanisms which can actually prop up inequalities. For Gutmann, such practices help 'to achieve the practical acquiescence of the politically subservient to the social order' and show an 'underlying acceptance of society as it is—its inevitability if not its justice' (1993: 75).[5] Similarly, for some, workplace 'resistance' is better understood as survival strategies or avoidance tactics which help workers get through the day and survive the drudgery and lack of control that characterises many jobs (Noon and Blyton, 2007). The argument is that while mundane 'resistance' may indicate people's *dissatisfaction* with their situation, it does not really present a fundamental challenge to the system which produces it, and indeed by providing coping mechanisms for subordinated groups actually serves to reproduce their situation.

From this perspective, dissent and noncompliance are not enough to discredit theories of false consciousness or hegemony, because people's dissatisfaction with their situation is understood as, at best, a very limited understanding of it—in line with Willis's (1977) notion of 'partial penetration'[6] or Gramsci's (1971) notion of 'contradictory consciousness'. Scott argues that the widespread nature of oppositional practices shows that subordinate classes are sceptical of dominant ideologies (1985: 317). But if people are 'resisting' unintentionally or unwittingly propping up power relations, does this leave theories of symbolic domination on stronger ground after all? Certainly, Gutmann (1993) argues that Scott has an inflated sense of the acuteness of people's perception of their situation. However, we should be wary of dichotomising people's practices into resistance *or* collusion, *true* consciousness or *false* consciousness. Mumby (2005: 38) concedes that work on resistance has sometimes 'imputed social actors with levels of agency and insight that sometimes stretch credulity' but argues we must move beyond a one-sided emphasis on either resistance or control, as this runs the risk of viewing social actors in either a 'romanticized' fashion or as 'unwitting dupes' (Mumby, 2005: 38). By contrast,

> the richest and most powerful conceptions are those that transcend the dichotomy that sees resistance as either (a) the practice of a wholly coherent, fully self-aware subject operating from a pristine, authentic space of resistance or (b) the activities of social actors that are subsumed within, and ultimately ineffectual against, a larger system of power relations. (Mumby, 2005: 37)

For those sceptical of claims made in the resistance literature, we cannot overlook the fact that acts of 'resistance' 'occur mostly in the prevailing systems of power' (Bayat, 2000: 545). But there is a danger of dismissing practices because they remain embedded in power relations or are based on partial understandings of social processes. This places an 'impossible burden' on resistance 'by judging it in terms of its capacity to transform society' (Ackroyd and Thompson, 1999: 23). Practices of resistance are often not internally coherent and frequently have unintended consequences, and 'what seems resistant can turn out to be collusive, and apparent accommodation can produce possibilities for change' (Mumby, 2005: 37). Because of this, many authors influenced by poststructuralism favour an analysis of 'the mutually constitutive relationship between dominant power relationships and counter-conducts' in which the forms resistance takes are closely linked to 'the regimes of power against which they are opposed' while 'simultaneously practices of government themselves are shaped by the manner in which they are resisted' (Death, 2010: 235, 240). There are also structural versions of this argument. Adnan, for example, sees the strategies of contention between groups of the rich and poor in Daripalla as shaped interactively in a dynamic trajectory (2007: 183), while Ackroyd and Thompson (1999) indicate the dynamic interactions of workers and management as each creatively innovate in response to the other's attempts to subvert/impose control. For many authors, resistance and control are coproduced and exist in a dialectical relationship (Mumby, 2005: 31).

This complexity in practices of resistance means that the 'intentions, consciousness and articulations of resistance actors' must be understood as being at least 'partly formed by the powerful discourses in which actors are situated' (Vinthagen and Johansson, 2013: 15). While this complexity is sometimes perceived as actually accommodation, consent or contradictory consciousness rather than 'resistance', others insist that resistance 'is not always pure' so that 'even while resisting power, individuals or groups may simultaneously support the structures of domination that necessitate resistance in the first place' (Hollander and Einwhoner, 2004: 549). A 'single activity may constitute both resistance and conformity to different aspects of power or authority' (Ibid.). [7]

> Actors may also challenge their own positions within a particular social structure, while not challenging the validity of the overall structure. For example, in the act of denying the identity of the 'scrounger', chronically unemployed men simultaneously support the attribution of this identity to others. . . . Similarly, transsexuals resist their own gender assignment while accepting the gender system as a whole. . . . Individuals may choose to resist in some situations but choose not to resist in others. Often these choices are linked to the web of relationships in which any individual is embedded; some of these relationships may sustain resistance, while others may not. As Leblanc (1999: 17) writes, 'Resisters, after all, remain within the social system they consist'. (Hollander and Einwhoner, 2004: 549)

As Bayat notes, many authors in the resistance paradigm focus 'eclectically on both intended and unintended practices as manifestation of "resistance"' (Bayat, 2013: 543). But there are good reasons for this: since it is not always easy to identify the intent of an action (particularly if the intent is disguised), because actions may be ambiguous or derive from a complex set of sometimes contradictory motives but also because practices which may not be intended by agents as 'resistance' nonetheless have the potential to transform relations of power and inequality. For Vinthagen and Johansson (2013: 18, original emphasis), 'no *particular* intention or consciousness . . . is necessary in order to detect "everyday resistance"' since people 'intend or recognize different things with the same acts'. For them, the key issue is resistance as a practice 'carried out in some kind of oppositional relation to power' rather than an intention or an outcome (Johansson and Vinthagen, 2016: 418). Here the emphasis is on oppositional practices which have the *potential* to transform power relations, whether or not they are intended as such. But for others, it is important to distinguish acts intended as 'resistance' from acts which might look like 'resistance' but which simply arise as the unintended consequences of everyday practices.

RESISTANCE, ENCROACHMENT AND EVERYDAY MODIFICATION: THE INDETERMINACY OF PRACTICES

We have already seen that acts of resistance can, unintendedly, prop up relations of power and control, but it also seems that practices which 'resist' power relations need not be intended as such, and the transformation of power relations can also occur as an unintended consequence of other everyday practices. Some authors (Bayat, 2000, 2013; Kerkvliet, 2009) argue that we must distinguish practices *intended* as resistance from practices which might *appear as* 'resistance' but which are simply the consequence of people going about their everyday activities. They argue that even if people are cutting corners, or breaking or reinterpreting the rules, these activities often simply result from various forms of self-help or self-organisation. This distinction is often conflated in studies of 'resistance', not least because forms of self-help or self-organisation can have unintended yet very significant transformative consequences. The argument here is that the noncompliant practices which emerge from strategies of self-help or self-organisation do not necessarily indicate a wider sense of injustice or opposition to inequality or power relations. Nonetheless, very significant social change can arise from these strategies of self-help.

Kerkvliet (2009: 230) gives the example of how a major reversal of national policy on collective farming occurred in Vietnam 'without social upheaval, without violence, without a change in government, without even organized opposition'. In the 1950s in Vietnam, the Communist Party government imposed cooperative farming on peasant households, but these cooperatives rarely functioned in the way intended, with individual households doing most of the actual work. By 1988, the policy was abandoned under the pressure of the everyday noncompliant practices of villagers which led to 'eventual collapse from within of the collective farming cooperatives' (Ibid.: 231). However, Kervliet (Ibid.: 240) argues that this noncompliance arose from 'everyday modifications and evasions' rather than 'everyday resistance', because the subversions were generally not 'acts of defiance', with a variety of intentions in play. People took collective land for themselves 'out of a conviction that they could farm it better individually', or as 'preemptive measures' to get grain they presumed other members would steal because 'people did not trust one another', or from 'rivalries between neighbouring villages' (Ibid.: 237–38). This shows the 'large number of ways people make "paths" of their own rather than adhere to the ways officials prescribed', with such deviations variously arising from people seeking 'to make work easier' or because 'they felt entitled to stray from prescribed courses' or because they saw others straying (Ibid.: 239). Such practices 'convey indifference to the rules' but are 'typically things people do while trying to "cut corners" so as to get by. Although they may approach becoming, or seem at first glance to be, forms of everyday resistance, they are not. They do not intentionally oppose superiors or advance claims at odds with superiors' interests' (Kerkvliet, 2009: 237).

Bayat makes a similar point about 'quiet encroachments' in cities in the Middle East, in ordinary people's reclamation of public spaces through activities such as squatting, illegal use of public utilities and unlicensed street vending. Taken in the aggregate, these encroachments are subversive, even transformative, practices, but they are not intended as such and emerge from people simply trying to live their lives as best they can under difficult circumstances:

> In Cairo or Tehran, for example, many poor families tap electricity and running water illegally from the municipality despite their awareness of their illegal behaviour. Yet, they do not steal urban services in order to express their defiance vis-a-vis the authorities. Rather, they do it because they feel the necessity of those services for a decent life; because they find no other way to acquire them. Hence, the significance of the unintended consequences of agents' daily activities. (Bayat, 2013: 43)

However, while such activities may derive from struggles for self-help rather than deliberate resistance to authority, if dignity, self-determination or a decent life can only be achieved by deliberately flouting the rules, this is scarcely an endorsement of the authorities or acquiescence to the status quo. The point here is that people are doing what they can to change their situation.

Nonetheless, it is important to recognise that people break or bend the rules for a variety of reasons, and nor can we simply assume that breaking the rules is always positive. Rules, conventions and dominant values do not just reflect the interests of the dominant, because rules and conventions also secure the cooperative activities that underpin all social arrangements, and values also reflect wider principles which people see as important (Sayer, 2005b: 955, 958–59). Dominant values are also often the product of previous struggles over justice and recognition. So while resistant practices may occur in pursuit of autonomy, may reject a dominant cultural code and even be 'anti-establishment', this does not make them progressive. For example, Simi and Futrell (2009) discuss how activists in the American 'White Power' movement engage in a 'form of everyday resistance' by concealing their racist, white supremacist attitudes in social situations (at work but also in wider family networks) where there are strong conventions against the expression of racist views. These White Power activists conceal their stigmatised views and anti-establishment practices in order to avoid interactional conflict, with this disguise 'part of a struggle about identity, commitment, and the power to resist others' labels' (Simi and Futrell, 2009: 91). These racist activists are far from the kinds of subaltern Scott was describing, but Simi and Futrell argue that their 'mundane everyday struggles' demonstrate the same kind of 'creative capacities for "persistence and inventiveness" . . . under social constraints' that Scott had in mind (Ibid.: 106).

Neither are struggles for workplace autonomy and self-organisation necessarily positive, as Lipsky's (1980: 3, xii) classic study of 'street-level bureaucrats'[8] demonstrates. To manage funding and time pressures and large caseloads, these front-line public service workers adopt informal routines in order to cope with and simplify their overburdened work situation. However, their informal routines often subvert the formal policies they are meant to implement in ways which are quite destructive for their clients. Lipsky highlights the negative side to these struggles for autonomy because the coping routines of street-level bureaucrats result in the rationing of services and the control of clients (for example, by making access to services difficult, making clients wait extended periods of time, selective triage and the 'creaming' off of clients most likely to meet official success criteria rather than those most in need) (Ibid.: xii). Street-level bureaucrats retain discretion to resist organisational pressures because they are engaged in complex tasks which the formal rules and guidelines can only partially cover (Ibid.: 15). But their informal routines not only distort official policy and adversely affect clients they are also highly selective in ways open to abuse and discrimination.

In work on 'resistance', there is a tension between exploring practices capable of resisting or transforming power relations and yet also wanting those practices to be progressive. This has sometimes resulted in a tendency to romanticise efforts to resist control or else the adoption of a selective focus on only the 'right' kinds of resistance. Ackroyd and Thompson (1999) prefer to speak of 'misbehaviour' rather than 'resistance', seeking to avoid some of these pitfalls. 'Misbehaviour' emerges from workplace self-organisation but consists of 'non-compliant' practices which deviate from expected standards of conduct and so can comprise some frankly objectionable and far from progressive activities. Ackroyd and Thompson argue that focusing on only the 'right' kinds of resistance (usually that which analysts endorse) means ignoring more problematic forms of misbehaviour—such as sexual or racial harassment, or bullying—and failing to understand 'misbehaviour' on its own terms, as very specific oppositional practices occurring within particular contexts. They distance their concept of 'misbehaviour' from that of 'resistance', arguing that the 'non-compliant' practices of misbehaviour are not simply a response to authority, since those misbehaving have their own specific and situated aims and agendas. Hence, 'non-compliant' practices of misbehaviour need to be seen *on their own terms*, as attempts to assert autonomy through informal self-organisation in specific contexts in which 'the self-organization of small groups is, more often than not, highly restrictive in its identification of means and ends' (Ibid.: 71). A similar point, with a more poststructural emphasis, is made by Mumby (2005: 38), who argues that a focus on 'the indeterminacy of organizational meanings and practices' 'refuses a monologic reading that reifies practice as either resistant or dominant'.

Other analysts suggest that too many accounts reify workplace 'resistance' and 'control' because they 'mask the complexity of the everyday experience of work' and 'neglect the questions of who is controlling and resisting whom and for what purposes' (Button, Mason and Sharrock, 2003: 60). Such reification overlooks how workers 'may simultaneously resist some aspects of management control of their activities and nevertheless seek to perform their allocated tasks to the best of their abilities', doing so 'both in order to achieve organizational goals and to maximise the intrinsic satisfaction of their work' (Ibid.). For example, a study of call-centre workers (Lankshear et al., 2001: 605) found that even under conditions of high surveillance (calls were taped and monitored), employees developed their own relatively autonomous understandings of professional performance which prioritised customer care over high-pressure selling. Here workers adopted practices which followed some management-defined organisational goals but resisted others (Ibid.: 605). This suggests that the identification of practices as 'resistance' or 'conformity' requires closer attention to the specific contexts and relations of practical action.

Many of the theorists examined in this chapter argue that it is the indeterminacy of social practices which creates the space for discretion, nonconformism, dissent or misbehaviour. This theme is particularly apparent in the arguments of de Certeau, Ackroyd and Thompson and poststructural accounts of 'resistance'. People find ways of using imposed systems for their own ends (de Certeau, 1984: 18) because the indeterminacy of meaning (of any regulation, practice or object) means there is always space and play for manoeuvre and reinterpretation. The 'ambiguity and indeterminacy of meaning' in organisations means 'struggle over meaning is always open-ended', creating the 'possibilities for constructing alternative, resistant, counterhegemonic accounts of organizing' (Mumby, 2005: 33). 'Control can never be absolute and in the space provided by the indeterminacy of labour, employees will constantly find ways of evading and subverting managerial organization and direction at work. This tendency is a major source of the dynamism within the workplace' (Ackroyd and Thompson, 1999: 47).

But while indeterminacy is frequently raised as the explanation of how 'routine' forms of noncompliance are possible within systems of regulation and control, the problem is that the indeterminacy of rules means that *both* conforming and nonconforming practices require people to interpret the appropriateness of rules in context. Even when we seek to obey them, rules must always be constantly worked at and renegotiated. And much rule-breaking behaviour in organisations is not noncompliance but rather the result of people's flexible interpretations of how to apply rules in the light of larger organisational priorities. For example, Zimmerman's (1970) famous study of 'intake' receptionists at a social welfare unit[9] found that receptionists frequently deviated from the rules governing allocation. However, they were not deliberately breaking the rules but rather 'acting-in-accord' with them, making allowances for unusual circumstances (such as a case worker spending a long time with an applicant). Receptionists changed the formal procedure when they felt that the practical circumstances of organising their shared work task meant it was 'reasonable' to do so; they were engaged in a 'for practical purposes' ordering of their task activities, undertaking a 'reasonable' adjustment of the rules, which gave them a 'sense of "doing good work"' (Ibid.: 233).

The question of when rule-breaking is an oppositional act must be decided in context, but such indeterminacy also raises a fundamental question of how rules, regulations or codes can *ever* constrain people's behaviour. The answer rests in how the collective and situational steering of practices shapes notions of reasonable conduct. The broader point here, as Chapter 7 explores, is that indeterminacy is routinely resolved in our ongoing practical action through the collective work of social ordering and sense-producing we all engage in to anchor and coordinate social relations. So while indeterminacy *is* a problem for the intelligibility and coordination of action, it is a problem that people routinely resolve — situationally, interactionally and above all *practically*. As a consequence, people generally do not experience the social world as indeterminate but on the contrary as objective, orderly and durable. To understand the constraints of the social world, and also the space for dissent and resistance, we must look further at how coordinated collective practice is achieved and sustained — and also undermined.

In this chapter, I have explored the argument that once we look less restrictively, the sheer extent of noncompliant and subversive practices becomes apparent, and it becomes much harder to argue that power and inequality are naturalised. Work on everyday evasion, insubordination and noncompliance identifies widespread dissent and mundane resistance among subordinate groups but argues that this dissent has too often been ignored or underestimated because the activities in question fail to fit the collective, organised and explicitly oppositional forms of protest expected by analysts. Theorists of mundane forms of 'everyday' resistance argue that accounts of symbolic legitimation and naturalisation have too readily been taken in by people's *public performance* of compliance, failing to recognise widespread but more subterranean forms of 'hidden' discontent expressed through concealed acts of nonconformism, subversion and rule-breaking. Such dissent is concealed because subordinates often have a vested interest in avoiding open displays of insubordination. In more authoritarian or repressive contexts, subordinates must use ambiguous or disguised forms of resistance to limit the risks of more overt mobilisation. However, clandestine forms of insubordination also occur in less repressive contexts, the result of people seeking to evade more mundane forms of regulation and constraint as best they can. Research on misbehaviour, tactics, counter-conduct and insubordination shows that the everyday functioning of organisations and institutions is heavily dependent on informal practices and self-organisation which often elude the official gaze or control. Such work also indicates the situational, coordinated and interactional nature of dissent and rule-breaking, in which people partly base their behaviour on what others are doing, and can get away with, in given contexts.

But if indeterminacy and self-organisation are endemic, and subversion, misbehaviour and dissent widespread, this returns us to the question of why relations of inequality and domination are so persistent. One obvious conclusion—and a central argument of this book—is that relations of inequality and subordination can be reproduced without symbolic domination and in the face of people's dissent through various processes of practical constraint. However, as this chapter shows, many analysts resist this conclusion. Those who question whether mundane resistance is really a force for social transformation see it instead as a coping mechanism which helps people to put up with controlling social environments but which also allows that control to continue. This represents the 'thin' theory of naturalisation, where people's local acts of 'letting off steam' do not change their acceptance of the inevitability, if not the justice, of wider arrangements. But we must pay serious attention to such 'everyday' forms of evasion, insubordination and noncompliance, because if enough people bend the rules there can be aggregate consequences out of all proportion to the individual actions themselves, and even the most banal and dispersed practices of recalcitrance can have transformative potential.

Others concede that rule-breaking activities are commonplace but argue that these are not really intended as resistance but are simply practices of self-help or self-organisation. The implication again is that 'real' resistance only really emerges in dissent which is capable of challenging wider relations of inequality rather than dissent which is simply aimed at changing someone's immediate situation. We must certainly analyse people's self-help and rule-breaking activities *on their own terms*, locating them within their ordinary practical concerns and contexts of activity and emerging as part of their struggles to resolve their problems of experience. However, to focus on the scope of subversion as the basis of 'real' resistance is to miss a broader question. Whether nonconformity represents resistance, misbehaviour or just corner-cutting modifications for the purposes of self-help, such manoeuvrings show that people do not straightforwardly naturalise their social arrangements as self-evident or inevitable. Rather, people constantly seek to adapt their circumstances as they find them to their own practical purposes, even if their ability to do so and the scope of their actions depends on the situational constraints they encounter. I now turn to reconsider the nature of that social constraint.

NOTES

1. Systems of patronage in which local power-brokers, landlords and employers wield great influence on people's livelihoods and security.
2. Lukes's 'third dimension of power' emphasises the capacity of power relations to shape a 'false or manipulated consensus', preventing people from having grievances 'by shaping their perceptions, cognitions, and preferences' in such a way that they accept their position as natural, unchangeable or as having no alternative (2005 [1974]: 28).
3. And in the case of Foucault, differences in emphasis in earlier and later discussions of power.
4. Governmentality as a form of power is about attempts to regulate the 'conduct of conduct' and, as such, extends well beyond the state or state institutions (Foucault, 2007a).
5. For Gutmann, 'if the subordinate classes already understand their social existence and there is no mystification in the form of fatalism, the primary explanation of their tolerance of the status quo must be military' (Gutmann, 1993: 83). But this argument operates with a very thin notion of the constraints on the practices of subordinates, since, as we have seen in Chapter 5, people's tolerance of the status quo may be affected by a range of concerns and sanctions extending well beyond military coercion (or naturalisation in the form of fatalism).
6. Where the working class have a partial recognition of their exploitation but are unable to fully understand or reject the capitalist power relations which produce it.
7. They give the example of women's bodybuilding, which resists the gendered expectation that women will not be muscular but conforms to the expectation that women should be concerned with bodily improvement.
8. Such as social workers, police officers, housing and benefit officers.
9. Who were meant to allocate case workers to applicants on a strict rotation basis.

SEVEN
Making Sense of Inequality

In thinking through our sense of inequality, and the question of why people so often—yet not always—put up with relations of inequality, the answer to which this book has repeatedly returned is less one of symbolic legitimation and more one of the various kinds of practical constraint to which people are subject. This is not to deny the existence of symbolic legitimation but to qualify its significance in reproducing inequality, not least because there are substantial limits to symbolic legitimation or the naturalisation of social arrangements. The conclusion of this book is that relations of inequality and subordination can be reproduced without widespread consent or ignorance—people can be sceptical of dominant values and beliefs, they can feel discontent, they can understand the constraints of their situation reasonably well, and yet they can still lack the capacity to change it. All this points to questions of social constraint. But how are we to understand that constraint?

The 'orthodoxy' on this sees social actors constrained 'by supra-individual forces and structures which are external to and transcend the actors' standpoint' (Hughes and Sharrock, 2007: 248). Here we see two forms of constraint: that of external, objective social structures but also the constraint of the partial perspectives which actors can form of these structures. The idea that actors only have a partial grasp of the social structures they inhabit is linked to the concept of naturalisation, the 'widespread assumption across social science' that practices 'impose themselves by virtue of their apparent natural necessity' and are therefore experienced as 'immutable and universal' (Greiffenhagen and Sharrock, 2009: 420). For many analysts, social relations take on a naturalised, objectified quality which comes to control their creators. As Chapter 1 argues, symbolic legitimation then becomes transmuted into a form of objective, practical constraint, but one requiring symbolic demystification to overcome. If people 'naturalise' a practice, for change to occur it is necessary 'to unmask this mistaken "naturalness" of people's beliefs' (Ibid.). And because actors' perspectives are distorted, it is the 'task of social science' to help unmask the 'arbitrary' and socially constructed nature of the world (Ibid.).

This chapter considers a range of objections to such arguments and offers a very different understanding of constraint: one focused less on power relations or social structures and their naturalisation and more on the constraining and enabling features intrinsic to all collective practices, including egalitarian ones. It is only once we understand how shared practices are collectively sustained that we can see why people develop a 'realistic' sense of what is possible and so often 'go along' with practices they do not necessarily commit to or support. While social arrangements *are* experienced as external, objective and constraining, this is the constraint of nothing more—but also nothing less—than the social relations required to enable practical activity. Rejecting the idea that social agents 'are confronted by a distant autonomous . . . structure' which 'precedes and imposes upon the individual', society is here explained 'merely by reference to the great flow of interactions between innumerable humans' (King, 2004: 230). If institutions such as corporations, governments or economies 'are continuously produced by those who are continuously producing themselves as members', then our explanation of 'social reproduction in the production of institutions' must be found 'in people's beliefs, and in the public practices by which shared beliefs are coordinated in collective action' (Harré, 1998: 39, 40).

Here organisations, institutions, rules and social codes are seen as the continuous accomplishment of practical interaction, constantly worked at and renegotiated, always subject to ongoing interpretation, change and revision. This makes such institutionalised phenomena no less constraining, but it does mean that the nature of their constraint must be seen differently. As Hughes and Sharrock (2007: 247, original emphasis) argue, 'it is an obvious fact that very large and complex arrangements of *collective* action can be built out of face-to-face encounters' into the sort of arrangements that other analysts call 'structures'. However, we can only explain how these structures are 'created, stabilised and operate if they are understood as complexes of social interaction created, sustained and renewed through the process of ongoing social activity' (Ibid.). A focus on the continuous production of social arrangements also means that people must have a reflexive, calculative awareness of the constraints they face in complexes of social interaction. So while social phenomena are indeed constraining, we must avoid the 'temptation' of seeing the social actor as 'subject to constraints of which he/she is unaware' and which 'are at work even when the actor believes that his/her actions are free' (Sharrock and Button, 1991: 155).

To set out this argument, I draw on accounts of social life influenced by a distinctive set of philosophical accounts: chiefly pragmatism (Dewey, 1922, 1938; Mead, 1934) but also phenomenology (Schütz, 1962, 1964) and ordinary language philosophy (Wittgenstein, 1953). There are many tributaries from these philosophies into social analysis (Ferguson, 2006; Ogien, 2015; Rouse, 2007a), but here I focus on those approaches which most show this influence: interactionism, ethnomethodology, later theories of social practices and actor-network theory (ANT) as well as some more avowedly pragmatist analysts. Such work shows considerable differences, not all of which can be dealt with here. Instead, I draw out some shared themes to explore the question of subjective inequality in a set of arguments which mark a decisive difference from many of the other approaches considered in this book.

The first theme is the implication of the role that indeterminacy plays in social life, in which social meaning is inherently ambivalent and only becomes determined through its *use in practice*, from doing things in the world. Starting from the 'ambivalence of the meaning of all social phenomena' (Schütz, 1964: 227), all these perspectives argue—with some qualifications—that practical action routinely resolves this ambivalence. Secondly, in setting out *how* indeterminacy is routinely resolved, there is an emphasis on the continual active work of social ordering and sense-producing that people must engage in to anchor and coordinate social relations. This mundane work—an ongoing stream of accounting, anchoring, aligning, coordinating and sanctioning activities—is a key element in the constitution of orderly social arrangements (and in how they are transformed). Thirdly, because people establish shared meaning and orderly arrangements through their practical activities, this makes meaning and social order a situationally anchored process. Such approaches therefore adopt a sceptical stance to generic concepts of social 'structure' or 'power' unanchored to concrete social arrangements, rejecting the reification of social arrangements into an 'objective' reality which exists at a different level from people's practical activities. Finally, the argument that meaning is established in practical use also results in an emphasis on the situated, practical nature of *all* knowledge, where the understandings through which people conduct their activities always take a practical character. Because knowledge is for practical purposes, in which 'my thinking is first and last and always for the sake of my doing' (James, 1983 [1890]: 960), our practical activity 'enters into the construction of the object known' (Dewey, 1984 [1929]: 18). This idea—that knowledge is inevitably tied to, and limited by, the practical engagements of actors— has implications for how we assess not just the understandings of practical actors but also that of social analysts.

It might seem strange for a book examining the subjectivities of inequality to focus on such approaches, not least because their minimalist approach to social ontology sometimes results in accusations that they neglect, or cannot address, issues of inequality and constraint, structure and power. The charge is that they are so tied to actors' particularistic points of views and interpretative capacities that they are incapable of broader analysis or critique. As King (2004: 160) notes, such approaches are variously accused of 'idealism' (reducing objective reality to individual interpretations of that reality), 'individualism' (reducing social reality to the individual) and—because 'social reality is never independent of the way humans understand it'—of being 'uncritical' because analysts 'must accept the account of reality provided by any individual no matter how deluded or interested'. Most of these criticisms, however, derive from a mischaracterisation of the phenomenological emphasis in such approaches:

> Objectivists misunderstand phenomenology as a doctrine that argues that the world is experienced as subjective (with the implication that the experienced world is divested of objective properties). In contrast . . . phenomenology's starting assumption is that the world is experienced as objective, i.e., that it is experienced as possessing just those properties—of externality, independence, publicity, durability, immutability—that objectivists treasure. (Greiffenhagen and Sharrock, 2008: 88–89)

In what follows, I consider the implications of seeing the social world as the constant accomplishment of its members. Such an emphasis addresses 'how objectivity is present in experience' (Greiffenhagen and Sharrock, 2008: 79) but produces a very different account of *how* the externality, durability, objectivity and constraint of social arrangements are constituted.

INDETERMINACY AND THE EVERYDAY ACCOMPLISHMENT OF SOCIAL ARRANGEMENTS

The indeterminacy of social life is such that no rule, norm or social code has an unambiguous meaning that can encompass all possible situations—which presents 'fundamental concerns' for any conception of social life based on 'rules, norms, conventions, or meanings' (Rouse, 2007a: 501–2). Such indeterminacy is often used to explain how 'routine' forms of noncompliance are possible within systems of regulation and control, creating 'gaps' in such systems. But if indeterminacy is an endemic feature of social arrangements, how are regulation and entrenched relations of inequality so persistent, or indeed possible? Social situations *are* fundamentally ambivalent, but we do not generally experience them as such, because their indeterminacy is routinely resolved in and through our practical actions. So while some theorists see indeterminacy as creating the space for discretion, nonconformity or dissent, others point out that social orderliness is *constituted through* the practical methods people routinely employ to deal with indeterminacy. What are these methods? Wittgenstein argues that 'there is a way of grasping a rule which is *not* an *interpretation*, but which is exhibited in what we call "obeying the rule" and "going against it" in actual cases' (Wittgenstein, 1953, I, para. 201, original emphasis). So '"obeying a rule" is a practice' (Ibid., para. 202, 242) where rule-following ultimately draws upon 'agreement in forms of life'. As a result, the 'concept of a "practice" is then widely invoked in social theory to identify the locus of this background understanding or competence that makes it possible to follow rules, obey norms, and articulate and grasp meanings' (Rouse, 2007a: 503). Nonetheless, as Rouse (Ibid.) notes, there are disagreements over *how* social practices 'govern, influence, or constitute the actions of individual practitioners'.

Many practices are organised around *constitutive* rules, which define what a practice is. To hit a ball with a stick only makes sense as 'playing baseball' if we follow the procedural rules which constitute baseball as a game, for example. The mutual intelligibility of practical action often depends on such constitutive rules, which are constraining but in a very particular way:

> Such rules, in a sense, do not determine someone's conduct, but rather determine *what can count as* a particular kind of conduct in various circumstances. They have, therefore, a major role as *enablers* of such conduct. Although it is certainly true that, as such, they also play a *constraining* role, such a role is routinely of a *conditional* sort, such that, for example, *if* you want to do X, then you *must* do, *have to* do, A, B and/ or C. (Coulter, 2009: 397, original emphasis)

But not all social rules are constitutive, because rules feature in a variety of different ways in practical activity. People 'do not so much follow rules as use them, manipulate them, ignore them, invoke them, or invent them whole cloth for practical purposes—to instruct others, to explain behaviour in retrospect, to anticipate behaviour, to normalize behaviour, to restore temporarily disrupted order, to find fault, to repair damaged rapport, or, most generally, simply to describe behaviour as the behaviour-that-it-is' (Hilbert, 2009: 166). The appropriateness of rules is 'contextually decided according to the needs of the situation' and 'heavily dependent upon interactional sequences which define the social situation' (Frega, 2015: para 14). Rules do not straightforwardly direct people's activities but rather are primarily 'a way, or set of ways, of causing activities to be seen as morally, repetitively, and constrainedly organized' (Wieder, 1974: 175, quoted in Emirbayer and Maynard, 2011: 239).

Others point to another constituent feature of social practices: their collective nature where, in order to take part, we must take account of the *regularities* in how people perform a practice. Practices as organised constellations of material activities performed by multiple people (Schatzki, 2012: 14) represent 'standardized' activities, organised by socially typical 'practical understandings' (Reckwitz, 2002: 210). Such understandings become established through 'a recursive process where the repetition of performances, in a similar fashion, by a great many different actors, establishes a way of doing things which is constraining upon others who seek to participate in the activity' (Warde, 2016: 150). But practices are 'temporally extended patterns of activity by multiple agents', so there remains a question of how these patterns are 'sustained, transmitted, and imposed' (Rouse, 2007a: 503).

The approaches I focus on in this chapter argue that the ongoing practical requirement to resolve indeterminacy results in a myriad of coordinating, sense-making, checking, aligning, accounting and sanctioning activities. It is these routine, often unnoticed activities which constitute and sustain orderly social arrangements, enable and transmit coordinated practices, and impose a range of practical constraints on our actions. There are major consequences of such an approach for how we think about both inequality and our subjective sense of inequality. An emphasis on the ongoing active creation of both mutual intelligibility and social life points towards the major significance of everyday, mundane activities in which the 'insubstantial' stuff of practical, situated interaction is *constitutive* of conventions, rules, institutions and organisations and produces our sense of the external and constraining world to which we adjust our actions accordingly. While social life is made up of individual performances, these 'take place, and are only intelligible, against the more or less stable background of other performances' (Rouse, 2007a: 505–6), whose widespread repetition 'create the impression that there are proper ways to go about the business of everyday life . . . a sense of an external, "objectivated" social reality, features people mutually recognize, and around which they organize their conduct and their interactions' (Warde, 2016: 152). 'Despite being in one sense a reified and contestable impression delivered by many actual performances', these conventions 'exert power' by defining 'an orthodoxy regarding how people should proceed in their daily lives' (Ibid.: 152).

Not everyone is happy to found the obduracy and durability of social life in such insubstantial stuff as practical action. Some look instead to institutions or to how objective social structures shape embodied dispositions in order to explain this. For Boltanski (2011: 55–7), for example, the diversity of people's points of view means that 'reality' (people's construction of the world) is always 'fragile', and people are faced with 'radical uncertainty', with different interpretations of reality (of what is and should be). But Boltanski argues that approaches focused on practical action place 'too much confidence in the ability of actors' to reduce uncertainty and instead sees formal institutions performing this role (Ibid.: 54, 22). Institutions, he asserts, establish legitimate principles of organisation through the orderly nature of their arrangements which regulate acceptable performances and—by defining, categorising and reference setting—stabilise 'reality' via signalling activities which establish what it is, in the process reducing uncertainty (Ibid.). For Boltanski, the 'reality' institutions impose upon people permits 'agreement' about what is going on and how it is legitimate to act, providing an authoritative determination of the nature of social life.

An alternative account, but one which also rejects the idea that social formations are 'made, unmade and remade in and through personal interactions' is Bourdieu's (1990a: 130) account of the dispositional habitus. Bourdieu argues that it is people's structurally generated dispositions which generate the regularity, obduracy and durability of their practices, where any interaction 'owes its form to the objective structures that have produced the dispositions of the interacting agents' (1990a: 58–59). The dispositions that underpin any practice derive from the shared structural conditions of existence through which people develop their tacit 'know-how' of how to act. Individuals' doxic 'sense' of how to behave provides the 'conductorless orchestration' which enables 'practices to be objectively harmonized without any calculation . . . and mutually adjusted in the absence of any direct interaction or . . . explicit coordination' (Ibid.). As Rafanell (2013: 185) notes, this 'portrays individuals as operating in a pre-existing, pre-given configuration of the social world in which micro-level interactions are deeply shaped by structural factors' and where 'resistance can only occur under profound crises that reveal to the oppressed the "arbitrary" nature of the world'.

Both Boltanski and Bourdieu emphasise the naturalised 'objectification' of social arrangements, in which social relations take on the status of 'real objects' beyond the consciousness or control of actors. Boltanski (2011: 62) argues that as institutions establish 'the whatness of what is', they become taken for granted as an objective reality, concealing the arbitrary nature of their social construction. As Susen notes (2014b: 184), in Boltanski's account, it is because social experience is 'institutionally consolidated and because institutions are socially naturalized that the reality of the world is structured and the world of reality remains unnoticed'. For Bourdieu (1990a: 130), the 'objectification' of institutions 'guarantees the permanence and cumulativity of material and symbolic acquisitions which can then subsist without the agent having to recreate them continuously'. These 'objective, institutionalized mechanisms' 'have the permanence and opacity of things' and 'live beyond the reach of individual consciousness and power' (Ibid.: 130). I shall return to the problems inherent in such arguments of naturalisation later. A more immediate difficulty, however, is that neither structurally sedimented dispositions nor the authoritative determination of reality by institutions can actually resolve the indeterminacy of practices.

Take the role of 'institutions'. The authoritative defining, categorising and reference-setting performed by institutions still leaves us with the problem of the situational indeterminacy of rules, categories or codes.

From a pragmatist perspective, 'it is a mistake both to consider that we grasp the world, first and foremost, by relying on our description and categorisation of things and to assert that we totally rely on institutional definitions of the "whatness of what is"' (Quéré and Terzi, 2014: 118). It is also unhelpful to make abstract statements about the role of 'institutions', since we must 'distinguish various kinds of institutions' (Ibid.: 116–17). While 'institutions are contemporaneous ways of doing, saying, and thinking which prevail in a society' which 'found both the intelligibility of an activity and its concerted accomplishment', there is a difference between 'the "institutions of social life" (such as greetings), which order the social life, and the "institutions of the administered life", which "shape people"' (Ibid.: 117–18). *All* types of institutionalised activity 'shape interactions and social activities', 'structure the skills of social actors' and 'imply a constraining aspect' (Ibid.: 118). But formal 'institutions'—in the sense that Boltanski understands them—only 'play a small part in the process' of shaping how we behave and think, because formal institutions 'overlap with many established customs that can hardly be attributed to any identifiable instigator' (Ibid.: 118). Quéré and Terzi point instead to the great array of ordinary practical actions which work to 'define "normality"', 'establish, maintain, and restore order' (Ibid.). As Chapter 6 indicates, informal practices and self-organisation are as much—if not more—constitutive of organisational life as the formal, official determination of reality, and we must look to ordinary practical action to understand how social orderliness is established.

Quéré and Terzi (2014: 110) argue that the idea that uncertainty is 'radical and generalised' only makes sense 'if we consider certainty as a mere intellectual and subjective matter', whereas a pragmatist stance focuses on knowledge as *a matter of practice*, with 'certainty' understood as 'a *practical attitude* that appears as complete trust in the accomplishment of actions' (Ibid.: 110, 111, original emphasis). Boltanski 'rightly' objects 'to the existence of an agreement of beliefs' but 'ignores a possible agreement in activities that would differ from the agreement of opinions or points of view' (Ibid.: 108). Quéré and Terzi (Ibid.: 111) draw on Dewey's (1938: 490) point that agreement in activities should not be confused with the 'intellectual acceptance of the same set of proposals'. Agreement between people does not require a 'convergence of beliefs or opinions' but instead consists of 'agreement in action' about 'ways of acting and their consequences' (Quéré and Terzi, 2014: 111).

A focus on 'agreement in action' might point us back to the 'conductorless orchestration' of Bourdieu's dispositional account of practices. But the restricted reflexivity in this account creates difficulties in explaining the coordination and mutual intelligibility of practices. Processes of reflexive monitoring, active coordination and alignment remain crucial to any account of practices, because dispositional regularities in practices are still subject to the problem of indeterminacy (of identifying various performances as instances of the 'same' practice) (Brandom, 1994; Rouse, 2007a, 2007b). People must engage in practical work within interaction to establish and sustain practices as 'the same', which means that any coordinated practice depends on the mutual *accountability* of its constituent performances:

> A practice is not a regularity underlying its constituent performances, but a pattern of interaction among them that expresses their mutual normative accountability. On this 'normative' conception of practices, a performance belongs to a practice if it is appropriate to hold it accountable as a correct or incorrect performance of that practice. Such holding to account is itself integral to the practice, and can likewise be done correctly or incorrectly. (Rouse, 2007a: 529–30)

Here the bounds of a practice are identified by how performances 'bear on one another', in which one performance 'expresses a response to another, for example, by correcting it, rewarding or punishing its performer, drawing inferences from it, translating it, imitating it (perhaps under different circumstances), circumventing its effects, and so on' (Rouse, 2007a: 530). The production of 'agreement in practice' does depend on the dispositions people share, but it also requires practices to be actively coordinated and standardised (Barnes, 2000: 64). Even habitual, routinised practice requires negotiation and alignment:

> The successful execution of routine social practices always involves the continual overriding of routine practices (habits, skills) at the individual level. Think of an orchestra playing a familiar work or a military unit engaged in a march-past. Any description of these activities as so many agents each following the internal guidance of habit or rule would merely describe a fiasco. Individual habituated competence is of course necessary in these contexts, but so too is constant active intervention to tailor individual performances to what other participants are doing, always bearing in mind the goal of the overall collective performance. (Barnes, 2000: 55–56)

People must actively monitor, coordinate and align shared practices, which means that habit and reflexive monitoring are *intertwined* features of how uncertainty and indeterminacy are routinely resolved in practical activity, where 'to be calculative, individuals have to be creatures of habit' while 'routine action is a form of calculative action' (Barnes, 1988: xiii, 44). Reflection and habit are component phases of ongoing action processes, emerging through the sequential unfolding, coordination and governance of action (Dewey, 1922). We reflect and reconstruct our practical reasoning when taken-for-granted practice becomes blocked, but the uncertainties of practical action make such blockages frequent (Ibid.). Habit and reflection are 'functionally coupled aspects of one and the same interaction cycle' and 'shape each other mutually' (Jung, 2010: 155). In thinking about how practices are sustained, 'we have to think of individuals who know the routines, who calculate on the basis of what they know, who consequently act routinely most of the time, and who thereby collectively reconstitute the objects of their knowledge and confirm what they know' (Barnes, 1988: 44).

To focus on agreement in practice 'is to cite something public and visible, something that is manifest in what members do', in which people 'reconstitute the system of shared practices by drawing upon it as a set of resources in the course of living their lives' (Barnes, 2001: 25–26). But such agreement is only made possible because people 'are interdependent social agents, linked by a profound mutual susceptibility, who constantly modify their habituated individual responses as they interact with others, in order to sustain a shared practice' (Ibid.: 32). Agreement in practice depends on people being able to view their actions from the viewpoint, and expectations, of others—a process of both socialised subjectivity but also of reflexive monitoring, of self and others (Mead, 1934: 135). Yet it also depends on some 'public, institutionalized medium of coordination' (Harré, 1998: 40) and 'methods for sanctioning and modifying our individual dispositions to keep them in line . . . mediated by verbal commentary, criticism, and evaluation, e.g., by saying "you can't" and "you must"' (Bloor, 2001: 101).

To argue that the social world is the everyday, 'worked-at' accomplishment of practical activity has important consequences for how we view the nature of social constraint and for our view of the role of people's everyday sense of inequality in producing the obduracy and externality of social arrangements. This does not make the social world ephemeral or easier to change than in a more structural account of social affairs, however. The social world is certainly not *experienced* as ephemeral or easy to change. A view of social life as being created anew on each and every enactment means in one sense it must be conceived as 'inherently *provisional*', with institutional phenomena always understood as 'local, and in a permanent state of change' (Rafanell, 2013: 192, 195, original emphasis). But social life is always enacted in, and through, collective activity and via a series of practical constraints. This makes social life just as obdurate, durable and constraining as in any structural account—but these features are realised in a different set of ways.

NOT JUST A MATTER OF INTERPRETATION: THE CONSTRAINTS OF PRACTICAL ACTION

Interactionism and ethnomethodology focus on the great array of practical activities which produce agreement in action and constitute the orderly nature of social life. Here the durable and constraining nature of social life is achieved through the rules of etiquette and procedural conventions which help produce orderly interactions; in the reflexive monitoring, checking, aligning and sanctioning activities through which we call each other to account to sustain coordinated action; and in the ordinary accounts and descriptions through which we signal, recognise and constitute the mutual intelligibility of what we are doing. To argue this is not to suggest that there is no such thing as social structures or to claim that actors are 'free to act in, or form interpretations of, the world' (Greiffenhagen and Sharrock, 2008: 73). On the contrary, when people 'experience moral principles, religious truths, stable bureaucratic policy, or objective reality, they are experiencing something tangibly *real*: social constraint' (Hilbert, 2009: 172). However, such constraint is located in our ordinary practical engagements where people 'mutually recognize the fact that they are obligated to each other', and this recognition serves as 'an utterly concrete power which binds humans together and sustains even the most apparently objective institution' (King, 2004: 17, 232). Practices and institutions arise from the ways in which people 'together agree how they should conduct themselves . . . look to each other to decide on how to go on and . . . hold each other mutually to that decision' (Ibid.: 232). This is nonetheless highly consequential for relations of inequality and power:

> An institution is a short-hand and simplified way of referring to these complex networks of individuals, whose daily interactions and practices, constitute the institution . . . [but] the individual with whom we have to cope in institutional relations is supported by a vast unseen network of other individuals, who give that individual power over us. Since the relationship we have with an individual bureaucrat presupposes the existence of large numbers of people who all recognize the network of individuals which is the institution, and therefore, empower that institution, it seems as if we confront something wholly impersonal, un-individual and objective. (King, 1999: 272)

Despite their objective appearance, any well-established value, convention or social rule is underpinned by social interaction, where it is 'the social process in group life that creates and upholds the rules, not the rules that create and uphold group life' (Blumer, 1969: 19). If the meaning and operation of any rule or practice is contingent on, and emergent within, ongoing sequences of interpretative interaction, 'an institution does not function automatically because of some inner dynamics of system requirements; it functions because people at different points do something, and what they do is the result of how they define the situation in which they are called on to act' (Ibid.). But people are never free to interpret their situation just as they wish.

In one sense social conditions are a matter of interpretation. Drawing on Blumer's premise that people act in terms of what things mean to them, Harris (2006: 228, 226) notes that the influence of 'objective' social hierarchies is 'mediated by the interpretations of the actors', which requires a focus on how people 'interpret indeterminate situations as putative examples of inequality'. However, there are significant limits to people's ability to subjectively interpret their social situation, and interactionism does not suggest that 'any individual can define social reality in whatever way he or she chooses' (Hughes and Sharrock, 2007: 248–49). Chapter 5 has already considered arguments (some drawing on interactionism) that people's sense of their situation and the problems they face are very variably understood and framed. But this is not a question of personal interpretation. Social arrangements are 'supra-individual' ways of ordering reality, which constrain individual interpretations and practices and cannot just be 'thought away' (Polletta, 2003: 101).

The key issue here is not questions of subjectivity (or the individual's 'point of view') but rather the *intersubjective* interpretive schemes that structure social life, those shared and agreed upon aspects of our mutually experienced social world which make any practical action possible (Schütz, 1964: 227). The focus is not on 'individual interpretations of what they are about' but on the 'shared understandings which are necessarily drawn upon by the participants' (King, 2004: 231). Social organisation is '"built in" to the very perceptions of the social actor' so that 'their comprehension of events is fundamentally of events within a "known" and regular social order' (Sharrock and Button, 1991: 61). So 'social structure' is 'a *socially sanctioned* scheme of interpretation' with 'such schemes . . . *embedded* in social settings' (Ibid.: 165, original emphasis). Someone asking a question 'is only adequately identified as (say) a teacher asking a lesson relevant question of a pupil against the "known in common" background of "life in schools", where events are conceived as "events in lessons" and where relations are to be subsumed under the categories "teacher" and "pupils"' (Ibid.: 162). And as I consider later, the settings which shape socially sanctioned schemes of interpretation are *socio-material*, so such schemes of interpretation are additionally constituted through materialised arrangements in which understandings are embedded in mundane artefacts and technologies. However, let us first consider some further consequences of the practical and intersubjective character of interaction.

The practical character of interaction means that 'defining the situation' must be understood as the resolution of a problem 'embedded in and carried through in socially organized circumstances' which must be 'solved with others to . . . figure out what, practically, the social actor can do in the circumstances' (Hughes and Sharrock, 2007: 253). To see the social actor as 'a *practical* actor' 'is to highlight that the actor will be *practically* constrained' as the 'very notion of "practical action"' is 'of action under conditions which are not all of one's choosing, are unlikely to be all of one's preference, which are perhaps intractable to one's manipulations' and where any practical action entails '"coming to terms" with its circumstances' (Sharrock and Button, 1991: 155, original emphasis).

Practical activities must be coordinated, and while interaction is predicated on mutual obligations to the orderliness of interactional sequences producing 'self-sustained restraints' on what we do (Goffman, 1983: 5), it is also achieved by people 'constantly correcting, sanctioning, criticizing [or] approving others' behaviors which impinge upon the stability of social interaction' (Frega, 2015: para. 16). So

> ubiquitous to all encounters is the constant checking of each other's responses, based on signs of recognition, acceptance, deference, rejection, withdrawal of recognition, loss of deference, etc. Goffman in particular argues that humans are emotionally vulnerable to others' judgements and evaluations, but in particular to signs of approval and disapproval, seeking signs of deference and recognition and earnestly trying to avoid 'loss of face' . . . this effectively results in individuals' reconfiguring their differing tendencies when aligning themselves to others. (Rafanell, 2013: 197)

But joint practice also depends on the mundane practical 'methods' that people deploy to establish the 'intersubjective intelligibility' of their actions, by making what they are doing 'witnessable' and 'account-able' to each other (Garfinkel, 1967). People coordinate themselves 'by actively achieving a sense of knowing things in common' (Emirbayer and Maynard, 2011: 237)—organising their activities so as to make them 'detectable, countable, recordable, reportable . . . analysable—in short, account-able' (Garfinkel, 1967: 33). During 'a substantial proportion of their daily lives, ordinary members of society are engaged in descriptive accountings of states of affairs to one another', but these 'accounting practices' work to 'locate, identify, describe, categorize, analyze, or otherwise provide for the sense of practical activities' and are the means by which members rein in indeterminacy 'in the course of realizing practical actions' (Heritage, 1984: 136–37; Garfinkel, 1967: 249, 250).

Throughout this book, I have looked at people's sense of inequality through their perceptions, accounts and practical sense of unequal social relations. Many analysts focus on how people's subjective sense of inequality approximates to 'objective' reality, assessing why their understandings might be limited or distorted. Garfinkel's concept of 'accountability', however, emphasises the *constitutive* role of people's accounts and descriptions. From this perspective, the social world is 'managed, maintained, and acted upon through the medium of ordinary descriptions' (Heritage, 1984: 179, 137). Because people are engaged in a constant process of making their own and others' actions intelligible through procedural methods of accountability, they always 'design their actions . . . so as to permit others, by methodically taking account of circumstances, to recognize the action for what it is' (Ibid.: 179). Rejecting a representational view of such descriptions, the focus is on 'what the actors might be accomplishing in and through their acts of reporting' (Ibid.: 138). The accounts and reports which enable coordinated practice variously 'name, characterize, formulate, explain, excuse, excoriate, or merely take notice', but the result is that members are always aware that their activities are 'subject to comment' and so design their actions 'with an eye to their accountability, that is, how they might look and how they might be characterized' (West and Zimmerman, 1987: 136).

Because we are subject to this 'condition of visible accountability', our actions 'become designed and shaped responsively' to the constraints imposed by such visibility (Heritage, 1984: 117). Take for example membership categories such as gender, which are here seen as a 'managed property of conduct' 'contrived with respect to the fact that others will judge and respond to us in particular ways' (West and Zimmerman, 1987: 127, 140). Gender 'is something that one *does*', as an accomplishment carried out 'in the virtual or real presence of others who are presumed to be oriented to its production' (Ibid.: 125, 126, 140). If 'we fail to do gender appropriately, we as individuals . . . may be called to account', but in adjusting our behaviour accordingly 'we simultaneously sustain, reproduce, and render legitimate' institutionalised gender arrangements (Ibid.: 146). To be 'held accountable' is 'to stand vulnerable to being ignored, discredited, or otherwise punished' if one's behaviour appears inconsistent with expectations—so compliance with expectation is 'strongly compelled, because the threat or actuality of being held account-able makes compliance the least interactively costly option' (Schwalbe et al., 2000: 441). Crucially, however, to 'do' gender is 'not always to live up to normative conceptions of femininity or masculinity', nor does it mean endorsing those normative conceptions, rather 'it is to engage in behaviour *at the risk of gender assessment*' (West and Zimmerman, 1987: 136, 125, original emphasis).

Members here 'constrain one another' though 'they often experience the constraint as coming from outside the immediate setting—as policy, as tradition, as culturally mandated, as structural' (Hilbert, 2009: 171). But while they may be experienced as external, institutions, normative orders or cultural systems are not *entities* but rather 'an array of practical, self-organizing and self-investigating phenomena' (Lynch, 2001: 140). Social institutions and normative orders are constituted in, and sustained through, the accounting frameworks by which we 'recognize' the social world as 'what it is' and adjust our actions accordingly, with structural phenomena understood as 'emergent products' of the 'communicative, perceptual, judgemental and other "accommodative" work whereby persons, in concert . . . establish, maintain, restore and alter the social structures that are the assembled products of the temporally extended courses of action directed to these environments as persons "know" them' (Garfinkel, 1963: 187–88).

From an interactionist perspective too, 'the activity of individuals when referring to the social world is *constitutive* rather than *descriptive*' in which 'the referral of social realities possesses a performative force' (Rafanell, 2013: 188, original emphasis). But individual acts of 'referring, labelling and using categories' only 'acquire constitutive force when performed by an aggregate of interconnected individuals', so it is *the collective basis* of this referring activity which is key (Ibid.: 189). However, 'all of us as individuals help to construct the world around us by using agreed categories' in which, for example, 'a "leader" is who and what we collectively take to be a leader and refer to as such' with leadership 'a *social institution* which both shapes social practices and the individuals or groups who are named as leaders' (Gorringe and Rafanell, 2015: 9, original emphasis). For 'most practical purposes' the individual may neglect his or her own contribution 'to the social reality in which [he or she] believes' (Barnes, 1988: 51). But while the 'contribution of any given individual to the constitution of social objects may be minute ... the nature of that object will nonetheless be *wholly and entirely constituted* by the totality of the individuals in the relevant society' where, for example, the 'gang-leader is constituted as such by gang-members' actions' or the 'share-price is constituted by market transactions' (Ibid.: 52, original emphasis).

Such a 'performative' understanding of social institutions (Barnes, 1988; Rafanell, 2013: 182) sees institutional phenomena constituted in the 'dynamics of micro-interactive activity in which individuals align themselves to others' beliefs and practices ... permeated by the monitoring, controlling and sanctioning of differing individual tendencies'. Social ordering arises from 'the pressures people exert upon each other ... from calculative conformity and the calculative sanctioning of others into conformity' (Barnes, 1988: 42). Individuals 'know what the routines are', and this knowledge 'leads them to act so that the normative order continues, so that their actions figure amongst the phenomena through which others know the normative order and are themselves able to act in ways which take account of its existence' (Ibid.: 44). As a result, such individuals 'have a sense of living in an ordered social context, a context not merely intelligible and describable but one that manifests some degree of pattern and predictability at the level of action' (Ibid.: 45).

A focus on the collective co-production and co-constitution of social life is sometimes seen as a consensual view of social arrangements. But this is less a question of consent and more a question of people 'recognizing' and adjusting to the socially ordered context they negotiate (and so help constitute). People 'go along' with interaction arrangements 'for a wide variety of reasons', and we 'cannot read from their apparent tacit support of an arrangement that they would, for example, resent or resist its change' (Goffman, 1983: 5). People have 'a disheartening capacity' for accepting 'miserable interactional arrangements' with a 'willingness to accept the way things are ordered' (Ibid.: 6). Conventions serve as a reference for future activity, so often 'the easiest thing ... is for everyone to do what everyone knows is the way everyone already knows' (Becker, 1982:

56). This is entirely consistent with people performing practices grudgingly, cynically, perfunctorily, as a matter of rote or a necessary evil. Such grudging performances occur for a variety of practical, contextual reasons: because of the weight of expectation; because we know it will help those who matter to us; because it enables us to do something else that we do value; because we worry how others might react if we do not; or simply because taking part is easier than swimming against the tide.

Participants may evaluate a system negatively 'and yet, given the knowledge they possess and the calculative procedures they employ, still see their own individual conforming actions within the system as the best possible', 'adjusting to contingencies they find themselves unable to change . . . a matter of interacting individuals making the best of things' (Barnes, 1988: 41, 124). Barnes (Ibid.: 21) points to the weaknesses in theoretical models which see the 'uncoerced component' in people's acceptance of the status quo as the product of manipulated consent or approval.

> Approval is altogether the wrong kind of notion to invoke in the explanation of the persistence of large-scale distributions of powers. If our failure to assail and demolish the existing power structure indicates a general approval for its existence, then presumably we also approve the Bass Rock, or Ben Nevis, which likewise we have failed to assail and demolish. And indeed there is a useful analogy lying latent here. If we could understand the sense in which we tolerate the mountain, acquiesce in its existence, drive round it instead of hacking through it, we might have a template for understanding something of our toleration of a distribution of power. (Barnes, 1988: 125)

Arguments which focus on the continuous accomplishment of social arrangements by their members do require qualification however. Materiality is an intrinsic feature of such arrangements, with all social phenomena 'nexuses of human practices and material arrangements' (Schatzki, 2010: 123, 129). Practices are already pre-structured through the objects which are an integral part of them, and this material aspect to social arrangements also works to frame our view of the world (Miller, 2010). The material dimension to social arrangements is not ignored in work focused on interaction[1] ; nonetheless, ANT and practice theorists argue for a greater focus on the further material component in how people experience the practical constraints of social arrangements, influencing 'which practical understanding and, consequently, which kinds of social practices are possible' so that 'social order and reproduction can be adequately understood only when we realize their double localization: as understanding incorporated in human bodies and as understanding materialized in artefacts' (Reckwitz, 2002: 212). Here there are affinities with the pragmatist view of practical activities as a continuous *transaction* between organism and environment (Dewey, 1958 [1929]; Dewey and Bentley, 1949; Quéré and Terzi, 2011: 272), which requires a focus on how the success or failure of practical activities is also bound up with things, objects and artefacts. A similar transactional view can be seen in the emphasis in later practice theories and ANT that 'the body is not merely interactive with its surroundings, but "intimately" involved with it' (Rouse, 2007: 513–14). As a result, people's understanding of their situation is 'not "inside" minds or cultures, but embodied in worldly phenomena, skills, equipment, institutions' (Rouse, 2002: 79).

The 'objectivation' of practices is constituted in the interactional and intersubjective, but these are socio-material processes. However, this materiality does not make social structures 'real' objective entities. It is still the collectively held nature of practical activity which governs or constrains individual actions, organises the contexts that people act in and on and produces the 'intelligibility' of our world (Rouse, 2007a: 505–6; Schatzki, 2015: 6). But the process by which people 'know' and experience the environment in which they 'intra-act' is mediated not just by 'situated interactions among knowers' but also 'by models, skills, instruments, standardized materials and phenomena' (Rouse, 2001: 204). So our sense of groups, institutions, organisations and social structures as durable entities and 'real' social objects does not just result from the constant work of interactive ordering but also through the socio-material assemblages by which we stabilise social arrangements (Callon and Latour, 1981). Nonetheless, while the material constitution of the social world adds to its visibility and durability, there remain substantial limits to this objectivation.

THE MATERIAL WORLD AND THE LIMITS TO OBJECTIVATION

The material constitution of social life means social ordering is a process of *socio-material assemblage*, in which the 'ambiguity of context in human societies is partially removed by a whole gamut of tools, regulations, walls and objects' (Callon and Latour, 1981: 299, 284). This helps constitute the durability of social arrangements in time and space. But this is not an argument for objective social structures, though the 'reach' of social arrangements in time and space *is* sometimes said to require a structural account. For theorists like Bourdieu, a 'fixation on readily visible orderliness' misses 'a "reality" that escapes immediate intuition because it resides in structures that are transcendent to the interaction they inform' (1977: 81; Bourdieu and Wacquant, 1992: 62). The claim here is not only that interactions are constituted by wider processes or relations but also that interactors can only ever have a partial grasp of that wider context, so a focus on their perspectives is itself partial. I shall address the question of partial perspectives later. But what of the wider relations—social, spatial and historical—within which any interaction sits? Certainly, in focusing on the situated nature of practice, it is important to recognise that any situation 'is an extensive duration, covering past, present and future events' (Dewey, 1938: 228) so that any 'present situation is not confined to the circumstances and details occurring here and now' (Quéré and Terzi, 2011: 272). Nevertheless, an emphasis on the sites and sequences of interaction does not commit us to the view that actors are constrained only 'by the most immediate circumstances' (Hughes and Sharrock, 2007: 252, 253). An emphasis on situations of practical interaction

> does not imply that persons in situations have no awareness of larger-scale social arrangements. . . . Two persons, here and now, may comprise the site where the defining is going on, but it would not be adequately defined to exclude say, that they are employees of a major multinational corporation, managing its international financial transactions in order to figure out how the company will be placed in the event of a stock market downfall. The point is that 'large-scale social structures' patently do constrain people's actions, but they do so by virtue of their meaning, through the way they are defined and through the chains of interaction that make up the continuing affairs of collectivities. (Hughes and Sharrock, 2007: 253)

However, the durability and reach of social arrangements is partly constituted through the material artefacts which 'permit the link to be made between one place and another, distant, one'; through the 'sensors, counters, radio signals, computers, listings, formulae, scales, circuit-breakers [and] servo-mechanisms' which help practices to 'endure beyond the present, in a matter other than our body' (Latour, 1990: 103; 1996b: 238, 240). But this does not mean that such interactions are simply 'an activation or materialization of what is *already* completely contained elsewhere in the structure' (Latour, 1996b: 231). Rather the argument is that social practices comprise not only '"intersubjective" relationships' but also the 'things' that are 'necessary' and '"equal" components' of a practice (Reckwitz, 2002: 208). These material elements 'help to stabilise social order' because 'their behaviour is predictable' (De Vries, 2016: 91). Artefacts must still be interpreted and used, 'handled' as part of a practical understanding, but they 'do not allow any arbitrary practical use and understanding' (Reckwitz, 2002: 210, 212). So 'when human agents have developed certain forms of know-how concerning certain things, these things "materialize" or "incorporate" this knowledge within the practice' and things become 'sites of understanding, in the form of *materialized understanding*' (Ibid.: 212, original emphasis). As a result, material objects are 'resources' which 'enable and constrain' practices (Ibid.).

Latour points to the 'formatted' nature of settings (2005: 211), where the intelligible, orderly nature of social arrangements depends on the 'array of mundane artefacts and technologies' which help constitute and regulate our social experience as, for example, in the layout of a lecture hall which 'suggests where the teacher will stand and where the students will be sitting' providing 'a *script* for their actions' (De Vries, 2016: 85–86, 97). In work organisations, the corner office, the reception desk, the office cubicle, the cleaner with no space but the cupboard she keeps her equipment in, all represent the formatted socio-material nature of the setting—which do not just reflect or signal inequalities but also enact them—steering people's sense of the space of possible practices and shaping expectations. Their material component helps make 'socio-material' arrangements 'durable' and—literally—objectifies them. We 'delegate' force, rules or moral codes to objects and technology (the seat belt, the speed camera, the algorithms that calculate tax or welfare eligibility, etc.) which then regulate practices to some extent independently of interpretative interaction (Latour, 1990; 2005). Algorithms in welfare services, policing, finance and insurance steer decision-making in activities such as job, welfare and loan application screening, resulting in an 'automating of inequality' (Eubanks, 2018). This often occurs in opaque, unregulated ways which exacerbate disadvantage, for example in the algorithms which target disadvantaged postcodes for pay-day loan adverts or in the predictive policing algorithms which concentrate patrols in poor neighbourhoods (O'Neil, 2016). Such objects do not merely 'reflect' the social, as the process of 'delegation' to objects often exceeds their designers' aims, and the delegates impose behaviour back (Latour, 1990). For example, in 'audit culture' the metrics used to quantify performance 'come to have a life or efficacy of their own' in which 'things are no longer measured by indicators, but rather indicators establish targets to aim toward' (Strathern, 2002: 307).

Our sense of 'objectivated' social arenas also occurs through specific techniques directed at making the social world 'visible' as a 'totality'—though for very particular practical purposes. These techniques occur through the practical activities of 'oligoptica' and 'centres of calculation', sites where people engage in detailed, very specific observations to coordinate and monitor the activities relevant to their job, in the process producing 'sturdy but extremely narrow views of the (connected) whole' (Latour, 2005: 181). In a university, for example, the dean's office is an oligopticon—a site which, in order to monitor and coordinate the many activities of the university, 'sees a narrow band of other sites very well' (Schatzki, 2015: 12). Oligoptica 'are present in abundance' in accounting, management, business organisation and statistical services (De Vries, 2016: 96). Our 'objectivated' sense of social arrangements is partly constituted through such activities: in planning and timetabling departments, finance offices, court rooms, statistical agencies, and so on (and in the maps, charts, spreadsheets, algorithms, tax and planning codes they generate). So while our lives are 'made up only of successive interactions', we 'should not forget the multiple panoptica that strive each day to sum up' our lives, shaping our sense of them (Latour, 1996b: 239).

These mapping and connecting activities enable denser associations, so oligoptica are also sites of power, here understood as 'the ways in which actors are defined, associated and simultaneously obliged to remain faithful to their alliances' (Callon, 1986: 224). Power is constituted through social alignments (Wartenburg, 1990) in which 'one agent's actions effectively exercise power over another only to the extent that other agents' actions are appropriately aligned with the actions of the dominant agent', so that, for example, 'judges exercise power over prisoners only if the actions of bailiffs, guards, appeals courts, and others are *appropriately* aligned with what the judge does' (Rouse, 2001: 204, original emphasis). The presence and effectiveness of alignments depends on 'subordinate agents' efforts to resist or bypass them as well as dominant agents' attempts to utilize, strengthen, or extend them' (Ibid.). But 'the *material* mediation of power by its circumstances' mean 'tools, processes, and physical surroundings' all 'belong to dynamic alignments of dominance, subordination, and resistance', so that 'just as practices should not be reduced to *social* practices, power should not be reduced to *social* power' (Rouse, 2001: 204, original emphasis).

But while the socio-material nature of practices contributes to their objectivation and constraint, there remain substantial limits to this. Institutional phenomena may be durable, but they never acquire the status of objective entities, and the very nature of their constitution means they can never be beyond the consciousness or control of the people who collectively constitute them. Objects provide a form of 'mundane governance', but this is a messy and contingent process, and we should not overstate the durability they afford (Woolgar and Neyland, 2013: 38). Social and political factors are never simply '*built into* the objects or technology' because there is 'nothing obvious or "natural", "inherent" or "given" about the capacities of objects and technologies' which are only 'contingently enacted' (Ibid.: 38, 13, 14, original emphasis). Just like other social relations, we must 'apprehend technology as being in a constant process of interpretation and understanding' (Ibid.: 39), always embedded within relations of accountability, available for mutual interrogation as part of joint sense-making, and so 'dependent on routine, moment to moment interaction through which sense is made of the system, and accountability accomplished' (Ibid.: 32).

Despite its socio-material nature, then, social life is still continually 'composed, made up, constructed, established, maintained, and assembled' (Latour, 2000: 114), with these processes of ordering always an 'iterative, precarious accomplishment' (Müller, 2012: 386). Rather than seeing institutions, organisations and structural arrangements as 'already gathered entities', there are only 'endless attempts at ordering' (Law, 1994: 101), as 'behind the façade of organizations . . . a plethora of humans and things need to be coordinated and brought together to make an organization capable of acting' and so always require 'permanent stabilizing' (Müller, 2012: 379). Even 'the largest organizations, the so-called global players', are 'just made up of local interactions in the sense that they connect one entity with another' (Müller, 2015: 35). It is because 'Wall Street is connected to many places' that it is 'more powerful, overarching', but this does not make it 'a wider, larger, less local, less interactive, less intersubjective place' (Latour, 2005: 178–79). In practice theory, too, while 'formal and often authoritative agents are an essential component of the ordering and coordination of many practices', practices must still be performed, and while people 'display serious commitment to the proper conduct' of practices, performances are always 'continual improvisations within more or less precise or fuzzy parameters' (Warde, 2016: 45, 46). Institutions remain 'nothing more than nexuses and sequences' of socio-material practices (Reckwitz, 2002: 211, 213). If within an 'organization' some practice 'bundles' focus on management or governance, this does not mean these 'form hierarchies or lie on different levels'. Instead such 'governance bundles' 'simply add, amid and alongside' the maze of practices of an organisation '*further* bundles of practices and arrangements that are linked to these networks and, together with them, compose a larger network of linked networks' (Schatzki, 2015: 11–12).

Similarly, the vision and control of oligoptica are limited. Those 'who have collected, compiled and computed' our lives do not constitute a social structure 'above' us, because they 'work in control rooms that are themselves just as localized, just as blind' (Latour, 2005: 240). Latour emphasises their restrictions, generating narrow knowledge for specific purposes' (Latour and Hermant, 2006: Plan 24). Oligoptica 'gain in coordination capacities only because they agree to lose . . . most of the information' and constantly reveal 'the fragility of their connections and their lack of control over what is being left in between their networks' (Latour and Hermant, 2005: Plan 18; Latour, 2005: 188). These marked limits to any oligopticon's grasp provide 'the space we need to be able to breathe more freely' and help avoid 'both the megalomania of those who dominate the collection of traces, and the paranoia of those who think they are dominated by them' (Latour and Hermant, 2006: Plan 52, 18). Schatzki (2015: 13) further emphasises the limits of power centres, arguing that 'a large phenomenon is brought about through *all* the activities and events that compose' it, so that power centres 'are not any more constitutive of, and only marginally more responsible for' the existence of an institution than 'the other bundles involved'.

> Social life is vast, and power centres can only effect so much. Their spheres of influence are limited, and myriad actions in other sites (bundles) must be performed in order for social affairs to move in the direction power centres seek. . . . Power centres certainly play a role in

many, if not practically all, instances of such events. More often than not, however, nets of cascading chains of action simply pass through power centres, and the character of the latter as power centres is not essential to what happens. (Schatzki, 2015: 13)

Accounts of socio-material objectivation qualify, but do not substantially alter, approaches which see social interaction as central to structural phenomena, so that durable social structures are not monolithic entities or opaque forces but rather the provisional, worked at product of the continuous actions of many aligned individuals. For some analysts this is a source of hope. By showing how inequalities 'are "done" or accomplished' in everyday encounters, we can also 'disclose ways in which the workings of these principles of division can be "undone"' (Emirbayer and Maynard, 2011: 248). While 'individuals may seem powerless in the face of vast systems and structures like capitalism', the insight that 'collective shared identity and knowledge through social interaction is more fundamental' to such institutions reveals 'the power that collectives of individuals can and could wield' (Gorringe and Rafanell, 2015: 2). The implication is that we have all the capacity to change things and that collective action 'can alter social structures even without taking power' (Gorringe and Rafanell, 2015: 1–2).

For Harré (2002: 121), any attempt at social change aimed at 'mythic large-scale social structures' or changing the 'morphology of institutions' will be less effective than interventions aimed at 'the minutiae of the rules and customs that go into the management of the social practice constitutive of each and every social order'. The 'efficacious agents' in the social world are not social structures but rather the people who 'shape their world, creating social structures, by following the rules of social engagement or acting in accordance with them' (Ibid.: 199). If our aim is the transformation of society, 'the place to act is at that point where the people actually generate the roles and acts that are constitutive of institutions and other social realities' (Ibid.). This insight helps to explain the effectiveness of the dispersed 'nonmovements' discussed in Chapters 5 and 6 and shows how even the most disadvantaged and powerless can exercise 'power from below'. Collective practices, however constrained, rest on patterns of mutual dependence and alignment so everyone involved has 'potential power over others who depend on them' (Piven, 2008: 39). These patterns of expectation and cooperation provide resources and leverage that comes from such interdependence (Ibid.: 39, 5). For Gorringe and Rafanell (2015: 2, 11), the power of collective action is not limited to actions aimed at changing state power but also rests in much more dispersed practices of dissent and alternative expressions of value aimed at 'subtle alterations in social relationships and patterns of knowledge'. Exercising such capacities is difficult, but when these 'disparate and diffused practices of dissent come together, tyrants are toppled and new worlds are envisaged' (Ibid.: 11). So the key question is 'how we might co-ordinate dispersed individuals in order to achieve change' (Ibid.). However, knowing how things work does not necessarily make them any easier to change. The collectively held nature of practices makes them hard to alter, with no easy answers and no royal road to change.

RESTRICTED VISIONS, PRACTICAL POINTS OF VIEW AND (THE DIFFICULTY OF) CHANGING THE WORLD

Objectivist and pragmatist-influenced accounts offer different arguments about how to achieve progressive social change. Much social analysis which identifies 'objective' social structures argues that the forces shaping people's lives are masked, naturalised or simply extend beyond their awareness, so that to effect change it is necessary to unmask the socially constructed nature of the world. Pragmatism, by contrast, focuses on people's understandings as part of their practical activities and their struggles to resolve their practical problems of experience. Here a reconstruction of people's understandings will be part of the resolution of their problems, but such a resolution is never simply a matter of changed perception. Understanding our difficulties does not necessarily mean we can resolve them. Problems of experience arise from the routine coordination of practical projects of action, and their resolution also means addressing the practical problems of living in association.

Consider the 'naturalisation' of social arrangements, where the 'objective' constraint of social structures is related to the partial perspectives which actors can form of them. Here social relations take on an external, 'objective' quality and become seen as natural or inevitable. This is the basis for criticisms of approaches which focus on situated practical activity. The criticism rests on the assumption that 'if there is to be any external constraint on the actions of individuals then it will need to be external to their consciousness' (Hughes and Sharrock, 2007: 248). This is a perspective which treats the social actor's viewpoint as 'deficient' in comparison to the 'privileged picture of the social world according to the sociological theorist' (Ibid.: 253) and where the 'critical' role of social analysis is to reveal the larger social whole which is unavailable to ordinary actors. Such arguments abound in social analysis. When Bourdieu (1984: 244; 1990b: 130–31) insists we must uncover the 'structure of objective relations which determines the possible form of interactions and of the representations the interactors can have of them', it is because he believes that the vision that people have of their social world is restricted, carried out under 'structural constraints' as 'views taken from a certain point'. This is why he objects to social analysis influenced by pragmatism and its emphasis on the situated, practical and partial nature of *all* knowledge.

For Bourdieu, a focus on the 'primary experience of the social world' and 'the relationship of familiarity with the familiar environment' means only accessing people's 'unquestioning apprehension of the social world which, by definition does not reflect on itself and excludes the question of the conditions of its own possibility' (1977: 3). The analyst must 'break the spell, the *illusio*' of practice, with the 'rigorous knowledge' of critique requiring 'a more or less striking rupture' with 'accepted belief' and 'the tacit presuppositions of common sense' (Bourdieu, 1990a: 82; Bourdieu, Accardo and Ferguson, 1999: 620).

Boltanski also argues that because actors only have a partial perspective on their situation, the job of social analysis is to locate their 'socially rooted' 'partial critiques' in a wider perspective which recognises their understandings as those of people who are 'subjected to structures which escape them' (2011: 6, 43). Seeing the world from the perspective of actors in the midst of their practical activity limits us to 'descriptions from below', and a more 'totalising' perspective is required which grasps the constraints and forces that influence people independent of their awareness (Ibid.: 43–44). This more 'objectivist', 'overarching' standpoint can 'provide disadvantaged actors' with 'tools to increase their critical capacities' and 'help them to contradict the individualizing meritocratic representations that contribute to their fragmentation and hence domination' (Ibid.). For Boltanski, the role of critique is to 'unmask' institutions in order to give dominated actors a more acute 'purchase on reality' so that they can recognise (and challenge) the '*provisional* and *revisable* character of . . . definitions of reality' imposed by institutions (Ibid.: 129, 155, original emphasis). Such a 'systematic critique of a particular social order' (Ibid.: 6) eludes a pragmatist approach (and ordinary actors) because starting from the position of reality as it appears to actors 'tends to produce an effect of closure of reality on itself' (Ibid.: 45), in effect representing the acceptance of naturalised social arrangements.

Certain versions of practice theory make the same argument, as Greiffenhagen and Sharrock (2008) note, pointing to Lave's (1988) distinction between 'arenas' (external social structures) and 'settings' (the aspects of arenas which are accessible and negotiable to actors). Lave argues that focusing on practical experience cannot 'account for macro-social, political economic structures' because these are 'arenas' which 'individuals can neither create nor negotiate directly' (1988: 150). Using the example of the supermarket, Lave and colleagues (1984) argue that to emphasise the point of view of actors effectively adopts a partial perspective, limiting our understanding of wider social structures:

> The supermarket as arena is the product of patterns of capital formation and political economy. It is not negotiable directly by the individual. It is outside of, yet encompasses the individual, providing a higher-order institutional framework within which the setting is constituted.

> At the same time, for individual shoppers the supermarket is a repeatedly experienced, personally ordered and edited version of the arena. In this aspect it may be termed a 'setting' for activity. Some aisles in the supermarket do not exist for a given shopper as part of his setting, while other aisles are multi-featured areas to the shopper who routinely seeks a particular familiar product. (Lave, Murtaugh and de la Rocha, 1984: 71)

By contrast, pragmatist accounts argue that all knowledge (including that of analysts) takes a practical character, and our practical problem-solving activities inevitably shape and limit our knowledge of the world, because our analysis is always 'purposeful, specific, and limited by the character of the trouble undergone' (Dewey, 1982 [1920]: 161). But while people always have partial, situated perspectives on their social world shaped by their practical engagements with it, these practical engagements vary enormously. Whether such engagements produce perspectives on the immediate situation or its wider connections depends on the practical activity in question, and 'the difference between the "negotiable" and the "non-negotiable" is made within experience' and is inherent 'in the structure of action . . . conceived as practical' (Greiffenhagen and Sharrock, 2008: 88–89).

So an understanding of people's supermarket experiences as partial involves a detachment from the practical character of people's understanding and 'consists of redefining the setting against which an action is portrayed in order to change the sense of that action' (Greiffenhagen and Sharrock, 2008: 86). Rather than viewing a visit to the supermarket 'against the background of daily chores', it is 'reimagined against the capitalist system as a totality (therefore portraying the trip to the supermarket as an external necessity imposed by capitalism)' (Ibid.). Through this change in perspective, 'shoppers' understandings of their supermarket visits are transformed into *mis*understandings'; however, 'the source of shoppers' "misunderstandings" is not their subjectivity (and the implied objectivity of the analyst), but rather a result of the fact that the analyst has reframed the relevances against which shoppers' descriptions are to be understood' (Ibid., original emphasis). Those aspects of supermarkets which make them an 'arena' of capitalism may not be a routine feature of *shoppers'* experience, but they are routine features of experience for individuals engaged in *different practices*—such as shareholders, managers, architects, engineers or marketing people (Ibid.: 86). While these features of supermarkets may not normally be 'negotiable' by shoppers, they are not beyond their 'intelligibility' (with common taken-for-granted understandings of supermarkets as profit-driven, for example), and although they 'may be beyond immediate and direct control of individual shoppers, they are not necessarily *completely* beyond their influence' (Ibid.). However, this is fundamentally a question of people's practical activities and purposes:

> Things that are inflexible givens for a brief shopping trip are not necessarily such in the context of commitment to a collective project of boycotting supermarket goods and protesting locations. Lave sees the difference in negotiability in ontological terms, resulting in a difference between the supermarket as 'setting' and as 'arena', where the former is available to shoppers and the latter to sociologists. In contrast . . . the difference in negotiability lies in the nature of the practical tasks and associated means involved (for example, between making day-to-day purchasing selections in the light of one's domestic circumstances and participating in collective activities aimed at confounding corporate management). These differences do not reflect differences between actors and sociologists, but between different kinds of actors engaged in different kinds of activities. (Greiffenhagen and Sharrock, 2008: 84–85)

An emphasis on the naturalisation of social arrangements implies that if only people could understand the arbitrary, socially constructed nature of their situation then its constraint would be undermined. Bourdieu, for example, sees the stable reproduction of inequality resting in processes of naturalisation, arguing that 'genuine scientific research embodies a threat to the "social order"' because it unmasks hidden power relations (Bourdieu and Hahn, 1970: 15, quoted in Swartz, 1992: 260). Constructionist accounts make a similar point when they argue that to demonstrate the conventionality of practices indicates 'alternative possibilities' (Bloor, 1994: 21). The aim of constructionist analysis then 'is to counterpose contingency to necessity, that is, to demonstrate that practices could be otherwise', so that we can reveal 'there is nothing necessary' about them (Greiffenhagen and Sharrock, 2009: 410). Boltanski shares this emphasis, arguing that people are ambiguously situated between social experience 'as it is' (where the world is externalised and reified into an apparently objective 'reality') and social experience 'as it is constructed' (where the given-ness of the social world can give way to the recognition of how it is socially and variably constructed) (2011: 51–53). He believes people engaging in practical action have a low level of reflexivity, because they operate in a taken-for-granted manner which does not question their situation and engage in 'realistic self-limitation of protests' depending 'on the degree to which social reality succeeds in getting actors to believe in its solidity and internalize their powerlessness to change test formats' (Ibid.: 34). The analyst must help expose the provisional and contingent definitions of reality imposed by institutions, in which exposing their social constructed nature will help undermine them (Ibid.: 129).

By contrast, the pragmatist perspective sees practical activity as inherently reflexive, because all practical activity 'directs and corrects itself from within its accomplishment' with the reflexivity of action 'displayed in the development and organization of everyday activities' (Quéré and Terzi, 2014: 100). Quéré and Terzi (2014: 113–14, 111) caution against accepting 'too easily fashionable discourses about the "social construction of reality" . . . considering the world as a senseless fact, on which meanings are imposed', because our sense of 'reality' is 'primarily related to our practical participation in the world—that is, to the explorations and investigations in which we engage in order to deal with it', in which 'things of the world appear to us as they are through what they make to us (or with us) when we face them in events, objects, and situations' and which we cope with 'by learning from our experiences, our successes, our failures, and from those of others'. While for given practical purposes people often take their social arrangements as 'given' or self-evident, this does not mean that they 'naturalize' such arrangements as unchangeable, nor does it mean revealing their socially constructed nature will undermine them. People's practical engagements *are* often strategies of negotiation and manoeuvre within environments which are taken as given, but this does not preclude other forms of practical activities emerging aimed at changing that environment, which entail very different understandings of it, for example as a set of unjust barriers to be collectively challenged. However, such practical engagements depend on people's varying resources and opportunities for practical action, which are never simply a matter of perspective.

As Greiffenhagen and Sharrock (2009: 423) note, any form of social convention that is widely institutionalised is likely to gain default status and become 'self-evident' simply by virtue of its pervasiveness in our everyday affairs. However, it is 'not that we cannot imagine other systems 'but rather that, all other things being equal, we will assume that this is the . . . system in play' (Ibid.). As Chapter 6 indicates, insubordination, noncompliance and strategic reinterpretation of the rules are commonplace, and not just in authoritarian contexts but also in the supposedly naturalised environments of 'complex domination'. And regardless of whether such deviations represent resistance, misbehaviour or are just corner-cutting modifications for the purposes of self-help, they show that people do not straightforwardly naturalise their social arrangements. Rather people constantly seek to adapt their circumstances as they find them to their own practical purposes. However, their ability to do so depends on the situational constraints they encounter.

The emphasis on naturalisation treats powerlessness as a matter of perception, neglecting the role of economic clout, coercion and other forms of practical constraint in maintaining inequalities (Jenkins, 2000 [1982]; Swartz, 1997, Stones, 2014: 227). The counter-argument is that 'individuals and groups often see clearly the arbitrary character of power relations but lack the requisite resources to change them' (Swartz, 1997: 289). Too often in social analysis 'individual reflexivity and impetus to change are conflated' because 'most people much of the time do not have control over the circumstances in which they find themselves, nor do they consider as sensible alternative courses of action' (Warde, 2014: 295). An emphasis on reflexivity in social change overestimates the degree of personal control that people have and neglects 'the importance of context, an external, collectively accessible, social and cultural environment wherein the mechanisms steering competent conduct are to be found' (Ibid.: 295; 2016: 101). The key question is people's concrete situation and the constraints on their capacity to effect particular outcomes. However, I have argued that such constraints must be understood as the constraints of collective practical activities.

People are not wrong, deluded or duped if they feel their social relations are external and constraining. Social relations are collectively ordered practices, encountered as features of a 'known' and 'external' socio-material environment, generally experienced as constraining socio-material conventions and routines which people must pragmatically negotiate. If we feel constraint in collective practices, this is the constraint of the many other people whose routines and conventions form our social-material environment, shape our expectations and accountability and constrain our room for manoeuvre. Such constraint is real enough, because it is certainly not easily changed. However, such constraint is also always situational and practical.

Here the weight of the world holding us in place in our practices is the weight of other people—not just the powerful, privileged or those in authority but everyone who participates in a practice, for whatever reason, and who so help to constitute that practice as a durable, 'public' feature of our socio-material environment. The stability of social arrangements arises from 'the pressures people exert upon each other', from 'people themselves, holding each other into some degree of conformity in practice' (Barnes, 1988: 42, 43). Because every individual has 'an incentive to a high level of conformity so long as all other individuals manifest a high level of conformity', there can be situations where few members actively support a routine collective practice in which all are engaged, yet each calculates that the others will carry on the practice (Ibid.: 37, 42). Of course, the degree of support for given social arrangements is ultimately an empirical matter, but the point here is that the self-interested activities of the powerful or the privileged are less important in sustaining unequal social arrangements than the conformity of everyone else. Knowing that other people will disobey a conventional practice or authority can result in the cascading acts of noncompliance which sometimes cause the sudden collapse of even the most authoritarian regimes. Rules only constrain us if sufficient numbers of others follow them (Harré, 1998: 40) and it is only as 'long as people believe that these rules are in place' that 'the activities that display institutions continue to exist'.

In situations 'where subordinates are divided', each group 'will find it difficult to do anything but comply so long as it calculates the consequences of its own actions in isolation'; however, such arrangements are always vulnerable to 'concerted deviance or concerted innovation' (Barnes, 1988: 99, 42). Rafanell (2013: 191–92, original emphasis) argues that a view of social life as 'the result of a *continuous* process of learning, negotiating, using, and checking with and against each other our practices, uses of rules, categories, beliefs, norms' offers an 'open-ended' understanding of social arrangements as being 'always in a permanent process of modification'. But there are limits to people's capacity to take advantage of this fluidity, because of the 'role of the collective' in the 'constitutive dynamics of performative activity' (Rafanell, 2009: 64). From this perspective, 'the consciousness of subordinates does not need to be "raised" . . . so much as co-ordinated' (Rafanell and Gorringe, 2010: 620). However, coordinated activity which tries to change the tide of established convention is hard to achieve. 'Why is it that in so many cases the potential for concerted disruption never becomes actual? It is because to act in concert requires communication, shared routines, organization, direction, control, and such things are often both technically difficult and risky to establish' (Barnes, 1988: 43).

Of course, the powerful and the privileged try to shape calculations around concerted disruption, and where 'individuals face even just a small amount of ordered, routinized repression, the problems of a successful concerted resistance may be truly formidable' (Barnes, 1988: 43). And there is a further set of obstacles to consider. The 'context' which people seek to change cannot just be 'reduced to institutions, norms or rules' because it is also 'a socio-technical arrangement', so the notion of social practices as a form of 'self-fulfilling prophecy' must also take into account how the performative constitution of social arrangements 'goes beyond human minds and deploys all the materialities comprising the socio-technical *agencements* that constitute the world in which these agents are plunged' (Callon, 2006: 22, 17). Since social change means changing 'complexes of social practices', it requires 'not only a transformation of cultural codes and of the bodies/minds of human subjects, but also a transformation of artefacts' and the material mediation of power in tools, processes and physical surroundings (Reckwitz, 2002: 213; Rouse, 2001: 204).

For Harré (1998: 40), the question is if 'the social world is reconstructible by creating new narratives, rules and so on . . . why is it so difficult to achieve? Why is the post-revolutionary society so similar to the society it purported to this place? Why were Stalin and the KGB so similar to the Tsar and the OGPU? Why is the regime of the Ayatollahs so similar to the regime of the Shah? Why was Napoleon so like Louis XIV?' (Ibid.). One answer, of course, rests in the fact that formal 'institutions' only play a small part in shaping how we behave and think, as a great array of ordinary and unremarked practical actions also define normality and maintain and restore order (Quéré and Terzi, 2014: 118). To effect social change, these unremarked practical customs must be changed too.

> The social world is constructed above all by the innumerable repetitions of small-scale social interactions, constrained by all sorts of almost unnoticed normative constraints. Doing the everyday things, such as walking down the street, greeting people, serving the dinner, hanging up the coats on a rainy day, greeting among men and women, and so on, and so on, call out unattended normative constraints, *immanent in which is the old social order, and also the new!* (Harré, 1998: 47–48, original emphasis)

In this book I have identified substantial problems with forms of social analysis which attribute the persistence of inequalities to the limited and distorted understandings that people have of their situation. We must certainly acknowledge the ongoing symbolic legitimation of inequalities, but these processes are uneven and incomplete in their grasp and always contested. My argument is that the 'problem' of people's restricted sense of inequality is actually less important in reproducing inequality than most accounts have assumed. If protest, everyday resistance, noncompliance, insubordination and critique are widespread—and there is considerable support for such a claim—the implication is that relations of inequality can be reproduced without widespread consent. For this reason, I argue that symbolic legitimation offers a very limited explanation of the persisting inequalities in social arrangements. I adopt an alternative pragmatist perspective on this issue which locates persistent inequalities not in people's distorted understanding of inequality but rather in the practical constraints they experience within collective arrangements. However, this also means adopting a different understanding of constraint: one focused less on power relations or social structures and their naturalisation and more on the constraining and enabling features intrinsic to all collective practices. It is only once we understand how shared practices are collectively sustained and experienced that we can see why people develop a 'realistic' sense of what is possible and so often 'go along' with practices they do not necessarily commit to or support. Social arrangements *are* most often experienced as external, objective and constraining, but this is the constraint of the social relations required to enable practical activity, in which organisations, institutions, rules and social codes are the continuous accomplishment of practical interaction, constantly worked at and renegotiated, always subject to ongoing interpretation, change and revision. This makes such institutionalised phenomena no less constraining, but it does mean their constraint operates differently.

Ultimately, there are no surprises about how we can change the social arrangements we reject, but also no easy answers. If social life is a continual round of ordering activities which both afford but also constrain our practices, then we need to look at the particular features of the situation being ordered to assess whether that constraint is positive or negative (and who it might be positive or negative for). And if social life is produced through this ongoing stream of accounting, anchoring, aligning, coordinating, assembling and sanctioning activities which constitute constraining collective practices, we can only reorder it through the exact same kinds of accounting, anchoring, aligning, coordinating, assembling and sanctioning activities. However, while they may ultimately help to change the world, such activities will always be attempts to resolve the situated practical problems of our collective experience, to overcome the obstacles and conflicts, difficulties and dangers that we face.

NOTE

1. Becker, for example, argues that conventional practices cluster 'packages of mutually adjusted activities, materials, and places' 'all of which must be changed if any one component is', which steers practices, often conservatively, because of the additional costs (in time, energy and resources) to innovation (1982: 134, 32, 28). Ethnomethodological studies have also focused on scientific and technological practices (Livingston, 2008).

EIGHT

Conclusion

Analysing Inequality

In this book I have argued that the 'problem' of people's restricted sense of inequality is less important in reproducing inequality than many analysts have assumed. Instead, I have adopted a pragmatist perspective which locates the constraints of social life and the durability of unequal arrangements in the practical nature of action and the ongoing stream of accounting, anchoring, aligning, coordinating, assembling and sanctioning activities which are necessary to any coordinated practice. This does not deny the force of dominant practices and values on our lives but does offer a different account of how they take their force, through how they form the 'known' environment to which we adjust our own practices. People constitute institutionalised social arrangements and shared practices by reflexively and calculatively drawing upon them as a set of resources in the course of living their lives (Barnes, 2001: 25–26). This locates the durability and constraint of social arrangements not in people's 'misrecognition' of them but rather in their processes of 'recognition'. Because we must 'recognise' social arrangements as 'what they are' in order to organise our activities, we adjust our actions accordingly and, regardless of our opinion about such arrangements, in so adjusting we help to reproduce them. Here people's collective sense of inequality is a constitutive one. This also means that while social arrangements are durable and constraining, the very nature of their constitution means they can never be beyond the reflexive awareness of the people who collectively constitute them. And while collective social arrangements are hard to swim against, and even harder to change, it is always possible to change shared practices through exactly the same kinds of accounting, anchoring, aligning, coordinating, assembling and sanctioning activities.

While for given practical purposes people often take their social arrangements as 'given' or self-evident, this does not mean that they 'naturalise' such arrangements as unalterable, nor does it mean that revealing their true nature will undermine them. People constantly seek to adapt their circumstances to their own practical purposes, but, their ability to do so depends on the situational constraints they encounter. People's practical engagements *are* often strategies of negotiation and manoeuvre within environments which are taken as given, but this does not prevent other forms of practical activities emerging aimed at more wholesale change of that environment, which entail very different understandings of it. Inevitably, strategies of negotiation and manoeuvre depend on people's varying resources and opportunities for practical action; the key question is people's concrete situation and the constraints on their capacity to effect particular outcomes. However, such constraints must be understood as the constraints of collective practical activities. People are not wrong if they feel their social relations are external and constraining. Social relations are collectively ordered practices, encountered as features of a 'known' and 'external' socio-material environment, generally experienced as constraining socio-material conventions and routines which people must pragmatically negotiate. If we feel constraint in collective practices, this is the constraint of the many other people whose routines and conventions form our social-material environment, shape our expectations and accountability and constrain our room for manoeuvre. Such constraint is real enough, because it is certainly not easily changed, but it is also always situational and practical. There are significant consequences of such an argument, not only for how we think about both 'inequality' and people's subjective 'sense' of inequality but also for critical social analysis—which I now turn to consider.

This argument rejects the kind of social analysis that Livingston (2008: 860) calls 'sociologies of the hidden social order', in which there are forces underlying the 'appearances of everyday life' which are inaccessible to practical actors and which must be made accessible by the special procedures of critical social science. Here the role of critical social analysis is to compare people's (mis)understandings of their situation to some notion of 'objective' material structure, a structure which is epistemologically available to the analyst but not to the partial perspectives of most ordinary actors. This form of social analysis sets up a model of the epistemological superiority of the analysts' grasp of the totality of social arrangements compared to the situated and limited perspectives of practical actors and, for critics, represents a static form of social theorising which 'always knows best' and where the failure of people to act in the ways that analysts expect is taken as a sign of false consciousness or symbolic domination rather than as evidence of the problems in analytical models (King, 1999: 285). The approach adopted in this book has more sympathies with sociologies of the 'witnessable social order' (Livingston, 2008) in which social orderliness is not only observable by and reflexively available to practical actors but is also constituted through their knowledgeable accounting and reflexive and calculative awareness. That knowledgeability is, however, situational and inevitably tied to and limited by the practical engagements of actors.

But what implications follow on from arguing that society is 'a self-describing enterprise' (Greiffenhagen and Sharrock, 2009: 424) constituted by knowledgeable actors in which all knowledge is a situated practical perspective? If we accept that social arrangements are always observable by and reflexively available to practical actors, what role does this leave for critical social analysis? Does this mean that practical actors are always competent agents who can never be wrong about their situation? And if social scientific knowledge is simply another type of situated, practical knowledge, what authority can analysts claim for social critique?

There are certainly implications of this stance for general social theory. Pragmatism proceeds from the notion that the Western intellectual tradition 'erroneously directs us away from lived experience, from concrete practices, toward theoretical abstractions' (Emirbayer and Maynard, 2011: 225), and pragmatism itself 'shuns grand abstractions' in favour of 'directly and practically looking at the limited and local truths as they emerge in concrete experience' (Plummer, 2007: 5). This results in the stance 'that there is no such thing or entity as "power" in a universal, transcendental, sense', with power not seen as 'some kind of entity whose essence can be revealed or abstracted from its situations of use' (Dennis and Martin, 2005: 208, 200). Because the establishment of shared meaning and social order is a situationally anchored (largely) interactional process, this results in a sceptical stance to generic concepts of social 'structure' or 'power' unanchored from concrete social arrangements, which rejects the reification of social arrangements into an 'objective' reality which exists at a different level from people's practical activities. Nonetheless, we can still assess the accuracy of people's accounts and understandings of their situation, though such assessment must always connect to the shared social meanings which shape practices, requiring a more hermeneutic approach to social analysis as a 'fusion of horizons' (Gadamer, 1975: 73; King, 1999: 285–86).

The argument is not 'that individuals can simply create reality in whatever way they want', because people are always 'restrained and limited by the way others have interacted in meaningful ways' (King, 1999: 285). So while knowledge may be 'accepted belief, generally held belief', it is nonetheless *practical* knowledge and therefore belief 'routinely implicated in social action' which we check and validate 'by observing what others do' (Barnes, 1988: 56, 60), with our activities relying 'irremediably on the practical confirmation or refutation of hypothetical ascriptions social members make about each other' as they 'correct and adjust expectations in the light of circumstances' (Quéré and Terzi, 2014: 112). Because experience, understanding and knowing are all aspects of *doing*, any organism not only 'acts upon its surroundings' but also 'undergoes the consequences of its own behaviour' (Kivinen and Ristela, 2003: 365). So while there may not be an objective structure with which to corroborate understandings, nonetheless there are 'meaningful networks of interactions against which interpretations can be correlated' (King, 1999: 285). For example, we can still 'demonstrate that the beliefs of certain dominant groups are ideological because they consistently misrepresent and obscure their actual relations with subordinate groups'; however, such a critique proceeds not by making reference to objective social structure but rather by referring 'to the ways the exploited experience, understand and resist their meaningfully produced but material relationship with their exploiters' (Ibid.: 285).

There are also analytical consequences which flow from the self-describing nature of social life. Because the properties of social life which seem 'objective, factual and trans-situational' are actually the 'managed accomplishments or achievements of local processes' (Zimmerman, 1978: 11), we must 'analyse situated conduct to understand how "objective" properties of social life achieve their status as such' (West and Fenstermaker, 1995: 19). People do things in a way that makes what they are doing analysable for the practical purposes of doing them (Garfinkel, 1967: 1; Livingston, 2008: 840), so terms like 'power', 'class', 'bureaucracy' and 'capitalism' are 'not labels for unambiguously given objects in the world' but rather are 'normatively negotiable designators carrying implications and expressing commitments in every act of description or explanation in which they are used' (Coulter, 1982: 41). While concepts of power, gender, race, inequality and so on are 'ubiquitously part and parcel of the vocabulary in and through which we socially organise and make sense of the world', we must 'investigate them in the local and historical circumstances of their production' (Hughes and Sharrock, 2007: 254–55). Because such concepts are part of people's ordinary social ordering and accounting activities, they are 'misleading when used to represent the ongoing details of that process' (Rawls, 2002: 18). Latour (2005) similarly argues that social analysts too often mistake the process through which social arrangements are assembled and made visible for a fixed object that is being described. For some, this limits both the scope of social analysis and the warrant for the critical knowledge-claims made by social analysts.

The self-describing nature of social life (in which terms like 'inequality' are ordering and accounting devices rather than referents to real objects that can be more or less accurately described) has for some resulted in the ethnomethodological 'posture of "indifference" to the versions of society propagated by its members' (Hughes and Sharrock, 2007: 255). Ethnomethodology 'sees itself as having no disciplinary license to criticise or evaluate' members' views, and while this does not preclude critique, it is only as 'citizens' that analysts can take political and moral stances 'not as ethnomethodologists' (Ibid.). This means a tight focus on how people actually do things and through which the orderliness of immediate settings are produced and sustained (Livingston, 2008: 842). But other analysts who emphasise the self-describing nature of social life reject these limitations. They draw different implications from the fact that our practices as social analysts are not easily separable from our other practices as social actors, with analysts always situated within the fields they study. The 'aspirations and norms of social science' do have to be understood within a framework in which the analysts' 'social-theoretical accounts of practices' are 'continuous with the "self-interpreting" character of social practices' (Rouse, 2007a: 525). But for Rouse (2007b: 10), a normative conception of social practices as contested and always containing their own meta-practices (of assessment, critique and inquiry) helps connect the critical and analytical efforts of social theorists to those of practical actors. The theorist's interpretation is, of course, ' itself situated within her own field of significant action' so 'her account will never reach completion or closure', but this does not mean that it is 'thereby rendered pointless', because the point of social theory 'is itself situated within the field of ongoing activity to which it contributes' (Rouse, 2007a: 525). Here critical reflection

> arises from within our practices of communication, understanding, production and exchange, and governance, that is, from the midst of our complex causal intra-actions in partly shared circumstances. Such reflections attempt to express what is already at issue and at stake in those practices, and they are accountable to the very issues and stakes they seek to articulate. There is no god's-eye view that offers a definitive standpoint from which to discern what those stakes really are. There are only ongoing efforts to forge a viable future together from within a shared but contested past and present. (Rouse, 2007b: 10)

For Rouse (2007b: 10), a normative conception of social practices as contested and always containing their own meta-practices helps us to understand how the analyses of social theorists can 'acquire authority and force'. The normative constitution of practices means they are always 'directed toward one another as mutually accountable to common stakes, albeit stakes whose correct formulation is always at issue within the practice' (Rouse, 2007b: 8). The normative accountability of practices means that the meaning of a practice is 'bound up with its *significance*, i.e., with what is at issue and at stake in the practice, to whom or what it *matters*, and hence with how the practice is *appropriately* or *perspicuously* described (Rouse, 2001: 202, original emphasis). If we emphasise the normative nature of practices, there can be no standpoint of 'epistemic sovereignty', 'outside' or 'above' practices through which we can 'establish or undermine their legitimacy once and for all' (Rouse, 2001: 205). But this does not prevent the force of critique; on the contrary it secures it. Hegemonic ideologies are always 'open to subversive readings', and there will always be 'conflicting interpretations' and 'marginal and alternative ways of knowing', all of which have the 'potential to support critical perspectives upon dominant practices of justification', and it is 'precisely because there are no self-certifying epistemic foundations immune from criticism' that dominant justifications 'can never be finally secured against alternative interpretations (Rouse, 2001: 207).

> An appropriate response to worries about irresistible power and seamless ideology is thus not to seek secure grounds for criticism, but to engage the specific forms of domination that seem troubling, to articulate insightful and effective criticisms of them, and to forge specific alignments and solidarities with others who might come to share such concerns. This . . . calls for a thicker conception of reflexivity than has usually been articulated. . . . Reflexivity has moral and political as well as rhetorical and epistemological dimensions: what do our writings and sayings *do*? To whom do we speak? What other voices and concerns do we acknowledge, make room for, or foreclose? Which tendencies and alignments do we reinforce and which do we challenge? Above all, to whom are we accountable? (Rouse, 2001: 207)

Latour sees ANT as a 'direct descendant' ethnomethodology (2003: 410) and shares the view that academic social analysis is simply another situated perspective undertaken for specific practical purposes—just one more resource among many in the assemblage of social arrangements. Rather than being 'an accurate description of what is happening out there' produced from a 'God's-eye privileged position', most social science is just 'one of many "master narratives" competing in the daily intricacies of practices for accountability with many other interpretations generated by the actors' (Latour, 2003: 41). However, 'there is no other way to build a society than thrashing out . . . constantly new interpretations of what gathers us together', and it is because of this that social theories can provide another resource for (re)assembling the social, albeit one 'competing on the ground' with many others, 'most of them more powerful, produced by the "actors themselves"' (Ibid.: 41). For Latour, this 'does not mean that social theories are not useful, respectable and accurate; it just means that they add their influence, detours, interpretations to the plot which they can in no way explain or replace' (2003: 41). The social sciences 'post-Garfinkel' are still connected to a political project, but it is precisely *because* 'society does not exist as a *sui generis* entity but as what has to be locally achieved' that social science can contribute to this local achievement (2003: 41). Thus, the 'pragmatic test' is to see whether social analysis 'does make a difference or not for the emergence of a public assembled along different lines' (Ibid.: 41–42).

What are the implications of such a pragmatic test for social analysis? Pragmatism eschews the ontological and epistemological prescriptions that proponents of ethnomethodology, ANT and practice theory are sometimes prone to as an unnecessary restriction on the problems and methods of inquiry. From a pragmatist perspective, inquiry is related to problem-solving in general, so 'inquiry is part of all social practice', and the relations between academic and lay inquiry are formed through collective efforts to resolve practical problems of experience (Bohmann, 1999: 461). Practical experience is also inherently normative, so a focus on the practical accomplishment of activities must also focus on the 'constitution and resolution of public problems' (Quéré and Terzi, 2011: 274, 272) and cannot exclude public and political experience. Nor is there any need for a god's-eye perspective from which to assess knowledge or engage in critique. Since knowledge is a tool for doing things within given situations, its validation derives from its practical use in which we must 'judge any idea by its consequences' (Dewey, 1948: 163). Because of the centrality of practice in pragmatism, 'the fact that everything is practical and can only be weighed in action', all theories are assessed as 'tools for action' (Kivinen and Piiroinen, 2006: 319). This results in 'a practical, problem-driven way of understanding social sciences' where social scientific conceptualisations 'must be operationalizable to things to be done' and their validity assessed 'by trying to act accordingly' (Kivinen and Piiroinen, 2006: 322).

However, such a stance is emphatically not an instrumental or technocratic approach to social science, in which experts must provide the solutions to ordinary people's problems. Firstly, inquiry is related to problem-solving in general and is a part of all social practice (Bohmann, 1999: 461), so there is no epistemological distinction between lay and scientific forms of knowledge; rather their differences are simply a question of different forms of practical engagement. For pragmatism, the success of scientific practice does not rest in its epistemological superiority or the more overarching or detached standpoint it adopts compared to the situated perspectives of ordinary practical actors. Rather the success of scientific inquiry rests in its democratic organisation, in which problems are resolved not by recourse to authority but by the inclusion of multiple perspectives and scrutiny which better support the development and testing of problem-solving strategies. Secondly, because pragmatism emphasises the 'cooperative practices of socially organized knowledge', there is always a practical problem of how best to achieve such cooperation (Bohman, 1999: 462, 465). Inquiry should be collective and plural, because problematic situations require collective practical interventions to understand and resolve them. 'Democratically organised' inquiry is more likely to be pragmatically successful because it will better incorporate the views and experiences of all those affected. Dewey (1954 [1927]) applies the same argument to the public and its problems, in which the generation of an inclusive public is key to transforming understanding of the nature of social problems. Here the best method is where 'anyone interested in a public issue contributes with equal ability and engages in an experimental approach to find a rational solution' (Ogien, 2014: 422). Such a public 'consists of all those who are affected by the indirect consequences of transactions to such an extent that it is deemed necessary to have those consequences systematically cared for' (Dewey, 1954 [1927]: 15–16).

Pragmatism transforms traditional theoretical or analytical questions into practical problems, seeing all knowledge and understanding, including social scientific knowledge, as a method of inquiry, part of the practical struggle to resolve problems of experience. People's understandings are embedded in their practical activities and their struggles to resolve their practical problems. When practice becomes blocked or difficult, this creates 'doubt' and 'perplexity', as we must anticipate alternative futures in which the way to proceed is unclear, which leads to reflection and deliberation and to reconstructions of our practical reasoning (Dewey, 1910: 9–10). In their practical engagements, people *are* knowledgeable, reflexive and calculative, but they are not always right or even competent, and nor are their practical activities inevitably successful. People can certainly be wrong, and we often are. But if we so closely tie people's capacity to be *wrong* to the workings of inequality, then it is hard to see how they can ever be *right*, for inequalities are marked and ubiquitous, and according to many theorists their obfuscating powers are mighty indeed.

Instead, we must locate people's doubt, confusion and error within their practical engagements and problems. We are always aware of the problems in our experience, as these represent difficulties of practice, but our difficulties in how to proceed also derive from the indeterminacy of the situation and how to resolve it, in which we 'are doubtful because the situation is inherently doubtful' (Dewey, 1938: 105–6). A reconstruction of people's understandings will be part of the resolution of their problems, but understanding these difficulties does not necessarily mean they can be resolved, because problematic situations require collective practical interventions which incorporate all those affected. Public problems like inequality are formidable and intractable, because such 'social problems have multiple causes' with solutions requiring 'coordination across many social domains' (Bohmann, 1999: 478). Furthermore, our understanding of our problems changes through our collective struggles to resolve them. How we understand and evaluate our situation—what Dewey (1939) termed 'valuation'—is a feature of coordinated activity and is always emergent and contextual:

> A person may articulate the problematic features of her situation in various ways: as obstacles, confusions, conflicts, unmet needs, dangers,

and so on. The test of a value judgment—whether it 'works'—is whether it successfully identifies an action that overcomes the obstacles, clears up the confusions, resolves the conflicts, satisfies the needs, avoids or eliminates the dangers, and so on. The standard of success for value judgments is thus developed internally to the practices at hand, relative to people's descriptions of their problems. . . . Of course, hypothesized solutions may fail in practice. This may lead agents to revise their understandings of their problems, rather than just trying alternative solutions to the same problems . . . descriptions of problems are open to experimental testing in tandem with proposed solutions. (Anderson, 2018: n.p.)

Those who are excluded or disadvantaged often lack a public voice or find institutions unresponsive, so pragmatism argues that practices of inquiry and the formation of publics should be democratic and inclusive in order that emergent publics can 'improve their lot and overcome their current disadvantages' (Bohmann, 1999: 478). Of course there are many obstacles to the formation of inclusive, transformative publics. The low accountability of public institutions, or their failure to reach all the people concerned, can result in 'a day-to-day management of a situation without any real influence on its causes', not least because many problems—for example, those related to the environment, conflict and migrations, financial transactions, urban development or labour regulation—do not match existing levels of political representation' and are 'often under the purview of institutions incapable of dealing with them (Terzi and Tonnelat, 2017: 530–31). And as Narayan (2016) argues, the reach of relations of inequality and interest groups (and their lack of accountability) means that many social problems require the formation of global publics. The development of a public 'must reach indirectly concerned circles of people', and the testing of its inquiry also requires a forming public to 'forge new skills and knowledge to deal with the problem at hand in emerging public environments' (Terzi and Tonnelat, 2017: 531). So the formation of publics 'goes hand in hand' with an 'active pedagogy of self and collective teaching through inquiry', though such education is less about the transmission of specific critical knowledge or values and more about supporting processes of self-reflection and inquiry which can act as 'a safeguard against the powers of administrations, interest groups and the pressure of unfounded opinions' (Ibid.).

Ogien (2014: 422–23) argues that one of the 'great contributions of pragmatism' to social analysis is how it focuses attention on 'the constitution of public problems', looking at 'the way in which groups of individuals come to engage in a procedure of "constituting the public problem" and to lead it to an end, with all the hesitations and impediments that this joint and pluralistic activity forces them to overcome', analysing 'how the relationship between experts and "public" come together, how a collective intelligence is formed through mutual investigation and how use of this resource enables the resolution of the problem under consideration'. Social scientists certainly have a role to play in the constitution of publics and in transforming the understanding of public problems, but the pragmatist emphasis on the 'social organization and distribution of knowledge' sees that role differently and more modestly, with the social analyst 'one among many reflective participants, engaging in an ongoing process of deliberation and self-reflection' (Bohmann, 1999: 476). This represents a 'politics of cooperative inclusion' that aims at resolving conflicts 'in ways that include all perspectives and interests' where the goal is 'not to control social processes or even to influence the sorts of decisions that agents might make' but rather 'to initiate public processes of self-reflection' (Ibid.: 478). Only by incorporating all those subject to the problem can there be a resolution, assessed in terms of its practical consequences. The success of such social inquiry 'may be measured by its practical consequences for the quality of discussion and debate in the public sphere' (Ibid.: 475).

Of course, a well-functioning public sphere may be suppressed, and even if there is a well-established one, it still 'may be difficult to initiate reflection on various social themes' (Bohmann, 1999: 475). From the perspective of critical theories, such as theories of symbolic legitimation, the eclipse of inclusive publics is often framed as a question of agents' systematically distorted grasp of their situation, which puts 'the critic once again in a position of epistemic superiority' (Ibid.: 475). But as de Sousa Santos (2014: ix) notes, the Western-centric critical tradition too often 'sees itself as a vanguard theory that excels in knowing about, explaining, and guiding rather than knowing with, understanding, facilitating, sharing, and walking alongside'. Such an emphasis on the epistemic superiority of the analyst is inimical to pragmatist notions of plural, cooperative and inclusive modes of inquiry. Pragmatism makes no 'strong claims' for epistemological sovereignty, 'since the critic's theory does not provide the practical warrant of critique' (Bohmann, 1999: 475). Social criticism is not underpinned by the 'best comprehensive social theory' but rather is a practical problem of the 'organization of critical reflection in a public sphere', which seeks to help citizens to 'transform existing frameworks for social cooperation and coordination' (Ibid.: 471).

Therefore, while successful inquiry is plural and collective, the evaluation of the knowledge produced is not entirely internal to the community of inquirers, since evaluation in and through practice means knowledge stands or falls through its practical consequences and transactions. As Kilpinen (2012: 65) notes, the practical basis of knowledge means 'knowledge is not a state of mind but something we *do* . . . and something that we do continuously (otherwise it would not amount to genuine knowledge)'. A pragmatist social science therefore 'treats social actors as knowledgeable social agents to which its claims are publicly addressed', but the aims of such inquiry are to 'initiate processes of self-reflection, the outcomes of which agents determine for themselves' and which must be 'verified by those participating in the practice' in which this practical verification is 'part of the process of inquiry itself' (Bohmann, 1999: 475, 471–72).

On one reading, the democratic commitments of pragmatists 'leave them with no substantive political point of view, only the cooperative and second-order testing of a variety of alternative procedures, goals, and frameworks' (Bohmann, 1999: 478). However, as Bohman argues, pragmatism's concept of inquiry also entails a substantive commitment to inclusive, democratic and egalitarian practices which creates a role for the social sciences to 'institutionalize reflection on institutionalized practices and their norms of cooperation' (1999: 478, 463). Social inquiry plays a significant part in examining 'the basis and terms of ongoing cooperation itself, particularly within the most basic social institutions' (Ibid.: 463). In addition to its 'reformist democratic politics', pragmatist social inquiry aims for a form of 'second-order reflection' by focusing on the operations of power within cooperation and collective practices of inquiry (Ibid.: 478). Just as all cooperative practices 'have a moment of inquiry', they 'also need a moment of self-reflection on such inquiry itself', and pragmatism 'takes practical inquiry one reflective step further', though this is 'a step that can only be carried out by a public' (Ibid.: 464). Because power depends on the alignment and cooperation of many actors, 'such cooperation may be publicly scrutinized and challenged to transform relations of power and authority into contexts of democratic accountability', so the aim is to increase 'the role of cooperation in the many collective enterprises in which citizens are now implicated, using the lever of the dependence of those practices and enterprises (even when hierarchical) on ongoing cooperation' (1999: 478). Nonetheless, it remains 'up to the participants themselves to solve the problem of cooperation' (Ibid.: 465).

Throughout this book I have considered the claim that ordinary people's understandings of inequality are restricted, paradoxical or mystified. I have argued that if we locate people's knowledge, beliefs and values about inequality within a more situated understanding of their practical engagements and concerns, then their sense of inequality seems less restricted and starts to make better sense. People *do* have a restricted point of view on inequality, but this must be understood in terms of how people acquire their sense of inequality through various kinds of pragmatic engagements, where their knowledge is generated as a means to practically navigate given situations. People's sense of inequality is ultimately a sense of constraint, but this takes many practical forms which must be analysed *on their own terms*, located within people's practical concerns and contexts of activity and emerging as part of their struggles to resolve their problems of experience. But while people always have partial, situated perspectives on their social world shaped by their practical engagements with it, these practical engagements vary enormously. Whether such engagements produce perspectives on the immediate situation or its wider connections depends on the practical activity in question and the collective capacity for such action.

A sense of inequality emerges as people navigate various practical problems of constraint. It is a sense of the constraints of low resources and low status, of insecurity and subordination, often experienced as a sense of obligations and limits, as fear and anxiety about how to cope; a sense of no choice and of situations we cannot control; it is a sense of our inability to live our lives as we want to and of having to do things we really would rather not; it is a sense of the world being run by powerful and remote people unaccountable to us; a sense of being forced to put up with disrespect, humiliation and indignity; a sense of lacking alternatives and of being unable to change our situation; a sense of 'that's just the way the world is' and 'you'll never really change things'. But a sense of inequality also emerges as part of people's problem-solving and problem-reconstructing activities. So a sense of inequality is also a sense of indignation and anger, a sense of injustice and unfairness, a sense of 'they can't get away with this' and 'we can't let this stand'. People are not wrong if they feel their social relations are external and constraining or if they feel a certain resignation about wider social relations being resistant to change, and their practical engagements *are* often strategies of negotiation and manoeuvre within environments which are taken as given. But this does not preclude other forms of practical activities aimed at changing that environment, and people's practical viewpoints and their resignation about inequality certainly do not prevent challenge, critique or resistance. However, such practical engagements depend on people's varying resources and opportunities for practical action.

Bibliography

Aboulafia, M. (1999). 'A (neo) American in Paris: Bourdieu, Mead, and pragmatism', in R. Shusterman (ed.), *Bourdieu: A Critical Reader*. Oxford: Wiley-Blackwell.
Abrahams, J., and Ingram, N. (2013). 'The chameleon habitus: Exploring local students' negotiation of multiple fields'. *Sociological Research Online*, 18(4): 21.
Ackroyd, S., and Thompson, P. (1999). *Organizational Misbehaviour*. London: Sage.
Adnan, S. (2007). 'Departures from everyday resistance and flexible strategies of domination: The making and unmaking of a poor peasant mobilisation in Bangladesh'. *Journal of Agrarian Change*, 7(2): 183–224.
Adorno, T. (1991). *The Culture Industry*. London: Macmillan.
Adorno, T., and Horkheimer, M. (1993). *Dialectic of Enlightenment*. New York: Continuum.
Ahmed, S. (2007). 'A phenomenology of whiteness'. *Feminist Theory*, 8(2): 149–68.
Alesina, A., and La Ferrara, E. (2005). 'Preferences for redistribution in the land of opportunities'. *Journal of Public Economics*, 89(5): 897–931.
Alvaredo, F., Chancel, L., Piketty, T., Saez, E., and Zucman, G. (2017). *The World Inequality Report 2018*, available at https://wir2018.wid.world/files/download/wir2018-full-report-english.pdf, accessed 10/03/2019.
Anderson, E. (2014). 'A world turned upside down: Social hierarchies and a new history of egalitarianism'. *Juncture*, 20: 258–67.
Anderson, E. (2018). 'Dewey's moral philosophy', in E. Zalta (ed.), *The Stanford Encyclopedia of Philosophy* (Fall edition), available at https://plato.stanford.edu/archives/fall2018/entries/dewey-moral/, accessed 21/02/2019.
Anderson, J. (1995). 'Translator's introduction' to A. Honneth, *The Struggle for Recognition*. Cambridge: Polity Press.
Andrews, D., and Leigh, A. (2009). 'More inequality, less social mobility'. *Applied Economics Letters*, 16(15): 1489–92.
Antonucci, L., Horvath, L., Kutiyski, Y., and Krouwel, A. (2017). 'The malaise of the squeezed middle: Challenging the narrative of the "left behind" Brexiter'. *Competition and Change*, 21(3): 211–29.
Archer, M. (2000). *Being Human*. Cambridge: Cambridge University Press.
Atkinson, A. (2015). *Inequality: What Can Be Done?* Cambridge, MA: Harvard University Press.
Atkinson, A., and Salverda, W. (2009). 'The changing distribution of earnings in OECD countries'. *Economica*, 76(304): 780–81.
Baaz, M., Lilja, M., and Vinthagen, S. (2017). *Researching Resistance and Social Change*. Lanham, MD: Rowman & Littlefield.
Bamfield, L., and Horton, T. (2009). *Understanding Attitudes to Tacking Economic Inequality*. York: Joseph Rowntree Foundation.
Barnes, B. (1988). *The Nature of Power*. Cambridge: Polity.
Barnes, B. (2000). *Understanding Agency*. London: Sage.
Barnes, B. (2001). 'Practice as collective action', in T. Schatzki, K. Knorr Cetina and E. von Savigny (eds.), *The Practice Turn in Contemporary Theory*. London: Routledge.
Bashi Treitler, V., and Boatcă, M. (2016). 'Dynamics of inequalities in a global perspective: An introduction'. *Current Sociology*, 64(2), 159–71.
Baumberg, B. (2014). 'Benefits and the cost of living: Pressures on the cost of living and attitudes to benefit claiming', in A. Park, C. Bryson and J. Curtice (eds.), *British Social Attitudes: The 31st Report*. London: NatCen Social Research.

Baumberg, B., Bell, K., Gaffney, D., with Deacon, R., Hood, C., and Sage, D. (2012). *Benefits Stigma in Britain*. London: Elizabeth Finn Care/Turn2us.

Baumberg Geiger, B. (2018). 'Benefit "myths"? The accuracy and inaccuracy of public beliefs about the benefits system'. *Social Policy and Administration*, 52(5): 998–1018.

Baumberg Geiger, B., and Meuleman, B. (2016). 'Beyond "mythbusting": How to respond to myths and perceived undeservingness in the British benefits system'. *Journal of Poverty and Social Issues*, 24: 291–306.

Baumberg Geiger, B., Reeves, A., and de Vries, R. (2017). 'Tax avoidance and benefit manipulation: Views on its morality and prevalence'. *British Social Attitudes the 34th Report*. London: NatCen Social Research.

Bayat, A. (2000). 'From "dangerous classes" to "quiet rebels": Politics of the urban subaltern in the global South'. *International Sociology*, 15(3): 533–57.

Bayat, A. (2013). *Life as Politics: How Ordinary People Change the Middle-East*. Palo Alto, CA: Stanford University Press.

Bayat, A. (2016). 'Foreword', to S. Fadaee (ed.), *Understanding Southern Movements*. Abingdon: Routledge.

Becker, H. (1982). *Art Worlds*. Berkeley: University of California Press.

Benford, R., and Snow, D. (2000). 'Framing process and social movements: An overview and assessment'. *Annual Review of Sociology*, 26: 611–39.

Bernabou, R., and Tirole, J. (2006). 'Belief in a just world and redistributive politics'. *Quarterly Journal of Economics*, 121(2): 699–746.

Bernburg, J. (2016). *Economic Crisis and Mass Protest: The Pots and Pans Revolution in Iceland*. London: Routledge.

Besen, Y. (2006). 'Exploitation or fun? The lived experience of teenage employment in suburban America'. *Journal of Contemporary Ethnography*, 35(3): 319–40.

Bhambra, G. (2016). 'Class analysis in the age of Trump (and Brexit): The pernicious new politics of identity '. *Sociological Review Blog*, 23 November, available at https://www.thesociologicalreview.com/blog/class-analysis-in-the-age-of-trump-and-brexit-the-pernicious-new-politics-of-identity.html, accessed 13/04/2019.

Bhambra, G. (2017). 'Brexit, Trump, and "methodological whiteness": On the misrecognition of race and class'. *British Journal of Sociology*, 68(S1): S214–32.

Bloor, D. (1991). *Knowledge and Social Imagery*. London: University of Chicago Press.

Bloor, D. (1994). 'What can the Sociologist of Knowledge say about 2 + 2 = 4?', pp. 21 –32 in P. Ernest (ed.), *Mathematics, Education and Philosophy: An International Perspective*. London: Falmer.

Bloor, D. (2001). 'Wittgenstein and the priority of practice', in T. Shatzki et al. (eds.), *The Practice Turn in Contemporary Theory*. London: Routledge.

Blumer, H. (1969). *Symbolic Interactionism*. Berkeley: University of California Press.

Blumer, H. (1971). 'Social problems as collective behaviour'. *Social Problems*, 18(3): 298–306.

Boggs, C. (1977). 'Marxism, prefigurative communism, and the problem of workers' control'. *Radical America*, 6: 99–122.

Bohman, J. (1998). 'Practical reason and cultural constraint: Agency in Bourdieu's theory of practice', in R. Shusterman (ed.), *Bourdieu: A Critical Reader*. Oxford: Wiley-Blackwell.

Bohmann, J. (1999). 'Theories, practices, and pluralism: A pragmatic interpretation of critical social science'. *Philosophy of the Social Sciences*, 29(4): 459–80.

Boltanski, L. (2011). *On Critique: A Sociology of Emancipation*. Cambridge: Polity Press.

Boltanski, L. (2012). *Love and Justice as Competences—Three Essays on the Sociology of Action*. Cambridge: Polity Press.

Boltanski, L., and Chiapello, E. (2007). *The New Spirit of Capitalism*. London: Verso.

Boltanski, L., and Thévenot, L. (1999). 'The sociology of critical capacity'. *European Journal of Social Theory*, 2: 359–78.

Boltanski, L., and Thévenot, L. (2006). *On Justification: Economies of Worth*. Princeton, NJ: Princeton University Press.

Bordo, S. (1993). 'Feminism, Foucault, and the politics of the body', in C. Ramazanoglu (ed.), *Up Against Foucault*. New York: Routledge.
Bottero, W. (2010). 'Intersubjectivity and Bourdieusian approaches to "identity"'. *Cultural Sociology*, 4(1): 3–22.
Bourdieu, P. (1977). *Outline of a Theory of Practice*. Cambridge: Cambridge University Press.
Bourdieu, P. (1984). *Distinction*. London: Routledge and Kegan Paul.
Bourdieu, P. (1990a). *The Logic of Practice*. Cambridge: Polity.
Bourdieu, P. (1990b). *In Other Words*. Cambridge: Polity.
Bourdieu, P. (1990c). *Photography: A Middle-Brow Art*. Cambridge: Polity.
Bourdieu, P. (1992a). *Language and Symbolic Power*. Cambridge: Polity.
Bourdieu, P. (1992b). 'In conversation: Doxa and common life', with Terry Eagleton. *New Left Review*, 191(1): 111–21.
Bourdieu, P. (1993a). *Sociology in Question*. London: Sage Publications.
Bourdieu, P. (1993b). *The Field of Cultural Production*. Cambridge: Polity.
Bourdieu, P. (1996). *The State Nobility: Elite Schools in the Field of Power*. Cambridge: Polity.
Bourdieu, P. (1998a). *Practical Reason*. Cambridge: Polity.
Bourdieu, P. (1998b). *The State Nobility*. Cambridge: Polity.
Bourdieu, P. (2000). *Pascalian Meditations*. Cambridge: Polity.
Bourdieu, P. (2001). *Masculine Domination*. Palo Alto, CA: Stanford University Press.
Bourdieu, P., Accardo, A., and Ferguson, P. (1999). *The Weight of the World: Social Suffering in Contemporary Society*. Palo Alto, CA: Stanford University Press.
Bourdieu, P., and Wacquant, L. (1992). *An Invitation to Reflexive Sociology*. Oxford: Polity.
Brandom, R. (1994). *Making It Explicit: Reasoning, Representing, and Discursive Commitment*. Cambridge, MA: Harvard University Press.
Breines, W. (1982). *The Great Refusal: Community and Organization in the New Left: 1962–1968*. New York: Praeger.
Bromley, C. (2003). 'Has Britain become immune to inequality?', in A. Park, J. Curtice, K. Thomson, L. Jarvis and C. Bromley (eds.), *British Social Attitudes: The 20th Report*. London: Sage and NCSR.
Brunori, P. (2017). 'The perception of inequality of opportunity in Europe'. *Review of Income and Wealth*, 63(3): 464–91.
Brunori, P., Ferreira, F., and Peragine, V. (2013). *Inequality of Opportunity, Income Inequality and Economic Mobility: Some International Comparisons*. IZA Discussion Paper No. 7155. Bonn, Germany: Institute for the Study of Labour (IZA), available at http://ftp.iza.org/dp7155.pdf, accessed 11/04/2019.
Buechler, S. (1995). 'New social movement theories'. *Sociological Quarterly*, 36(3): 441–64.
Butler, J. (1999). 'Performativity's Social Magic', in R. Shusterman (ed.), *Bourdieu: A Critical Reader*. Oxford: Blackwell.
Button, G., Mason, D., and Sharrock, W. (2003). 'Disempowerment and resistance in the print industry? Reactions to surveillance-capable technology'. *New Technology, Work and Employment*, 18(1): 50–61.
Cai, Y. (2010). *Collective Resistance in China: Why Popular Protests Succeed or Fail*. Palo Alto, CA: Stanford University Press.
Calhoun, C. (1993). '"New social movements" of the early nineteenth century'. *Social Science History*, 17: 385–427.
Callon, M. (1986). 'Some elements of a sociology of translation: Domestication of the scallops and the fishermen of St Brieuc Bay', in J. Law (ed.), *Power, Action and Belief: A New Sociology of Knowledge*. London: Routledge.
Callon, M. (2006). 'What does it mean to say that economics is performative?' CSI Working Papers, 005. Paris: Centre de Sociologie de l'Innovation, ffhalshs-0091596f, available at https://halshs.archives-ouvertes.fr/halshs-00091596/document, accessed 01/03/2019.

Callon, M., and Latour, B. (1981). 'Unscrewing the big leviathan: How actors macro-structure reality and how sociologists help them to do so', in K. Knorr-Cetina and A. Cicourel (eds.), *Advances in Social Theory and Methodology: Towards an Integration of Micro- and Macro-Sociologies*. Boston, MA: Routledge.

Carriero, R. (2016). 'More inequality, fewer class differences: The paradox of attitudes to redistribution across European countries'. *Comparative Sociology*, 15: 112–39.

Castell, S., and Thompson, J. (2007). *Understanding Attitudes to Poverty in the UK: Getting the Public's Attention*. York: Joseph Rowntree Foundation.

Castells, M. (1997). *The Power of Identity*. Cambridge, MA: Blackwell.

Celikates, R. (2006). 'From critical social theory to a social theory of critique. On the critique of ideology after the pragmatic turn'. *Constellations: An International Journal of Critical and Democratic Theory*, 13: 21–40.

Chambers, J., Swan, L., and Heesacker, M. (2014). 'Better off than we know: Distorted perceptions of incomes and income inequality in America'. *Psychological Science*, 25: 613–18.

Chin, C., and Mittelman, J. (1997). 'Conceptualising resistance to globalisation'. *New Political Economy*, 2(1): 25–37.

Clarke, G., and Sison, M. (2005). 'Voices from the top of the pile: Elite perceptions of poverty and the poor in the Philippines', in E. Reis and M. Moore (eds.), *Elite Perceptions of Poverty and Inequality*. London: Zed Books.

Cojocaru, A. (2014). 'Fairness and inequality tolerance: Evidence from the Life in Transition Survey'. *Journal of Comparative Economics*, 42(3): 590–608.

Cole, W. (2018). 'Poor and powerless: Economic and political inequality in cross-national perspective, 1981–2011'. *International Sociology*, 33(3): 357–85.

Collins, C., and Hoxie, J. (2017). *Billionaire Bonanza: The Forbes 400 and the Rest of Us*. Washington, DC: Institute of Policy Studies, available at https://inequality.org/wp-content/uploads/2017/11/BILLIONAIRE-BONANZA-2017-Embargoed.pdf, accessed 15/04/2018.

Collinson, D. L., and Ackroyd, S. (2005). 'Resistance, misbehaviour and dissent', pp. 305–26 in S. Ackroyd, R. Batt, P. Thompson and P. Tolbert (eds.), *The Oxford Handbook of Work and Organization*. Oxford: Oxford University Press.

Combahee River Collective. (1983). 'A black feminist statement', in B. Smith (ed.), *Home Girls: A Black Feminist Anthology*. New York : Kitchen Table: Women of Color Press.

Corak, M. (2013). 'Income inequality, equality of opportunity, and intergenerational mobility'. *Journal of Economic Perspectives*, 27(3): 79–102.

Cornish, F., Haaken, C., Moskovitz, L., and Jackson, S. (2016). 'Rethinking prefigurative politics'. *Journal of Social and Political Psychology*, 4(1): 114–27.

Coulter, J. (1982). 'Remarks on the conceptualization of social structure'. *Philosophy of the Social Sciences*, 12(1): 33–46.

Coulter, J. (2009). 'Rule-following, rule-governance and rule-accord: Reflections on rules after Rawls'. *Journal of Classical Sociology*, 9(4): 389–403.

Crenshaw, K. (1989). 'Demarginalizing the intersection of race and sex: A black feminist critique of antidiscrimination doctrine, feminist theory, and antiracist politics' . *University of Chicago Legal Forum*, 140: 139–67.

Crenshaw, K. (1991). 'Mapping the margins: Intersectionality, identity politics, and violence against women of color'. *Stanford Law Review*, 43(6): 1241–99.

Cribb, J., Norris Keiller, A., Waters, T. (2018). *Living standards, poverty and inequality in the UK: 2018*, IFS Report, No. R145, Institute for Fiscal Studies (IFS), London, http://dx.doi.org/10.1920/re.ifs.2019.0145.

Crossley, N. (2002). *Making Sense of Social Movements*. Milton Keynes: Open University Press.

Crossley, N., and Ibrahim, J. (2012). 'Critical mass, social networks and collective action: Exploring student political worlds'. *Sociology*, 46(4): 596–612.

Cruces, G., Perez-Truglia, R., and Tetaz, M. (2013). 'Biased perceptions of income distribution and preferences for redistribution: Evidence from a survey experiment'. *Journal of Public Economics*, 98: 100–112.
Currier, A., and Thomann, M. (2016). 'Gender and sexual diversity organizing in Africa', in S. Fadaee (ed.), *Understanding Southern Movements*. Abingdon: Routledge.
Curtice, J. (2010). 'Thermostat or weather vane? How the public has reacted towards the new Labour government', in A. Park, J. Curtice, K. Thomson, M. Phillips, E. Clery and S. Butt (eds.), *British Social Attitudes: The 26th Report*. London: Sage.
Curtice, J. (2016). 'Role of government', in E. Clery, J. Curtice and R. Harding (eds.), *British Social Attitudes: The 34th Report*. London: NatCen Social Research.
Curtis, J., and Andersen, R. (2015). 'How social class shapes attitudes on economic inequality: The competing forces of self-interest and legitimation'. *International Review of Social Research*, 5: 4–19.
Dallinger, U. (2010). 'Public support for redistribution: What explains cross-national differences?'. *Journal of European Social Policy*, 20(4): 333–49.
Death, D. (2010). 'Counter-conducts: A Foucauldian analytics of protest'. *Social Movement Studies*, 9(3): 235–51.
Deaton, A. (2013). *The Great Escape: Health, Wealth and the Origins of Inequality*. Princeton, NJ: Princeton University Press.
de Certeau, M. (1980). 'On the oppositional practices of everyday life'. *Social Text*, 3(Autumn): 3–43.
de Certeau, M. (1984). *The Practice of Everyday Life*. Berkeley: University of California Press.
Deess, E. (1997). 'Collective life and social change in the German democratic republic'. *Mobilization: An International Quarterly*, 2(2): 207–25.
Dennis, A., and Martin, P. (2005). 'Symbolic interactionism and the concept of power'. *Sociology*, 56(2): 191–213.
De Sousa Santos, B. (2014). *Epistemologies of the South: Justice against Epistemicide*. Boulder, CO: Paradigm Publishers.
De Vries, G. (2016). *Bruno Latour*. Cambridge: Polity Press.
Dewey, J. (1910). *How We Think*. Boston: DC Heath and Co.
Dewey, J. (1922). *Human Nature and Conduct*. New York: Henry Holt.
Dewey, J. (1938). *Logic: The Theory of Inquiry*. New York: Henry Holt.
Dewey, J. (1939). *The Theory of Valuation*. Chicago: University of Chicago Press.
Dewey, J. (1954) [1927]. *The Public and Its Problems*. Athens: Swallow/Ohio University Press.
Dewey, J. (1958) [1929]. *Experience and Nature*. New York: Dover.
Dewey, J. (1982) [1920]. 'Reconstruction in philosophy' , in J. A. Boydston (ed.), *The Middle Works of John Dewey*, vol. 12. Carbondale: Southern Illinois University Press.
Dewey, J. (1984) [1929]. 'The quest for certainty', in J. A. Boydston (ed.), *The Later Works of John Dewey*, vol. 4. Carbondale: Southern Illinois University Press.
Dewey, J., and Bentley, A. (1949). *Knowing and the Known*. Boston: Beacon Press.
Domhoff, W. (2017). *Wealth, Income, and Power*, available at www2.ucsc.edu/whorulesamerica/power/wealth.html, accessed on 11/04/2019.
Dorling, D. (2014). *Inequality and the 1%*. New York: Verso Books.
Dorling, D. (2016). 'Brexit: The decision of a divided country'. *British Medical Journal*, 354: i3697.
Dorling, D. (2017). *The Equality Effect: Improving Life for Everyone*. Oxford: New Internationalist.
Dorling, D., and Tomlinson, S. (2019). *Rule Britannia: Brexit and the End of Empire*. London: Biteback.
Dreyfus, H. (2003). '"Being and power" revisited', in A. Milchman and A. Rosenberg (eds.), *Foucault and Heidegger: Critical Encounters*. Minneapolis: University of Minnesota Press.
DuBois, W. E. B. (1935). *Black Reconstruction*. New York: Harcourt, Brace.

Duprat, M. H. (2018). 'The dynamics of inequality: Is there a general pattern?'. *Econote*, 42, Societe Generale Economic and Sectoral Studies Department, available at https://www.societegenerale.com/sites/default/files/2018/the-dynamics-of-inequality.pdf, accessed 02/03/2019.

Duru-Bellat, M., and Tenret, E. (2012). 'Who's for meritocracy? Individual and contextual variations in the faith'. *Comparative Education Review*, 56(2): 223–47.

Dyer, R. (2000). 'The matter of whiteness', in L. Back and J. Solomos (eds.), *Theories of Race and Racism*. London: Routledge.

Eagleton, T. (1991). *Ideology: An Introduction*. London: Verso.

Eagleton, T. (1992). 'In Conversation: Doxa and Common Life' (with Pierre Bourdieu). *New Left Review*, 191(1): 111–21.

Edmiston, D. (2018). 'The poor "sociological imagination" of the rich: Explaining attitudinal divergence towards welfare, inequality, and redistribution'. *Social Policy and Administration*, 53: 1–15.

Edwards, G. (2014). *Social Movements and Protest*. Cambridge: Cambridge University Press.

Emirbayer, M., and Maynard, D. (2011). 'Pragmatism and ethnomethodology'. *Qualitative Sociology*, 34(1): 221–61.

Engelhardt, C., and Wagener, A. (2014). 'Biased perceptions of income inequality and redistribution', *Hannover Economic Papers* (HEP) dp-526, Leibniz Universität Hannover, Wirtschaftswissenschaftliche Fakultät.

Epstein, B. (1991). *Political Protest and Cultural Revolution*. Berkeley: University of California Press.

Eubanks, V. (2018). *Automating Inequality: How High-Tech Tools Profile, Police, and Punish the Poor*. New York: St. Martin's Press.

Evans, M., and Kelley, J. (2004). 'Subjective social location: Data from 21 nations'. *International Journal of Public Opinion Research*, 16(1): 3–38.

Evans, M., and Kelley, J. (2017). 'Communism, capitalism, and images of class: Effects of reference groups, reality, and regime in 43 nations and 110,000 individuals, 1987–2009'. *Cross-Cultural Research*, 51(4): 315–59.

Evans, M., Kelley, J., and Kolosi, T. (1992). 'Images of class: Public perceptions in Hungary and Australia'. *American Sociological Review*, 57: 461–82.

Evans, S., and Boyte, H. (1986). *Free Spaces: The Sources of Democratic Change in America*. New York: Harper and Row.

Evans, T. (2009). Managers, Professionals and Discretion in Street-Level Bureaucracies. Conference of the Social Policy Association, 13, available at https://historyofsocialwork.org/1969_Lipsky/2009,%20Evans,%20Managers,%20professional%20and%20discretion%20in%20street-level%20bureaucracies%20OCR%20C.pdf, accessed 06/01/2019.

Evans, T. (2011). 'Professionals, managers and discretion: Critiquing street-level bureaucracy'. *British Journal of Social Work*, 41(2): 368–86.

Fadaee, S. (2012). *Social Movements in Iran: Environmentalism and Civil Society*. Abingdon: Routledge.

Fadaee, S. (2016). 'Introduction: Genesis of social movement theory and Southern movements', in S. Fadaee (ed.), *Understanding Southern Movements*. Abingdon: Routledge.

Fadaee, S. (2017). 'Bringing in the South: Towards a global paradigm for social movement studies'. *Interface: A Journal for and about Social Movements*, 9(2): 45–60.

Fanon, F. (1967a) [1961]. *The Wretched of the Earth*. Harmondsworth: Penguin.

Fanon, F. (1967b) [1961]. *Toward the African Revolution*. New York: Grove Press.

Fanon, F. (1986) [1952]. *Black Skin, White Masks*. London: Pluto Press.

Ferguson, H. (2006). *Phenomenological Sociology*. London: Sage.

Finseraas, H. (2009). 'Income inequality and demand for redistribution: A multilevel analysis of European public opinion'. *Scandinavian Political Studies*, 32(1): 94–119.

Flacks, R. (1976). 'Making history vs. making life: Dilemmas of an American Left'. *Sociological Inquiry*, 46(3–4): 263–80.

Flacks, R. (1988). *Making History: The American Left and the American Mind*. New York: Columbia University Press.
Flacks, R. (2004). 'Knowledge for what? Thoughts on the state of social movement studies', in J. Goodwin and J. M. Jasper (eds.), *Rethinking Social Movements: Structure, Meaning and Emotion*. Lanham, MD: Rowman & Littlefield.
Fleming, C., Lamont, M., and Welburn, J. (2012). 'African Americans respond to stigmatization: The meanings and salience of confronting, deflecting conflict, educating the ignorant and "managing the self"'. *Ethnic and Racial Studies*, 35(3): 400–417.
Flemmen, M., and Savage, M. (2017). 'The politics of nationalism and white racism in the UK'. *The British Journal of Sociology*, 68: S233–64.
Fong, C. (2001). 'Social preferences, self-interest, and the demand for redistribution'. *Journal of Public Economics*, 82(2): 225–46.
Foucault, M. (1976). *The History of Sexuality, Vol. 1: An Introduction*. New York: Random House.
Foucault, M. (1979). *Discipline and Punish: The Birth of the Prison*. Harmondsworth: Penguin.
Foucault, M. (1982). 'The subject and power'. *Critical Inquiry*, 8(4): 777–95.
Foucault, M. (2000). 'Omnes et singulatim: Towards a critique of political reason', in J. D. Faubian (ed.), *Power: Essential Works of Foucault 1954–1984*, vol. 3. New York: The New Press.
Foucault, M. (2007a). *Security, Territory, Population: Lectures at the College de France 1977–1978*. Edited by M. Senellart. Basingstoke: Palgrave Macmillan.
Foucault, M. (2007b). 'What is critique', in S. Lotringer (ed.), *The Politics of Truth*. Los Angeles, CA: Semiotext(e).
Francis, D., and Hester, S. (2004). *An Invitation to Ethnomethodology*. London: Sage.
Frankenberg, R. (2000). 'White women, race matters: The social construction of whiteness', in L. Back and J. Solomos (eds.), *Theories of Race and Racism*. London: Routledge.
Franks, A. S., and Scherr, K. C. (2019). 'Economic issues are moral issues: The moral underpinnings of the desire to reduce wealth inequality'. *Social Psychological and Personality Science*, 10(4): 553–62.
Fraser, N. (1994). 'Pragmatism, feminism, and the linguistic turn', in S. Benhabib, J. Butler, D. Cornell, and N. Fraser (eds.), *Feminist Contentions: A Philosophical Exchange*. New York: Routledge.
Fraser, N. (2001). 'Recognition without ethics?'. *Theory, Culture and Society*, 18(2–3): 21–42.
Fraser, N. (2008). 'Abnormal justice'. *Critical Inquiry*, 34: 393–422.
Fraser, N., and Honneth, A. (2003). *Redistribution or Recognition? A Political-Philosophical Exchange*. New York: Verso.
Frega, R. (2015). 'The normative structure of the ordinary'. *European Journal of Pragmatism and American Philosophy* (Online), VII-1, available at http://ejpap.revues.org/370, accessed 12/11/2018.
Friedman, S. (2016). 'Habitus clivé and the emotional imprint of social mobility'. *Sociological Review*, 64: 129–47.
Funk, C. (2000). 'The dual influence of self-interest and societal interest in public opinion'. *Political Research Quarterly*, 53(1): 37–62.
Gadamer, H. (1975). *Truth and Method*. London: Sheed and Ward.
Gamson, W. (1992a). *Talking Politics*. Cambridge: Cambridge University Press.
Gamson, W. (1992b). 'The social psychology of collective action', in A. Morris and C. Mueller (eds.), *Frontiers in Social Movement Theory*. New Haven, CT: Yale University Press.
Gamson, W. (1995). 'Constructing social protest', in H. Johnston and B. Klandermans (eds.), *Social Movements and Culture*. Minneapolis: University of Minnesota Press.
Gamson, W., and Meyer, D. (1996). 'Framing political opportunity', in D. McAdam, J. McCarthy, and M. Zald (eds.), *Comparative Perspectives on Social Movements: Political*

Opportunities, Mobilizing Structures, and Cultural Framings. Cambridge: Cambridge University Press.
Garfinkel, H. (1963). 'A conception of, and experiments with, "trust" as a condition for stable concerted actions', in O. J. Harvey (ed.), *Motivation and Social Interaction.* New York: Ronald Press.
Garfinkel, H. (1967). *Studies in Ethnomethodology.* Cambridge: Polity Press.
Gest, J., Reny, T., and Mayer, J. (2018). 'Roots of the radical right: Nostalgic deprivation in the United States and Britain'. *Comparative Political Studies,* 51(13): 1694–1719.
Gimpelson, V., and Treisman, D. (2017). *Misperceiving Inequality.* NBER Working Paper No. 21174, available at http://www.nber.org/papers/w21174, accessed 05/01/2018.
Gimpelson, V., and Treisman, D. (2018). 'Misperceiving inequality'. *Economics and Politics,* 30: 27–54.
Glasius, M., and Pleyers, G. (2013). 'The global moment of 2011: Democracy, social justice and dignity'. *Development and Change,* 44(3): 547–67.
Goffman, E. (1959). *The Presentation of Self in Everyday Life.* New York: Anchor Books.
Goffman, E. (1963). *Stigma: Notes on the Management of Spoiled Identity.* Upper Saddle River, NJ: Prentice Hall.
Goffman, E. (1974). *Frame Analysis: An Essay on the Organization of Experience.* Cambridge, MA: Harvard University Press.
Goffman, E. (1983). 'The interaction order'. *American Sociological Review,* 48(1): 1–17.
Gomberg, P. (2007). *How to Make Opportunity Equal: Race and Contributive Justice.* Oxford: Blackwell.
Goodwin, J., and Jasper, J. M. (2004a). 'Introduction', to J. Goodwin and J. M. Jasper (eds.), *Rethinking Social Movements: Structure, Meaning and Emotion.* Lanham, MD: Rowman & Littlefield.
Goodwin, J., and Jasper, J. M. (2004b). 'Caught in a winding, snarling vine: The structural bias of political process theory', in J. Goodwin and J. M. Jasper (eds.), *Rethinking Social Movements: Structure, Meaning and Emotion.* Lanham, MD: Rowman & Littlefield.
Gorringe, H. (2005). *Untouchable Citizens.* New Delhi: Sage.
Gorringe, H., and Rafanell, I. (2007). 'The embodiment of caste'. *Sociology,* 41(1): 97–114.
Gorringe, H., and Rafanell, I. (2015). 'Power and social transformation: Understanding power from below'. *Transnational Institute,* available at https://www.tni.org/en/briefing/power-and-social-transformation-understanding-power-below, accessed 03/04/2018.
Graeber, D. (2014). *The Democracy Project.* London: Penguin.
Gramsci, A. (1971). *Selections from the Prison Notebooks of Antonio Gramsci.* Edited and translated by Quintin Hoare and Geoffrey Nowell Smith. New York: International Publishers.
Greenhouse, C. (2005). 'Hegemony and hidden transcripts: The discursive arts of neoliberal legitimation'. *American Anthropologist,* 107(3): 356–68.
Greiffenhagen, C., and Sharrock, W. (2008). 'Where do the limits of experience lie? Abandoning the dualism of objectivity and subjectivity'. *History of the Human Sciences,* 21(3): 70–93.
Greiffenhagen, C., and Sharrock, W. (2009). 'Two concepts of attachment to rules'. *Journal of Classical Sociology,* 9(4): 405–27.
Guha, R. (2000). *Environmentalism: A Global History.* Oxford: Oxford University Press.
Gurr, T. (1970). *Why Men Rebel.* Princeton, NJ: Princeton University Press.
Gusterson, H. (2017). 'From Brexit to Trump: Anthropology and the rise of nationalist populism'. *American Ethnologist,* 44(2): 209–14.
Gutmann, M. C. (1993). 'Rituals of resistance: A critique of the theory of everyday forms of resistance'. *Latin American Perspectives,* 20(2): 74–92.
Habermas, J. (1981). 'New social movements'. *Telos,* 49: 33–37.
Habermas, J. (1987). *The Theory of Communicative Action: Vol. 2, Lifeworld and System, A Critique of Functional Reason.* London: Polity Press.

Hacking, I. (2002). *Historical Ontology*. Cambridge, MA: Harvard University Press.
Hadler, M. (2005). 'Why do people accept different income ratios? A multi-level comparison of thirty countries'. *Acta Sociologica* 48(2): 131–54.
Haenfler, R., Johnson, B., and Jones, E. (2012). 'Lifestyle movements: Exploring the intersection of lifestyle and social movements'. *Social Movement Studies*, 11(1): 1–20.
Hall, S. (1986). 'Gramsci's relevance for the study of race and ethnicity'. *The Journal of Communication Inquiry*, 10(2): 5–27.
Hall, S., Leary, K., and Greevy, H. (2014). *Public Attitudes to Poverty*. York: Joseph Rowntree Foundation.
Han, C. (2012). 'Satisfaction with the standard of living in reform-era China'. *China Quarterly*, 212: 919–40.
Harré, R. (1998). 'When the knower is also known', in T. May and M. Williams (eds.), *Knowing the Social World*. New York: Open University Press.
Harré, R. (2002). 'Social reality and the myth of social structure'. *European Journal of Social Theory*, 5(1): 111–23.
Harris, C. (1993). 'Whiteness as property'. *Harvard Law Review*, 106(8): 1707–91.
Harris, S. (2006). 'Social constructionism and social inequality'. *Journal of Contemporary Ethnography* 35: 223–35.
Hassell, J. (2018). 'Is income inequality rising around the world?', available at https://ourworldindata.org/income-inequality-since-1990, accessed 13/04/2019.
Hauser, O., and Norton, M. (2017). '(Mis)perceptions of inequality'. *Current Opinion in Psychology*, 18: 21–25.
He, X., and Reynolds, J. (2017). 'Bootstraps, buddies, and bribes: Perceived meritocracy in the United States and China'. *Sociological Quarterly*, 58(4): 622–47.
Hecht, K. (2017). *A Relational Analysis of Top Incomes and Wealth: Economic Evaluation, Relative (Dis)advantage and the Service to Capital*. International Inequalities Institute Working Paper 11. London: London School of Economics and Political Science.
Henley, J. (2016). 'White and wealthy voters gave victory to Donald Trump, exit polls show'. *The Guardian*, 9 November, available at https://www.theguardian.com/us-news/2016/nov/09/white-voters-victory-donald-trump-exit-polls, accessed 11/05/2019.
Heritage, J. (1984). *Garfinkel and Ethnomethodology*. Cambridge: Polity.
Hilbert, R. (2009). 'Ethnomethodology and social theory', in B. Turner (ed.), *The New Blackwell Companion to Social Theory*. Hoboken, NJ: Blackwell.
Hill Collins, P. (2012). 'Social inequality, power, and politics: Intersectionality and American pragmatism in dialogue'. *Journal of Speculative Philosophy*, 26(2): 442–57.
Hills, J. (2015). *Good Times Bad Times: The Welfare Myth of Them and Us*. Bristol: Policy Press.
Hirsch, E. (1990). *Urban Revolt: Ethnic Politics in the Nineteenth-Century Chicago Labor Movement*. Berkeley: University of California Press.
Hirschman, A., and Rothschild, M. (1973). 'The changing tolerance for income inequality in the course of economic development'. *Quarterly Journal of Economics*, 87(4): 544–66.
Hochschild, A. (2016). *Strangers in Their Own Land: Anger and Mourning on the American Right*. New York: The New Press.
Hollander, J., and Einwhoner, R. (2004). 'Conceptualizing resistance'. *Sociological Forum*, 19(4): 533–54.
Holloway, J. (2010). *Crack Capitalism*. London: Pluto Press.
Holmwood, J. (2014). 'Beyond capital? The challenge for sociology in Britain'. *British Journal of Sociology*, 65(4): 607–18.
Hong, L., and Kongshøj, K. (2014). 'China's welfare reform: An ambiguous road towards a social protection floor'. *Global Social Policy*, 14(3): 352–68.
Honneth, A. (1992). 'Integrity and disrespect: Principles of a conception of morality based on the theory of recognition'. *Political Theory*, 20(2): 187–201.
Honneth, A. (1995). *The Struggle for Recognition*. Cambridge: Polity Press.

Honneth, A. (2003). 'Redistribution as recognition: A response to Nancy Fraser', in N. Fraser and A. Honneth (eds.), *Redistribution or Recognition? A Political-Philosophical Exchange*. New York: Verso.
hooks, b. (2003). *Rock My Soul: Black People and Self-Esteem*. New York: Washington Square Press.
Hossain, N., and Moore, M. (2005). 'So near and yet so far: Elites and imagined poverty in Bangladesh', in E. Reis and M. Moore (eds.), *Elite Perceptions of Poverty and Inequality*. London: Zed Books.
Huber, J., and Form, W. (1973). *Income and Ideology*. New York: Free Press.
Hudson, J., and Lunt, N., with Hamilton, C., Mackinder, S., Meers, J., and Swift, C. (2016a). 'Nostalgia narratives? Pejorative attitudes to welfare in historical perspective: Survey evidence from Beveridge to the British social attitudes survey'. *Journal of Poverty and Social Justice*, 24(3): 227–43.
Hudson, J., and Lunt, N., with Hamilton, C., Mackinder, S., Meers, J., and Swift, C. (2016b). 'Exploring public attitudes to welfare over the Longue Durée: Re-examination of survey evidence from Beveridge, Beatlemania, Blair and beyond'. *Social Policy and Administration*, 50(6): 691–711.
Hudson, J., Patrick, R., and Wincup, E. (2016). 'Introduction to themed special issue: Exploring "welfare" attitudes and experiences'. *Journal of Poverty and Social Justice*, 24(3): 215–26.
Hughes, J., and Sharrock, W. (2007). *Theory and Methods in Sociology*. Basingstoke: Palgrave Macmillan.
Ingram, N. (2011). 'Within school and beyond the gate: The complexities of being educationally successful and working class'. *Sociology*, 45(2): 287–302.
Ingram, N., and Abrahams, J. (2015). 'Stepping outside of oneself: How a cleft-habitus can lead to greater reflexivity through occupying "the third space"', in J. Thatcher, N. Ingram, C. Burke and J. Abrahams (eds.), *Bourdieu: The Next Generation*. London: Routledge.
International Monetary Fund. (2018). *How to Operationalize Inequality Issues in Country Work*. IMF Policy Paper, available at https://www.imf.org/en/Publications/Policy-Papers/Issues/2018/06/13/pp060118howto-note-on-inequality, accessed 10/04/2019.
Irwin, S. (2015). 'Class and comparison: Subjective social location and lay experiences of constraint and mobility'. *British Journal of Sociology*, 66(2): 259.
Irwin, S. (2018). 'Lay perceptions of inequality and social structure'. *Sociology*, 52(2): 211–27.
Jæger, M. (2013). 'The effect of macroeconomic and social conditions on the demand for redistribution: A pseudo-panel approach'. *Journal of European Social Policy*, 23(2): 147–61.
Jagd, S. (2011). 'Pragmatic sociology and competing orders of worth in organizations'. *European Journal of Social Theory*, 14(3): 343–59.
James, W. (1983) [1890]. *The Principles of Psychology*. Cambridge, MA: Harvard University Press.
Janmaat, J. G. (2013). 'Subjective inequality: A review of international comparative studies on people's views about inequality'. *European Journal of Sociology/Archives Européennes de Sociologie* 54(3): 357–89.
Jasper, J. (1997). *The Art of Moral Protest*. Chicago: University of Chicago Press.
Jasper, J., and Poulsen, J. (1995). 'Recruiting strangers and friends: Moral shocks and social networks in animal rights and anti-nuclear protests'. *Social Problems*, 42(4): 493–512.
Jenkins, R. (2000) [1982]. 'Pierre Bourdieu and the reproduction of determinism', in D. Robbins (ed.), *Pierre Bourdieu*, vol. 2. London: Sage.
Jensen, T. (2014). 'Welfare commonsense, poverty porn and doxosophy'. *Sociological Research Online*, 19(3): no pagination.
Jensen, T., and Tyler, I. (2015). 'Benefits broods: The cultural and political crafting of anti-welfare commonsense'. *Critical Social Policy*, 35(4): 470–91.

Jermier, J., Knights, D., and Nord, W. (eds.). (1994). *Resistance and Power in Organizations*. London: Routledge.

Johansson, A., and Vinthagen, S. (2016). 'Dimensions of everyday resistance: An analytical framework'. *Critical Sociology*, 42(3): 417–35.

Jung, M. (2010). 'John Dewey and action', in M. Cochran (ed.), *The Cambridge Companion to Dewey*. Cambridge: Cambridge University Press.

Kalati, N., and Manor, J. (2005). 'Elite perceptions of poverty and poor people in South Africa', in E. Reis and M. Moore (eds.), *Elite Perceptions of Poverty and Inequality*. London: Zed Books.

Kantola, A., and Kuusela, H. (2018). 'Wealth elite moralities: Wealthy entrepreneurs' moral boundaries'. *Sociology*, 53(2): 368–84.

Karadja, M., Mollerstrom, J., and Seim, D. (2017). 'Richer (and holier) than thou? The effect of relative income improvements on demand for redistribution'. *Review of Economics and Statistics*, 99(2): 201–21.

Keller, T., Medgyesi, M., and Toth, I. (2010). 'Analysing the link between measured and perceived income inequality in European countries'. Research Note No. 8, European Commission, Directorate-General Employment, Social Affairs and Equal Opportunities, Brussels.

Kelley, J., and Evans, M. (1993). 'The legitimation of inequality: Occupational earnings in nine nations'. *American Journal of Sociology*, 99(1): 75–125.

Kelley, J., and Zagorski, K. (2005). 'Economic change and the legitimation of inequality: The transition from socialism to the free market in Central-East Europe'. *Research in Social Stratification and Mobility*, 22: 321–66.

Kelley, N., Warhurst, C., and Wishart, R. (2018). 'Work and welfare', in D. Phillips, J. Curtice, M. Phillips and J. Perry (eds.), *British Social Attitudes: The 35th Report*. London: NatCen Social Research.

Kenworthy, L., and Pontusson, J. (2005). 'Rising inequality and the politics of redistribution in affluent countries'. *Perspectives on Politics*, 3(3): 449–71.

Kerkvliet, B. J. T. (2009). 'Everyday politics in peasant societies (and ours)'. *Journal of Peasant Studies*, 36(1): 227–43.

Kerr, W. (2014). 'Income inequality and social preferences for redistribution and compensation differentials'. *Journal of Monetary Economics*, 66(C): 62–67.

Khan, S., and Jerolmack, C. (2013). 'Saying meritocracy and doing privilege'. *Sociological Quarterly*, 54(1): 9–19.

Kiatpongsan, S., and Norton, M. (2014). 'How much (more) should CEOs make? A universal desire for more equal pay'. *Perspectives on Psychological Science*, 9(6): 587–93.

Kilpinen, E. (2012). 'Human beings as creatures of habit', in A. Warde and D. Southerton (eds.), *The Habits of Consumption: Studies across Disciplines in the Humanities and Social Sciences* 12: 45–69. Helsinki: Helsinki Collegium for Advanced Studies.

Kim, H., Huh, S., Choi, S., and Lee, Y. (2018). 'Perceptions of inequality and attitudes towards redistribution in four East Asian welfare states'. *International Journal of Social Welfare*, 27: 28–39.

King, A. (1999). 'Against structure: A critique of morphogenetic social theory'. *Sociological Review* 47(2): 199–227.

King, A. (1999). 'The impossibility of naturalism: The antinomies of Bhaskar's realism'. *Journal for the Theory of Social Behaviour*, 29(3): 267–88.

King, A. (2004). *The Structure of Social Theory*. Abingdon: Routledge.

Kivinen, O., and Piiroinen, T. (2004). 'The relevance of ontological commitments in social sciences: Realist and pragmatist viewpoints'. *Journal for the Theory of Social Behaviour*, 34(3): 231–48.

Kivinen, O., and Piiroinen, T. (2006). 'Toward pragmatist methodological relationalism: From philosophizing sociology to sociologizing philosophy'. *Philosophy of the Social Sciences*, 36(3): 303–29.

Kivinen, O., and Ristela, P. (2003). 'From constructivism to a pragmatist conception of learning'. *Oxford Review of Education*, 29(3): 363–75.

Koenig, M. (2017). 'Exploring the micro-politics of recognition'. *Ethnic and Racial Studies*, 40(8): 1261–70.
Krinsky, J., and Crossley, N. (2014). 'Social movements and social networks: Introduction'. *Social Movement Studies*, 13(1): 1–21.
Kristeva, J. (1982). *Powers of Horror: An Essay on Abjection*. New York: Columbia University Press.
Kuhn, A. (2019). 'The subversive nature of inequality: Subjective inequality perceptions and attitudes to social inequality'. *European Journal of Political Economy* (Online), available at www.sciencedirect.com/science/article/pii/S0176268016301756?via%3Dihub, accessed 14/05/2019.
Lamont, M. (2016). 'Getting respect: Responding to stigma and discrimination: Presidential talk to the district of Columbia sociological society, February 11, 2016'. *Sociologist* (May), available at http://thesociologistdc.com/all-issues/getting-respect-responding-to-stigma-and-discrimination/, accessed 09/08/2018.
Lamont, M., and Mizrachi, N. (2012). 'Ordinary people doing extraordinary things: Responses to stigmatization in comparative perspective'. *Ethnic and Racial Studies*, 35(3): 365–81.
Lamont, M., Moraes Silva, G., Welburn, J., Guetzkow, J., Mizrachi, J., Herzog, H., and Reis, E. (2016). *Getting Respect Responding to Stigma and Discrimination in the United States, Brazil, and Israel*. Princeton, NJ: Princeton University Press.
Lankshear, G., P. Cook, D. Mason, S. Coates and G. Button. (2001). 'Call Centre Employees' Responses to Electronic Monitoring: Some Research Findings', *Work Employment and Society*, 15(3): 595–605.
Larsen, C. (2016). 'How three narratives of modernity justify economic inequality'. *Acta Sociologica*, 59(2): 93–111.
Latour, B. (1990). 'Technology is society made durable'. *Sociological Review*, 38(1): 103–31.
Latour, B. (1993). *We Have Never Been Modern*. Cambridge, MA: Harvard University Press.
Latour, B. (1996a). 'On actor-network theory. A few clarifications plus more than a few complications'. *Soziale Welt*, 47: 369–81.
Latour, B. (1996b). 'On interobjectivity'. *Mind, Culture, and Activity*, 4: 228–44.
Latour, B. (2000). 'When things strike back: A possible contribution of "science studies" to the social sciences'. *British Journal of Sociology*, 51(1): 107–23.
Latour, B. (2005). *Reassembling the Social: An Introduction to Actor-Network-Theory*. Oxford: Oxford University Press.
Latour, B., and Hermant, E. (2006). 'Paris: invisible city'. Available at http://www.bruno-latour.fr/virtual/EN/index.html, accessed 17/12/2018.
Lave, J. (1988). *Cognition in Practice: Mind, Mathematics, and Culture in Everyday Life*. Cambridge: Cambridge University Press.
Lave, J., Murtaugh, M., and de la Rocha, O. (1984). 'The dialectic of arithmetic in grocery shopping', in B. Rogoff and J. Lave (eds.), *Everyday Cognition: Its Development in Social Context*. Cambridge, MA: Harvard University Press.
Law, J. (1994). *Organizing Modernity*. Oxford: Blackwell.
Lawler, S. (2011). 'Symbolic violence', in D. Southerton (ed.), *Encyclopaedia of Consumer Culture*. London: Sage.
Lears, J. (1985). 'The concept of cultural hegemony: Problems and possibilities'. *American Historical Review*, 90(3): 567–93.
Leblanc, L. (1999). *Pretty in Punk: Girls' Gender Resistance in a Boys' Subculture*. New Brunswick, NJ: Rutgers University Press.
Lemieux, C. (2014). 'The moral idealism of ordinary people as a sociological challenge: Reflections of the French reception of Luc Boltanski and Laurent Thévenot's *On Justification*', in S. Susen and B. Turner (eds.), *The Spirit of Luc Boltanski*. London: Anthem Press.
Lerner, M. (1980). *The Belief in a Just World: A Fundamental Delusion*. New York: Plenum.

Levy, R. (1991). 'Structure-blindness: A non-ideological component of false consciousness'. *International Journal of Sociology and Social Policy*, 11(6–8): 61–70.
Lilja, M., Baaz, M., Schulz, M., and Vinthagen, S. (2017). 'How resistance encourages resistance: Theorizing the nexus between power, "organised resistance" and "everyday resistance"'. *Journal of Political Power*, 10(1): 40–54.
Linos, K., and West, M. (2003). 'Self-interest, social beliefs, and attitudes to redistribution: Re-addressing the issue of cross-national variation'. *European Sociological Review*, 19(4): 393–409.
Lipsky, M. (1980). *Street-Level Bureaucracy: The Dilemmas of Individuals in Public Service*. New York: Russell Sage Foundation.
Lister, R. (2003). *Poverty*. Cambridge: Polity Press.
Littler, J. (2013). 'Meritocracy as plutocracy: The marketising of "equality" within neoliberalism'. *New Formations: A Journal of Culture/Theory/Politics*, 80–81: 52–72.
Liu, S., and Shi, W. (2017). 'Worker struggles and factory occupation in China during the current economic crisis'. *Social Movement Studies*, 16(3): 355–60.
Livingston, E. (2008). 'Context and detail in studies of the witnessable social order'. *Journal of Pragmatics*, 40(5): 840–62.
Lora-Wainwright, A. (2017). *Resigned Activism: Living with Pollution in Rural China*. Cambridge, MA: MIT Press.
Lübker, M. (2004). 'Globalisation and perceptions of inequality'. *International Labor Review*, 143(1–2): 91–128.
Lübker, M. (2014). 'Income inequality, redistribution, and poverty: contrasting rational choice and behavioral perspectives'. *Review of Income and Wealth*, 60(1): 133–54.
Lukes, S. (2005). *Power: A Radical View*, 2nd edition. Basingstoke: Palgrave Macmillan.
Luo, X. (1998). 'What affects attitudes towards government's role in solving unemployment? A comparative study of Great Britain and the United States'. *International Journal of Public Opinion*, 10(2): 121–44.
Lupu, N., and Pontusson, J. (2011). 'The structure of inequality and the politics of redistribution'. *American Political Science Review*, 105(2): 316–36.
Lynch, M. (2001). 'Ethnomethodology and the logic of practice', in T. Schatzki, K. Knorr Cetina and E. von Savigny (eds.), *Practice Turn in Contemporary Theory*. London: Routledge.
Madsen, R. (2011). 'Review of *Myth of the Social Volcano: Perceptions of Inequality and Distributive Injustice in Contemporary China* by Whyte; *Collective Resistance in China: Why Popular Protests Succeed or Fail* by Cai'. *American Journal of Sociology*, 117(3): 967–70.
Marmot, M. (2002). 'The influence of income on health: Views of an epidemiologist'. *Health Affairs*, 21(2): 31–46.
Marshall, G., and Swift, A. (1996). 'Merit and mobility: A reply to Peter Saunders'. *Sociology*, 30(2): 375–86.
Martinez-Alier, J. (2002). *The Environmentalism of the Poor*. Cheltenham: Edward Elgar.
Marx, K. (1990) [1867]. *Capital*. London: Penguin Classics.
Marx, K. (2000) [1859]. *The 18th Brumaire of Louis Bonaparte*, 2nd edition, in D. McLennan (ed.), *Karl Marx, Selected Writings*. Oxford: Oxford University Press.
McAdam, D. (1982). *Political Process and the Development of Black Insurgency, 1930–1970*. Chicago: University of Chicago Press.
McAdam, D. (1986). 'Recruitment to high-risk activism: The case of freedom summer'. *American Journal of Sociology* 92(1): 64–90.
McAdam, D. (1995). '"Initiator" and "spinoff movements": Diffusion processes in protest cycles', in M. Traugott (ed.), *Repertoires and Cycles of Collective Action*. Durham, NC: Duke University Press.
McAdam, D., McCarthy, J., and Zald, M. (1988). 'Social movements', in N. Smelser (ed.), *Handbook of Sociology*. Beverly Hills, CA: Sage.
McAdam, D., and Paulsen, R. (1993). 'Specifying the relationship between social ties and activism'. *American Journal of Sociology*, 99(3): 640–67.

McAdam, D., Tarrow, S., and Tilly, C. (2001). *Dynamics of Contention*. New York: Cambridge University Press.

McAdam, D., Tilly, C., and Tarrow, S. (2009). 'Comparative perspectives on contentious politics', in M. Lichbach and A. Zuckerman (eds.), *Comparative Politics: Rationality, Culture, and Structure: Advancing Theory in Comparative Politics*. Cambridge: Cambridge University Press.

McCall, L. (2013). *The Undeserving Rich: American Beliefs about Inequality Opportunity and Redistribution*. Cambridge: Cambridge University Press.

McCall, L. (2016). 'Political and policy responses to problems of inequality and opportunity: Past, present, and future', in I. Kircsh and H. Braun (eds.), *The Dynamics of Opportunity in America: Evidence and Perspectives*. New York: Springer.

McCall, L., and Chin, F. (2013). 'Does knowledge of inequality affect beliefs about inequality?'. Paper presented at the Midwest Political Science Association meeting, Chicago, 11–14 April 2013. Available at http://faculty.wcas.northwestern.edu/~jnd260/cab/CAB2013McCall.pdf, accessed 24/03/2019.

McCall, L., and Orloff, A. (2017). 'The multidimensional politics of inequality: Taking stock of identity politics in the U.S. Presidential election of 2016'. *British Journal of Sociology*, 68(S1): S34–56.

McCall, L., Burk, D., Laperrière, M., and Richeson, J. (2017). 'Rising inequality shapes opportunity beliefs'. *Proceedings of the National Academy of Sciences*, 114(36): 9593–98.

McCarthy, J. D., and Zald, M. N. (1977). 'Resource mobilization and social movements: A partial theory'. *American Journal of Sociology*, 82: 1212–41.

McKenzie, L. (2015). *Getting By: Estates, Class and Culture in Austerity Britain*. Bristol: Policy Press.

McNamee, S., and Miller, R. (2004). 'The meritocracy myth'. *Sociation Today*, 2(1).

McNamee, S. J., and Miller, R. K. (2009). *The Meritocracy Myth*. Lanham, MD: Rowman & Littlefield.

McNay, L. (1999). 'Gender, habitus and the field: Pierre Bourdieu and the limits of reflexivity'. *Theory, Culture & Society*, 16(1): 95–117.

McRobbie, A. (2015). *Be Creative*. Cambridge: Polity.

Mead, G. H. (1934). *Mind, Self and Society*. Edited by C. Morris. Chicago: University of Chicago Press.

Medgyesi, M. (2013). 'Increasing income inequality and attitudes to inequality: A cohort perspective'. AIAS, GINI Discussion Paper 94, available at http://www.gini-research.org/system/uploads/598/original/94.pdf?1393500304, accessed 21/03/2018.

Meltzer, A., and Richard, S. (1981). 'A rational theory of the size of government'. *Journal of Political Economy*, 89(5): 914–27.

Melucci, A. (1985). 'The symbolic challenge of contemporary movements'. *Sociological Research*, 52: 789–816.

Melucci, A. (1989). *Nomads of the Present*. London: Hutchinson Radius.

Melucci, A. (1996). *Challenging Codes: Collective Action in the Information Age*. Cambridge: Cambridge University Press.

Merolla, D., Hunt, M., and Serpe, R. (2011). 'Concentrated disadvantage and beliefs about the causes of poverty: A multi-level analysis'. *Sociological Perspectives*, 54(2): 205–27.

Meyer, D. (2004). 'Protest and political opportunities'. *Annual Review of Sociology*, 30: 125–45.

Mijs, J. (2019). 'The paradox of inequality: Income inequality and belief in meritocracy go hand in hand'. *Socio-Economic Review*, 0(0): 1–29, available at https://static1.squarespace.com/static/55e8aafee4b011f0abb1b06d/t/5c483fe7c74c5023692e12de/1548238828312/Mijs.+2019.+Paradox+of+Inequality.pdf, accessed 05/04/2014.

Milanovic, B. (2016). *Global Inequality: A New Approach for the Age of Globalization*. Cambridge, MA: Harvard University Press.

Miller, D. (2010). *Stuff*. Cambridge: Polity Press.

Minkoff, S., and Lyons, J. (2017). 'Living with inequality: Neighborhood income diversity and perceptions of the income gap'. *American Politics Research*, 47(2): 329–36.

Mirshak, N. (2019a). 'Rethinking resistance under authoritarianism: Civil society and non-contentious forms of contestation in post-uprisings Egypt'. *Social Movement Studies*, 18(6): 702–19.
Mirshak, N. (2019b). 'Education as resistance: Egyptian civil society and rethinking political education under authoritarian contexts'. *Critical Sociology*, https://doi.org/10.1177/0896920519856398.
Mitchell, T. (1990). 'Everyday metaphors of power'. *Theory & Society*, 19: 545–77.
Mols, F., and Jetten, J. (2017). *The Wealth Paradox: Economic Prosperity and the Hardening of Attitudes*. Cambridge: Cambridge University Press.
Moore, M., and Hossain, N. (2005). 'Elites, poverty and public policy: From structure to strategy', in E. Reis and M. Moore (eds.), *Elite Perceptions of Poverty and Inequality*. London: Zed Books.
Morris, A. (1984). *The Origins of the Civil Rights Movement*. New York: Free Press.
Müller, J.-W. (2016). *What Is Populism?* Philadelphia: Philadelphia Press.
Müller, M. (2012). 'Opening the black box of the organization: Socio-material practices of geopolitical ordering'. *Political Geography*, 31: 379–88.
Müller, M. (2015). 'Assemblages and actor-networks: Rethinking socio-material power, politics and space'. *Geography Compass*, 9(1): 27–41.
Mumby, D. K. (2005). 'Theorizing resistance in organization studies: A dialectical approach'. *Management Communications Quarterly*, 19(1): 19–44.
Mutz, D. (2018). 'Status threat, not economic hardship, explains the 2016 presidential vote'. *PNAS*, 11(44): E4330–39.
Narayan, J. (2016). *John Dewey: The Global Public and its Problems*. Manchester: Manchester University Press.
Newman, B., Johnston, C., and Lown, P. (2015). 'False consciousness or class awareness? Local income inequality, personal economic position, and belief in American meritocracy'. *American Journal of Political Science*, 59: 326–40.
Niehues, J. (2014). 'Subjective perceptions of inequality and redistributive preferences: An international comparison'. *Quarterly Journal of Empirical Economic Research*, no. 2, Cologne Institute of Economic Research, Germany.
Nilsen, A. G. (2016). 'Power, resistance and development in the global South: Notes towards a critical research agenda'. *International Journal of Politics, Culture and Society*, 29: 269–87.
Nolan, B., Salverda, W., Checchi, D., Marx, I., McKnight, A., György Tóth, I., and de Werfhorst, H. (eds.). (2014). *Changing Inequalities and Societal Impacts in Rich Countries: Thirty Countries' Experiences*. Oxford: Oxford University Press.
Noon, M., and Blyton, P. (2007). *The Realities of Work*, 3rd edition. New York: Palgrave.
Norton, M. I., and Ariely, D. (2011). 'Building a better America—one wealth quintile at a time'. *Perspectives on Psychological Science*, 6: 9–12.
Norton, M. I., and Ariely, D. (2013). 'American's desire for less wealth inequality does not depend on how you ask them'. *Judgment and Decision Making*, 8: 393–94.
Nozick, R. (1974). *Anarchy, State and Utopia*. New York: Basic Books.
Oakley, K., Laurison, D., O'Brien, D., and Friedman, S. (2017). 'Cultural capital: Arts graduates, spatial inequality, and London's impact on cultural labor markets'. *American Behavioral Scientist*, 61(12): 1510–31.
Oberhauser, A., Krier, D., and Kusow, A. (2019). 'Political moderation and polarization in the heartland: Economics, rurality, and social identity in the 2016 U.S. presidential election'. *Sociological Quarterly*, 60(2): 224–44.
Oddsson, G. (2010). 'Class awareness in Iceland'. *International Journal of Sociology and Social Policy*, 30(5/6): 292–312.
Oddsson, G., and Bernburg, J. G. (2018). 'Opportunity beliefs and class differences in subjective status injustice during the Great Recession in Iceland'. *Acta Sociologica*, 61(3): 283–99.
OECD. (2011). *Divided We Stand: Why Inequality Keeps Rising*. Paris: OECD Publishing. Available at https://read.oecd-ilibrary.org/social-issues-migration-health/the-

causes-of-growing-inequalities-in-oecd-countries_9789264119536-en#page1, accessed 11/04/2019.
OECD. (2015). *In It Together: Why Less Inequality Benefits All*. Paris: OECD Publishing. Available at read.oecd-ilibrary.org/employment/in-it-together-why-less-inequality-benefits-all_9789264235120-en#page1, accessed 11/04/2019.
OECD. (2019). *Under Pressure: The Squeezed Middle-Class*. Paris: OECD Publishing. Available at https://doi.org/10.1787/689afed1-en, accessed 15/04/2019.
Ogien, A. (2014). 'Pragmatismes et sociologies'. *Revue Française de Sociologie*, 55: 563–79. Translation by Toby Matthews, *Revue Française de Sociologie*, 55(3): 414–28. Available at https://www.cairn-int.info/article-E_RFS_553_0563--pragmatisms-and-sociologies.htm, accessed 31/10/2018.
Ogien, A. (2015). 'Pragmatism's legacy to sociology respecified'. *European Journal of Pragmatism and American Philosophy* (Online), VII–1, available at http://ejpap.revues.org/371, accessed 12/11/2018.
Ohlström, M. (2011). 'Experiences and justice: On the limits of recognition'. *European Journal of Philosophy and Public Debate*, 3(5): 205–10.
Oliver, P., and Johnston, H. (2000). 'What a good idea! Ideologies and frames in social movement research'. *Mobilization*, 4(1): 37–54.
Olson, M. (1965). *The Logic of Collective Action*. Cambridge, MA: Harvard University Press.
O'Brien, D., Laurison, D., Miles, A., and Friedman, S. (2016). 'Are the creative industries meritocratic? An analysis of the 2014 British Labour Force Survey'. *Cultural Trends*, 25(2): 116–31.
O'Neil, C. (2016). *Weapons of Math Destruction: How Big Data Increases Inequality and Threatens Democracy*. New York: Crown.
Orton, M., and Rowlingson, K. (2007). *Public Attitudes to Economic Inequality*. York: Joseph Rowntree Foundation.
Osberg, L., and Smeeding, T. (2006). '"Fair" inequality? Attitudes toward pay differentials: The United States in comparative perspective'. *American Sociological Review* 71: 450–73.
Oxfam. (2014). *Working for the Few: Political Capture and Economic Inequality*. Briefing Paper 178, Oxfam International, available at www.oxfam.org/sites/www.oxfam.org/files/bp-working-for-few-political-capture-economic-inequality-200114-summ-en.pdf, accessed 05/01/2019.
Oxfam. (2017). *An Economy for the 99%*. Briefing Paper, Oxfam International, available at www.cdn.oxfam.org/s3fs-public/file_attachments/bp-economy-for-99-percent-160117-en.pdf, accessed 05/01/2019.
Oxfam. (2019). *Public Good or Private Wealth*. Briefing Paper, Oxfam International, available at oxfamilibrary.openrepository.com/bitstream/handle/10546/620599/bp-public-good-or-private-wealth-210119-en.pdf, accessed 05/04/2019.
Pahl, R., Rose, D., and Spencer, L. (2007). *Inequality and Quiescence: A Continuing Conundrum*. ISER Working Paper 2007–22. Colchester: University of Essex.
Pascale, C.-M. (2007). *Making Sense of Race, Class, and Gender*. Abingdon: Routledge.
Patrick, R. (2016). 'Living with and responding to the "scrounger" narrative in the UK: Exploring everyday strategies of acceptance, resistance and deflection'. *Journal of Poverty and Social Justice*, 24(3): 245–59.
Payne, G. (1992). 'Competing views of contemporary social mobility and social divisions', in R. Burrows and C. Marsh (eds.), *Consumption and Class*. Basingstoke: Macmillan.
Payne, G., and Grew, C. (2005). 'Unpacking "class ambivalence": Some conceptual and methodological issues in accessing class cultures'. *Sociology*, 39(5): 893–910.
Pearce, N., and Taylor, E. (2013). 'Government spending and welfare', in A. Park, C. Bryson, E. Clery, J. Curtice and M. Phillips (eds.), *British Social Attitudes: The 30th Report*. London: NatCen Social Research.

Pemberton, S., Fahmy, E., Sutton, E., and Bell, K. (2016). 'Navigating the stigmatised identities of poverty in austere times: Resisting and responding to narratives of personal failure'. *Critical Social Policy*, 36(1): 21–37.
Peterson, E. W. (2017). 'Is economic inequality really a problem? A review of the arguments'. *Social Sciences*, 6(4): 1–25.
Pheterson, G. (1986). 'Alliances between women: Overcoming internalized oppression and internalized domination'. *Signs*, 12: 146–60.
Pickerill, J., Krinsky, J., Hayes, G., Gillan, K., and Doherty, B. (eds.). (2015). *Occupy! A Global Social Movement*. Abingdon: Routledge.
Pierson, P. (1993). 'When effect becomes cause: Policy feedback and political change'. *World Politics*, 45(4): 595–628.
Piketty, T. (2013). *Capital in the Twenty-First Century*. Cambridge, MA: Harvard University Press.
Piven, F. (2008). 'Can power from below change the world?'. *American Sociological Review*, 73(1): 1–14.
Piven, F., and Cloward, R. (1979). *Poor People's Movements: Why They Succeed, How They Fail*, 2nd edition. New York: Vintage Books.
Piven, F., and Cloward, R. (1991). 'Collective protest: A critique of resource mobilization theory'. *International Journal of Politics, Culture, and Society*, 4(4): 435–58.
Piven, F., and Cloward, R. (2005). 'Rule making, rule breaking, and power', in T. Janoski, R. Alford, A. Hicks and M. Schwartz (eds.), *The Handbook of Political Sociology: States, Civil Societies, and Globalization*. Cambridge: Cambridge University Press.
Plummer, K. (2007). 'Herbert Blumer', in R. Stones (ed.), *Key Sociological Thinkers*, 2nd edition. New York: Palgrave Macmillan.
Polletta, F. (1999). '"Free spaces" in collective action'. *Theory and Society*, 28(1): 1–38.
Polletta, F. (2003). 'Culture is not just in your head,' in J. Goodwin and J. Jasper (eds.), *Rethinking Social Movements*. Lanham, MD: Rowman & Littlefield.
Polletta, F., and Jasper, J. (2001). 'Collective identity and social movements'. *Annual Review of Sociology*, 27: 283–305.
Polletta, F., and Hoban. (2016). 'Why consensus? Prefiguration in three activist eras'. *Journal of Social and Political Psychology*, 4(1): 286–301.
Pontusson, J., and Rueda, D. (2010). 'The politics of inequality: Voter mobilization and left parties in advanced industrial states'. *Comparative Political Studies*, 43(6): 675–705.
Power, S., Allouch, A., and Brown, P. (2016). 'Giving something back? Sentiments of privilege and social responsibility among elite graduates from Britain and France'. *International Sociology*, 31(3): 305–23.
Puwar, N. (2004). *Space Invaders: Race, Gender and Bodies out of Place*. London: Berg.
Pyke, K. (2010). 'What is internalized racial oppression and why don't we study it? Acknowledging racism's hidden injuries'. *Sociological Perspectives*, 53(4): 551–72.
Quéré, L., and Terzi, C. (2011). 'Some features of pragmatist thought still remain insufficiently explored in ethnomethodology'. *Qualitative Sociology*, 34: 271–75.
Quéré, L., and Terzi, C. (2014). 'Did you say "pragmatic"? Luc Boltanski's sociology from a pragmatist perspective', in S. Susen and B. Turner (eds.), *The Spirit of Luc Boltanski*. London: Anthem Press.
Rafanell, I. (2009). 'Durkheim's social facts and the performative model: Reconsidering the objective nature of social phenomena', in G. Cooper, A. King, and R. Rettie (eds.), *Sociological Objects: Reconfigurations of Social Theory*. London: Routledge.
Rafanell, I. (2013). 'Micro-situational foundations of social structure: An interactionist exploration of affective sanctioning'. *Journal for the Theory of Social Behaviour*, 43 (2): 181–204.
Rafanell, I., and Gorringe, H. (2010). 'Consenting to domination? Theorising power, agency and embodiment with reference to caste'. *Sociological Review*, 58(4): 604–22.
Ragnarsdottir, B., Bernburg, J., and Olafsdottir, S. (2013). 'The global financial crisis and individual distress: The role of subjective comparisons after the collapse of the Icelandic economy'. *Sociology*, 47(4): 755–75.

Rawls, A. (1987). 'The interaction order *sui generis*: Goffman's contribution to social theory'. *Sociological Theory*, 5(2): 136–49.
Rawls, J. (1971). *A Theory of Justice*. Cambridge, MA: Harvard University Press.
Reay, D. (2005). 'Beyond consciousness? The psychic landscape of social class'. *Sociology*, 39(5): 911–28.
Reckwitz, A. (2002). 'Toward a theory of social practice'. *European Journal of Social Theory*, 5(2): 243–63.
Reckwitz, A. (2002). 'The status of the "material" in theories of culture: from "social structure" to "artefacts"'. *Journal for the Theory of Social Behaviour*, 32(2): 195–217.
Reeskens, T., and van Oorschot, W. (2013). 'Equity, equality, or need? A study of popular preferences for welfare redistribution principles across 24 European countries'. *Journal of European Public Policy*, 20(8): 1174–95.
Reis, E. (2005). 'Perceptions of poverty and inequality among Brazilian elites', in E. Reis and M. Moore (eds.), *Elite Perceptions of Poverty and Inequality*. London: Zed Books.
Reny, T., Collingwood, L., and Valenzuela, A. (2019). 'Vote switching in the 2016 election: How racial and immigration attitudes, not economics, explain shifts in white voting'. *Public Opinion Quarterly*, 83(1): 91–113.
Ribeiro Thomaz, O. (2005). 'Haitian elites and their perceptions of poverty and inequality', in E. Reis and M. Moore (eds.), *Elite Perceptions of Poverty and Inequality*. London: Zed Books.
Richards, J. (2008). 'The many approaches to organisational behaviour. A review, map and research agenda'. *Employee Relations*, 30(6): 653–78.
Ringen, S., and Ngok, K. (2013). *What Kind of Welfare State is Emerging in China?* UNRISD Working Paper 2013–2, United Nations Research Institute for Social Development, available at www.unrisd.org/80256B3C005BCCF9/%28httpAuxPages%29/28BCE0F59BDD3738C1257BE30053EBAC/$file/Ringen%20and%20Ngok.pdf, accessed 23/10/2018.
Riskin, C. (2014). 'Inequality and the reform era in China', in S. Fan, S. Kanbur, S. Wei, et al. (eds.), *The Oxford Companion to the Economics of China*. Oxford: Oxford University Press.
Roberts, K. (2001). *Class in Modern Britain*. New York: Palgrave.
Roex, K. L., Huijts, T., and Sieben, I. (2019). 'Attitudes towards income inequality: "Winners" versus "losers" of the perceived meritocracy'. *Acta Sociologica*, 62(1): 47–63.
Rose, D. (2006). *Social Comparisons and Social Order*. ISER Working Paper 2006–48. Colchester: University of Essex.
Roser, M., and Ortiz-Ospina, E. (2016). 'Income inequality', available at https://ourworldindata.org/income-inequality, accessed 13/04/2019.
Rosset, J., Giger, N., and Bernauer, J. (2013). 'More money, fewer problems? Cross-level effects of economic deprivation on political representation'. *West European Politics*, 36(4): 817–35.
Rouse, J. (2001). 'Two concepts of practices', in T. Schatzki, K. Knorr Cetina and E. von Savigny (eds.), *The Practice Turn in Contemporary Theory*. London: Routledge.
Rouse, J. (2007a). 'Practice theory'. *Division I Faculty Publications*. Paper 43, available at http://wesscholar.wesleyan.edu/div1facpubs/43, accessed 31/10/2018.
Rouse, J. (2007b). 'Social practices and normativity'. *Philosophy of the Social Sciences*, 37(1): 1–11.
Rowlingson, K., Orton, M., and Taylor, E. (2010). 'Do we still care about inequality?', in A. Park, J. Curtice, E. Clery and D. Bryson (eds.), *British Social Attitudes: The 27th Report: Exploring Labour's Legacy*. London: Sage.
Runciman, W. G. (1966). *Relative Deprivation and Social Justice*. London: Routledge Kegan Paul.
Sachweh, P., and Olafsdottir, S. (2012). 'The welfare state and equality? Stratification realities and aspirations in three welfare regimes'. *European Sociological Review*, 28(2): 149–68.

Salverda, W., Nolan, B., Checchi, D., Marx, I., McKnight, A., György Tóth, I., and de Werfhorst, H. (eds.). (2014). *Changing Inequalities in Rich Countries: Analytical and Comparative Perspectives*. Oxford: Oxford University Press.
Savage, M. (2000). *Class Analysis and Social Transformation*. Buckingham: Open University.
Savage, M. (2003). 'A new class paradigm'. *British Journal of Sociology of Education*, 24(4): 535–41.
Savage, M., Bagnall, G., and Longhurst, B. (2001). 'Ordinary, ambivalent and defensive: Class identities in the Northwest of England'. *Sociology*, 35 (4): 875–92.
Sayer, A. (1999). 'Bourdieu, Smith and disinterested judgement'. *Sociological Review*, 47(3): 403–31.
Sayer, A. (2005a). 'Class, moral worth and recognition'. *Sociology*, 39(5): 947–63.
Sayer, A. (2005b). *The Moral Significance of Class*. Cambridge: Cambridge University Press.
Sayer, A. (2009). 'Contributive justice and meaningful work'. *Res Publica*, 15: 1–16.
Sayer, A. (2011). 'Habitus, work and contributive justice'. *Sociology*, 45(1): 7–21.
Sayer, A. (2012). 'Capabilities, contributive injustice and unequal divisions of labour'. *Journal of Human Development and Capabilities*, 13(4): 580–96.
Schaffner, B., MacWilliams, M., and Nteta, T. (2018). 'Explaining white polarization in the 2016 vote for president: The sobering role of racism and sexism'. *Political Science Quarterly*, 33(1): 9–34.
Schatzki, T. (2010). 'Materiality and social life'. *Nature and Culture*, 5(2): 123–49.
Schatzki, T. (2012). 'A primer on practices', in J. Higgs, R. Barnett, S. Billett, M. Hutchings and F. Trede (eds.), *Practice-Based Education: Perspectives and Strategies*. Rotterdam: Sense.
Schatzki, T. (2015). 'Spaces of practices and of large social phenomena'. Espaces-Temps.net, 24 March, available at https://www.espacestemps.net/en/articles/spaces-of-practices-and-of-large-social-phenomena/, accessed 29/10/2018.
Schor, J. (1998). *The Overspent American*. New York: Harper.
Schröder, M. (2017). 'Is income inequality related to tolerance for inequality?'. *Social Justice Research*, 30(1): 23–47.
Schütz, A. (1962). *The Problem of Social Reality: Collected Papers I*. The Hague: Martinus Nijhoff.
Schütz, A. (1964). *Studies in Social Theory: Collected Papers II*. The Hague: Martinus Nijhoff.
Schwalbe, M., Godwin, S., Holden, D., Schrock, D., Thompson, S., and Wolkomir, M. (2000). 'Generic processes in the reproduction of inequality: An interactionist analysis'. *Social Forces*, 79(2): 419–52.
Scott, J. C. (1976). *The Moral Economy of the Peasant*. New Haven, CT: Yale University Press.
Scott, J. C. (1985). *Weapons of the Weak: Everyday Forms of Peasant Resistance*. New Haven, CT: Yale University Press.
Scott, J. C. (1989). 'Everyday forms of resistance'. *Copenhagen Papers*, 4: 33–62.
Scott, J. C. (1990). *Domination and the Arts of Resistance: Hidden Transcripts*. New Haven, CT: Yale University Press.
Scott, J. C. (2012). *Two Cheers for Anarchism: Six Easy Pieces on Autonomy, Dignity, and Meaningful Work and Play*. Princeton, NJ: Princeton University Press.
Seccombe, K., James, D., and Walters, K. (1998). '"They think you ain't much of nothing": The social construction of the welfare mother'. *Journal of Marriage and the Family*, 60: 849–65.
Sen, A. (1985). *Commodities and Capabilities*. Amsterdam: North-Holland.
Sennett, R., and Cobb, J. (1972). *The Hidden Injuries of Class*. Cambridge: Cambridge University Press.
Sennett, R., and Cobb, J. (1977). *The Hidden Injuries of Class*. Cambridge: Cambridge University Press.

Sharrock, W., and Button, G. (1991). 'The social actor: Social action in real time', in G. Button (ed.), *Ethnomethodology and the Human Science*. Cambridge: Cambridge University Press.
Sherman, R. (2017). *Uneasy Street: The Anxieties of Affluence*. Princeton, NJ: Princeton University Press.
Shildrick, T., and McDonald, R. (2013). 'Poverty talk: How people experiencing poverty deny their poverty and why they blame "the poor"'. *Sociological Review*, 61: 285–303.
Shott, S. (1979). 'Emotion and social life: A symbolic interactionist analysis'. *American Journal of Sociology*, 84(6): 1317–34.
Simi, P., and Futrell, R. (2009). 'Negotiating white power activist stigma'. *Social Problems*, 56(1): 89–110.
Sivaramakrishnan, K. (2005a). 'Some intellectual genealogies for the concept of everyday resistance'. *American Anthropologist*, 107(3): 346–55.
Sivaramakrishnan, K. (2005b). 'Introduction to "moral economies, state spaces, and categorical violence"'. *American Anthropologist*, 107(3): 321–30.
Skeggs, B. (1997). *Formations of Class and Gender: Becoming Respectable*. London: Sage.
Skeggs, B. (2004). *Class, Self, Culture*. London: Routledge.
Skeggs, B. (2009). 'Haunted by the spectre of judgement: Respectability, value and affect in class relations', in K. P. Sveinsson (ed.), *Who Cares about the White Working Class?* London: Runnymede Trust.
Skeggs, B. (2011). 'Imagining personhood differently: Person value and autonomist working-class value practices'. *Sociological Review*, 59(3): 496–513.
Skeggs, B. (2012). 'Feeling class: Affect and culture in the making of class relations', in G. Ritzer (ed.), *The Wiley-Blackwell Companion to Sociology*. Cowley: Blackwell.
Skeggs, B. (2014). 'Values beyond value? Is anything beyond the logic of capital?'. *British Journal of Sociology*, 65(1): 1–20.
Skeggs, B., and Loveday, V. (2012). 'Struggles for value: Value practices, injustice, judgment, affect and the idea of class'. *British Journal of Sociology*, 63(3): 472–90.
Skocpol, T., and Amenta, E. (1986). 'States and social policies'. *Annual Review of Sociology*, 12: 131–57.
Slater, T. (2011). 'From "criminality" to marginality: Rioting against a broken state'. *Human Geography: A New Radical Journal*, 4(3): 106–15.
Smith, A. (1984) [1759]. *The Theory of Moral Sentiments*. Indianapolis, IN: Liberty Fund.
Snow, D. (2004). 'Social movements as challenges to authority: Resistance to an emerging conceptual hegemony'. *Research in Social Movements, Conflicts and Change*, 25: 3–25.
Snow, D., and Benford, R. (1988). 'Ideology, frame resonance, and participant mobilisation'. *International Social Movement Research*, 1: 197–217.
Snow, D., and Benford, R. (1992). 'Master frames and cycles of protest', in A. Morris and C. Mueller (eds.), *Frontiers in Social Movement Theory*. New Haven, CT: Yale University Press.
Snow, D., Cress, M., Downey, L., and Jones, A. (1998). 'Disrupting the "quotidian": Reconceptualizing the relationship between breakdown and the emergence of collective action'. *Mobilization*, 1998, 3(1): 1–22.
Snow, D., Rochford, E., Worden, S., and Benford, R. (1986). 'Frame alignment processes, micromobilization and movement participation'. *American Sociological Review*, 51(4): 464–81.
Solt, F. (2008). 'Economic inequality and democratic political engagement'. *American Journal of Political Science*, 52(1): 48–60.
Spicer, A., and Böhm, S. (2007). 'Moving management: Theorizing struggles against the hegemony of management'. *Organization Studies*, 28(11): 1667–98.
Steinberg, M. (1998). 'Tilting the frame: Considerations on collective action framing from a discursive turn'. *Theory and Society*, 27(6): 845–72.

Steinberg, M. (1999). 'The talk and back talk of collective action: A dialogic analysis of repertoires of discourse among nineteenth-century English cotton spinners'. *American Journal of Sociology*, 105(3): 736–80.
Steinberg, M. (2002). 'Toward a more dialogic analysis of social movement culture', in D. S. Meyer, N. Whittier and B. Robnett (eds.), *Social Movements: Identity, Culture and the State*. Oxford: Oxford University Press.
Stewart, A., Prandy, K., and Blackburn, R. M. (1980). *Social Stratification and Occupations*. London: Macmillan.
Stiglitz, J. (2014). 'Inequality is not inevitable'. Available at https://opinionator.blogs.nytimes.com/2014/06/27/inequality-is-not-inevitable/, accessed 13/04/2019.
Stiglitz, J. (2016). *The Great Divide: Unequal Societies and What We Can Do about Them*. New York: W. W. Norton.
Stones, R. (2014). 'Strengths and limitations of Luc Boltanski's On Critique', in S. Susen and B. Turner (eds.), *The Spirit of Luc Boltanski*. London: Anthem Press.
Strathern, M. (2000). 'Introduction', to M. Strathern (ed.), *Audit Cultures*. London: Routledge.
Susen, S. (2014a). 'Luc Boltanski: His life and work—an overview', in S. Susen and B. Turner (eds.), *The Spirit of Luc Boltanski*. London: Anthem Press.
Susen, S. (2014b). 'Is there such a thing as a "Pragmatic Sociology of Critique"? Reflections on Luc Boltanski's "On Critique"', pp. 173–210 in S. Susen and B. S. Turner (eds.), *The Spirit of Luc Boltanski: Essays on the 'Pragmatic Sociology of Critique'*. London: Anthem Press.
Susen, S. (2014c). 'Towards a dialogue between Pierre Bourdieu's "Critical Sociology" and Luc Boltanski's "Pragmatic Sociology of Critique"', pp. 313–48 in S. Susen and B. S. Turner (eds.), *The Spirit of Luc Boltanski: Essays on the 'Pragmatic Sociology of Critique'*. London: Anthem Press.
Svallfors, S. (2004). 'Class, attitudes and the welfare state: Sweden in comparative perspective'. *Social Policy and Administration*, 38(2): 119–38.
Svallfors, S. (2006). *The Moral Economy of Class: Class and Attitudes in Comparative Perspective*. Palo Alto, CA: Stanford University Press.
Swartz, D. (1997). *Culture and Power: The Sociology of Pierre Bourdieu*. Chicago: University of Chicago Press.
Tarrow, S. (1989). *Democracy and Disorder: Protest and Politics in Italy, 1965–1975*. Oxford: Oxford University Press.
Tarrow, S. (1994). *Power in Movement: Collective Action, Social Movements and Politics*. Cambridge: Cambridge University Press
Tarrow, S. (2008). 'Charles Tilly and the practice of contentious politics'. *Social Movement Studies*, 7(3): 225–46.
Taylor, M., and O'Brien, D. (2017). '"Culture is a meritocracy": Why creative workers' attitudes may reinforce social inequality'. *Sociological Research Online*, 22(4): 27–47.
Taylor-Gooby, P. (2013). 'Why do people stigmatise the poor at a time of rapidly increasing inequality, and what can be done about it?'. *Political Quarterly*, 84(1): 31–42.
Taylor-Gooby, P., and Taylor, E. (2015). 'Benefits and welfare: Long-term trends or short term reactions?', in J. Curtice and R. Ormston (eds.), *British Social Attitudes 32*. London: NatCen Social Research.
Terzi, C., and Tonnelat, S. (2017). 'The publicization of public space'. *Environment and Planning A*, 49(3): 519–36.
Therborn, G. (2013). *The Killing Fields of Inequality*. Cambridge: Polity.
Thévenot, L. (2011). 'Power and oppression from the perspective of the sociology of engagements: a comparison with Bourdieu's and Dewey's critical approaches to practical activities'. *Irish Journal of Sociology*, 19(1): 35–67.
Thompson, P., and Ackroyd, S. (1995). 'All quiet on the workplace front? A critique of recent trends in British industrial sociology'. *Sociology*, 29(4): 615–33.
Tilly, C. (2004). *Contention and Democracy in Europe, 1650–2000*. Cambridge: Cambridge University Press.

Tilly, C. (2008). *Contentious Performances*. Cambridge: Cambridge University Press.
Tóth, I., Horn, D., and Medgyesi, M. (2013). 'Rising inequalities: Will electorates go for higher redistribution?', in W. Salverda, B. Nolan, D. Checchi, I. Marx, A. McKnight, I. Tóth and H. de Werfhorst (eds.), *Changing Inequalities in Rich Countries: Analytical and Comparative Perspectives*. Oxford: Oxford University Press.
Touraine, A. (1981). *The Voice and the Eye: An Analysis of Social Movements*. Cambridge: Cambridge University Press.
Touraine, A. (2002). 'The importance of social movements'. *Social Movement Studies*, 1(1): 89–95.
Trump, K.-S. (2017). 'Income inequality influences perceptions of legitimate income differences'. *British Journal of Political Science*, 48: 929–52.
Turner, B. (2011). 'Book review: Luc Boltanski on critique. A sociology of emancipation'. *Sociological Review*, 59(4): 864–69.
Tyler, I. (2013). *Revolting Subjects: Social Abjection and Resistance in Neo-liberal Britain*. London: Zed Books.
Tyler, I. (2018). 'Resituating Erving Goffman: From stigma power to Black Power'. *The Sociological Review*, 66(4): 744–76.
Tyler, I., and Slater, T. (2018). 'Rethinking the sociology of stigma'. *Sociological Review*, 66(4): 721–43.
Van Oorschot, W. (2002). 'Individual motives for contributing to welfare benefits in the Netherlands'. *Policy and Politics*, 30(1): 31–46.
Van Oorschot, W., Reeskens, T., and Meuleman, B. (2012). 'Popular perceptions of welfare state consequences: A multi-level, cross-national analysis of 25 European countries'. *Journal of European Social Policy*, 22(2): 181–97.
Van Steckelenburg, J., and Klandermans, B. (2013). 'The social psychology of protest'. *Current Sociology*, 61(5–6): 886–905.
Verme, P. (2014). 'Facts and perceptions of inequality', in P. Verme, B. Milanovic, S. A. Sahar El Tawila, M. Gadallah and E. A. A. El-Majeed (eds.), *Inside Inequality in the Arab Republic of Egypt*. Washington, DC: World Bank.
Vincent, J. (1990). *Anthropology and Politics: Visions, Traditions, and Trends*. Tucson: University of Arizona Press.
Vinthagen, S., and Johansson, A. (2013). 'Everyday resistance: Exploration of a concept and its theories'. *Resistance Studies Magazine*, 1: 1–45.
Wagner, P. (2014). 'A renewal of social theory that remains necessary: The sociology of critical capacity twenty years after,' in S. Susen and B. Turner (eds.), *The Spirit of Luc Boltanski*. London: Anthem Press.
Walley, C. (2017). 'Trump's election and the "white working class": What we missed'. *American Ethnologist*, 44(2): 231–36.
Warde, A. (2014). 'After taste: Culture, consumption and theories of practice'. *Journal of Consumer Culture*, 14(3): 279–303.
Warde, A. (2016). *The Practice of Eating*. Cambridge: Polity Press.
Wartenberg, T. (1990). *The Forms of Power*. Philadelphia: Temple University Press.
Weiß, A. (2017). 'Sociological theories of global inequalities'. *Sociology*, 51(6): 1318–24.
West, C. (1989). *The American Evasion of Philosophy: A Genealogy of Pragmatism*. Madison: University of Wisconsin Press.
West, C., and Fenstermaker, S. (1995). 'Doing difference'. *Gender and Society*, 9(1): 8–37.
West, C., and Zimmerman, D. (1987). 'Doing gender'. *Gender and Society*, 1(2): 125–51.
Whyte, M. K. (2010a). *Myth of the Social Volcano: Perceptions of Inequality and Distributive Injustice in Contemporary China*. Palo Alto, CA: Stanford University Press.
Whyte, M. K. (2010b). 'Fair versus unfair: How do Chinese citizens view current inequalities?', in J. C. Oi, S. Rozelle and X. Zhou (eds.), *Growing Pains: Tensions and Opportunity in China's Transformation*. Stanford, CA: Shorenstein Center.
Whyte, M. K . (2011). 'Myth of the social volcano: Popular responses to rising inequality in China', in W. C. Kirby (ed.), *The People's Republic of China at 60*. Cambridge, MA: Harvard University Asia Center.

Whyte, M. K . (2016). 'China's dormant and active social volcanoes'. *China Journal*, 75: 9–37.
Whyte, M. K., and Han, C . (2009). 'The social contours of distributive injustice feelings in contemporary China', in D. S. Davis and W. Feng (eds.), *Creating Wealth and Poverty in Post-Socialist China*. Palo Alto, CA: Stanford University Press.
Wilkinson, R., and Pickett, K. (2009). *The Spirit Level*. London: Penguin.
Wilkinson, R., and Pickett, K. (2018). *The Inner Level*. London: Penguin.
Willis, P. (1977). *Learning to Labour*. London: Saxon House.
Willis, P. (1983). 'Cultural production and theories of reproduction', in Barton, L., and Walker S. (eds.), *Race, Class, and Education*. London: Croom Helm.
Wittgenstein, L. (1953). *Philosophical Investigations*. London: Macmillan.
Wlezien, C. (1995). 'The public as thermostat: Dynamics of preferences for spending'. *American Journal of Political Science*, 39: 981–1000.
Woolgar, S., and Neyland, D. (2013). *Mundane Governance*. Oxford: Oxford University Press.
Wong, L. (2004). 'Market reforms, globalization and social justice in China'. *Journal of Contemporary China*, 13(38): 151–71.
World Economic Forum. (2015). 'Deepening income inequality'. Available at http://reports.weforum.org/outlook-global-agenda-2015/top-10-trends-of-2015/1-deepening-income-inequality/, accessed 09/04/2019.
Xie, Y., and Zhou, X. (2014). 'Income inequality in today's China'. *Proceedings of the National Academy of Sciences*, 111(19): 6928–33.
Yan, F. (2013). 'A little spark kindles a great fire? The paradox of China's rising wave of protest'. *Social Movement Studies*, 12(3): 342–48.
Yates, L. (2015). 'Rethinking prefiguration: Alternatives, micropolitics and goals in social movements'. *Social Movement Studies*, 14(1): 1–21.
Young, M. (1962). *The Rise of the Meritocracy: 1870–2033*. Harmondsworth: Penguin.
Zagefka, H., and Brown, R. (2006). 'Predicting comparison choices in intergroup settings: A new look', in S. Guimond (ed.), *Social Comparison and Psychology*. Cambridge: Cambridge University Press.
Zimmerman, D. (1978). 'Ethnomethodology'. *American Sociologist*, 13: 6–15.
Zimmerman, D. (1970). 'The practicalities of rule use', in J. D. Douglas (ed.), *Understanding Everyday Life: Toward the Reconstruction of Sociological Knowledge*. London: Routledge and Kegan Paul.
Zuo, J., and Benford, R. (1995). 'Mobilization processes and the 1989 Chinese democracy movement'. *Sociological Quarterly*, 36(1): 131–56.

Index

abjection and abjectification, 105
Abrahams, J., 94
accountability, 187–188
Ackroyd, S., 157–159, 160, 163, 164, 166, 170, 171
activism, 125, 131–132, 136
actor network theory (ANT), 190, 212, 213
Adnan, S., 152, 166
affective inequality, 19–20, 89–92
affective sanctioning, 111–116
African Americans, 110
agency, human, 131, 157
agreement in action/practice, 182–183, 184
Ahmed, S., 73
American dream, the, 37, 70
Anderson, E., 214–215
Anderson, J., 108
ANT. *See* actor network theory
anti-discipline, 156
anti-globalisation activists, 131–132
Arab Spring (2010–2014), 139, 150
attitudes research, 26–27, 52
audit culture, 107
authoritarian rule, 14, 16, 23–24, 121, 122, 139, 146, 151, 153, 202
awareness of one's subordination, 111

Barnes, B., 12, 111, 183–184, 189, 190, 209
Bashi Treitler, V., 9
Baumberg Geiger, B., 46–47
Bayat, A., 139–141, 142, 145, 150, 163, 164, 165, 166, 167, 168
Becker, H., 189
Benford, R., 130
Bernauer, J., 6
Bernburg, J. G., 63–64
Bezos, Jeff, 42

Bhambra, G., 8, 40
Blackburn, R. M., 16
Blumer, H., 122–123, 185
BNP. *See* British National Party
Boatcă, M., 9
Boggs, C., 137
Böhm, S., 145–146
Bohman, J., 90, 214–217
Boltanski, L., 91–92, 97–98, 99–100, 101, 105, 106–107, 180–182, 198, 200
Bordo, S., 79, 83
Bourdieu, P., 18–20, 59, 64, 69, 71, 78–81, 83–84, 90, 93–94, 95–96, 155, 181, 182, 191, 197–198, 200; criticisms of, 93
Brazil, 109
Brexit, 8, 27, 30, 45–51, 65, 68, 105, 108
British National Party (BNP), 61
British Social Attitudes Survey, 41, 49
Buffett, Warren, 42
Button, G., 186

Cairo, 169
call-centre workers, 170
Callon, M., 191, 194
capitalism, 4, 9, 16–18, 100, 102, 106, 145, 154
caste system, 112–114
Chiapello, E., 100
Chin, C., 162
Chin, F., 70
China, 4, 27, 31–32, 33–35, 130, 136
citizenship rights, 139
city planning, 155
civil liberties, 6–7
civil rights movement, 127
civil society, 18
civil society organisations (CSOs), 150–151

class divisions, 13–14, 17, 66, 79, 95, 119, 159
Clinton, Hillary, 39
Cloward, R., 123–124, 125–126, 127–129, 141
cognitive liberation, 120, 129
Cole, W., 6
collective action, 120, 128–129, 130, 160, 196, 208
collective refusal, 121, 126, 128, 143, 145
colonialism, 77, 81, 139
commitments, 96, 115
common sense, 19, 71–72, 74–76
Communist Party, 34
constitutive value, 179
cooperative practices, 217
coping mechanisms, 173
Cornish, F., 137
Coulter, J., 179, 210
counter-conduct, 163
counter-framing, 130
Cruces, G., 43
CSOs. *See* civil society organisations
cultural dopes, 83, 98
cultural sector, 68
culture, concepts of, 133
Currier, A., 136

Dalits, 112–113
Dallinger, U., 30
Daripalla, Bangladesh, 152, 166
Death, D., 134, 166
de Certeau, M., 154–156, 160, 163, 171
de Sousa Santos, B., 216
Dewey, J., 182, 192, 199, 213–214
discourses, *dominant* and *challenging*, 133–134
disrespect, 89, 92, 101–102, 108
disruption, social, 127
dissent, 22–24, 92, 116, 121–122, 139, 140, 142–144, 146, 147, 165, 172–173; in disguised form, 151–152; limits to, 106–110
docile subjects, 147
domination, forms of, 14
Duprat, M. H., 4
Duru-Bellat, M., 36

Eagleton, T., 17, 18, 81, 83, 84

Eastern Europe, 31, 139
economic inequality, 25, 53, 57
educational provision, 49, 50
Edwards, G., 121, 123, 136–137, 142, 158, 159–160
egalitarian social structure, 28–29
Egypt, 150
Einwhoner, R., 162, 167
elite groups, 6, 16, 69, 120, 139
Emirbayer, M., 209
encroachments, 140–141, 148; *quiet*, 150, 168
entrepreneurs, 69
Epstein, B., 137
equality, general preference for, 28–29, 37–38
ethical beliefs, 96
ethnomethodology, 184, 210–211, 212
Evans, M., 41–42
existential inequality, 9
existential tests, 99–100, 107–108

Fadaee, S., 121, 136, 139
fairness, sense of, 26, 31, 96–97
false consciousness, 57, 64, 165, 208
Fanon, F., 77, 81
feminism, 79, 83
Flacks, R., 126–127, 136
Fleming, C., 103
Foucault, Michel, 134, 147, 153, 159, 163, 164
framing, 129–130, 132, 133, 141
Frankfurt School, 18
Fraser, N., 102, 103
free rider problem, 123
Frega, R., 179, 187
Friedman, S., 94
Futrell, R., 164, 169

Gamson, W., 120, 131
Garfinkel, H., 187, 188, 212
Gates, Bill, 42
GDP. *See* gross domestic product
gender relations, 63, 79, 188
Giger, N., 6
Gimpelson, V., 41, 42
Gini coefficient, 29
global corporations, 131

global financial crisis (2008), 13, 62, 63, 64, 131
Global North, 14–15, 136, 138, 153
Global South, 136, 138–139, 145
globalisation, 4
Goffman, E., 104, 160, 187, 189
Goodwin, J., 124
Gorringe, H., 92, 111–114, 115, 128–129, 196, 203
Gramsci, A., 18, 19, 151, 153, 163, 165
green campaigns, 136
Greenhouse, C., 153
Greiffenhagen, C., 175, 178, 185, 198–201, 209
grievances, 119–120, 121, 141; as distinct from actual inequality, 2; failure to act in the face of, 122–124
gross domestic product (GDP), 30
grudging performances, 190
Gutmann, M. C., 149–150, 165

habitus, 18, 19, 78, 80, 92, 93–94, 95, 155, 181; *torn*, 93–94
Hacking, I., 10–11
Haenfler, R., 138
Harré, R., 176, 196, 203, 204
Harris, S., 185
hegemony, 153, 165; cultural, 18; Gramscian concept of, 151, 153, 163
Heritage, J., 187
Hermant, E., 195
Hilbert, R., 179, 188
Hills, J., 46
Hochschild, A., 39
Hollander, J., 162, 167
Holloway, J., 122
Honneth, A., 89, 91–92, 101–102, 108
hooks, b., 76–77, 82
Hudson, J., 49–50, 52
Hughes, J., 175, 176, 186, 191–192, 197, 210
Hungary, 50

Iceland, 62–63, 65, 70
idealism, 178
income distribution, 37–38; position in the hierarchy, 42–43, 52, 57, 65–66
indeterminacy of social life, 178–179
India, 4, 112

individualism, 178
inequality: aversion to, 31; concern about, 4, 5, 27–28, 37–38; context of, 27, 31; different meanings of, 9–10; effects of, 10; measurement of, 4–5, 9, 33, 35, 40; misrecognition of, 2, 14, 16, 27–28, 40–41, 58–60, 80, 85, 86; perceptions of and attitudes to, 1, 16, 26–28, 35, 38, 40, 40–41, 42–45, 48–49, 51–53, 124; persistence of, 2, 3, 13, 59, 92, 100–101, 106, 110, 115, 147, 164, 204, 207; practical experience of, 3; in relation to discontent, 26, 39; sense of, 1–3, 9, 10, 12–16, 19–20, 25, 27, 60, 64, 89, 115, 175, 187, 204, 207, 217–218; social aspect of, 9–10, 11, 36, 45; subjective, 2, 10–11, 13, 14–16, 60, 64, 180; tolerance of, 15–16, 27–32, 36–37, 45, 60, 70, 80, 86, 126, 142, 175
information society, 135
infrapolitics, 148
Ingram, N., 94
injustice, 34
institutions and institutional mechanisms, 180–182
interaction, 189–190, 191–192, 210
interactionism, 184, 185–186, 188–189
interdependent power, 128
internalisation of inequality, 19, 20, 58, 65, 76–81, 92
international comparisons, 26–27, 28–30
International Monetary Fund, 5, 131
Iran, 136, 203
Irwin, S., 64, 65, 85–86
Israel, 109

Jæger, M., 40
James, W., 177
Jasper, J. M., 124
Jensen, T., 46
Jetten, J., 7–8
Johansson, A., 162, 166–167
Johnson, B., 138
Jones, E., 138
Jung, M., 183

Kelley, J., 41–42

Kerkvliet, B. J. T., 161, 162, 168
Kiatpongsan, S., 41
King, A., 176, 178, 185, 186, 209–210
Kitchen Revolution, 63
Kivinen, O., 210, 213
Kristeva, J., 105

labour market structure, 68
labour process theory, 159
Lamont, M., 103–104, 109
Latour, Bruno, 191–194, 195, 210, 212
Lave, J., 198, 200
Lawler, S., 79, 81
Lears, J., 19
Lemieux, C., 100
LGBTI movements, 136
liberal democracies, 14, 153
liberal welfare regimes, 30
liberation movements, 126–127
lifestyle movements, 138
Linos, K., 35–36
Lipsky, M., 169–170
Liu, S., 34–35
Livingston, E., 208
Louis XIV, 203
Loveday, V., 94
Lübker, M., 30
Lukes, S., 153
Lunt, N., 50
Lynch, M., 188

McAdam, D., 127, 129, 130
McCall, L., 28, 37–38, 40, 44–45, 49, 70
McCarthy, J. D., 125
McDonald, R., 74
McKenzie, L., 94
McNamee, S. J., 67
Madsen, R., 33–34
Maoist era, 32–33
market reforms, 31
Marshall, G., 60
Marx, Karl, 17
masculinity, 73
maximum limit on individual incomes, 32
Maynard, D., 209
Mead, G. H., 91, 101
Medgyesi, M., 41
media coverage, 45, 72

Melucci, A., 135
meritocratic principles, 28, 31, 35–36, 36, 43–44, 67–70
methodological localism, 15
Middle East, 140, 141, 150
Mijs, J., 27–28, 44
Miller, R. K., 67
Mirshak, N., 151
Mittelman, J., 162
Mizrachi, N., 103, 109
mobilisation, 123, 142–143, 150; barriers to, 120–121, 124–125, 131, 133; collective, 134; conditions for, 125–129
mobility, social, 5–6
Mols, F., 7–8
moral evaluation, 20, 51, 91, 92, 93, 95, 97, 114
Mubarak, Hosni, 150
Müller, M., 195
Mumby, D. K., 145, 157, 161, 164, 166, 170, 171
mutual dependence underlying social life, 128–129

Napoleon, 203
Narayan, J., 215
National Health Service (UK), 49, 50, 51
naturalisation: definition of, 175; of inequality, 2–3, 13–15, 17, 19, 86, 89, 120, 146, 147, 172, 200–201, 208; limits to, 19–23
neoliberalism, 4, 104, 108, 131
new social movement (NSM) theories, 134–136
Ngok, K., 33
normalisation of inequality, 71–75
normative practices, 211–212
normative principles, 92, 95, 97–100
Norton, M., 41
NSM theories. *See* new social movement theories

objectivism, 178
Occupy movement, 131–132
Oddson, G., 63–64
Ogien, A., 214
Ohlström, M., 101

Olafsdottir, S., 26
oligoptica, 193–194, 195
opportunity, 38, 40–41, 62
orders of worth, 99
organisational misbehaviour, 157–159, 170
organisational studies, 161, 162, 164
organisational theory, 157

Pahl, R., 60, 66
paradox of inequality, 27, 28–29, 32
Pascale, C.-M., 66, 71, 72
Pemberton, S., 75
pensions, 49, 50
la perruque, 156
phenomenology, 178
Piiroinen, T., 213
Piven, F., 123–124, 125–126, 127–129, 141, 200
Plummer, K., 209
political equality and engagement, 6–7
Polletta, F., 132–133, 137
populism, 7–8
post-material turn, 134, 136
poststructuralism, 161, 163–164, 170, 171
poverty: and poverty reduction, 4–5, 34, 41, 43, 45–48, 69, 74–75; stigmatising views of, 74
power relations, 12, 18, 21–22, 23–24, 123, 127–128, 146–147, 148, 153, 162, 163, 165–166, 167–168, 170
power, transcripts of, 151
powerless groups, 'weapons' of, 149
practice theory, 194, 213
pragmatism, 209, 213–214, 215, 216–217
Prandy, K., 16
prefiguration, 138
pride, 112
protest against inequality, 119–122, 123, 126, 133, 139, 142–144; constraints on, 127, 143
public problems, 122
public spheres, 99, 216
publics, constitution of, 216
Puwar, N., 73

quality of life activism, 136
Quéré, L., 182, 200–201, 209–210, 213

racism, 8–9, 39, 61, 77–78, 104, 169
Rafanell, I., 103, 109, 112, 128–129, 181, 184, 187, 196, 202–203
Ragnarsdottir, B., 63
Rawls, J., 210
reality tests, 99–100
receptionists, 171
Reckwitz, A., 190
recognition, 89–91; denial of, 101–103, 108, 115; mutual, 102
red state paradox, 39
redistribution of income and wealth, 30, 32, 36, 37, 38, 40, 42, 45, 47, 48–49, 51, 103
reference group comparisons, 33, 43, 60, 64–66
reflexivity, 92, 93–94, 201–202; critical, 3, 80, 210; level of, 200
regulation, 156
reification, 171
relative contentment, 62
resignation in the face of inequality, 17, 21, 120, 130–131, 143, 146
resistance to inequality, 19, 22–23, 145–154, 160–162, 163, 165, 167, 169, 172–173; definition of, 161; as distinct from compliance, 160; diversity in forms of, 161–162; *everday* type, 148–149, 149–151, 152–153, 154, 160, 162, 167; *mundane* forms of, 144, 145–147, 149, 153–154, 160, 172–173; *organised* but *hidden*, 150; *overt* and *covert*, 152; transmission of, 152
resistance studies, 147, 154, 160, 163
resource inequality, 9
Ringen, S., 33
rioting, 65, 105, 108
'rising tide lifts all boats', 42, 61
Ristela, P., 210
Rose, D., 60, 62
Rosset, J., 6
Rouse, J., 178–179, 180, 183, 190–191, 211, 212
rule-breaking, 171–173, 202
rule-following, 178
rule-making, 128
Runciman, W. G., 2, 60–61

Sachweh, P., 26
Sayer, A., 53, 65, 67–68, 90–92, 93, 95–97, 101, 103, 116
Scandinavian countries, 50, 51
Schatzki, T., 195–196
Schütz, A., 177
Schwalbe, M., 188
Scott, J. C., 16, 17, 19, 21, 81, 84, 121, 141, 143, 146, 148–152, 153–154, 160–161, 162, 163, 165, 169
Seccombe, K., 74
segregation, 44, 105
self-help strategies, 167, 169, 173
self-interest models of welfare, 29–30
self-limiting subordinate groups, 78
Sen, A., 77
shame, 92, 95, 112, 116
shared practices, 183–184, 204, 207
shared understandings, 186
shared values, 95
Sharrock, W., 175, 176, 178, 185, 186, 191–192, 197–201, 209, 210
Shi, W., 34–35
Shildrick, T., 74
shoe-wearing in public, 113–114
shop-floor cultures, 162
Simi, P., 164, 169
al Sisi, Fattah, 150
situated perspectives, 213
Skeggs, B., 73–74, 92, 94–95, 108
Slater, T., 106
Slovakia, 50
SMS. *See* social movement studies
Snow, D., 129–130, 134, 137
social *nonmovements*, 138–141
social analysis, 198, 211, 212–213
critical, 208–209
social arrangements, 12–15, 17–18, 20–21, 23–24, 147–148, 173, 176–177, 180, 181, 184, 186, 190, 191–192, 197, 201, 202, 203, 204, 207–209; collective, 23–24; consent to and dissent from, 15, 110, 116; critique of, 20
social change, 197, 203
social constraint, 175, 176
social construction, 175, 200, 201
social interaction, 185

social movement studies (SMS), 119–122, 123, 124, 125, 126, 129, 142, 143
social movements, 22, 33, 108, 120–121, 125, 128, 134, 137, 138, 139, 141–142, 145, 149–150, 159
social problems, 122–123
social relations, 175–176, 197, 202, 208, 218; constraint as a feature of, 23–24; resistance to change with regard to, 3
social reproduction, 176
social sanctioning, 111–112, 113
social science, 212–213, 216–217
social theory, 210–212
social unrest, 34
Spencer, L., 60
Spicer, A., 145–146
Stalin, Joseph, 203
Steinberg, M., 132, 133
Stewart, A., 16
Stiglitz, J., 5
stigmatisation, 103–105, 109
Stones, R., 107, 107–108
street-level bureaucrats, 170
strike action, 133
subaltern groups, 148, 149, 162–163
subversion, 153, 162, 164, 165, 172–173
supermarkets, 198–200
Susen, S., 99, 100, 108, 181
Svallfors, S., 26
Swartz, D., 21, 201
Sweden, 30
Swift, A., 60
symbolic domination, 58–59, 64–65, 77, 80–81, 90, 92, 94, 97, 104, 106, 124, 208
symbolic legitimation, 120, 175–176, 204, 216; of inequality, 2–4, 14–15, 16–17, 19–20, 21, 22–23
symbolic violence, 79, 81, 83

tactics of the weak, 154, 156
taxation, 6
Taylor, E., 46
Taylor-Gooby, P., 46
the Tea Party, 61
technological change, 4–5
Tehran, 169

television shows, 66, 72
Tenret, E., 36
Terzi, C., 182, 200–201, 209–210, 213, 215
Therborn, G., 9–10
thermostat effect, 46, 48, 49–50
Thévenot, L., 98, 99
thick theory, 17, 81, 212
thin theory, 17, 21, 23, 81, 120, 173
Thomann, M., 136
Thompson, P., 157–159, 160, 164, 166, 170, 171
Tiananmen Square, 130
Tonnelat, S., 215
Treisman, D., 41, 42
trickle-down economics, 5–6
Trump, Donald, 8–9, 39, 61
Tyler, I., 46, 104–106, 108

United Kingdom Independence Party (UKIP), 61
United States, 27, 37–38, 40, 45, 61, 66, 67, 70, 71, 74, 109, 127
universalism regarding welfare, 30

Van Oorschot, W., 30, 50
Vietnam, 168

Vinthagen, S., 162, 166–167
vital inequality, 9

Wacquant, L., 79
Warde, A., 179–180, 195, 201
warfare, 127
Welburn, J., 103
welfare systems, 29–30, 32, 39, 46–51
West, C., 188
West, M., 35–36
White Power movement, 169
whiteness and white privilege, 72–73
Whyte, M. K., 26, 31–32, 33–34
Willis, P., 165
Wittgenstein, L., 178–179
women's social relations, 74, 79, 83
World Economic Forum, 6
World Inequality Report, 5
World Trade Organization, 131

Yates, L., 137

Zakat tithe, 149
Zald, M. N., 125
Zimmerman, D., 171, 188, 210
Zuo, J., 130

About the Author

Wendy Bottero is Reader in Sociology at the University of Manchester, UK.

Lightning Source UK Ltd.
Milton Keynes UK
UKHW012006171220
375438UK00001B/80